INTERNATIONAL ARCHITECTURE & INTERIORS
Series directed by Matteo Vercelloni

NEW
OFFICES
IN USA

MATTEO VERCELLONI
EDITED BY SILVIO SAN PIETRO
PHOTOGRAPHS BY PAUL WARCHOL

EDIZIONI L'ARCHIVOLTO

IDEAZIONE E CURA DEL PROGETTO
Silvio San Pietro
Matteo Vercelloni

TESTI
Matteo Vercelloni

FOTOGRAFIE
Paul Warchol

REDAZIONE
Matteo Vercelloni

PROGETTO GRAFICO
Morozzi & Partners

REALIZZAZIONE GRAFICA E IMPAGINATO
Clini Reclaim (Silvia Clini)
Silvio San Pietro

TRADUZIONI
Andrew Ellis

SI RINGRAZIANO
Gli architetti e gli studi di progettazione per la cortese collaborazione e per aver fornito i disegni dei loro archivi.
Si ringraziano inoltre tutti coloro che hanno reso possibile la realizzazione di questo volume, e in particolare
Gian Paolo Cielo, Mirella Casadei, Claudio Giani, Osvaldo Petris e Loris Cuzzani.
We are grateful to the architects and designers who have kindly contributed to this project and have provided drawings
from their files.

[ISBN 88-7685-100-3]

A norma della legge sul diritto d'autore e del codice civile è vietata la riproduzione di questo libro,
di parti di esso, di disegni, planimetrie e fotografie con qualsiasi mezzo, elettronico, meccanico, per mezzo di fotocopie,
microfilms, registrazioni o altro. L'Editore perseguirà ogni violazione dei propri diritti esclusivi in sede giudiziaria.

© Copyright 1998
EDIZIONI L'ARCHIVOLTO
Via Marsala 3 - 20121 Milano
Tel. 02 / 2901.0424 - 2901.0444
Fax 02 / 2900.1942 - 659.5552
e-mail: archivolto@homegate.it

I edizione novembre 1998

INDICE GENERALE
CONTENTS

PREFACE / PREFAZIONE Matteo Vercelloni 6

ALTSCHILLER REITZFELD DAVIS TRACY-LOCKE NEW YORK, NY. Smith-Miller + Hawkinson Architects 14

APPLE COMPUTER INC. GLASTONBURY, CT. STUDIOS Architecture 22

BABCOCK & BROWN CORPORATE HEADQUARTERS SAN FRANCISCO, CA. STUDIOS Architecture 30

BURGER KING CORPORATE WORLD HEADQUARTERS MIAMI, FL. NBBJ Architecture Design Planning 38

CLEARY GOTTLIEB STEEN & HAMILTON LAW OFFICE NEW YORK, NY. Kohn, Pedersen, Fox, Associates P.C. 46

D.E. SHAW & COMPANY NEW YORK, NY. Steven Holl Architects 54

ESQUIRE MAGAZINE/THE HEARST MAGAZINE COMPANY NEW YORK, NY. Francois de Menil Architect, P.C. 64

FISCHER, FRANCIS, TREES & WATTS NEW YORK, NY. Linda Jacobs - Jon Nathanson Architects 72

HENRI BEAUFOUR INSTITUTE WASHINGTON, DC. Williams & Dynerman Architects 80

HUMMER WINBLAD VENTURE PARTNERS SAN FRANCISCO, CA. Holey Associates Architects 92

KIRSHENBAUM BOND & PARTNERS NEW YORK, NY. Asfour & Guzy Associates Architects 96

LANCASTER GROUP WORLDWIDE, INC. NEW YORK, NY. Quantrell Mullins & Associates Inc. 104

NEW LINE CINEMA-EAST NEW YORK, NY. Smith Miller+Hawkinson Architects 116

OFFICE HEADQUARTERS NEW YORK, NY. TsAO & McKown Architects 126

PUTNAM, LOVELL, DEGUARDIOLA & THORNTON SAN FRANCISCO, CA. Architecture + Light 134

SILICON GRAPHICS COMPUTER SYSTEMS MOUNTAIN VIEW, CA. STUDIOS Architecture 140

SONY MUSIC INTERNATIONAL MIAMI BEACH, FL. TAS Design 146

SQUIRE, SANDERS & DEMPSEY CLEVELAND, OH. STUDIOS Architecture 156

STEVE GOLD PRODUCTIONS NEW YORK, NY. Carl D'Aquino Interiors, Inc. 168

TIME OUT NEW YORK, NY. Margaret Helfand Architects 174

TOMMY BOY NEW YORK, NY. Turett Collaborative Architects 184

VARET MARCUS & FINK WASHINGTON, DC. STUDIOS Architecture 194

W. B. DONER BALTIMORE, MD. KressCox Associates, P.C. 204

TECHNICAL DATA / SCHEDE TECNICHE 215

BIOGRAPHIES / BIOGRAFIE 225

PREFACE

Dedicated to the new generation of office interiors in the United States, this fourth book in the series "International Architecture & Interiors" complements the previous books on interiors, apartment and house design, restaurants, and other types of developed space in America. With respect to the subjects covered so far, however, in the U.S. office design has played a pivotal role in the architectural history of the country's cities, epitomized by the hallmark landscape of office skyscrapers. The scope of this book is not to discuss the development of American office design but, as with the previous publications, to propose an up-to-date panorama on the evolving interior landscape of the American office, and the stylistic models employed in defining functions and distribution, the different ways of dealing with the interior design of spaces for qualified forms of work, which are not geared to quantity and mere rationalization of functions in relation to corporate profits.

Besides having in common the analysis and documentation of a designated aspect of American interior design, what ties this present publication with the previous books, underlining the critical coherence of the unfolding series and the continuity of the visual format, is the rigor and quality of the photographic coverage, which is once again entrusted to Paul Warchol, a U.S. photographer of international renown, who provides the reader with a vivid exposition of the twenty-three chosen projects, but also the atmospheres and lights of these work spaces, the colors, and details of their architectural solutions.

In America the architecture of office buildings has undeniably been a fundamental point of reference for the development of languages, types, and forms in the urban landscape of the major cities across the country. From the so-called speculative office building of the 1800s, to the ensuing wave of "elevator buildings" with their skyward development, followed by the first skyscrapers of the 1920s and '30s, which soon set a standard for the American inner-city skyline and continue to be a hallmark even today, office design has provided the functional dictate, the absolute theme for the development of new and different architectural types within the urban setting.

The interiors presented in this book are housed in structures of varying kinds: in "mature," block-type buildings, in more recent open-plan spaces focused around a core of services and having curtain-wall facades, in skyscrapers with narrow floor plans, but also in spaces formerly used as warehouses and storage depots, factory lofts converted into harmonious workspaces, thanks to the remodeling projects of the designers.

Unconventional offices, which combine an increasing number of functions linked to new forms of comfort. This is the case of the headquarters of the Tommy Boy rap music company designed by Turett Collaborative Architects in New York, where a former, two-story loft space has given a home to offices and meeting rooms flanked by gyms for aerobics, yoga, and weightlifting at the disposal of the company staff. Spaces dedicated to body care and rest rooms are combined with the traditional layout of workspaces and production areas, with new emphasis on the arrangement of working areas that give priority to the psychological implications of returning to the same place each day to work. From this point of view, the interiors assembled in this book pay particular attention to using natural light to the best possible advantage, harvesting it from the perimeter windows and filtering it through to the interior by means of translucent paneling and extensive internal glazing that provides a kind of internal facade, as it were. This customized paneling on the one hand enhances the interior landscape of the working environment, and on the other addresses the vital issue of illuminating the inner areas of the office floor (usually organized as contained open spaces), where once such areas were supplied with artificial lighting only. The task of interior transformation, this reconfiguring of new work places within neutral, empty environments that appear on the real estate market or turn up as functional spaces of a different kind, is a common feature of the projects presented here which, albeit in different ways and for different reasons, each emerge victorious from the architectural shell they occupy, a shell that is largely seen as an inhabitable receptacle, an anonymous container equipped with facilities, to be reconfigured from the point of view of ergonomics, function, and architecture. Anonymous spaces to be retooled to suit the corporate image the client wishes to project through the architectural scheme, in the same way in which the now venerable "speculative office systems" in Chicago (such as the Monadnock Building by Burham & Root, 1889–91; and the Home Insurance

Building by William Le Baron Jenney, 1884–85) endowed the massive, impressing facades with the monolithic persona of the trading companies and banking groups that occupied them. Architecture tuned to the client is perhaps the key feature shared by the first office blocks, which constituted the utmost in prime real estate at the time. In this sense, architecture (as in the case of restaurants, shops, and malls in general) becomes a form of communication with a message produced by the synergy of various separate disciplines (marketing, advertising techniques, optimization of the functional distribution of space in relation to productivity, self-image, etc.)[1]. Never so much as in the design of offices in the recent past has the architectural solution acquired the appearance of a human institution with a keen symbolic value[2]. On the question of office block design, Louis Sullivan, one of the fathers of modern architecture in the U.S., stated that such a building must be tall, its very height expressing strength and power[3]. A series of symbolic characteristics that have over time yielded to a sea of anonymous, uniform geometric curtain-wall frontages of unbroken glazing, a skin protecting the building or open-plan skyscraper designed to exploit the space to the utmost advantage for functional and distributive purposes. The sweeping open schemes originally devised for the typing pools soon accommodated drones of office clerks, who thereby lost their right to an office of their own (and hence their personality), and instead were herded into "bullpens," large standard workspaces common to new office design that were featured in many a movie – and not only in the States – as in the films of Billy Wilder devoted to white-collar workers, and in Jacques Tati's wistful caricature *Playtime* (1967), but also in more recent films such as *Gattaca* (1997) where, in a not-too-distant future we find ranks of svelte but alienating high-tech workstations arranged in infinite lines across vast open-plan environments similar to those devised by Frank Lloyd Wright – the Marin County Civic Center at San Rafael, California (1967). The ethic of total optimization underlying the bullpen scheme brought with it a drastic decline in work ambient quality, a factor that quickly weighed on the well-being and mood of the clerks, who felt themselves increasingly depersonalized. The loss of identity of the individual office worker is directly tied to the lack of character of the office architecture and the layout of its interiors. While the curtain wall was emblematic of this formal banalization of office architecture, with its routinized pattern of glazing, the unobstructed open plan with its service area at the center so as to allow optimum flexibility, became the rule for the interiors. The projects presented in this book mark an important leap ahead in rethinking office architecture, a serious reversal of the philosophy of interior design that offers new circulation schemes and mixes widely diverse types of workspace: from the individual, closed-off office to the twin unit that nonetheless insures due privacy for each of the occupants, the small working pools that eschew the bullpen ethic, carefully integrated with the general layout and enhanced with colored stairways and juxtapositions of varied building materials that flout standardization or uniformity. Each of the office designs chosen for this book stands out for its compositional features, its architectural language, and its overall impact, testifying to an objective eclecticism and degree of freedom necessary for defining offices of varying kinds: for attorney partnerships (Varet Marcus & Fink, Washington, D.C.; Squire, Sander & Dempsey, Cleveland, by Studios; Cleary Gottlieb Steen & Hamilton, New York, by Kohn Pedersen Fox Assoc.), where we find more outspoken intimations of tradition and legacy in the accurate choice of furnishings; offices for film and music production companies, noted computer corporations, and food retail chains, in which the compositional latitude is geared to constructing a memorable corporate self-image and a striking internal landscape played out through the variety of floor plans and forms employed (Sony Music International, Miami, by TAS Design; Steve Gold Productions, New York, by Carl D'Aquino; New Line Cinema, New York, by Smith Miller + Hawkinson; Apple Computer, Glastonbury, by Studios; Burger King, Miami, by NBBJ). Eye-catching compositional invention, creative attention to the general visual impact, and the discerning choice of industrial materials are the main feature of the offices of such publishing houses as the magazine *Esquire* by Francois deMenil, and the celebrated weekly *Time Out* by Margaret Helfand in New York. Occasionally there are explicit architectonic references to museum design; some of the offices chosen seem to play on an art-gallery concept, underlining the parallels of a space that acquires the same distributive system as the office. Such is the case with the banking consultants D. E. Shaw in

---

1. On this subject, note Piera Scuri's study, Cultura e percezione dello spazio - Nuovi ambienti di lavoro in America e in Italia (Dedalo, Bari 1990); in the second chapter she affirms that "American offices are largely the product of research conducted by psychologists, anthropologists, ethologists, and management organizations on samples of the population belonging to the American middle class. Open plans, workstations, and certain formal solutions (such as the decorative and "stimulating" use of artworks in the circulation areas of the American multinationals) "work" but only where applied to the social group for which the studies were realized".
2. See Gli uffici, by Michele Furnari, in the series "Guide per progettare" (Laterza, Bari 1995); especially chapters 2 and 4.
3. L. Sullivan, "The tall office building artistically considered," in Lipcott's Magazine, March 1896.

New York, in which Steven Holl seized the chance to explore the redistribution of natural light via refraction; another example is provided by the new headquarters of Babcock & Brown in San Francisco, by Studios; and not least the Henri Beaufour Institute's new offices by Williams & Dynerman.
Despite the sheer diversity of the projects selected for publication here, they share a common urge to create an office landscape that focuses more and more on the distributive needs of those who move and work therein, insisting on a strong, stimulating environment. This heralds the end of an epoch characterized by a bias toward uniquely quantitative parameters, in favor of more complex specifications (ergonomic and functional, environmental and architectonic) in which quality in the broadest sense has become the design keyword.

Matteo Vercelloni

PREFAZIONE

Dedicato all'architettura d'interni degli uffici americani, quarto volume della collana "International Architecture & Interiors", questo libro si affianca in modo sinergico ai precedenti titoli dedicati agli interni residenziali, alle case unifamiliari e ai ristoranti, spazi e architetture costruiti per lo più negli Stati Uniti. Tuttavia, rispetto agli altri argomenti trattati, il tema degli uffici appare nella storia dell'architettura americana come uno dei soggetti di riferimento principali e anche come uno dei settori di sviluppo di architetture topiche per la città statunitense, di cui il grattacielo è indubbiamente tra i più rappresentativi. Questo libro non intende occuparsi dello sviluppo dell'architettura degli uffici made in Usa ma, come per gli altri volumi della collana vuole proporre al lettore un panorama aggiornato sul divenire del paesaggio interno dell'ufficio americano, sulle figure chiamate a definirne funzioni e percorsi, sui diversi modi di affrontare il progetto d'interni per spazi di lavoro qualificati, non più solo chiamati a rispondere a esigenze quantitative e di semplice funzionamento razionale rapportati al maggiore profitto dell'azienda. Oltre al comune tema di analisi e di aggiornata documentazione di un aspetto dell'architettura d'interni americana, quello che lega questo volume ai primi tre della collana, sottolineando il valore di un discorso critico unitario e in divenire ma anche la validità di un percorso iconografico di consolidata continuità d'immagine, è il rigore e la qualità della lettura fotografica condotta anche in questa occasione da Paul Warchol, fotografo americano di fama internazionale, che restituisce al lettore con estrema chiarezza il senso progettuale delle ventitré soluzioni selezionate, ma anche le atmosfere e le luci di questi spazi di lavoro, i colori e i dettagli delle loro soluzioni architettoniche. Come abbiamo prima accennato, l'architettura del palazzo per uffici ha costituito in America uno tra i temi di riferimento fondamentali per lo sviluppo di linguaggi, tipi e forme del paesaggio urbano delle principali città. Dagli edifici a blocco degli ultimi decenni del secolo scorso (il cosiddetto *speculative office building*) a quelli appena successivi più slanciati in altezza e dotati dei primi ascensori (gli *elevator building*), sino ai grattacieli degli anni '20 e '30 che caratterizzano con forza lo skyline urbano dei centri direzionali statunitensi, per divenire il tipo edilizio di riferimento del paesaggio americano anche dei nostri giorni, l'ufficio ha costituito la ragione funzionale, il tema assoluto per lo sviluppo di nuove e differenti architetture a scala urbana. Gli interni che presentiamo in questo volume si trovano in molti edifici di questo tipo: in vecchi palazzi a blocco, in edifici più recenti a open spaces con cuore servizi centrale e facciate in curtain wall, in grattacieli dalla pianta più stretta, ma anche in spazi un tempo usati come magazzini e depositi, in loft trasformati in calibrati spazi di lavoro, grazie agli interventi d'interni compiuti dai progettisti. Uffici non convenzionali, che raggruppano sempre più funzioni legate anche a nuove forme di comfort. É il caso degli uffici della casa di produzione di musica rap "Tommy Boy", progettati da Turett Collaborative Architects a New York, dove in un vecchio edificio a loft sovrapposti, accanto agli uffici e alle sale riunione si affiancano sale per aerobica, per lo yoga e per il sollevamento pesi a disposizione degli impiegati dell'azienda. Spazi dedicati alla cura del corpo e sale per riposare si aggiungono così alle tradizionali stanze per lavorare e produrre, annunciando nuove attenzioni verso la configurazione di spazi di lavoro in cui deve emergere anche la sensazione psicologica di avere voglia di tornare tutti i giorni a lavorare nello stesso luogo. Da questo punto di vista tutte le soluzioni raccolte nel volume rivolgono grande attenzione all'impiego e alla valorizzazione della luce naturale che viene sempre catturata dalle facciate finestrate e portata all'interno grazie all'impiego di pareti in parte vetrate e ricche di aperture traslucide, appositamente progettate dagli architetti come facciate interne. Studiate quinte architettoniche che se da un lato arricchiscono la figura del paesaggio interno dell'ambiente lavoro, dall'altro risolvono l'importante problema di illuminare con luce naturale gli spazi più centrali (in genere organizzati in piccoli open space) un tempo trattati con sola luce artificiale. Proprio questo lavoro di progettazione d'interni, questo configurare nuovi luoghi di lavoro nell'ambito di spazi neutri e vuoti, offerti dal mercato immobiliare o trovati come preesistenze funzionali d'altro tipo, caratterizza tutti i progetti selezionati che in diversi modi si discostano, per tensione figurativa e soluzione progettuale, dall'architettura che li accoglie, assunta il più delle volte come sorta di scatola abitabile, di contenitore anonimo dotato di servizi, da configurare e da caratterizzare dal punto di vista ergonomico, funzionale e architettonico. Spazi anonimi da 'riprogettare' in funzione dell'immagine che l'azienda vuole comunicare proprio attraverso la soluzione architettonica, nello stesso modo in cui un tempo i lontani e severi *speculative office building* di Chicago (Monadnock Building di Burnham & Root, 1889-91; Home

Insurance Building di William Le Baron Jenney, 1884-85, per fare solo due esempi) traducevano nelle loro possenti e monumentali soluzioni di facciata la 'forza' e il 'monolitico spessore' delle compagnie commerciali e dei gruppi finanziari che li occupavano. L'architettura ad immagine e somiglianza del suo diretto fruitore è forse il concetto che più accomuna gli interni che presentiamo alle caratteristiche dei primi edifici per uffici che costituivano un tempo l'investimento immobiliare per eccellenza. L'architettura, oltre a essere una materia specifica, diventa in questo senso (come nel caso dei ristoranti, dei negozi e degli spazi commerciali in senso lato) una forma di comunicazione che si integra a un messaggio prodotto dalla sinergia di varie discipline (marketing, tecniche pubblicitarie, ottimizzazione nella distribuzione funzionale degli spazi in rapporto alla resa produttiva, immagine, ecc.[1] Mai forse come nell'architettura del palazzo per uffici americano di un vicino passato la soluzione architettonica acquista l'aspetto di "un'istituzione umana con un alto valore simbolico"[2]. Louis Sullivan, uno dei padri dell'architettura moderna americana, a proposito del palazzo per uffici sottolineava come l'edificio "deve essere alto, deve possedere la forza e la potenza dell'altezza, la gloria e l'orgoglio dell'esaltazione"[3]; una serie di caratteristiche simboliche che si sono perse nel tempo, per arrivare all'uniformità anonima e muta della facciata geometrica in *curtain wall*, il rivestimento continuo in vetro, pelle di protezione del palazzo o grattacielo a pianta libera dove organizzare l'open space di massimo sfruttamento funzionale-distributivo. Il grande spazio libero destinato in origine alle dattilografe viene in seguito occupato anche dagli impiegati che perdono così il diritto alla propria stanza (e quindi alla loro personalità) e vengono distribuiti e massificati in serie nel *bullpen* (letteralmente "recinto dei buoi"), spazi di lavoro comuni a ogni grande ufficio e ben raffigurati in molti film non solo americani: dai capolavori di Billy Wilder dedicati al mondo dei 'colletti bianchi', alla sagace caricatura di Jacques Tati nel film "Playtime" (1967), ma anche in film recenti come "Gattaca" (1997), dove in un futuro non troppo lontano troviamo una serie di eleganti quanto alienanti postazioni di lavoro ultratecnologiche disposte in serie infinita, come negli uffici degli anni passati, in grandi *open space* ambientati in una delle ultime opere di Frank Lloyd Wright, il Marin County Civic Center a San Rafael in California (1967). Alla maggiore densità 'ottimizzata' nell'open space-bullpen corrispondeva una diminuzione della qualità dell'ambiente di lavoro che finiva per riflettersi sulla psicologia e l'umore dell'impiegato, sempre più spersonalizzato. La perdita di personalità e carattere del singolo lavoratore dell'ufficio trovava così la sua traduzione architettonica anche nella mancanza di immagine dell'edificio per uffici e dei suoi spazi interni. Se il *curtain wall* divenne il simbolo standardizzato di questa riduzione formale dell'architettura chiamata a disegnare una sorta di anonimo *tartan* per i prospetti, lo spazio vuoto a pianta libera, con servizi centrali per 'massima flessibilità', fu assunto come regola degli interni. I progetti che presentiamo in questo libro sembrano in qualche modo riscattare il valore del progetto di architettura per gli uffici, chiamato a definire con forza nuovi spazi interni, a ridisegnare e reinventare percorsi e figure che mescolano sempre più diverse tipologie di spazi di lavoro: dall'ufficio singolo a quello doppio, entrambi separati con massima garanzia di privacy, a piccole zone collettive, ben diverse dagli alienanti *bullpen*, calate con calibrata regia nella disposizione generale in cui non mancano attenzioni a raffinate scale cromatiche e ad accostamenti materici, che si distaccano con convinzione da ogni tipo di standardizzazione e uniformità. Ognuno degli uffici selezionato per questo volume è diverso dall'altro per regia compositiva, linguaggio architettonico e figura complessiva, testimoniando l'oggettivo eclettismo e grado di libertà necessari a definire uffici di vario genere: per avvocati (Varet Marcus & Fink a Washington; Squire, Sander & Dempsey a Cleveland di Studios; Cleary Gottlieb Steen & Hamilton, a New York di Kohn Pedersen Fox Ass.), dove troviamo richiami più espliciti alla tradizione e al rigore dell'immagine anche nell'accurata scelta degli arredi; uffici per case di produzione cinematografiche e musicali, di note aziende di computer e di generi alimentari fast-food, in cui la libertà compositiva è tesa alla costruzione di un'immagine aziendale innovativa e alla creazione di paesaggi interni inconsueti e giocati sulla varietà di percorsi e figure (Sony Music International a Miami di TAS Design; Steve Gold Productions a New York di Carl D'Aquino; New Line Cinema a New York di Smith Miller + Hawkinson; Apple Computer a Glastonbury di Studios; Burger King a Miami di NBBJ). Ricerche compositive particolari e di grande interesse per immagine d'insieme e uso dei materiali industriali impiegati con intelligenza e creatività, caratterizzano anche alcuni uffici editoriali come quello di "Esquire

---

1. Vedi a tale proposito "Cultura e percezione dello spazio - Nuovi Ambienti di lavoro in America e in Italia" di Piera Scuri, edizioni Dedalo, Bari 1990. Al capitolo secondo si afferma: "Gli uffici americani sono in gran parte il prodotto di ricerche condotte da studiosi di psicologia, antropologia, etologia e organizzazione manageriale su campioni di popolazione appartenente alla middle class americana. L'open space, le work station, alcune soluzioni formali (ad esempio l'uso decorativo e 'stimolatorio' delle opere d'arte nei quartieri generali delle multinazionali americane) 'funzionano' ma in riferimento al gruppo sociale per il quale sono stati studiati e realizzati."
2. Vedi "Gli uffici", di Michele Furnari, Guide per progettare, Editori Laterza, Bari 1995. In particolare i Cap. 2 e 4.
3. L. Sullivan "The tall office buiilding artistically considered" ("Considerazioni sull'arte degli edifici alti per uffici") in "Lippincot's Magazine", marzo 1896.

Magazine" di Francois deMenil e del famoso settimanale "Time Out" di Margaret Helfand a New York. Non mancano poi riferimenti all'architettura di allestimento museale; alcuni degli uffici selezionati sembrano ricordare nell'immagine proposta la dimensione figurativa della galleria d'arte, sottolineando il valore e l'importanza dell'immagine offerta che acquista lo stesso peso del funzionamento distributivo dell'ufficio. É il caso del progetto per la compagnia di consulenza finanziaria D.E. Shaw a New York di Steven Holl, occasione per sperimentare un discorso compositivo sulla rifrazione della luce o della sede dell'istituto bancario Babcock & Brown a San Francisco di Studios, ma anche l'Henri Beaufour Institute a New York di Williams & Dynerman.

Alla diversa immagine dei progetti selezionati risponde il comune sforzo progettuale di creare dei paesaggi interni fortemente costruiti, che sottolineano un'attenzione sempre crescente per la definizione di spazi di lavoro dove alla funzionalità distributiva richiesta dai diversi fruitori corrisponde un'immagine architettonica dal forte carattere, che sembra sempre più sottolineare la fine degli anni caratterizzati dalle sole esigenze quantitative per rispondere a richieste più complesse (ergonomiche e funzionali, ambientali e architettoniche) in cui la qualità in senso lato appare come riferimento fondamentale.

Matteo Vercelloni

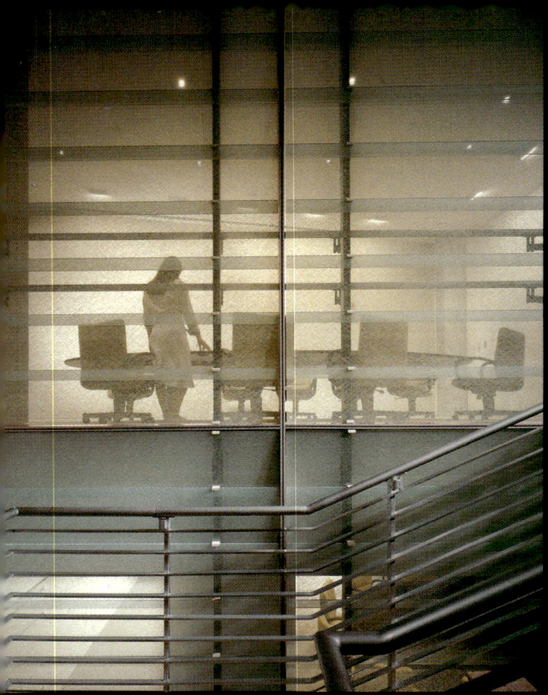
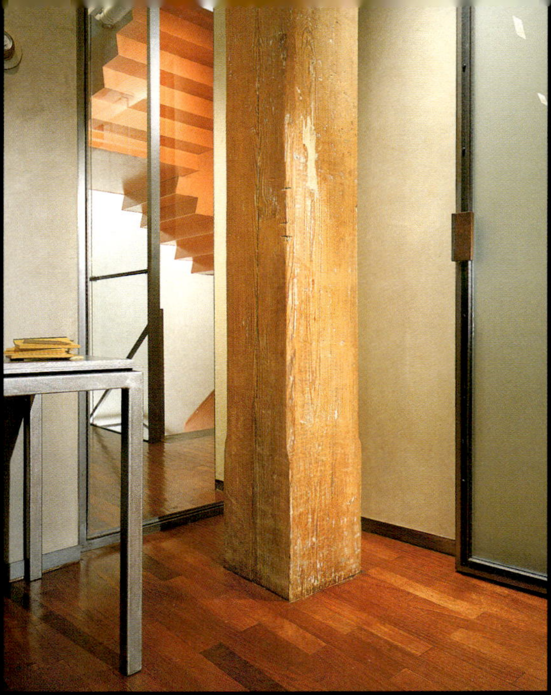
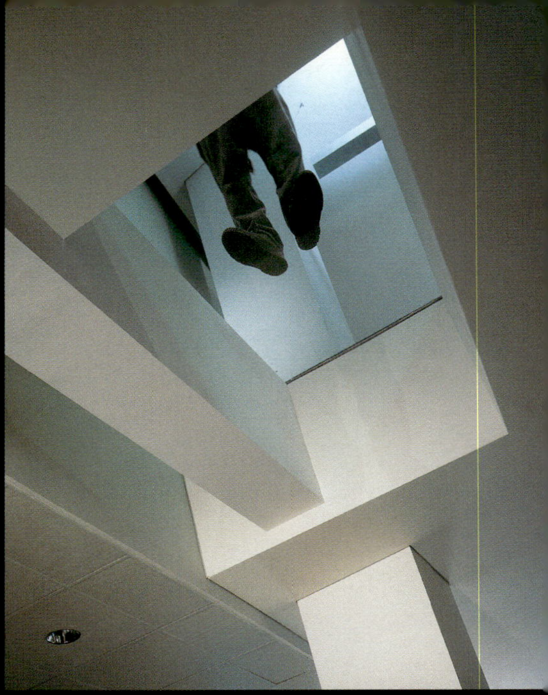
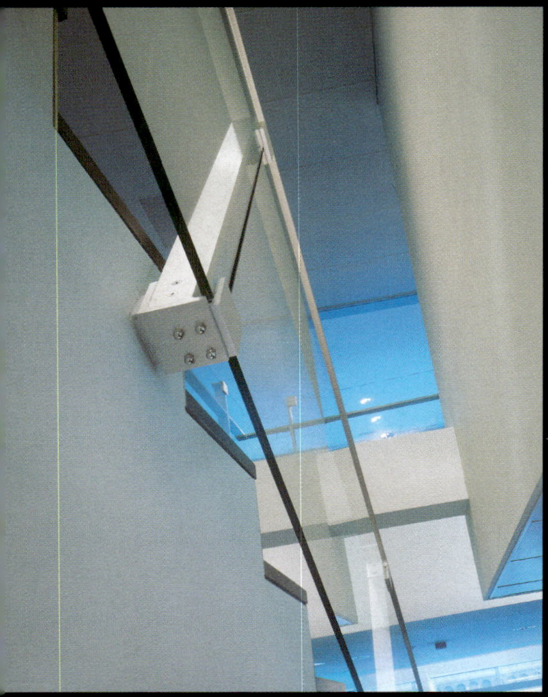
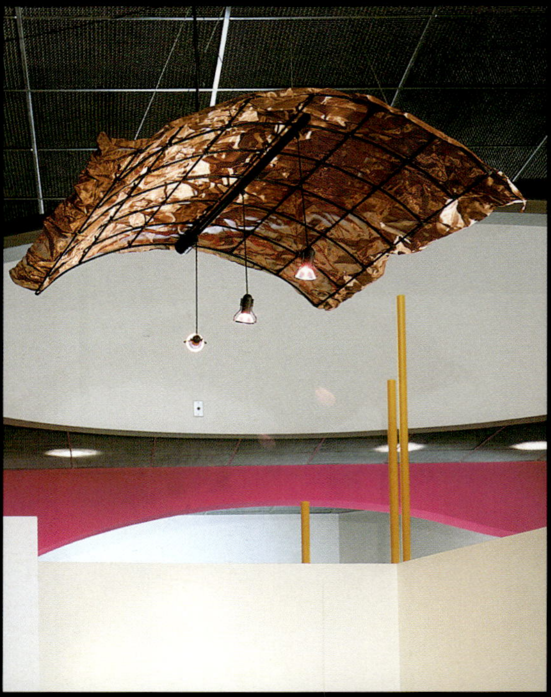
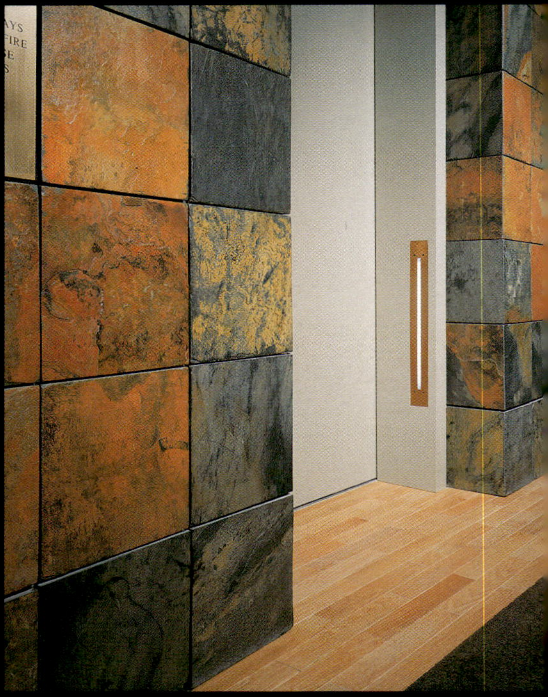
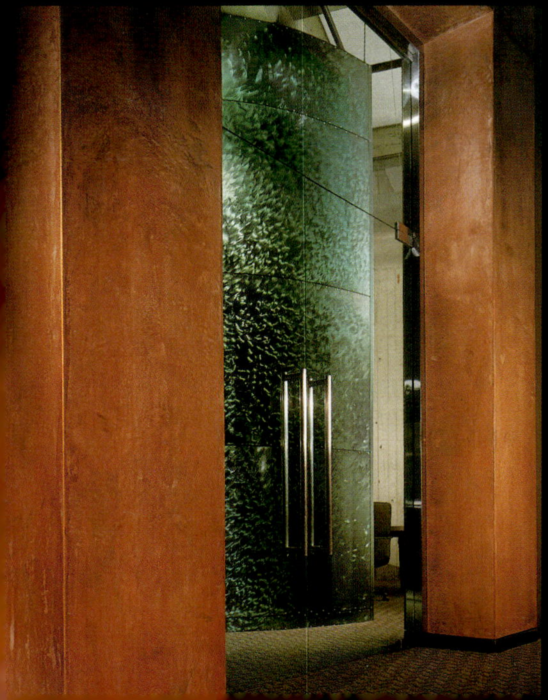

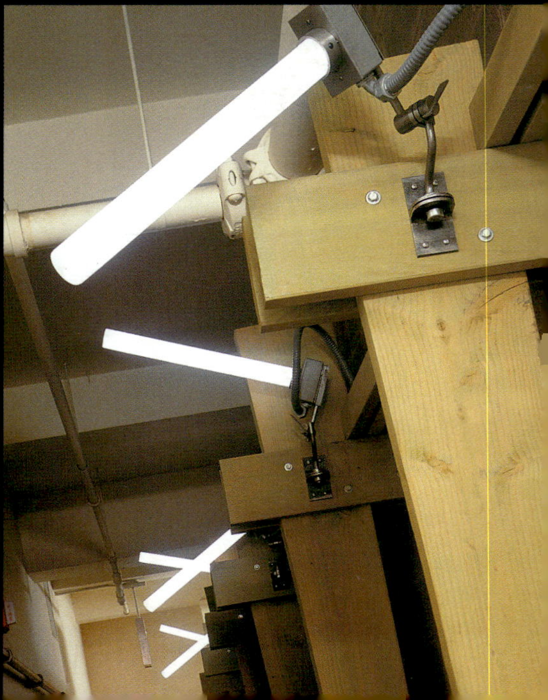

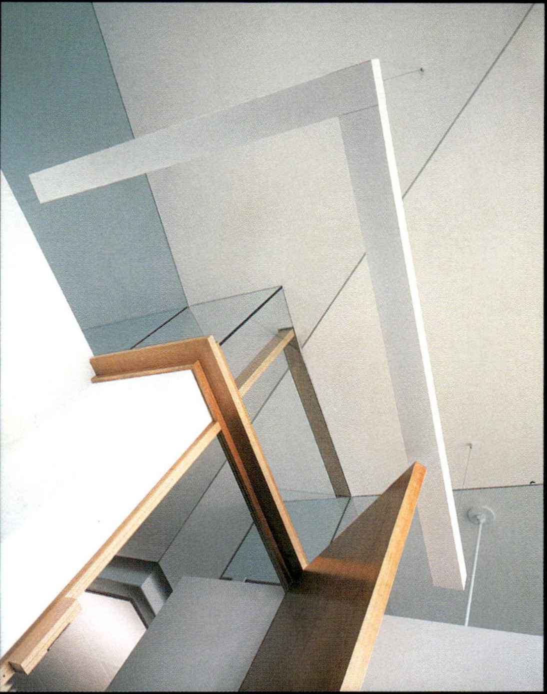
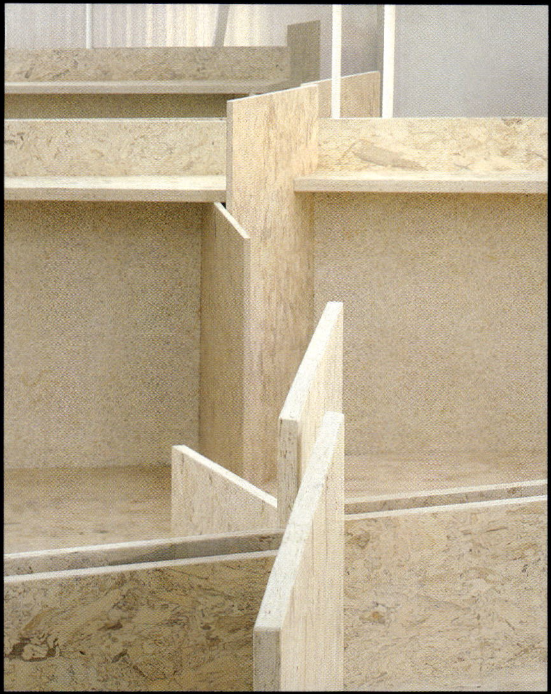
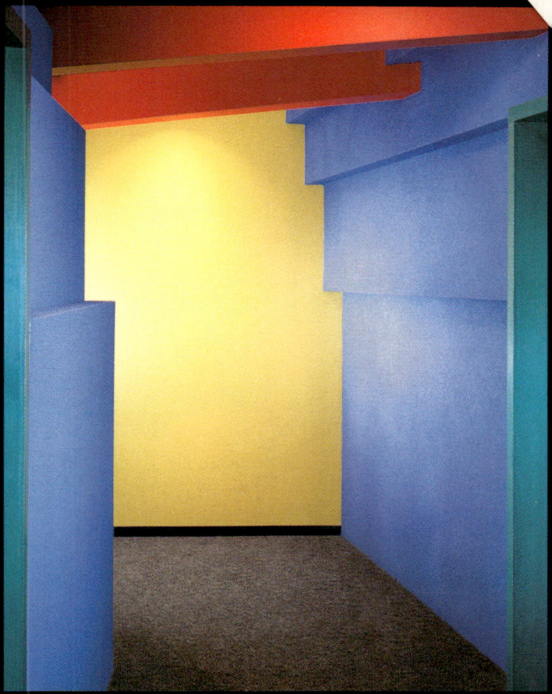
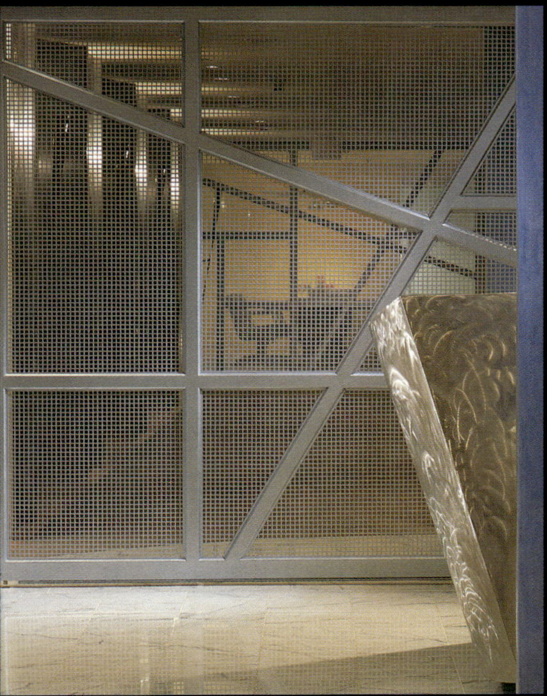
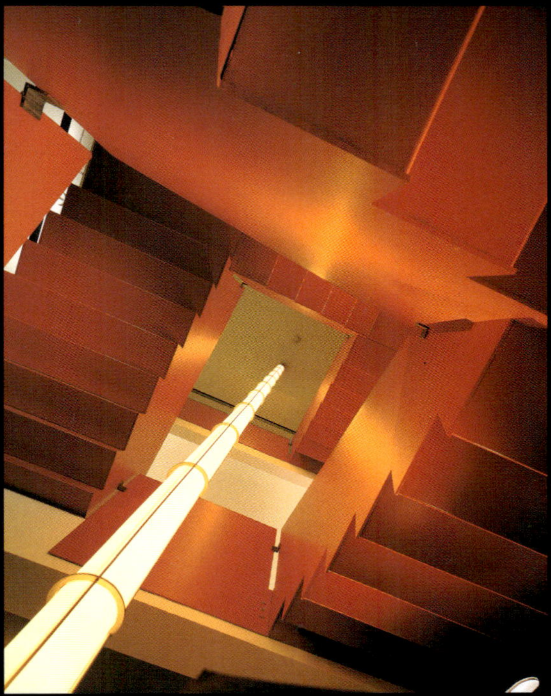
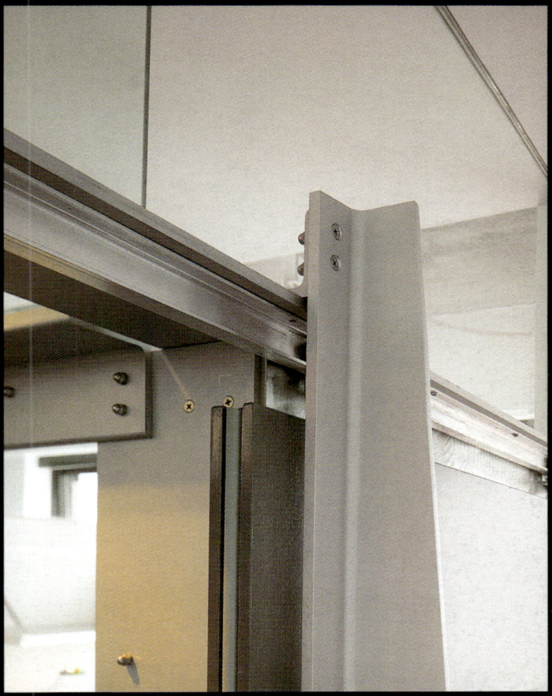
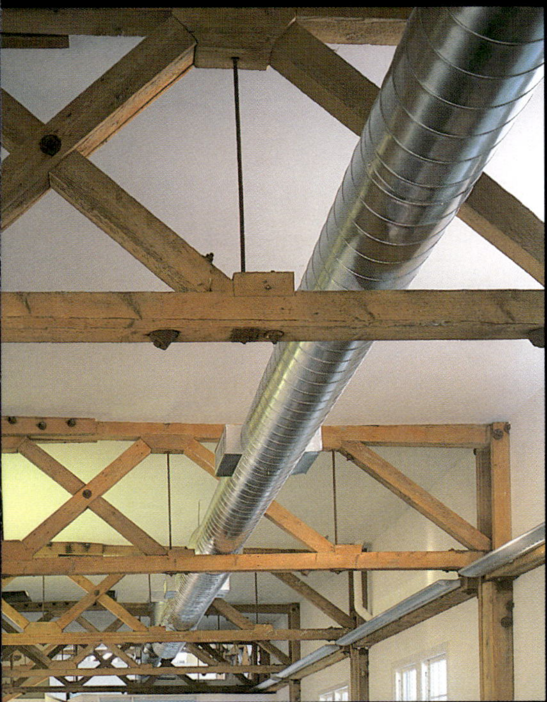
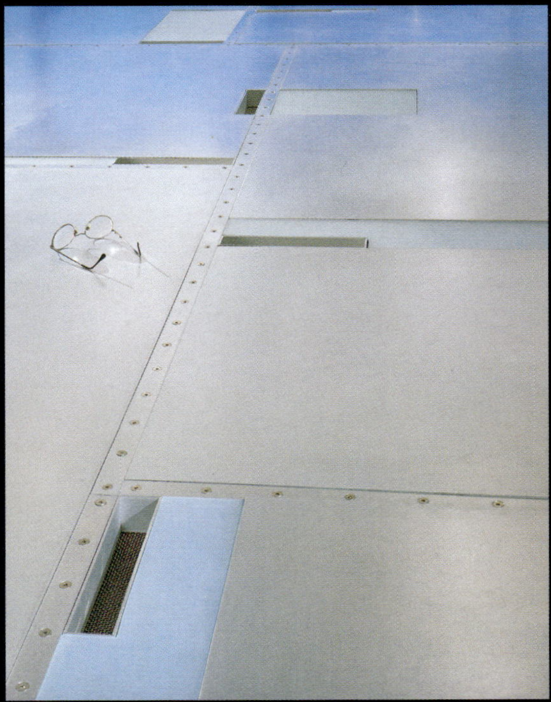
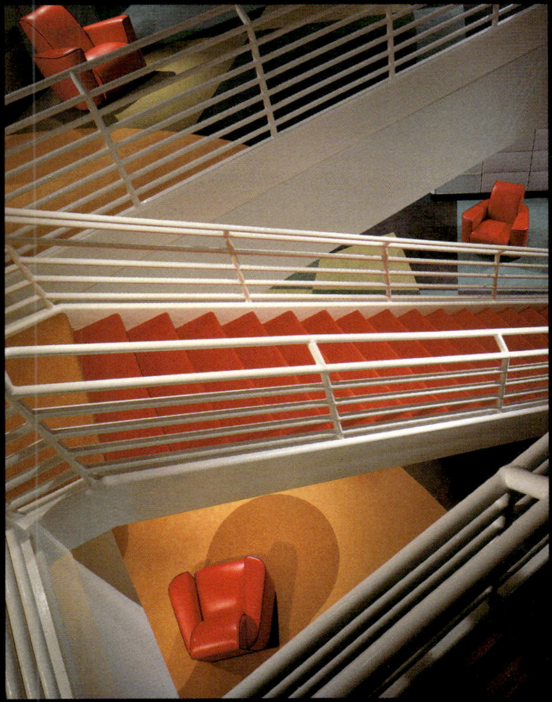

ALTSCHILLER REITZFELD DAVIS TRACY-LOCKE
Smith-Miller + Hawkinson Architects. New York, NY, 1990

The plan of the building presents a standard format comprising a central block with service facilities and an open working area modulated by the windows on three sides of the building. The keynote of the redesign was to exploit the natural light sources and optimize the inner areas, while affording a good view of the panoramic vistas over the city. In general terms, the designers opted to distributed all the enclosed spaces that required a certain degree of privacy around the perimeter. Single and twinned workstations, executive offices, and meeting rooms are therefore given perimeter priority along the three sides with daylight illumination; while along the blind wall runs a long, narrow open working area with a succession of individual workstations. The inner area, which develops around the service and stair core, houses various alternated typological solutions so as to create a diversity of architectural situations and environments: small open areas, meeting rooms, and separate offices create a compositive sequence modulated by the regular, straight circulation route of the perimeter corridor, and is interrupted only by the entrance lobby and reception area and the skewed angle of the executive suite, a device that serves to emphasize the careful orchestration of the whole. The precise architectural grammar, composed of a narrowed-down choice of materials: various aluminum fittings, steel, sandblasted glazing, painted ash, gray industrial carpeting, exposed concrete soffits, and by a rigorous sequence of differently formed volumes and spaces, lending a general sense of unity to the interiors as a whole. The huge sliding door hung from a girder at the entrance, marking the visitor's first impact with the design, gives onto the brightly lit reception area. Overhead, a lowered plasterboard bulkhead carves out the arrival area, forming a deft composition complementing the blue wooden furniture of the reception, and the white partitions of the corridors alternating with transparent panels to harvest the natural light filtering in from outside. These custom panels are set in aluminum frames, on which ride the sliding doors, echoing the entrance motif, albeit on a smaller scale.

La pianta dell'edificio presentava la tradizionale tipologia con blocco centrale-servizi e spazio a open space scandito dalle aperture presenti su tre lati di facciata. Spunto primario dell'intervento è stato quello di sfruttare al meglio la luce naturale ottimizzando la distribuzione interna e valorizzando anche alcune viste panoramiche della città. Dal punto di vista delle scelte generali si è optato per distribuire lungo i tre lati finestrati tutti quegli spazi che richiedevano una separazione e una garanzia di privacy. Postazioni operative singole e doppie, uffici per i dirigenti e sale riunioni occupano così la prima fascia di lavoro ricavata lungo i tre lati illuminati con luce naturale, mentre lungo il lato cieco sono stati disposti, in un open space stretto e lungo, una serie di posti di lavoro affiancati. La zona interna, sviluppata intorno al blocco servizi-scale, ospita varie soluzioni tipologiche alternate tra loro anche per creare diverse situazioni architettoniche e ambientali: piccoli open space, sale riunioni e uffici indipendenti creano la sequenza compositiva interna scandita dal percorso regolare e rettilineo del corridoio perimetrale che trova nella zona ingresso-reception e nell'angolo ruotato degli uffici direzionali due episodi di rottura che sottolineano la studiata regia compositiva dell'insieme. Una grammatica architettonica precisa, composta da una ristretta scelta di materiali (alluminio in diverse finiture, acciaio, vetro trasparente e sabbiato, legno di frassino dipinto, moquette industriale grigia e soffitto lasciato in cemento a vista) e da una rigorosa sequenza di soluzioni volumetrico-spaziali, caratterizza il percorso architettonico interno e l'immagine unitaria d'insieme. La porta scorrevole fissata a una putrella a vista dell'ingresso, figura di riferimento iniziale, si apre sulla luminosa zona reception. Un volume in cartongesso scende dal soffitto e segna la zona di arrivo unendosi, in una sintesi compositiva attenta e calibrata, ai mobili in legno blu della reception e ai setti bianchi del corridoio alternati all'accurato disegno delle pareti divisorie pensate per filtrare la luce esterna. Le pareti sono composte da lastre di vetro sabbiato e trasparente, sostenute da una struttura in alluminio su disegno su cui sono fissate anche le porte scorrevoli grigie che riprendono, in scala minore, la soluzione di quella dell'ingresso.

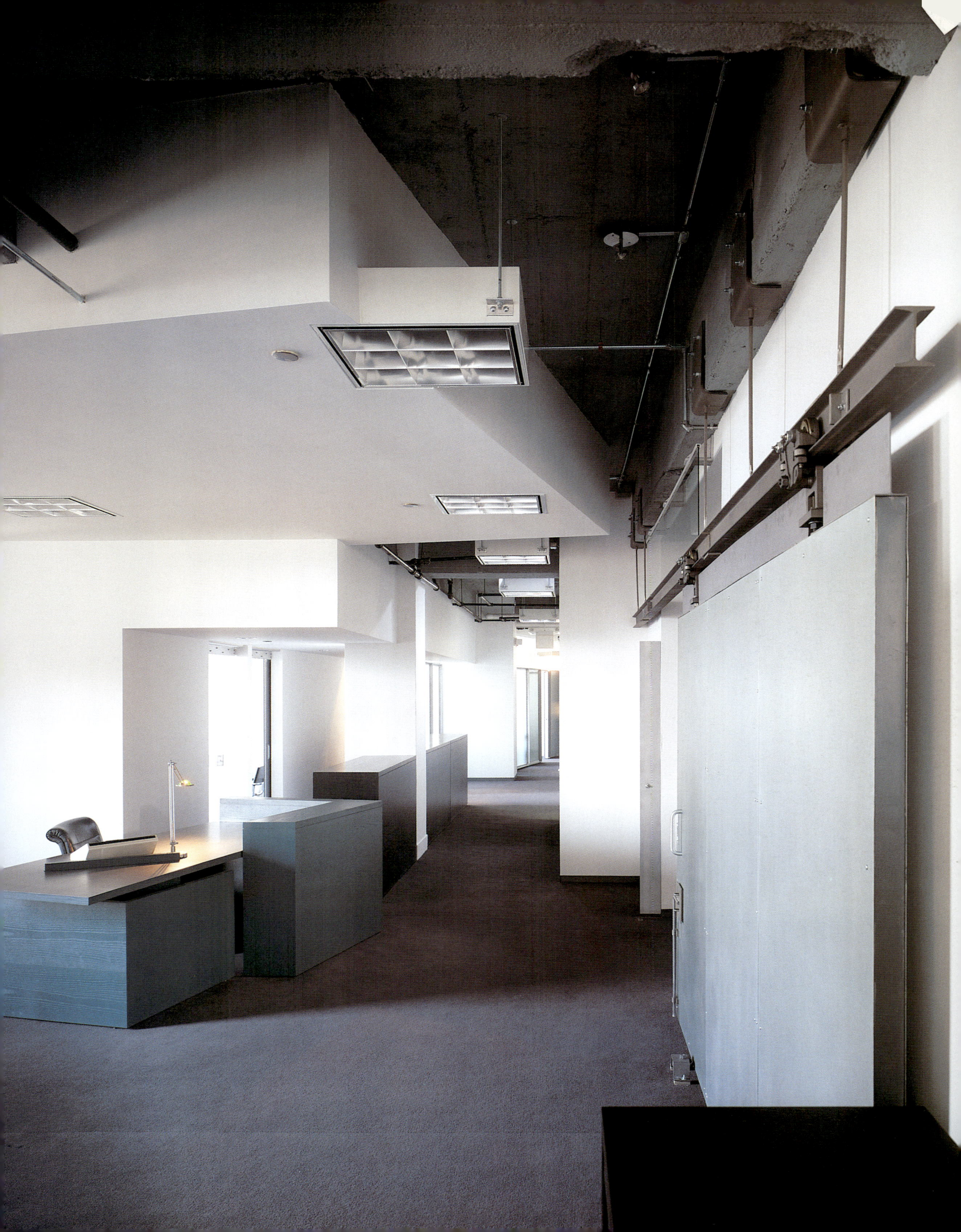

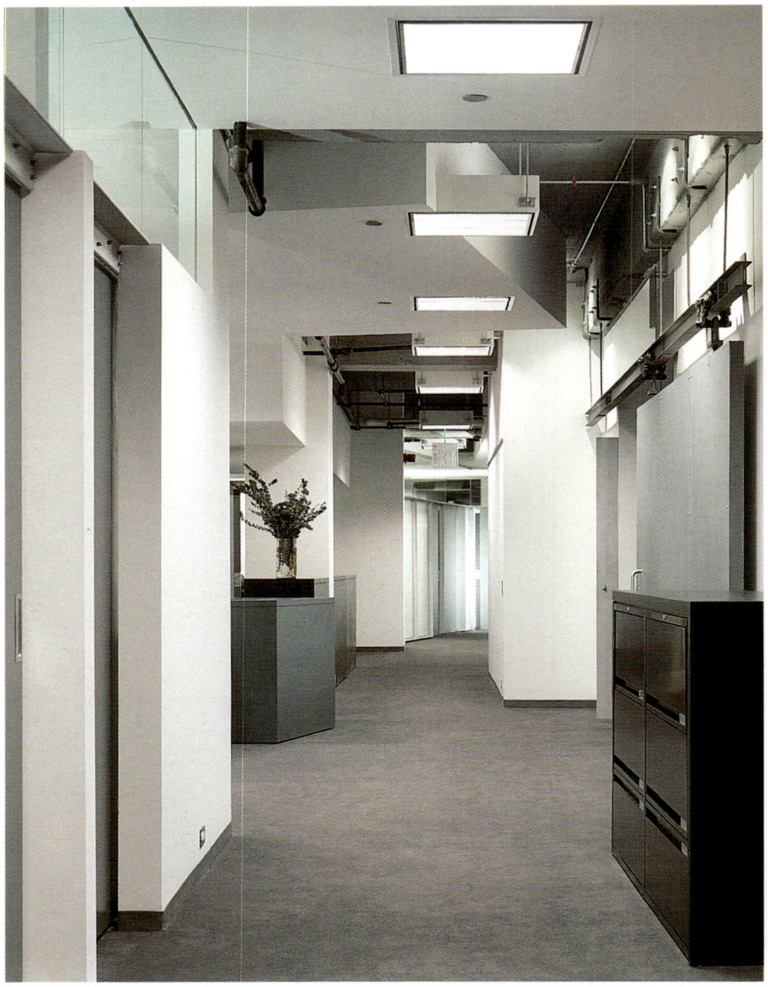

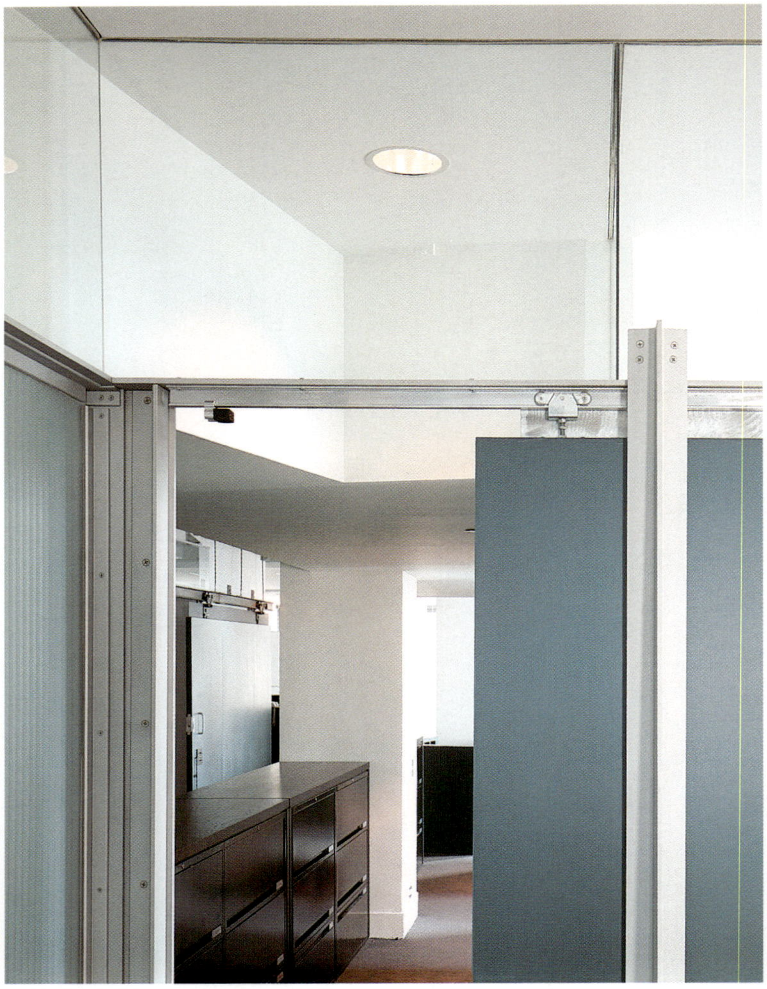

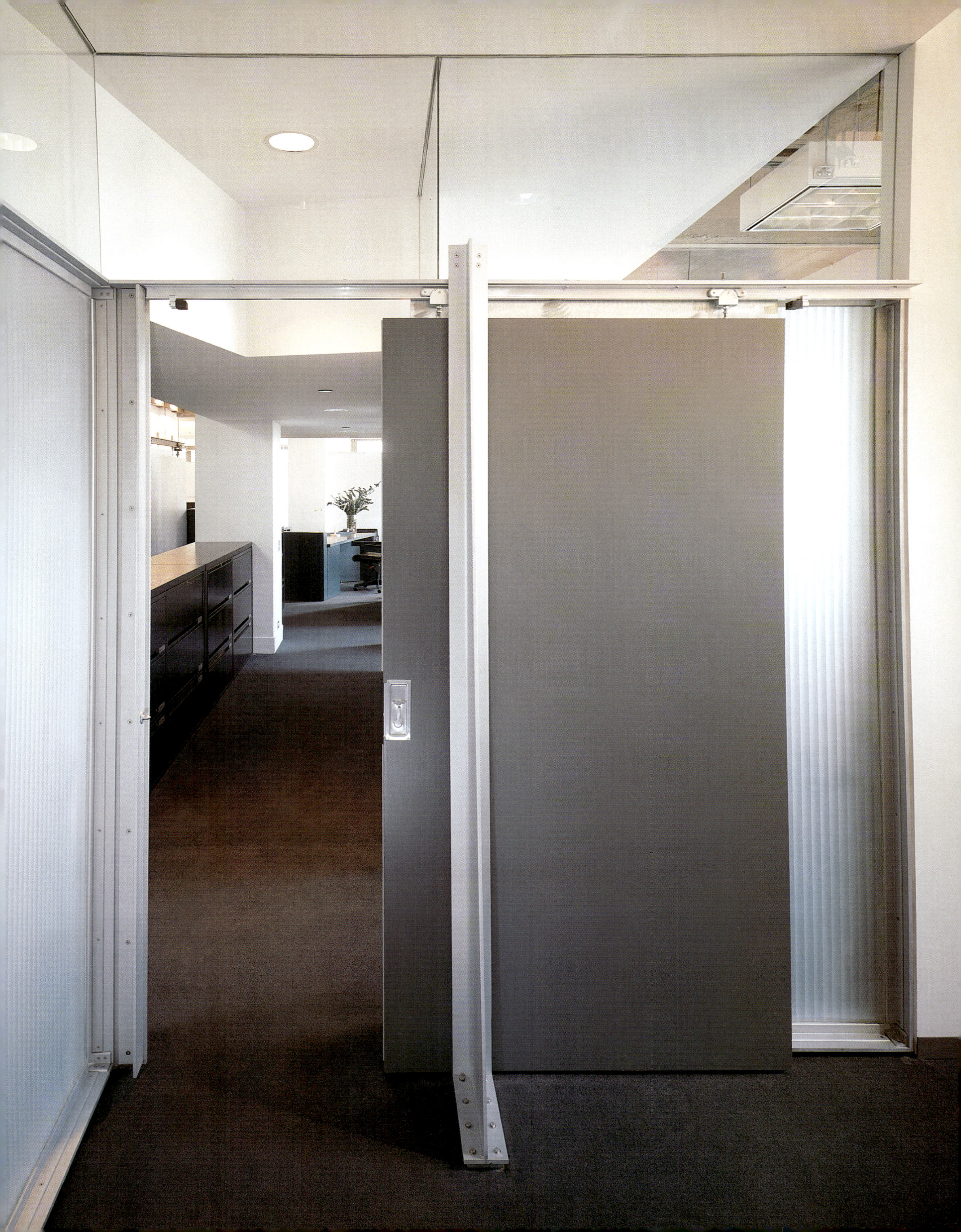

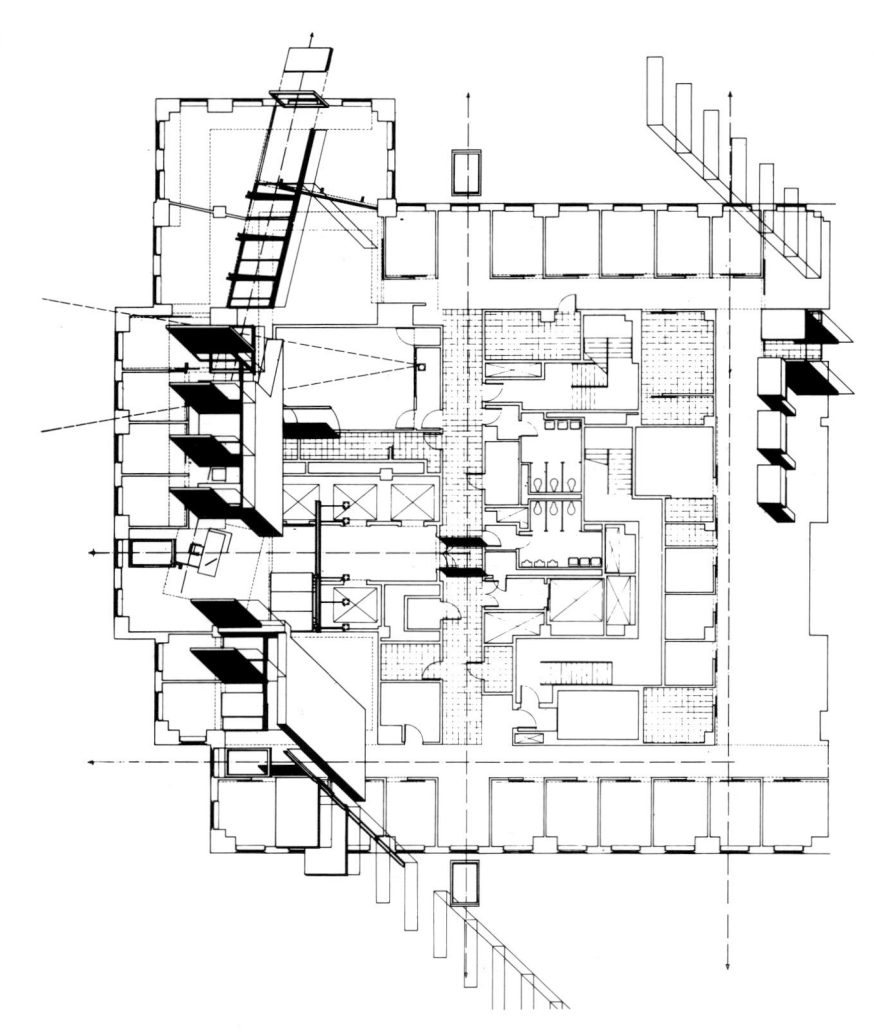

Axonometric conceptual draving of plan
Pianta con elementi in assonometria

Plan / Pianta

19

20

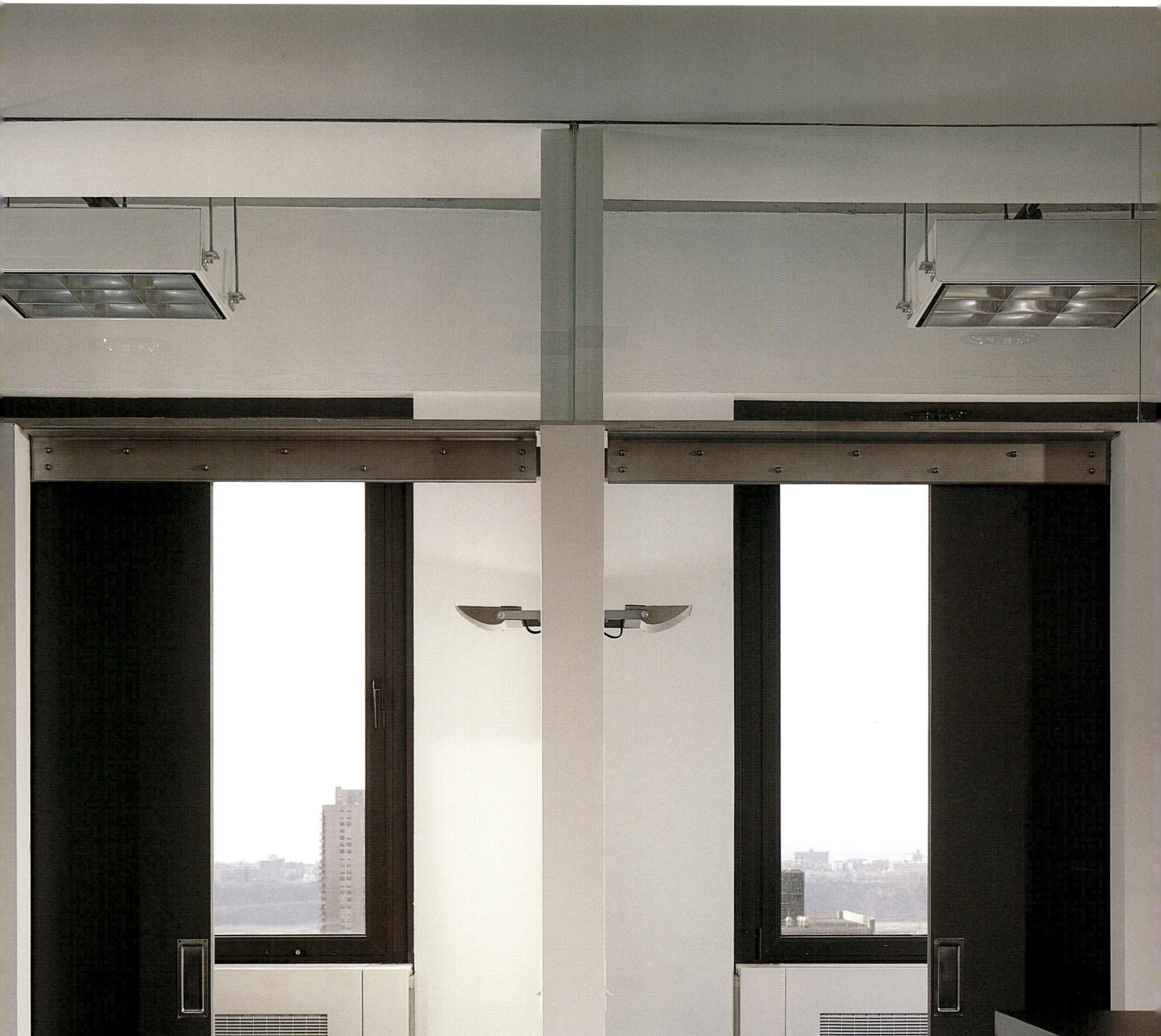

APPLE COMPUTER INC.
STUDIOS Architecture. Glastonbury, CT, 1990

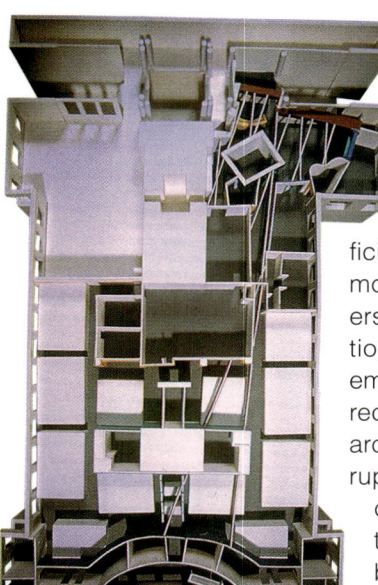

Spread out over an ample, single-level open space, this working environment wisely eschews the hackneyed format of the traditional office layout of workstation enclosures corralled by low partitions with white, square-tiled ceilings and recessed fluorescent strip lighting. Although the new design maintains something of the standard open-plan arrangement, it artfully breaks up the visuals with architectural inserts that slice through the entire space, characterizing the initial and closing areas in particular. The entrance itself is devised as a self-sufficient unit, standing off from the rest of the open space. A series of strikingly colored, modulated walls in bright yellow, blue, purple, and strong red are surmounted by ersatz, irregularly patterned roof beams set off from the false ceilings. This composition offers a resonant context for the reception area, where a curved yellow desk emerges from the red wall and dovetails with a sturdy blue cylinder. Just beyond the reception area, opposite the entrance, a conference room offers a small, self-sufficient architectural unit announced by a wall composed of staggered horizontal bands interrupted by the solid wooden surround of the door, whose design replicates the concept of the small entrance door, with its panes of sanded glass. This lively architectural composition is taken up again at the extreme opposite end of the offices, at the back of the operations area. A curving purple wall encloses the office cafeteria, where lowered ceilings have been omitted to allow full view of the original structural beams and the ceiling in corrugated white metal. Here the hallway carpeting gives way to pale gray linoleum floor with twin dark strips running obliquely toward the back of the room. In order to link the main reference motifs at either end of the office suite, a series of false beams similar to those at the entrance zigzag through the open space weaving a brightly colored geometric network. Together with the lively hues of the perimeter walls, the network of beams gives an otherwise humdrum interior a decisive stylistic and chromatic counterpoint that successfully enlivens the entire work space.

Ricavato su un unico livello a open space, questo ambiente di lavoro vuole sfuggire alla monotonia del tradizionale ufficio, formato da postazioni separate da basse pareti attrezzate sormontate da un anonimo controsoffitto a quadrotti bianchi in cui sono posizionate le luci al neon incassate. L'intervento, se da un lato mantiene le tradizionali postazioni di lavoro a open space, dall'altro ne stravolge l'immagine con inserti architettonici di rottura che vogliono attraversare con forza l'intero spazio, caratterizzandone gli spazi iniziali e di chiusura. L'ingresso è così proposto come un ambiente che prende le distanze da quello dell'open space; una serie di colorate e studiate pareti architettoniche che alternano giallo, azzurro e viola al rosso acceso delle irregolari travi posticce che scendono dal controsoffitto formano una scena di forte impatto per incorniciare il banco reception, composto da un volume giallo in curva incastrato in un forte cilindro azzurro. Di fianco alla reception e di fronte all'ingresso, una sala riunione si propone come piccola e compiuta architettura composta da pareti viola a fasce orizzontali descrescenti interrotte dall'innesto di un massiccio infisso di legno azzurro con vetrate sabbiate che ripete la soluzione del portoncino d'ingresso. Questa colorata composizione architettonica viene ripresa nella zona all'estremità opposta, sul fondo dell'open space operativo. Una parete in curva di colore viola contiene la zona caffetteria dell'ufficio, dove è stato smantellato il controsoffitto a quadrotti per mettere a nudo le travi strutturali e il soffitto in lamiera grecata tinteggiati di bianco. Qui la moquette grigia è stata sostituita con un pavimento di linoleum grigio chiaro segnato da due fasce scure poste in diagonale. A unire questi due episodi architettonici di riferimento, posti alle estremità dell'ufficio, una serie di travi posticce, come quelle costruite nell'ingresso, si sviluppa lungo il controsoffitto dell'open space, disegnando colorati e forti segni geometrici che, insieme ad alcune pareti perimetrali tinteggiate in tonalità vivaci, portano all'interno di uno spazio anonimo e ripetitivo un deciso contrappunto stilistico e cromatico in grado di cambiare l'immagine dell'intero ambiente di lavoro.

23

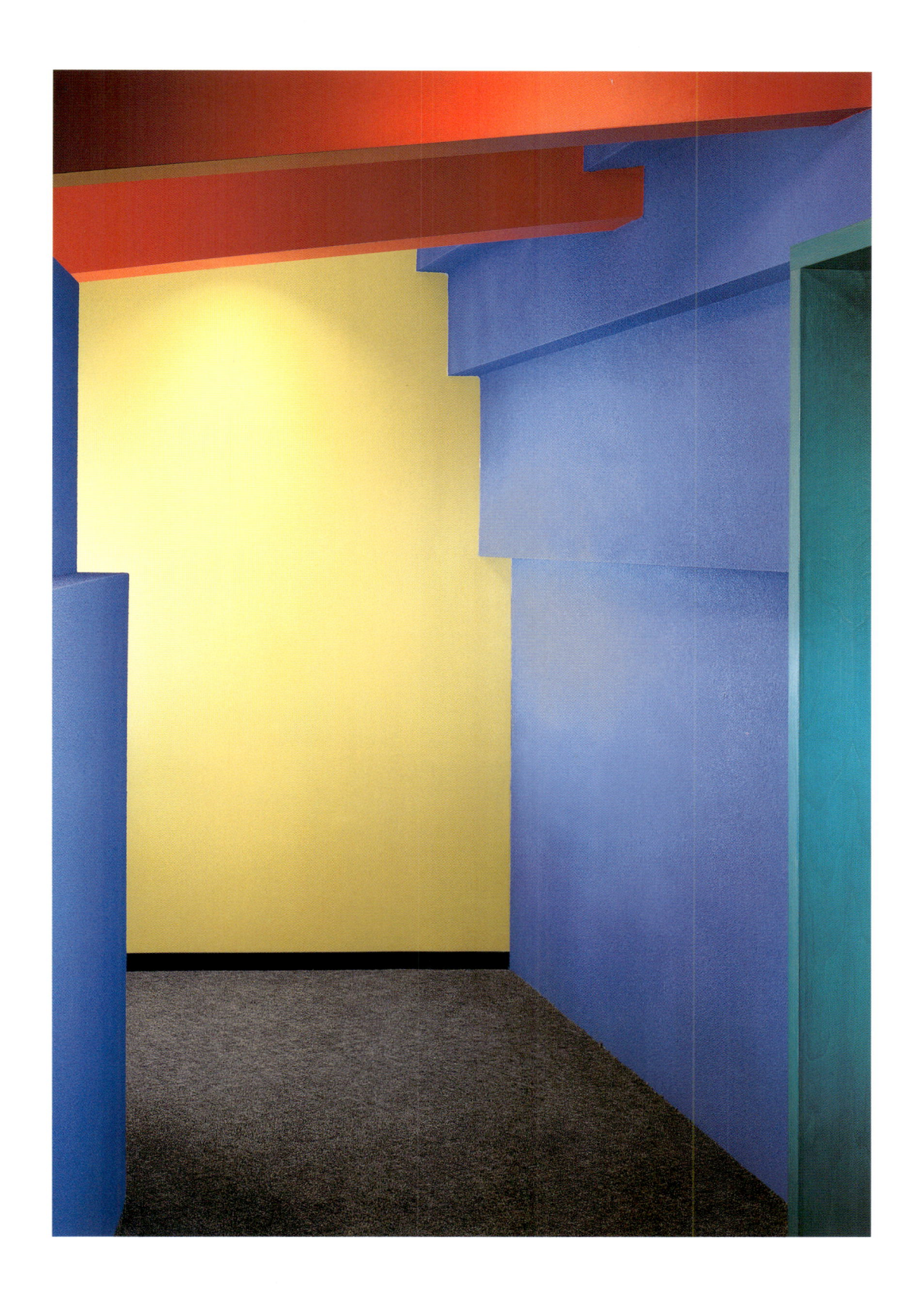

Axonometric / Assonometria

Plan / Pianta

25

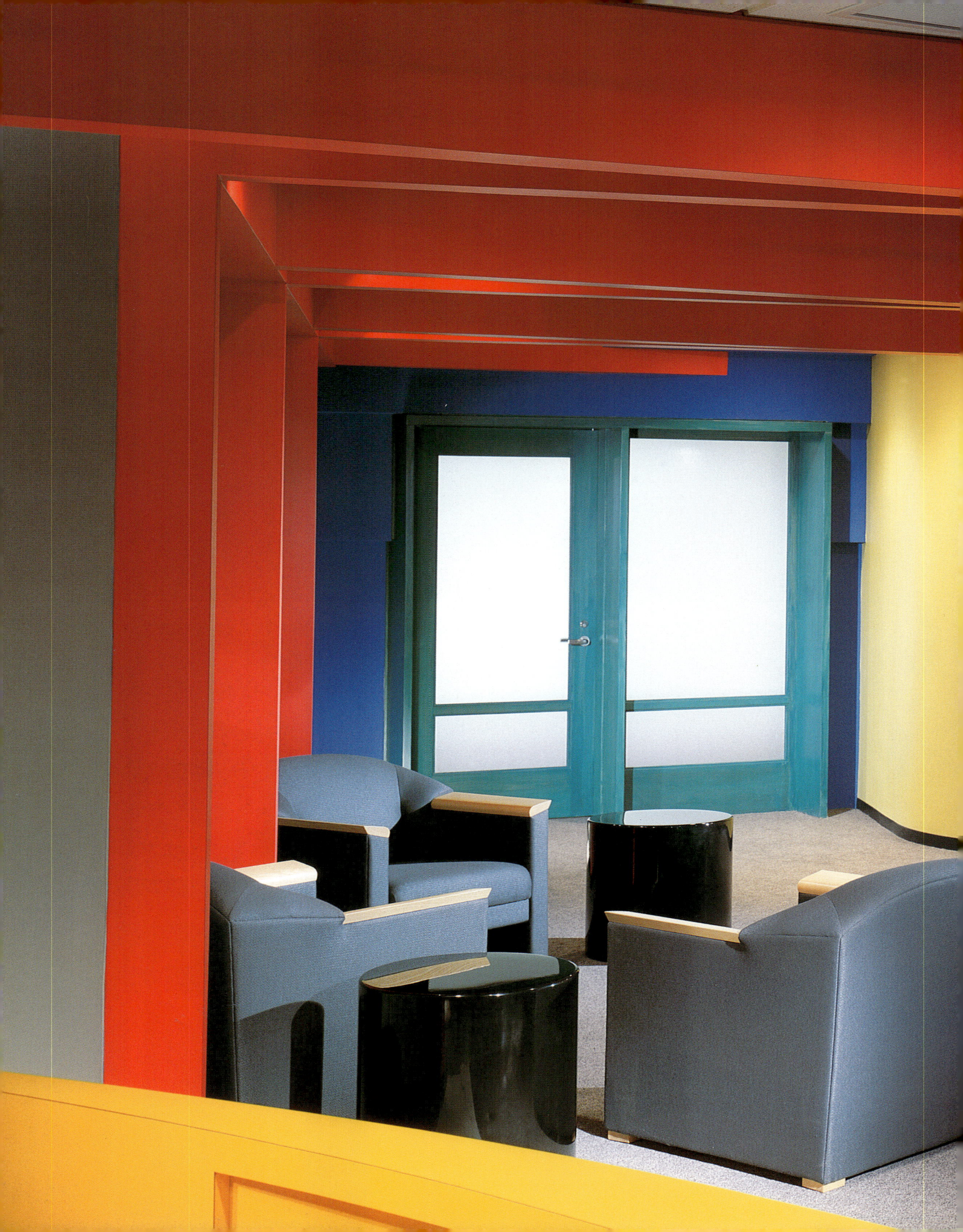

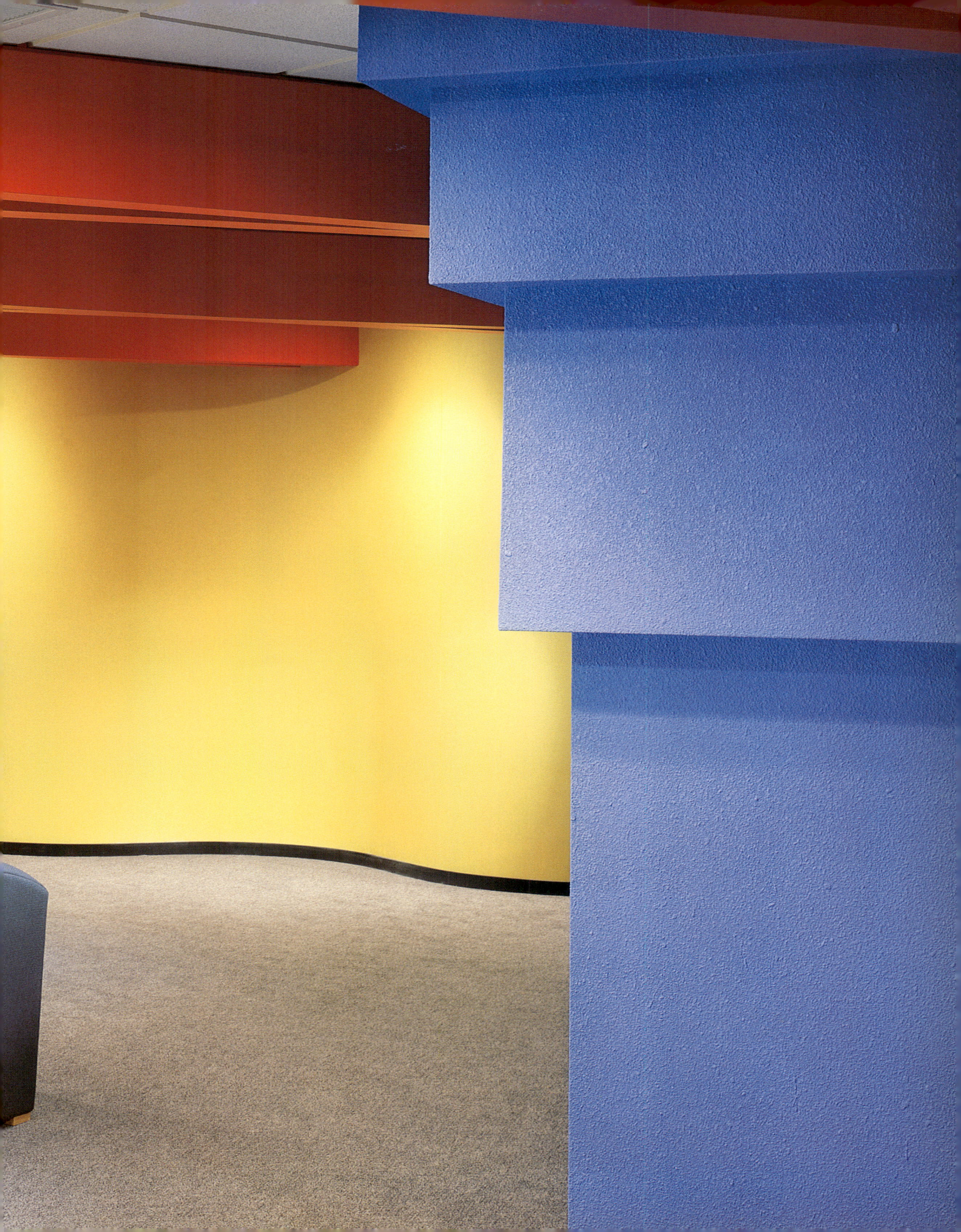

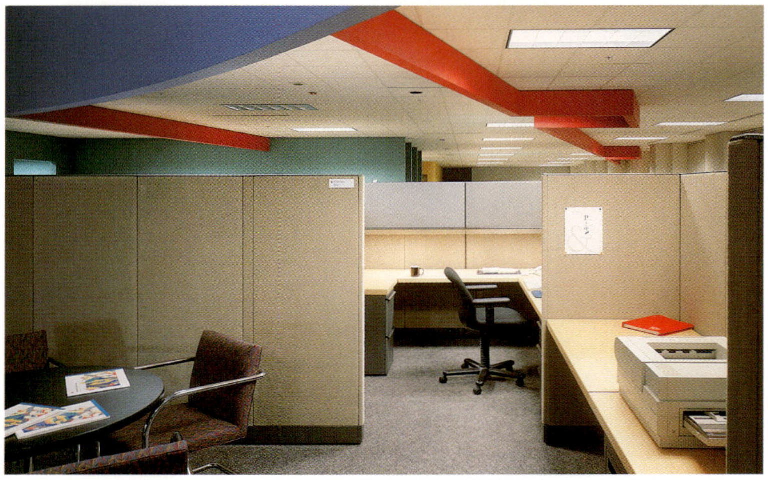

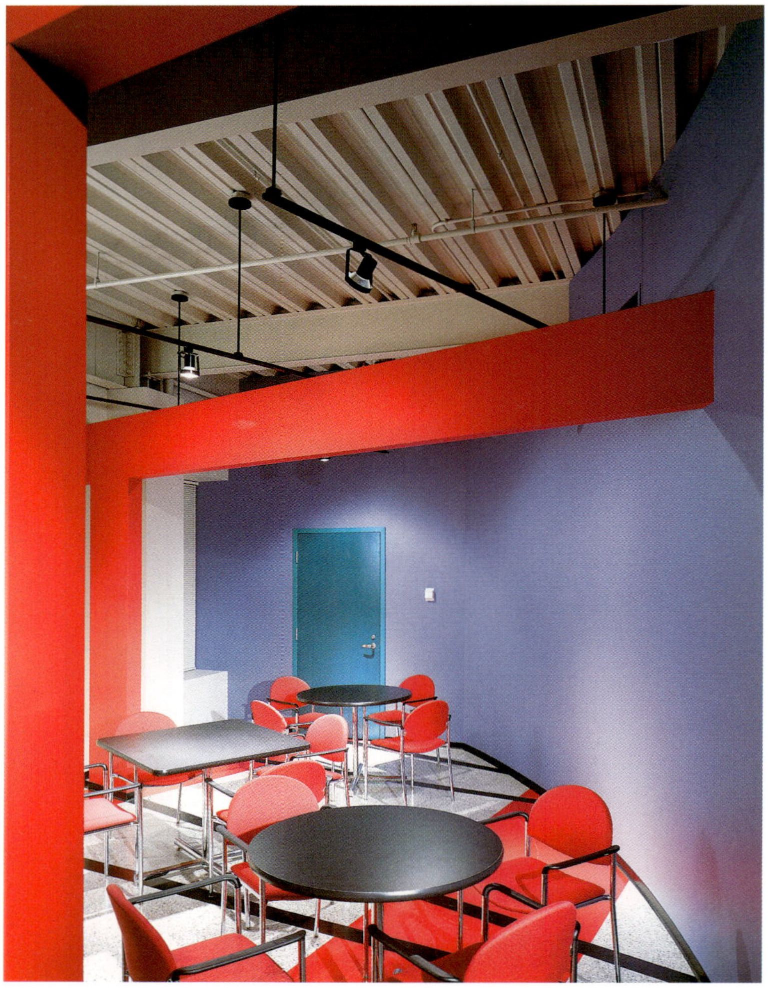

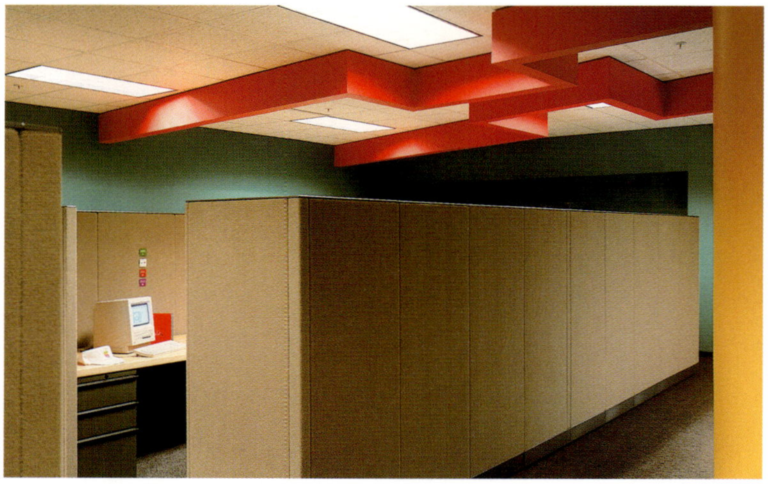

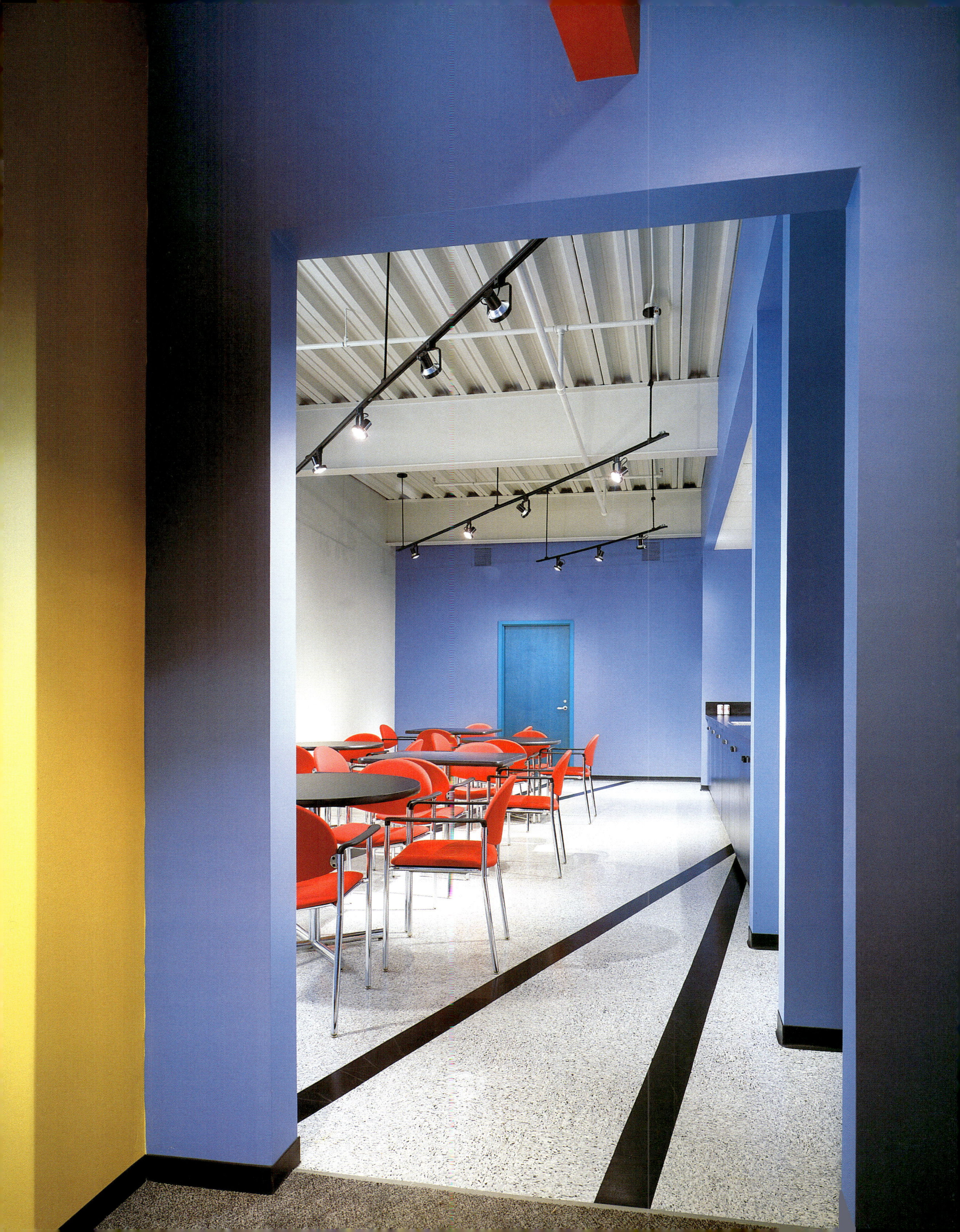

BABCOCK & BROWN
STUDIOS Architecture. San Francisco, CA, 1992

Installed on the top floor of a brick building constructed in 1926 on the Market Street waterfront, the headquarters of this banking corporation expressly required an architectural solution that adequately reflected the group's corporate philosophy: a space that would express the entrepreneurial élan, with a pinch of assertiveness. The original rectangular plan of the space is composed of an orthogonal network of beams and pillars in reinforced concrete, and was conceived as a neutral container to be reconfigured with a complex and unconventional working environment. Distributed below a ceiling of concrete and undulating metal sheeting, punctuated here and there by large skylights, are the various separate operative units whose arrangement the architects say is based on a medieval town plan. Stripped to expose the brickwork, which is interrupted periodically by broad archways, the entire perimeter has been equipped with individual offices, exclusive conference rooms, and comfortable zones for waiting and informal meetings. The layout takes full advantage of the disposition of the windows, successfully harnessing the natural light in the inner section, thanks to the glazed partition walls. This outer band represents the "city walls," so to speak, within which the new complex scheme of the offices develops by means of a series of architectural elements, their urban connotations rescaled to a new dimension. The work zones are distributed on various split levels, linked via carefully planned circulation routes that follow an elliptical plan, around which the entire design revolves. Two sturdy stucco arches, one gray, one brick-red, bridged by a vault-like canopy of sheet steel, characterize the entrance lobby, which gives onto a conference room; compact, eye-catching designs mark the complex central zone animated by a series of raised platforms and a series of ceiling elements that frequently complement the forms below. Materials such as steel (sometimes worked, as in the partition in the conference room overlooking the bay), aluminum, concrete, stucco, and glass, are used alongside industrial elements such as the large lamps hanging from the ceiling, and the exposed ducting, as if hinting at the original function of the building.

Ricavata all'ultimo piano di un edificio in mattoni costruito nel 1926 lungo il waterfront di Market Street, la sede di questo Istituto Bancario richiedeva espressamente una soluzione architettonica in sintonia con la filosofia del Gruppo: uno spazio che esprimesse vivacità imprenditoriale e una giusta dose di aggressività operativa. La pianta rettangolare regolare, segnata da una maglia ortogonale di travi e pilastri in cemento armato, è stata così assunta come spazio neutro in cui configurare un ambiente di lavoro complesso e non convenzionale. Sotto il soffitto in cemento e in lamiera grecata lasciati a vista, interrotto da ampi lucernari, sono stati distribuiti i diversi luoghi di lavoro secondo un principio compositivo ispirato, dicono i progettisti, alla città medioevale. Il perimetro, scandito dalle pareti di mattoni interrotte da ampie aperture ad arco, è stato interamente occupato da uffici operativi indipendenti, esclusive sale riunioni e confortevoli zone di attesa e per riunioni informali. La distribuzione ha sfruttato al meglio la disposizione delle aperture catturando la luce naturale anche nella zona interna grazie alle pareti divisorie in vetro. Questa fascia perimetrale rappresenta le 'mura della città'; nell'interno si sviluppa la nuova complessa immagine dell'ufficio, che attraverso una serie di elementi architettonici compiuti, traslati dalle forme urbane e tradotti nella dimensione d'interni, organizza su vari livelli diverse zone di lavoro connesse tra loro da studiati percorsi distributivi, previsti lungo un'ellisse di riferimento attorno cui si dispongono i vari segni del progetto. Due archi in stucco grigio e rosso mattone, connessi tra loro da una volta in lamiera, caratterizzano ingresso e reception aperta verso la sala conferenze; piccole e forti architetture sono distribuite nella complessa zona centrale movimentata da pedane e da una serie di elementi a soffitto pensati come forti volumi sospesi, spesso complementari delle forme sottostanti. Materiali come l'acciaio (a volte lavorato, come nella quinta della sala riunioni affacciata sulla Baia), l'alluminio e il cemento, lo stucco e il vetro, si affiancano a elementi industriali, come le grandi lampade che scendono dal soffitto e i condotti metallici a vista degli impianti, ricordando il carattere originario dell'edificio.

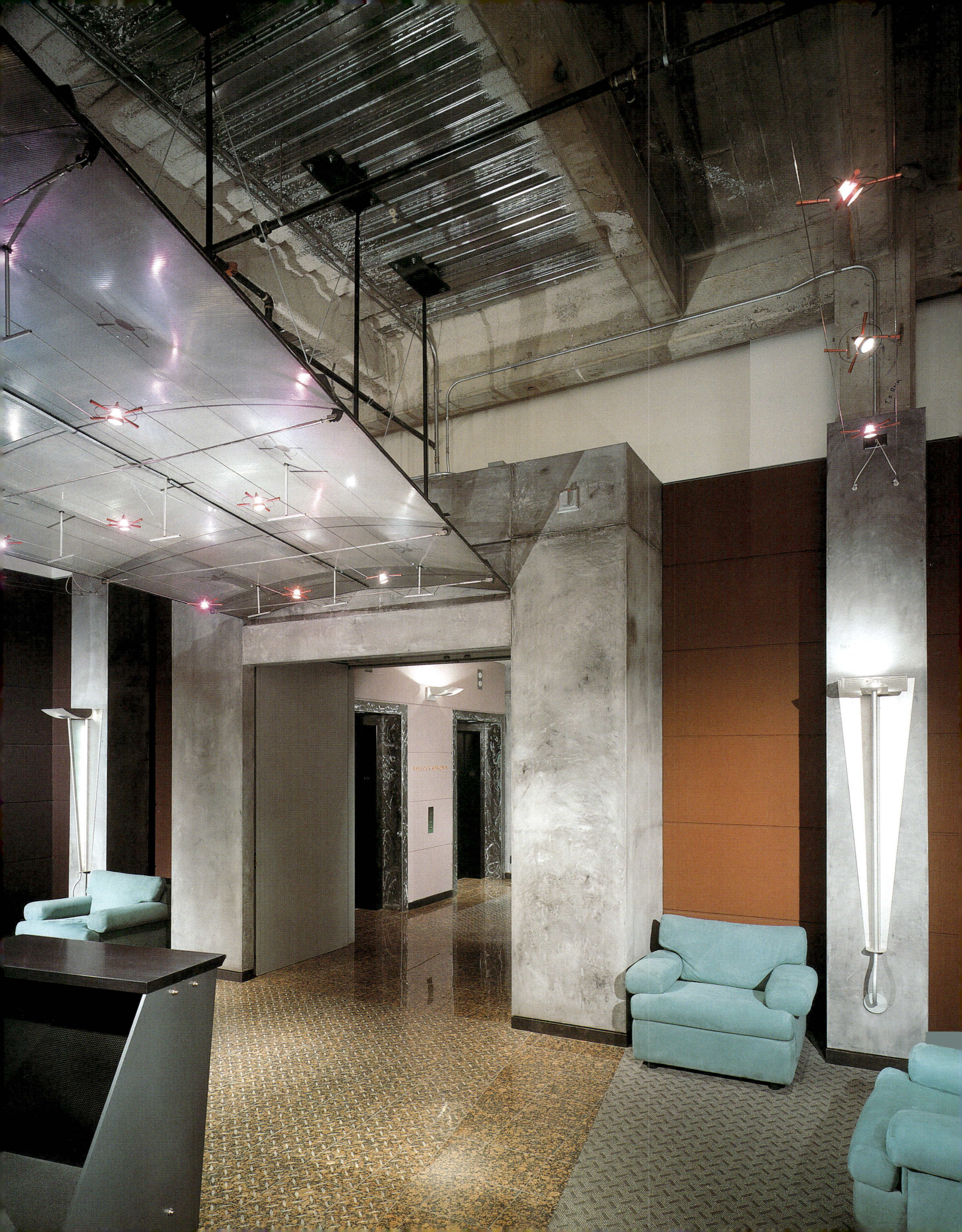

Transversal section / Sezione trasversale

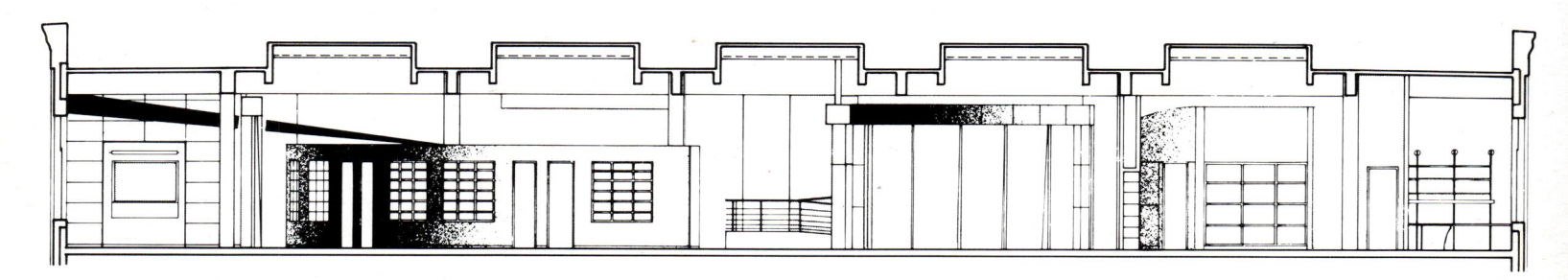

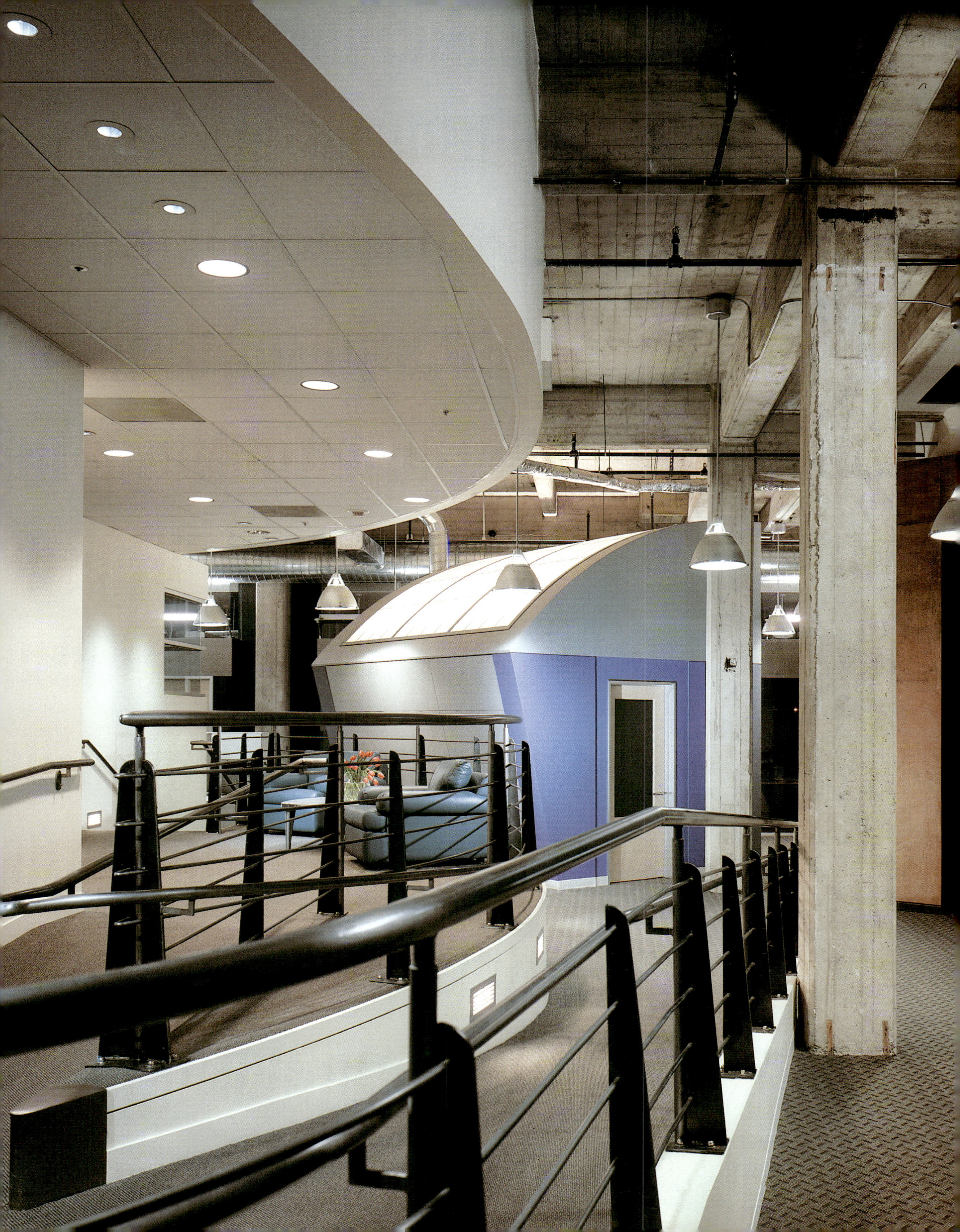

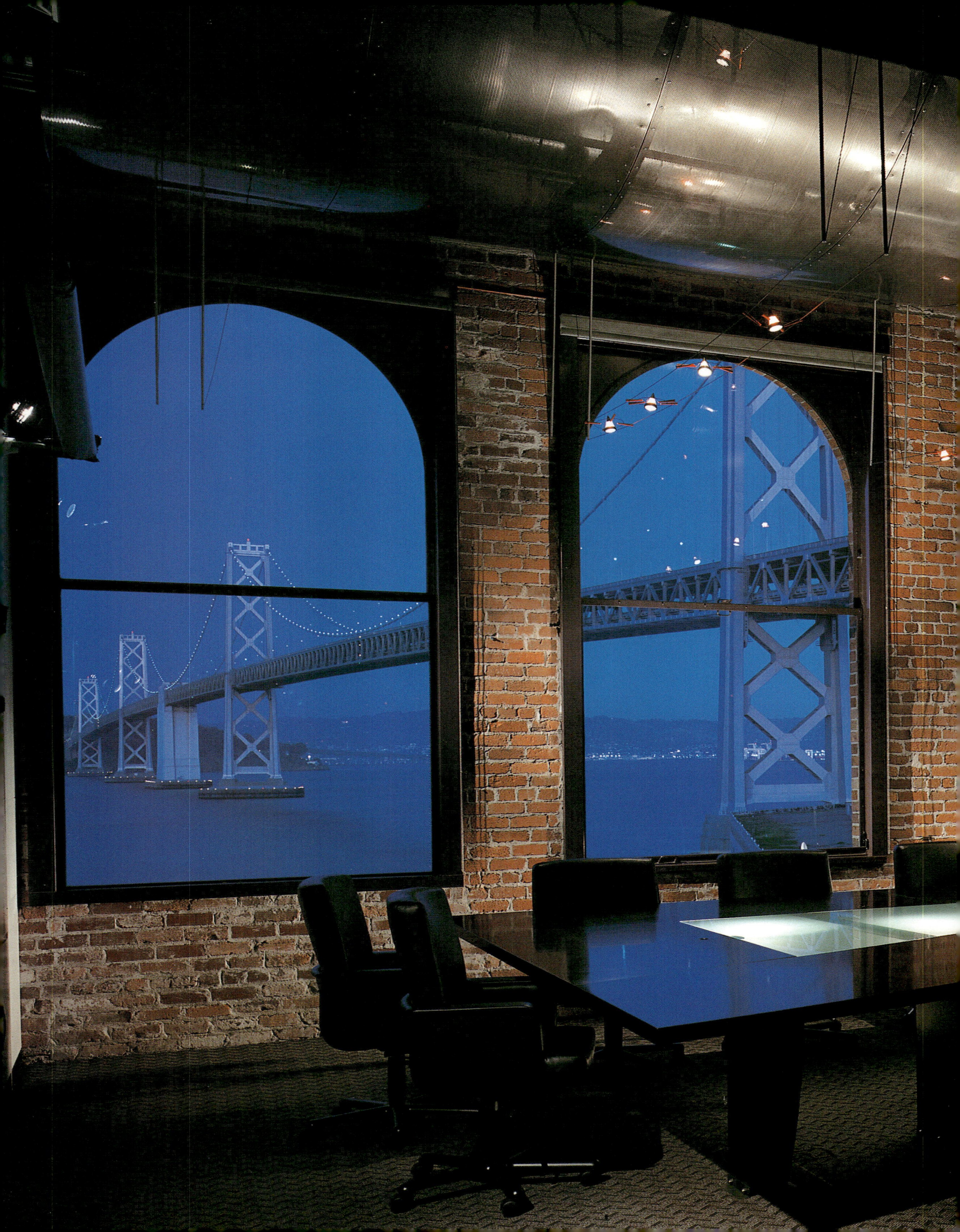

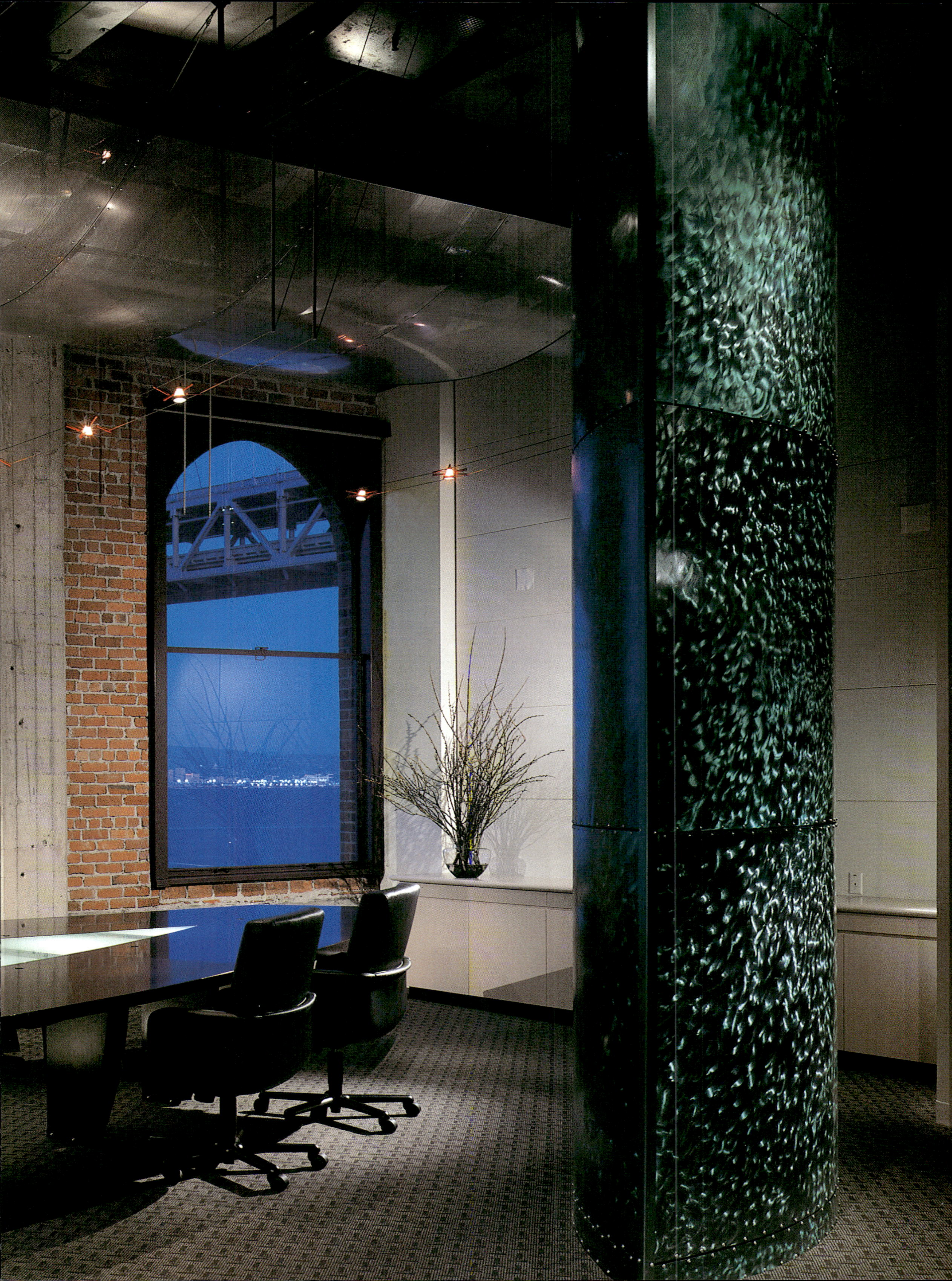

Plan / Pianta
1. Elevator lobby / Arrivo ascensori
2. Reception / Reception
3. Conference / Sale conferenze
4. Soft seating / Salottino di attesa per riunioni informali
5. Workout / Piccola palestra
6. Lockers room & showers / Spogliatoi e servizi igienici
7. Coffee / Saletta caffè
8. Workroom / Piccola cucina

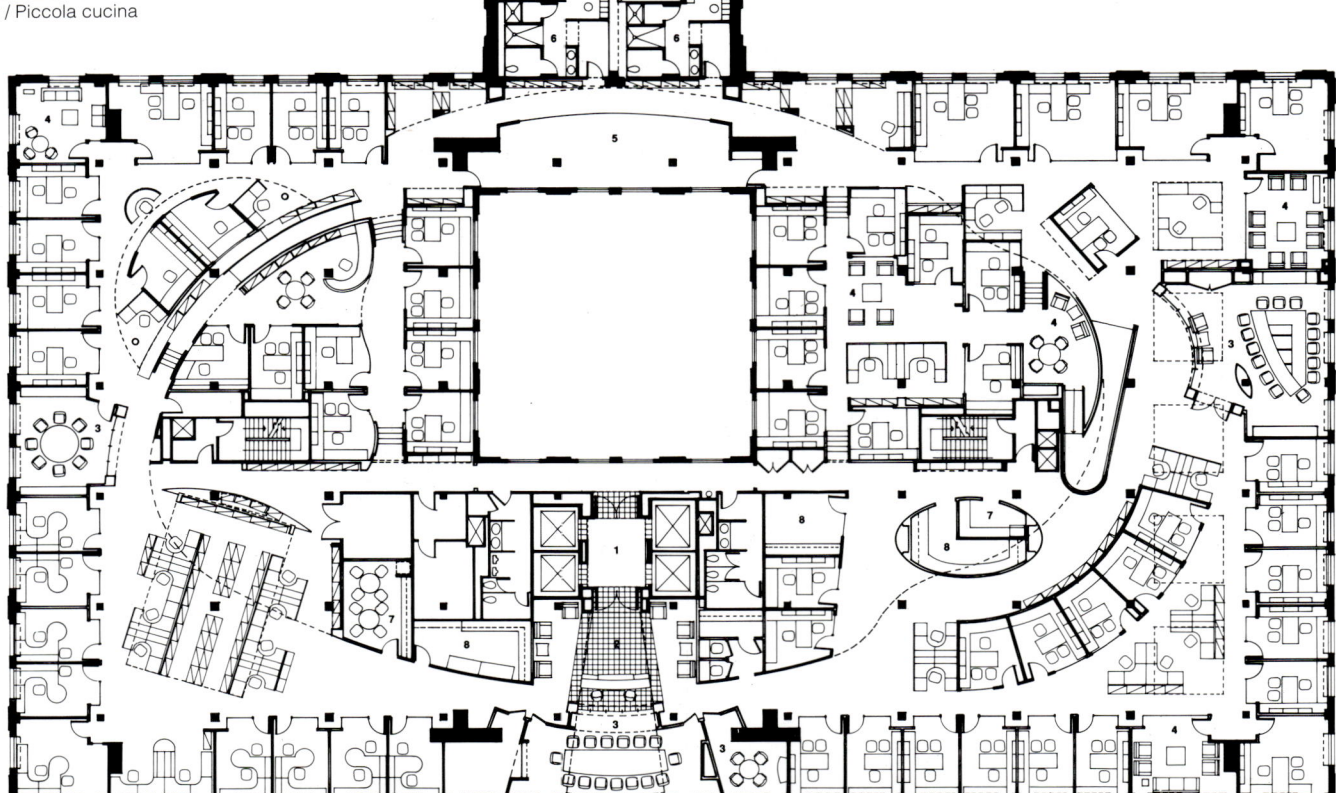

Axonometric plan / Vista assonometrica

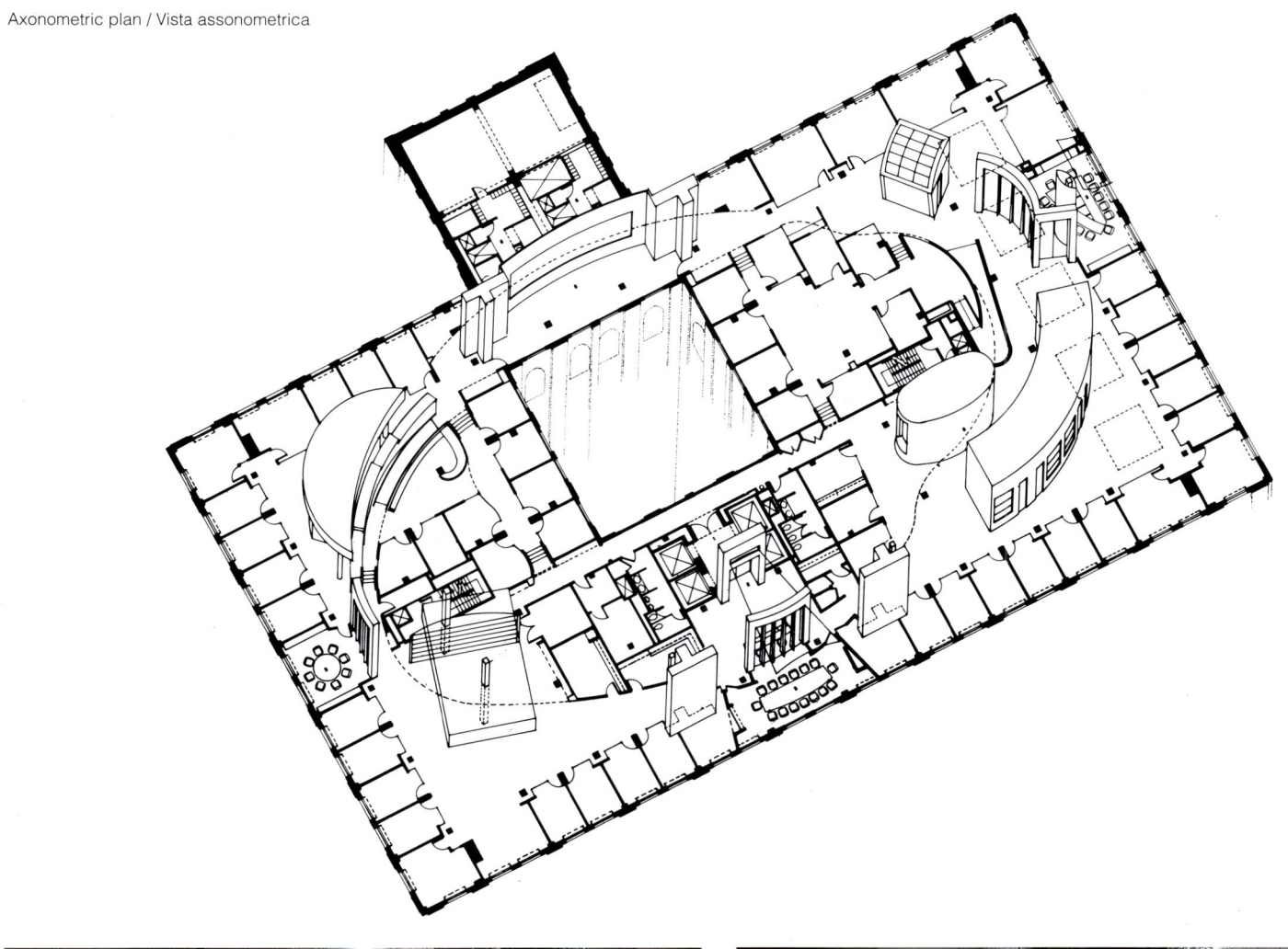

BURGER KING
NBBJ Architecture Design Planning. Miami, FL, 1993

Summarily demolished by Hurricane Andrew in 1992, the Burger King headquarters in Miami has been completely rebuilt: the style of the new interiors, echoing the general atmosphere of the company's fast-food joints, fulfills the functional needs while providing a collective workplace that does not encroach on the executive offices and other individual units. The headquarters' three floors are linked by an all-new system of internal stairways featuring white ship-style tubular banisters common to the city's renowned Deco architecture, an allusion to the waterfront landscape, with a kind of interior main-street ambiance composed of forms laid at various diagonals to comply with the irregular zigzag shape of the building. The main circulation route, along which the various workspaces are distributed, is composed of a series of neatly gauged juxtapositions, architectural inventions, and variety of materials that intermix dynamically, with curving and oblique walls in bright colors, paneling in horizontal rectangles for the partition walls that end short of the ceiling in glazed panels; other walls in sanded glass form large cubes (a whimsical, giant-size replica of the soda-pump found in fast-food restaurants) that channel off the main circulation route from the meeting and conference rooms. Management quarters and individual offices are shut off from the rest by sliding panels; large openings screened off by partitions with glazed sections give onto open-space areas, in which the white workstations are equipped with an assortment of colored chairs. The lively chromatic scheme of the main corridor, the office chairs, and the variegated types of furnishings of the conference rooms, is reiterated in the design and palette of the carpeting, which covers all the available floorspace: an abstract geometrical pattern with ample curved shapes, the sea and sky blue of Miami is complemented by a range of hues that wryly advertise the company's hallmark sauces: thick catsup reds, mustard and maionese yellows, and not least the inevitable green of fresh lettuce…

Devastata nell'estate del 1992 dall'uragano Andrew, la sede della Burger King di Miami è stata completamente ristrutturata: la nuova immagine, ricordando nell'atmosfera generale il carattere *fast food*, oggetto della produzione del Gruppo, risponde alle esigenze funzionali e a quelle della ricerca di un senso di lavoro collettivo senza disturbare la privacy degli uffici direzionali e singoli. Uniti i tre livelli con un nuovo dinamico sistema di scale interne, caratterizzate dalla ringhiera di tipo navale in tubi in ferro orizzontali tinteggiati di bianco, impiegata in molte architetture déco della città, ci si è voluti rapportare al paesaggio ubano del *waterfront* anche creando una sorta di *Main Street* interna, composta da varie figure disposte in diagonale seguendo la pianta irregolare dell'edificio. Il percorso collettivo di riferimento, da cui distribuire le diverse tipologie di spazi di lavoro, accoglie una serie di calibrati accostamenti, soluzioni architettoniche e diversi materiali che mischiano in un dinamico confronto pareti colorate in curva e oblique a tutt'altezza, rivestimenti a pannelli rettangolari orizzontali per elementi divisori che non raggiungono il soffitto; alte vetrate sabbiate formano dei grandi cubi (ironica versione gigante di quelli del ghiaccio delle bibite dei *fast food*) che separano il percorso interno dalle sale riunioni e conferenze. Uffici direzionali e singoli sono separati da alte porte scorrevoli colorate, mentre ampi varchi, schermati da pareti divisorie con zone vetrate, si aprono verso gli open space dove sono organizzate le funzionali postazioni operative bianche, cui si affiancano le sedie di vari colori. I vivaci colori presenti nella *Main Street* e ripresi dalle sedie di lavoro e dalla variegata selezione degli arredi per le sale riunione vengono sottolineati nel disegno e e nella tavolozza cromatica della moquette policroma che si estende per tutto lo spazio disponibile. All'interno di un disegno geometrico astratto, che mischia ampi riquadri con forme curvilinee, il blu e l'azzurro del mare di Miami si affianca a una scelta di colori volutamente ispirata a quella dei condimenti dell'Hamburger prodotto dal Gruppo: rosso per il ketchup e i pomodori, ocra per la senape, giallo per la maionese e verde per l'immancabile foglia di lattuga.

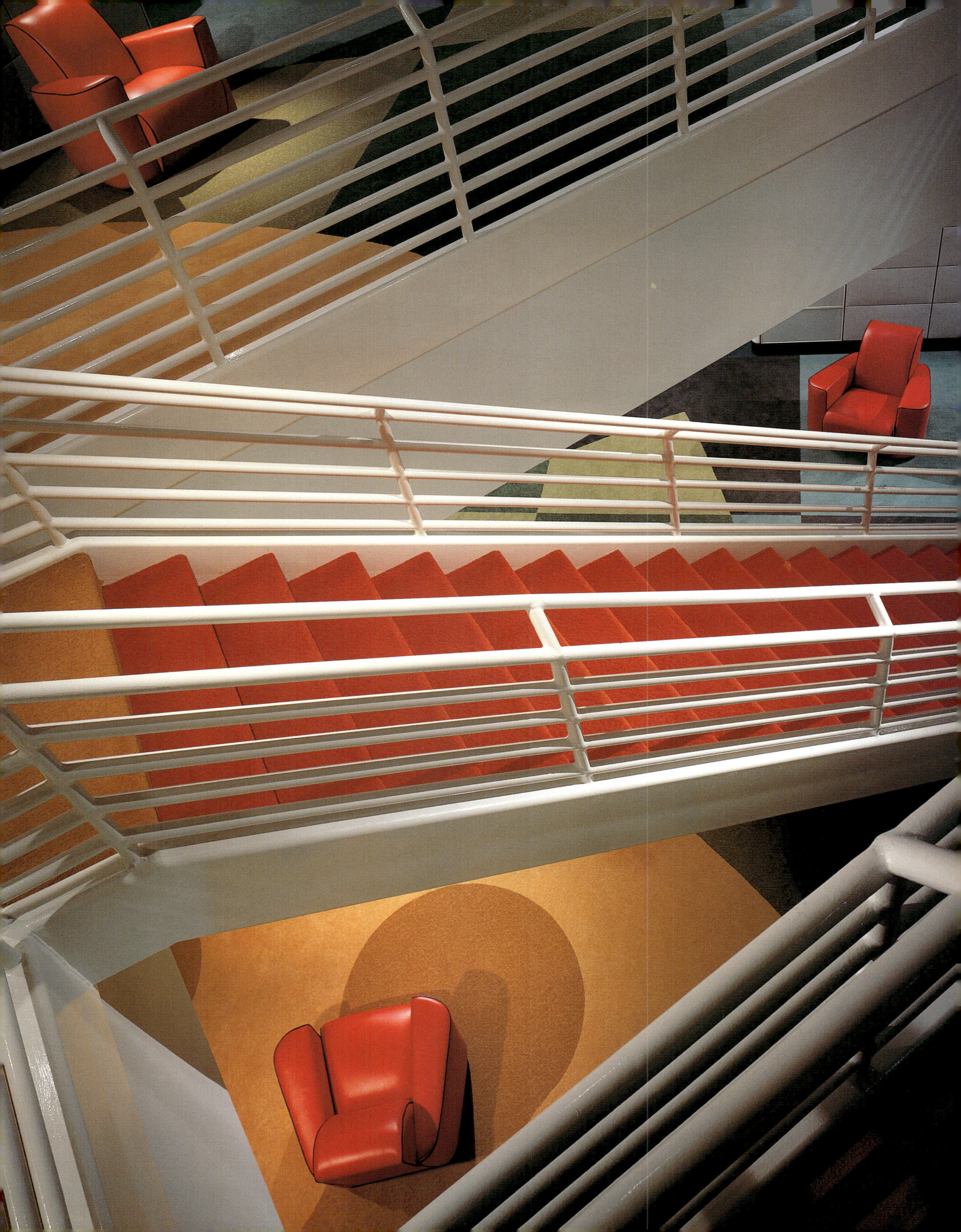

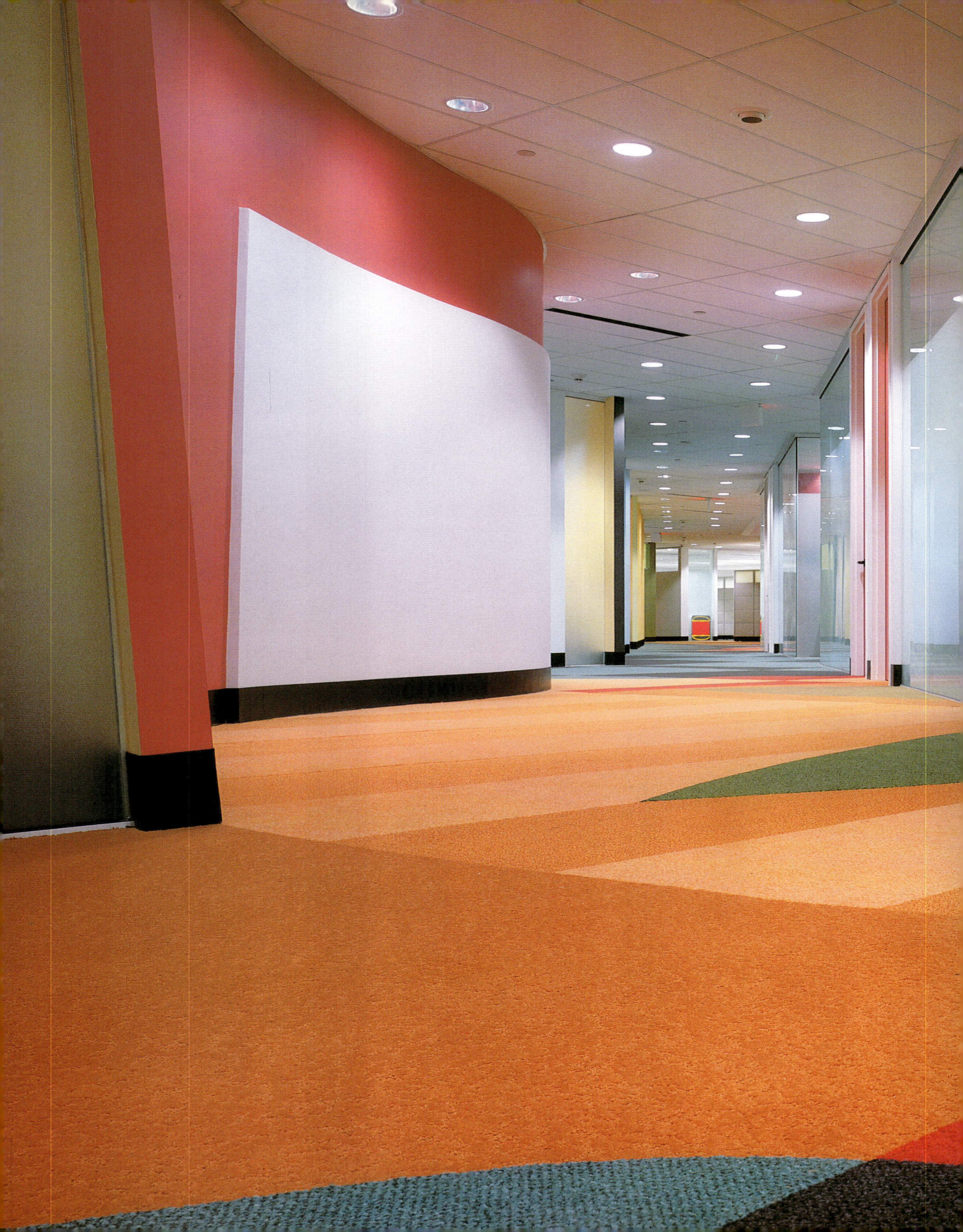

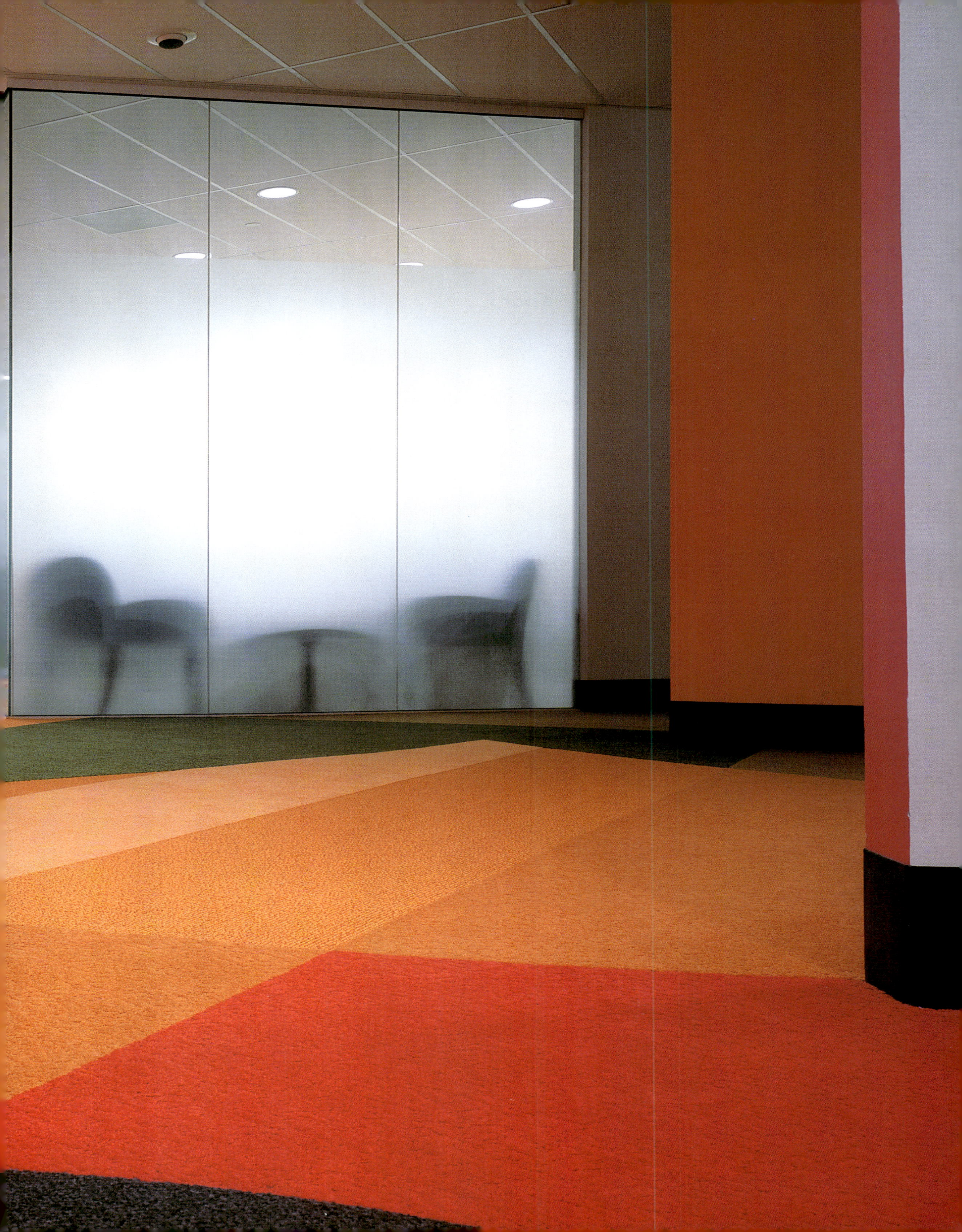

42

43

Plan / Pianta

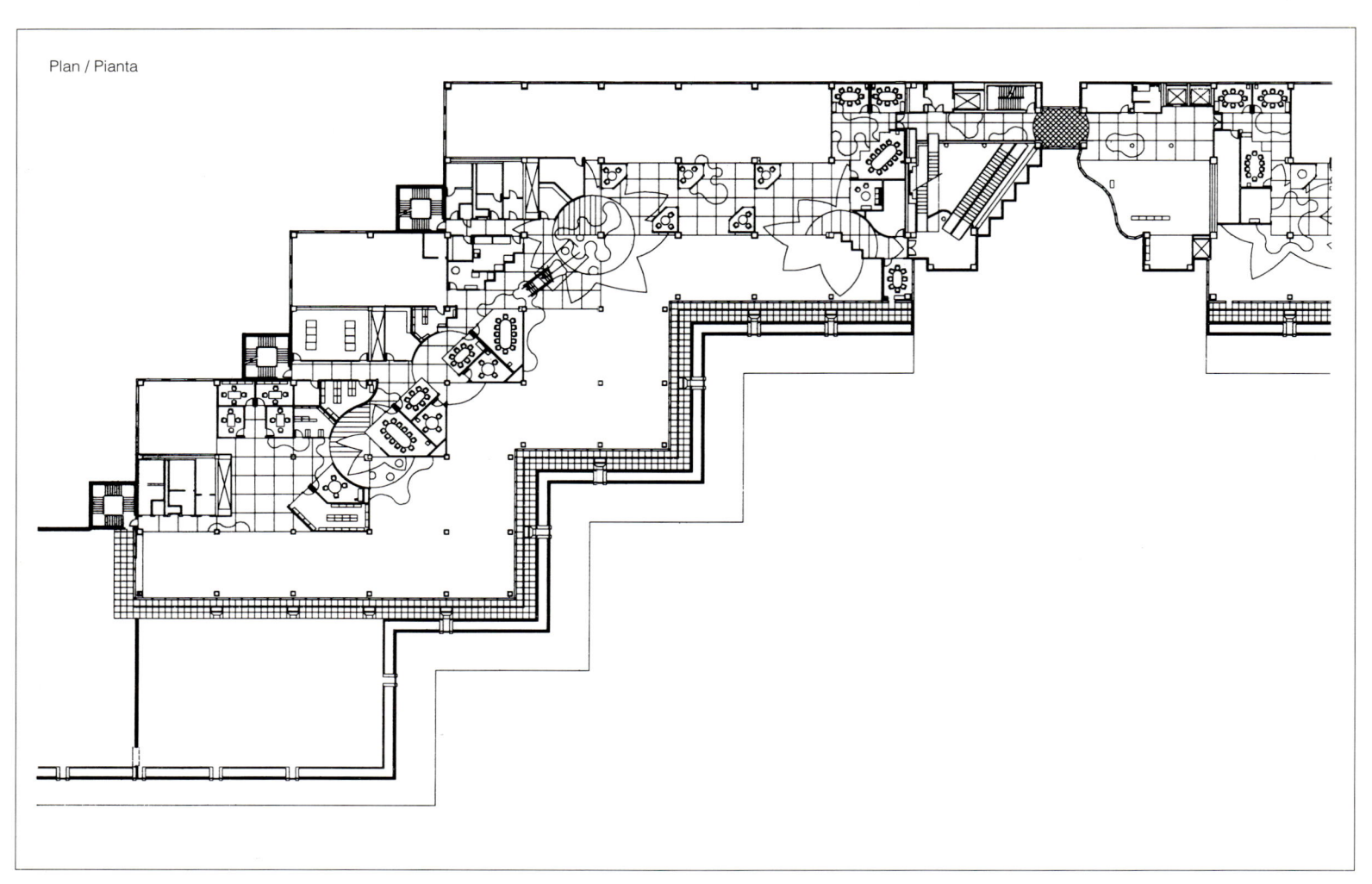

44

45

CLEARY GOTTLIEB STEEN & HAMILTON

Kohn, Pedersen, Fox, Associates P.C. New York, NY, 1990

This major legal consultancy is arranged on six stories in a large, uniformly rectangular building, and the layout of the interiors follows a strict rationale in which function is the keyword. The airy workspaces, which include open-plan collective areas, private office units, meeting rooms of varying dimensions, libraries and archives, recording and conference rooms, a snack lounge and a staff restaurant - all meticulously organized from a functional standpoint and with regard to the overall image and chosen furnishings - pivot on a pair of key architectural features that regulate the entire project, namely, the two multi-level atria that were obtained by demolishing the existing load-bearing structures. These two elements provide the pivot for the complex disposition of the interiors, by which a first band of independent workspaces are arranged along most of the glazed facades; whereas the internal spaces are organized on an open-plan scheme, with reception and secretarial facilities, and individual or collective workstation areas distributed around the less well-lit, central area, where the stair and elevator block is situated, alongside which are lodged the restrooms, a series of archive units, and assorted meeting rooms. The larger of the two multistory atria is set strategically along the building's facade, so as to offer a striking view of the Brooklyn Bridge and create an exceptional internal promenade leading off to each of the separate work areas. The fine oak used for most of the furniture and shelving is preluded in the staircases and the flooring in the two-level linkage area; whereas in the larger atrium, which extends upward on three stories, we find strikingly designed doorways faced in wood that emphasize the vertical thrust of the full-height design. This qualified architectural space, rich in compositive invention and creative detail (such as the carefully studied metal banister design), is characterized by a floor in dark stone (used here and there for the vertical cladding also) enhanced with white geometrical inserts that endorse the idea of "public space" within the building as a whole.

Questo grande studio legale è organizzato su sei piani di un grande edificio a pianta rettangolare regolare, strutturato secondo una rigida logica razionale di funzionamento degli spazi. La vasta tipologia degli ambienti di lavoro (open space, sale lavoro collettive e uffici privati singoli, sale riunione di diverse dimensioni, librerie e archivi, sale registrazione e per conferenze, una caffetteria e una mensa interna) studiati in ogni dettaglio sia dal punto di vista funzionale, sia per quanto riguarda l'immagine e le scelte d'arredo, si affiancano a due episodi architettonici di riferimento cui si rapportano gli ambienti del progetto complessivo: i grandi atri a più livelli ottenuti demolendo le strutture portanti esistenti. Intorno a questi due episodi si sviluppa la complessa regia distributiva che organizza una prima fascia di spazi di lavoro indipendenti lungo gran parte delle facciate vetrate, mentre nell'interno si organizzano ambienti open space con segreterie, reception e postazioni di lavoro singole o collettive, distribuite intorno alla zona centrale più buia, dove il blocco ascensori-scale è affiancato dai servizi, da una serie di sale archivio e da qualche sala riunione. Il maggiore dei due vani multipiano è organizzato in posizione strategica lungo la facciata che offre la migliore vista sul panorama della città, sui moli e sul Brooklyn Bridge, configurandosi così anche come sorta di eccezionale passeggiata interna da percorrere per raggiungere i diversi spazi di lavoro. Il legno di quercia impiegato per gran parte di arredi e librerie viene annunciato dal rivestimento della scala e dal parquet che caratterizzano il vano di collegamento su due livelli, mentre in quello di dimensioni maggiori, che si sviluppa per l'altezza di tre piani, troviamo dei grandi portali architettonici rivestiti in legno che sottolineano lo slancio verticale della soluzione a tutt'altezza. Questo qualificato spazio architettonico, ricco di soluzioni compositive e di dettaglio (come l'accurato disegno della ringhiera metallica), è segnato da un pavimento di pietra scura (usata a tratti anche come rivestimento verticale) con inserti geometrici bianchi che concorre a denunciarne il carattere di 'spazio pubblico' all'interno dell'architettura complessiva.

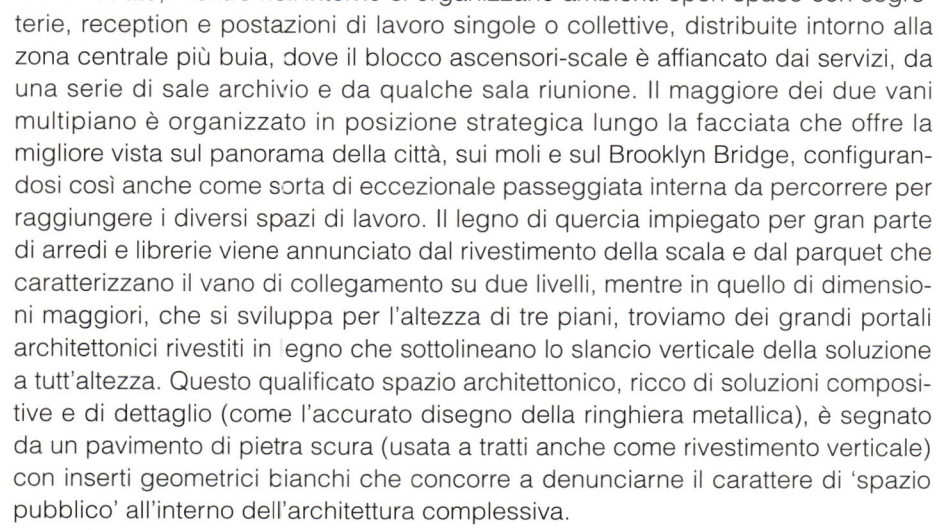

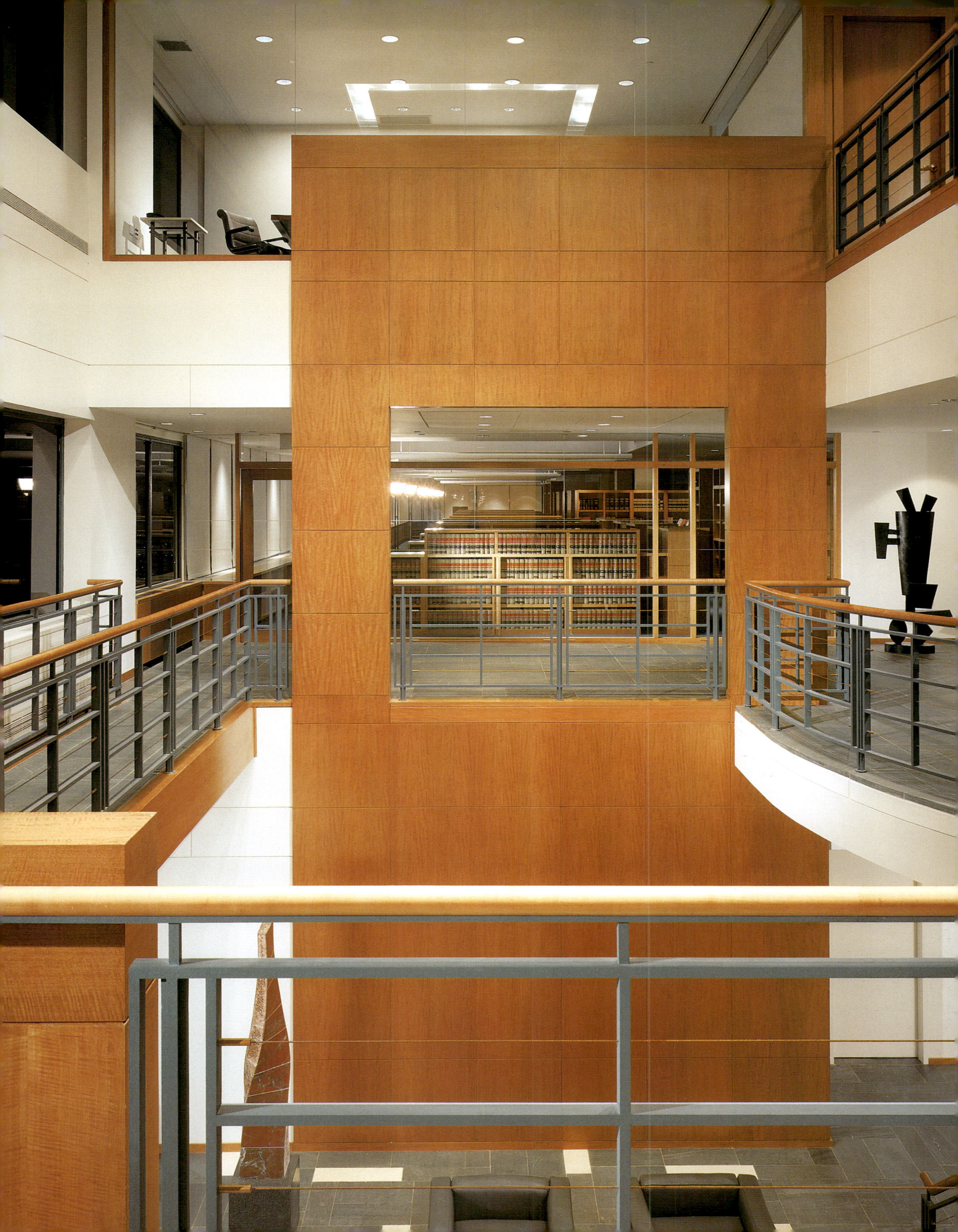

48

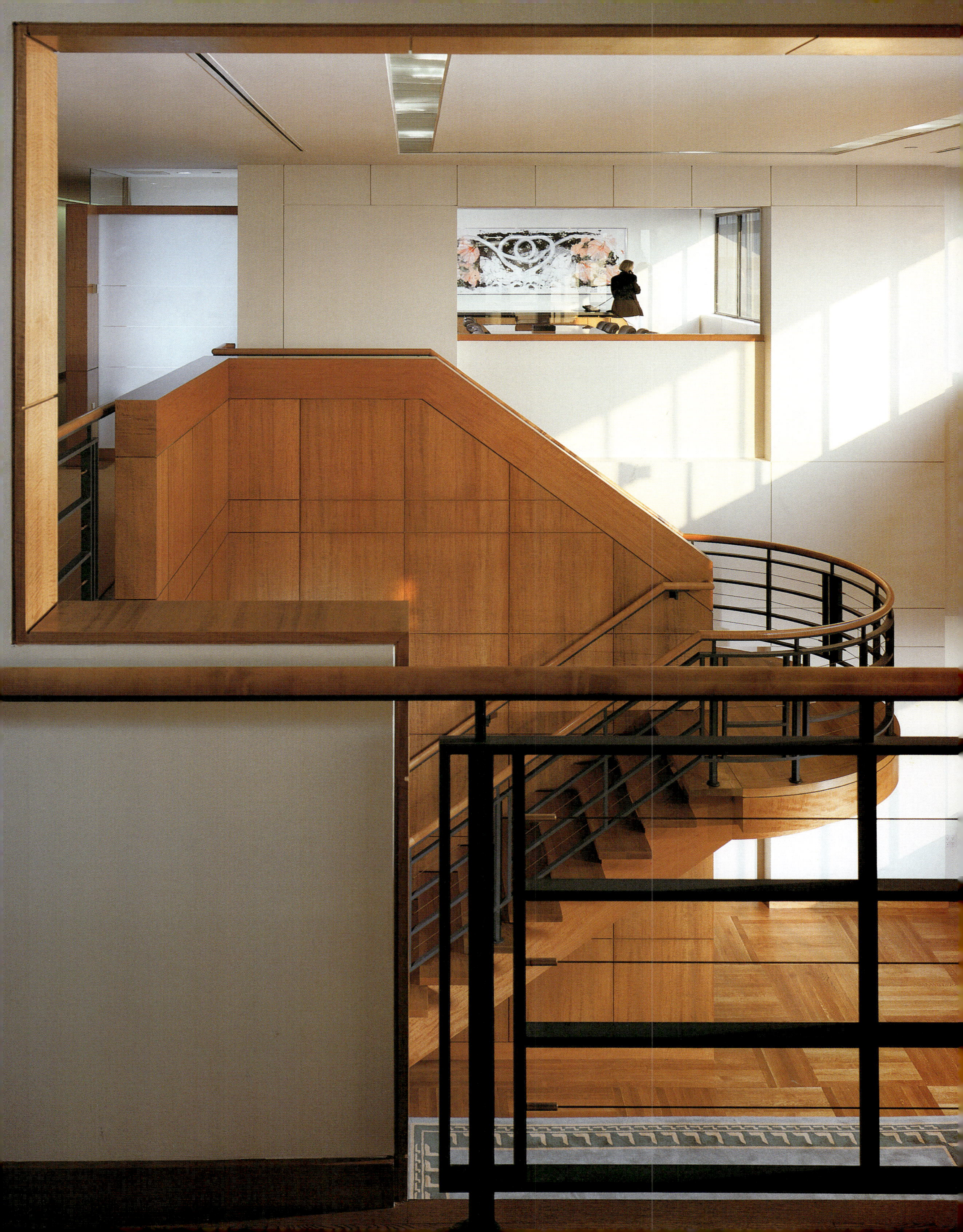

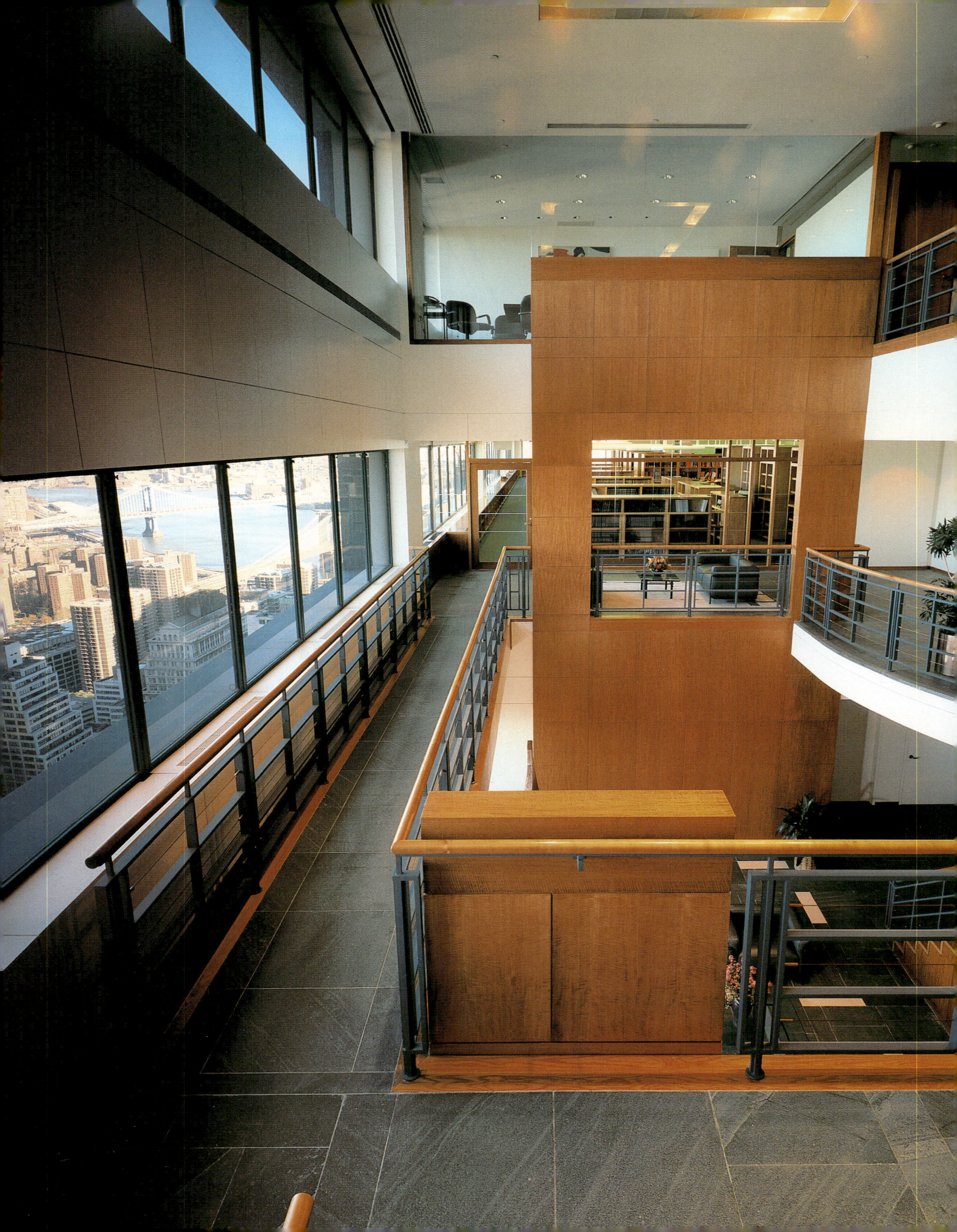

51

Plan / Pianta

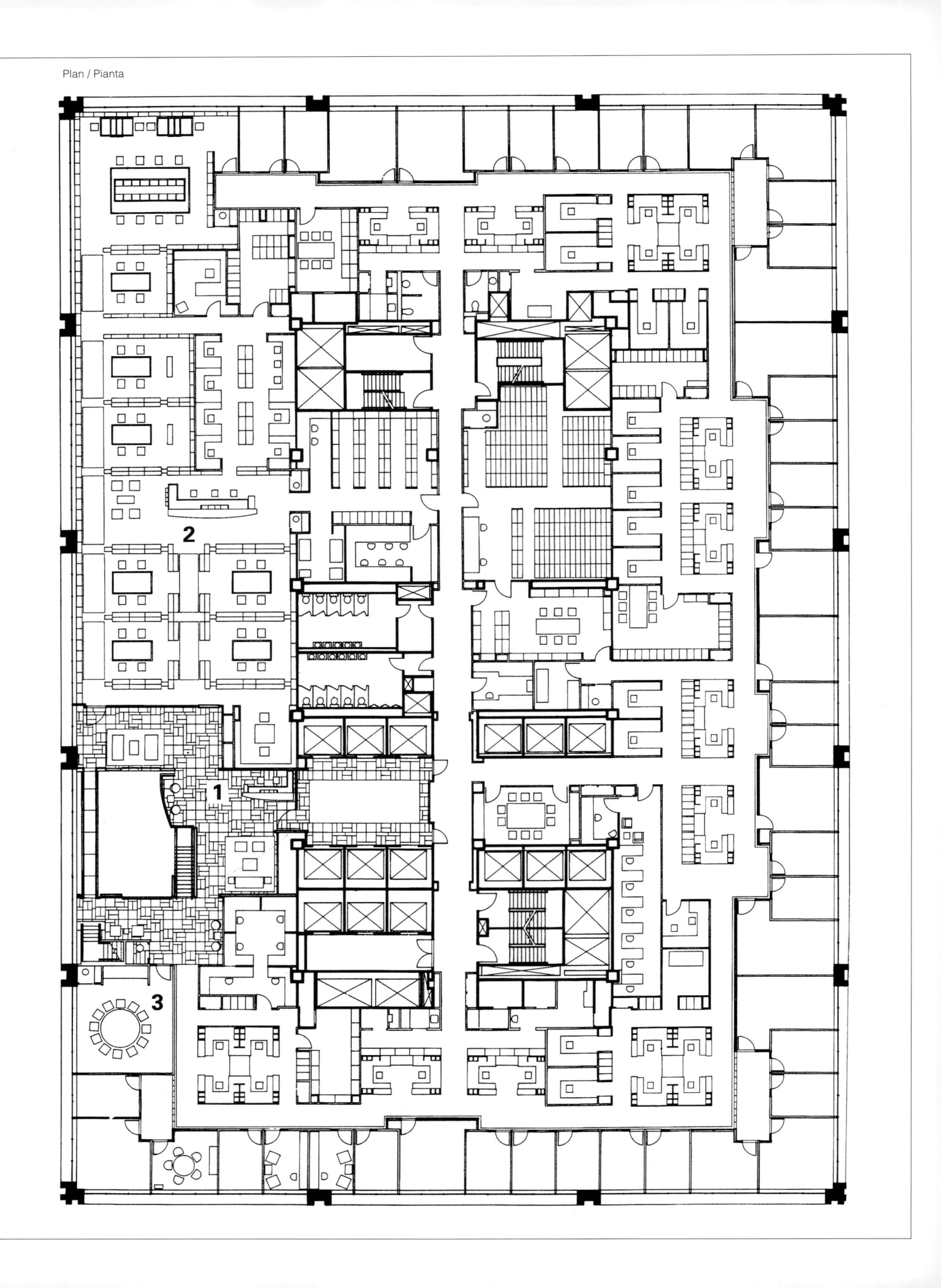

53

D.E. SHAW & COMPANY
Steven Holl Architects. New York, NY, 1991

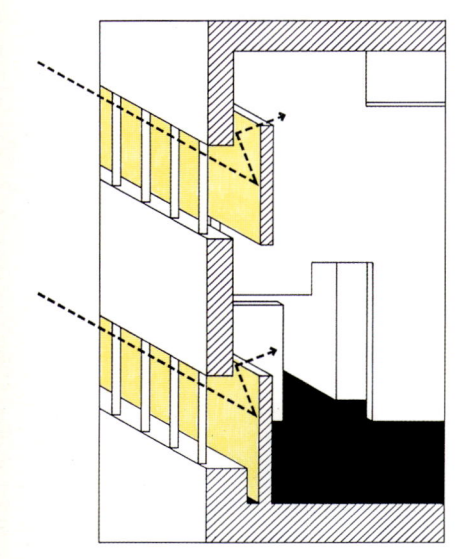

The uppermost two stories of a skyscraper in downtown Manhattan have been taken over by the corporate headquarters of this leading investment bank and financial consultancy. The definition of the image of these interiors, in harmony with the somewhat intangible sophistication of the high-key services offered by the client, provided an excellent opportunity to explore and investigate the phenomenon of reflected light and colors. The regular floor plan of the premises has been divided into two separate functional sections in correspondence with the entrance hall, which offers a central architectural hinge. On the right lie the smaller, individual offices; and on the left, an area given over to meeting and conference rooms of various sizes, flanking the edp center (which boasts over two hundred powerful processors connected via satellite to each stock market round the world). The unusual and enigmatic atrium rises to a height of two stories, its striking experimental design lending weight to the overall design philosophy of the interiors, offering the visitor a sensation that is more typical of a museum or art installation than of a suite of offices. Tall white walls rise up to form an enclosure of sculpted surfaces mounted with hidden light sources that give dramatic emphasis to the cut-out shapes, creating a pattern of dovetailed forms that include sections at skirting level too, illuminating the floor, which boasts a polished black finish. The light sources, gently tinted in various colors, reflect back from the white sections to great effect. The custom-built furniture pieces, moreover, are designed to be an integral part of the overall geometrical composition. Like its surroundings, the contrasting dark wooden reception desk is composed of interlocking geometric planes, and looks across the atrium at the waiting area, which is furnished with elementary metal seats and a low table. In a nearby conference room, a large irregularly contoured table whose top is animated by glass inserts and penholder grooves is brightly lit by a series of cylindrical pendant lamps of varying dimensions and heights, creating an elegant arrangement that aptly adds a lightweight touch to the general design of the space.

Negli ultimi due piani di un grattacielo nel centro di Manhattan è stata ricavata la sede di una società che opera nel campo di sofisticate consulenze finanziarie. La definizione dell'immagine interna, in sintonia con il carattere intangibile e di alto livello dei servizi offerti dalla committenza, è stata occasione per approfondire un percorso progettuale di sperimentazione sul fenomeno della riflessione di luce e colori. La pianta rettangolare dell'edificio è stata suddivisa in due settori funzionali in corrispondenza della zona ingresso. Questo si propone così come nodo architettonico centrale, da cui si sviluppano, a destra, una serie di uffici operativi indipendenti, a sinistra, una zona dedicata a sale riunioni di varie dimensioni, affiancate dalla centrale operativa dei computer (più di duecento, miniaturizzati e di grande potenza, collegati a satelliti e alle Borse di tutto il mondo). Oggetto architettonico a doppio livello, inconsueto ed enigmatico, l'atrio sottolinea nella sua immagine sperimentale e di grande impatto la filosofia complessiva dell'intervento, offrendo al visitatore la sensazione di entrare in un ambiente più vicino alla dimensione museale, o di allestimento artistico, che a quello di uno spazio di lavoro. Una serie di alte pareti bianche sovrapposte, a formare un'intercapedine in cui sono posizionate le sorgenti luminose, disegnano le suggestive sculture luminose ritagliate nel perimetro architettonico. La studiata composizione delle geometrie parietali forma una successione di incastri tra superfici che, distaccandosi in precisi punti dal pavimento nero lucido e dal soffitto, definiscono i vani luminosi e i passaggi del grande spazio architettonico centrale. Le sorgenti luminose a diversi colori sono proiettate sulle superfici che ne riflettono con efficacia tonalità e sfumature. Gli arredi su disegno sono parte integrante della composizione geometrica complessiva. Il banco reception, in legno scuro, si propone come calibrato assemblaggio di superfici, affiancandosi alle sedute e ai tavolini metallici della zona attesa. Dal soffitto di una sala riunioni, a illuminare il tavolo di metallo con inserti in vetro e nicchie in rete portapenne, scendono lampade cilindriche di diverse dimensioni che disegnano un elegante sistema di luce in grado di caratterizzare con leggerezza lo spazio complessivo.

Diagram of reflected color.

Particolare assonometrico del sistema di riflessione della luce sulle pareti dell'ingresso.

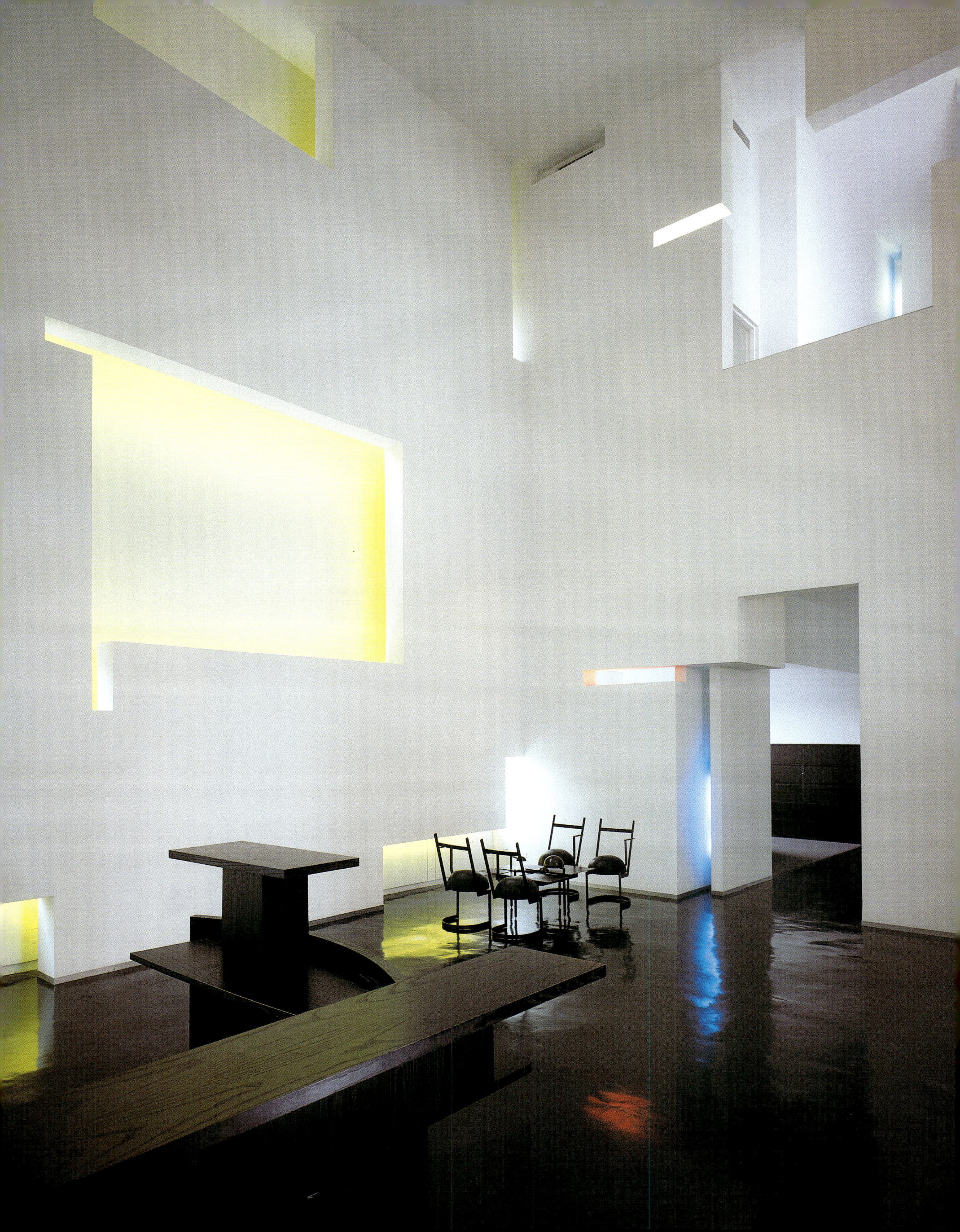

56

57

58

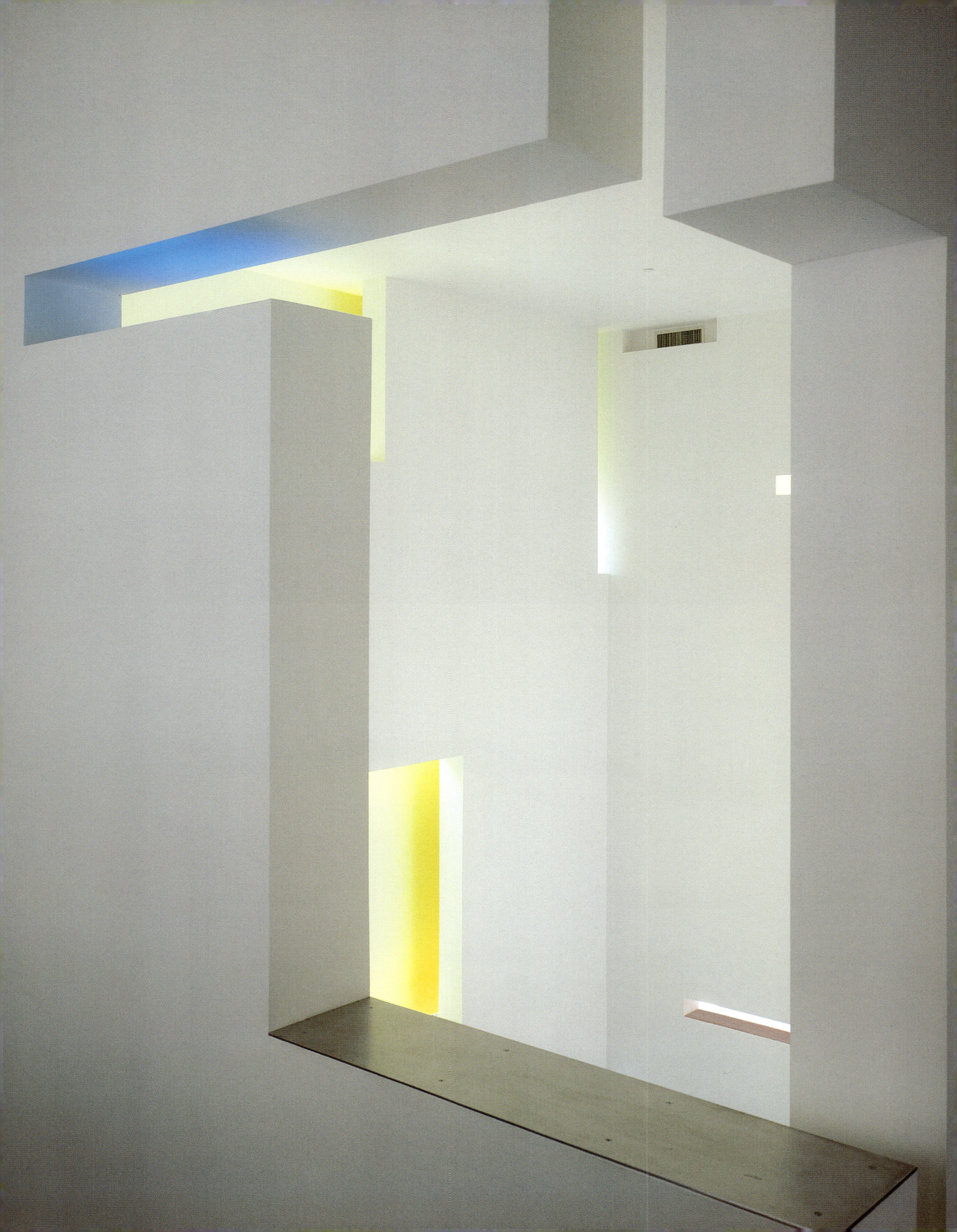

Axonometric / Assonometria

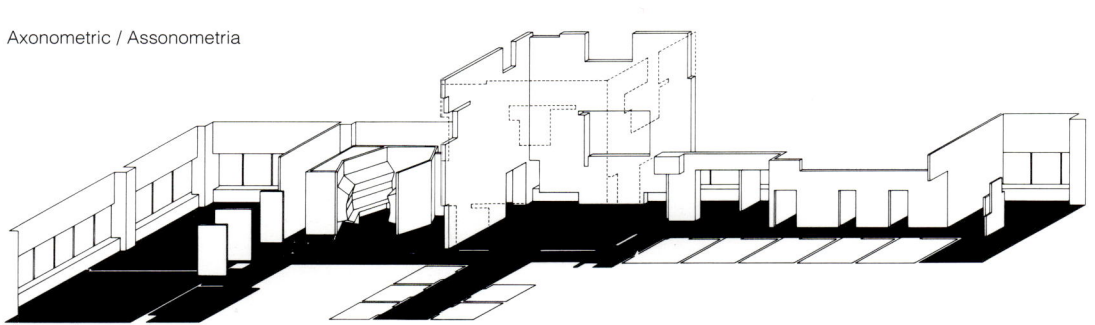

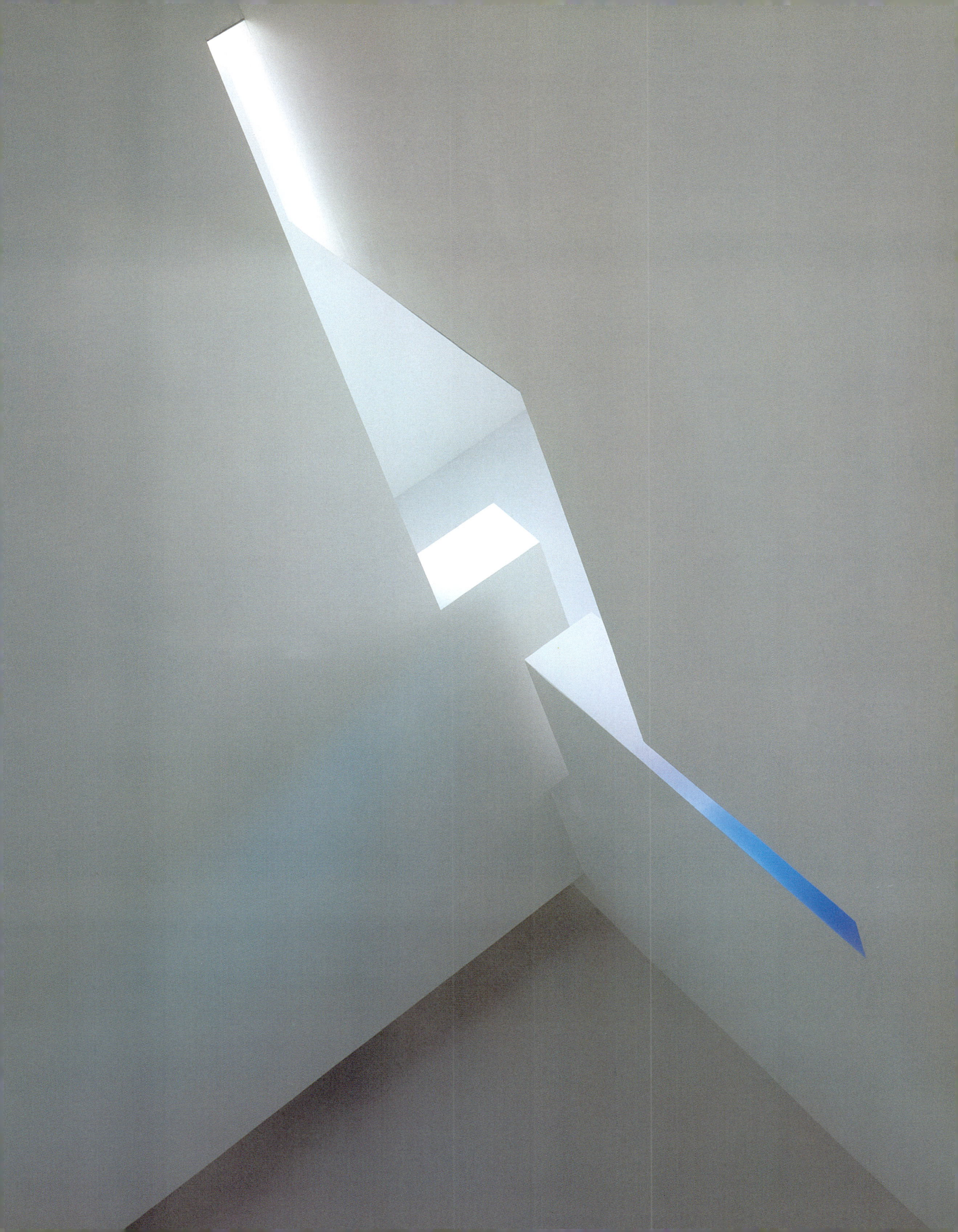

62

Plan / Pianta

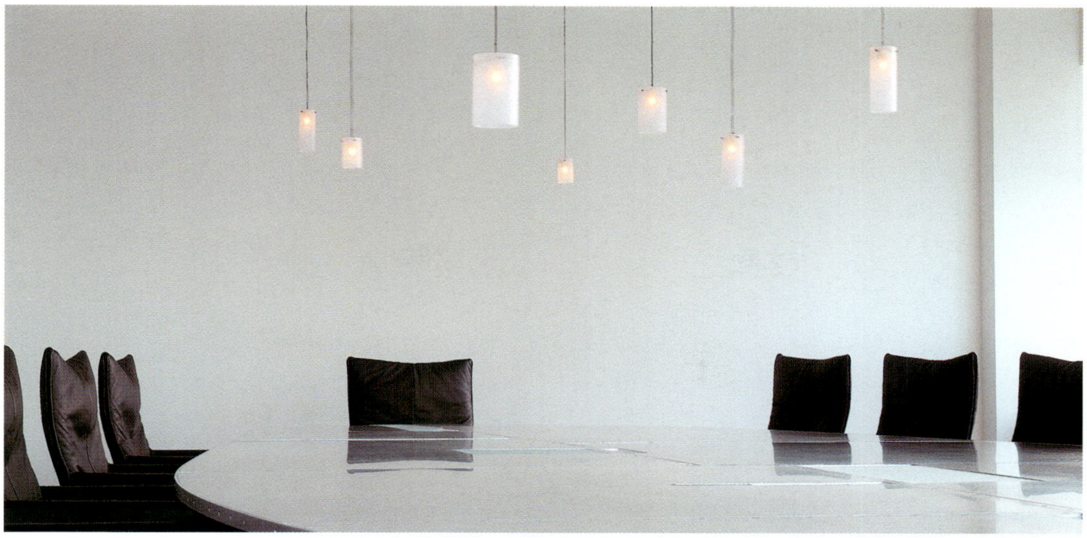

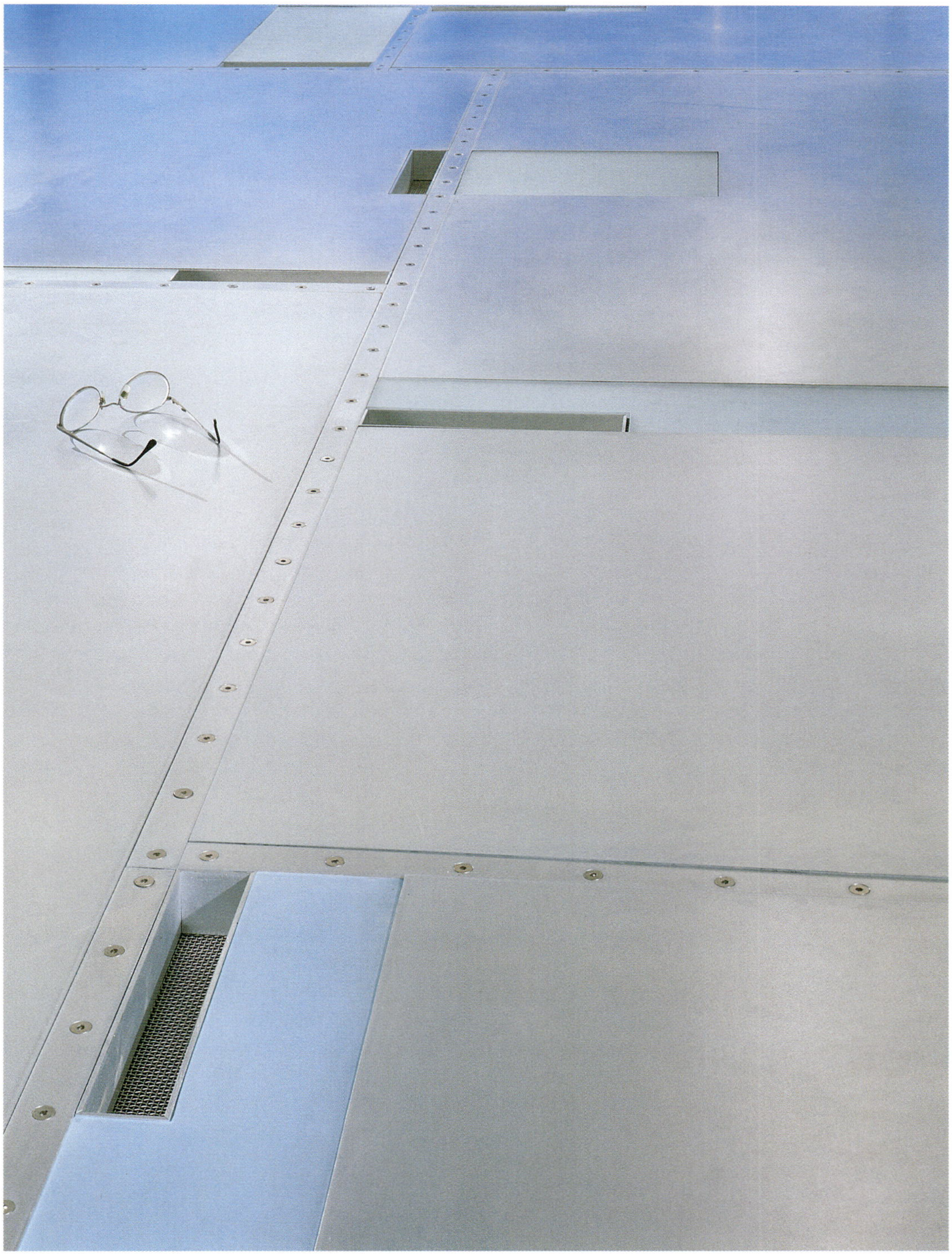

ESQUIRE MAGAZINE

Francois de Menil Architect, P.C. New York, NY, 1993

The new headquarters of *Esquire* magazine are installed in an industrial building constructed in the 1920s in midtown Manhattan. Here, the various offices for the editorial board, art directors, pasting up, and final editing, are all distributed on the last three stories of the building. The initial input for the project was to channel as much natural light as possible into the interior workspaces. The project also involved underlining the place's past as an industrial building. By organizing the service area alongside the stairways lining the front with a few apertures, and the archive area in the terminal part with a blind wall, the new distribution has made the best use of the existing windows along the facade, providing a series of offices and meeting rooms that have been accorded the necessary privacy and self-sufficiency. Some existing windows were left unobstructed so as to illuminate the central area, thereby conveying natural light to the interior of the open-plan area at the center, where it is captured by the partition walls that screen off the central operations area from the offices around the building's perimeter: a steel framework holds large panes of translucent paneling that terminate in glazed sections. The lighting systems of the central area are optimized with fluorescent ceiling units mounted in "shed" style between the regular pattern of the exposed ceiling girders. Alongside the new internal stairway a curved wall made from opaque polycarbonate and repeated on each of the three stories, closes off the meeting rooms while providing a source of reflected light on the central space where the workstations are located. These have a kind of meccano-like design with industrial zinc profiles to which untreated medium-density panels are attached. In addition to allowing maximum spatial flexibility, the workstation design contributes to the overall coherence of this "revisitation" of the industrial setting on which the project is based, from the choice of materials (floors in shiny black vinyl, door and window frames in steel, and staircases in iron with molded metal treads), to the individual architectural solutions.

In un edificio industriale costruito negli anni '20 nella midtown di Manhattan è stata ricavata la redazione della rivista Esquire che ha occupato gli ultimi tre livelli del regolare blocco edilizio distribuendovi gli uffici delle sue diverse sezioni (editoriale, arte e produzione, publishing). Imput iniziale del progetto era quello di portare all'interno degli spazi di lavoro la maggiore quantità di luce naturale possibile. Inoltre veniva espressa l'esigenza di valorizzare la memoria industriale dell'edificio originario. Organizzando la zona servizi di fianco al vano scala lungo il fronte con poche aperture e la zona archivi nella parte terminale con muro cieco, la nuova distribuzione ha sfruttato al meglio le aperture esistenti nella facciata organizzando una serie di uffici e sale riunione a cui sono state garantite la necessaria privacy e autonomia. Alcune finestre esistenti sono state lasciate libere di affacciarsi verso la zona centrale, portando all'interno della pianta libera la luce naturale che viene comunque catturata grazie alla soluzione delle pareti divisorie che separano la zona operativa centrale dagli uffici perimetrali: un infisso di acciaio sostiene ampie lastre di vetro traslucido sormontate per tutta la fascia superiore da vetrate trasparenti. L'illuminazione artificiale nella zona centrale viene ottimizzata dalle lampade fluorescenti a soffitto ubicate, a mo' di shed industriale, tra la scansione regolare delle travi a vista. Di fianco alla nuova scala interna una parete in curva, costruita in policarbonato opaco e ripetuta su tutti e tre i livelli, chiude le sale riunione e si pone come riuscito schermo luminoso riflettente che aggiunge luce all'open space in cui sono posizionate le postazioni di lavoro. Queste, costruite come una sorta di divertito 'meccano' con profilati zincati industriali cui sono fissati pannelli di medium density non trattato, oltre a garantire la massima flessibilità e componibilità, concorrono a formare la generale immagine di riuscita rilettura di un passato industriale cui l'intero progetto si rapporta, dalla scelta dei materiali (pavimento in vinile nero lucido, infissi di acciaio e scala in ferro con gradini in lamiera stampata) alle singole soluzioni architettoniche.

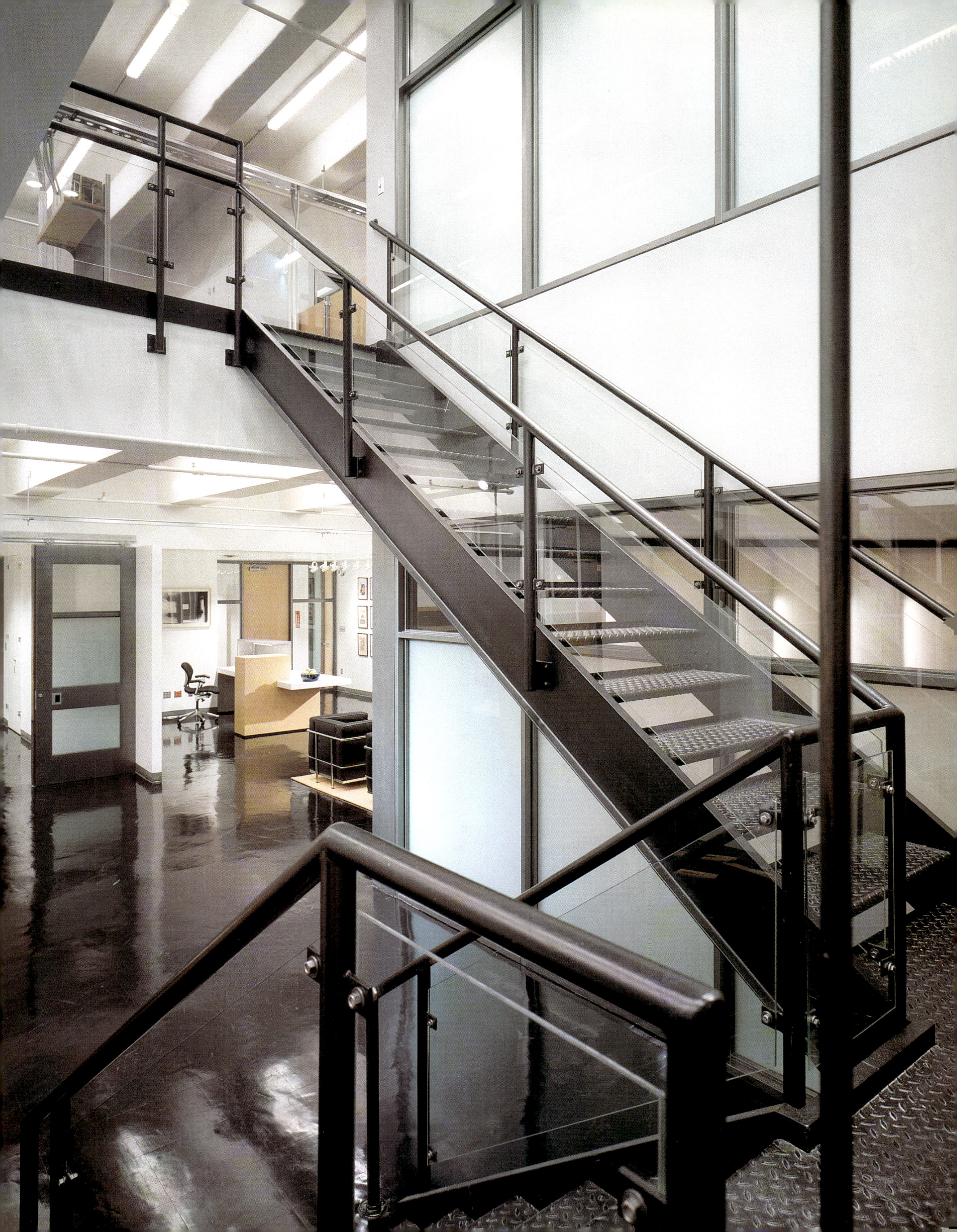

Perspective of 7th Floor Work Space / Vista prospettica di una zona operativa al 7° piano

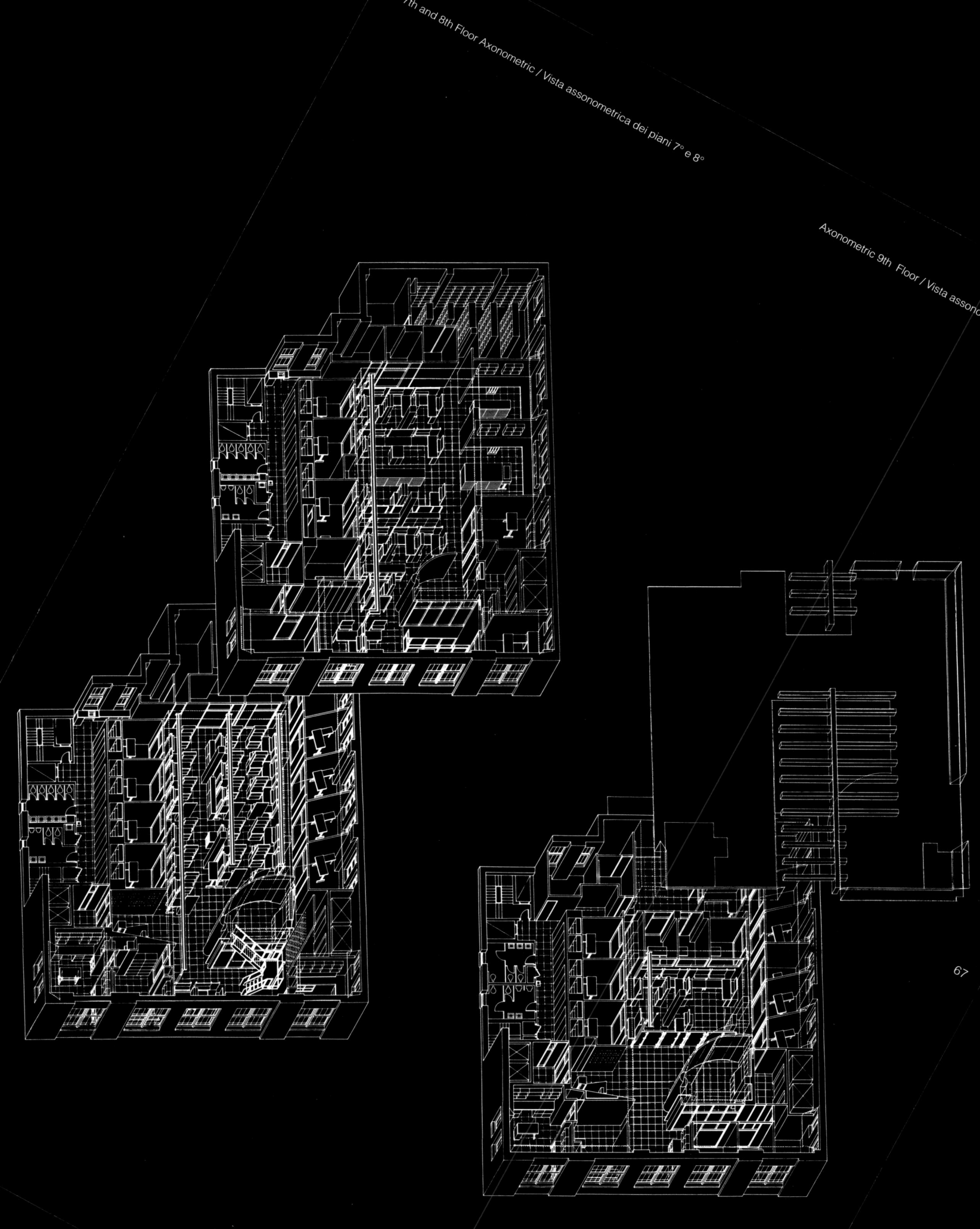

7th and 8th Floor Axonometric / Vista assonometrica dei piani 7° e 8°

Axonometric 9th Floor / Vista assono

67

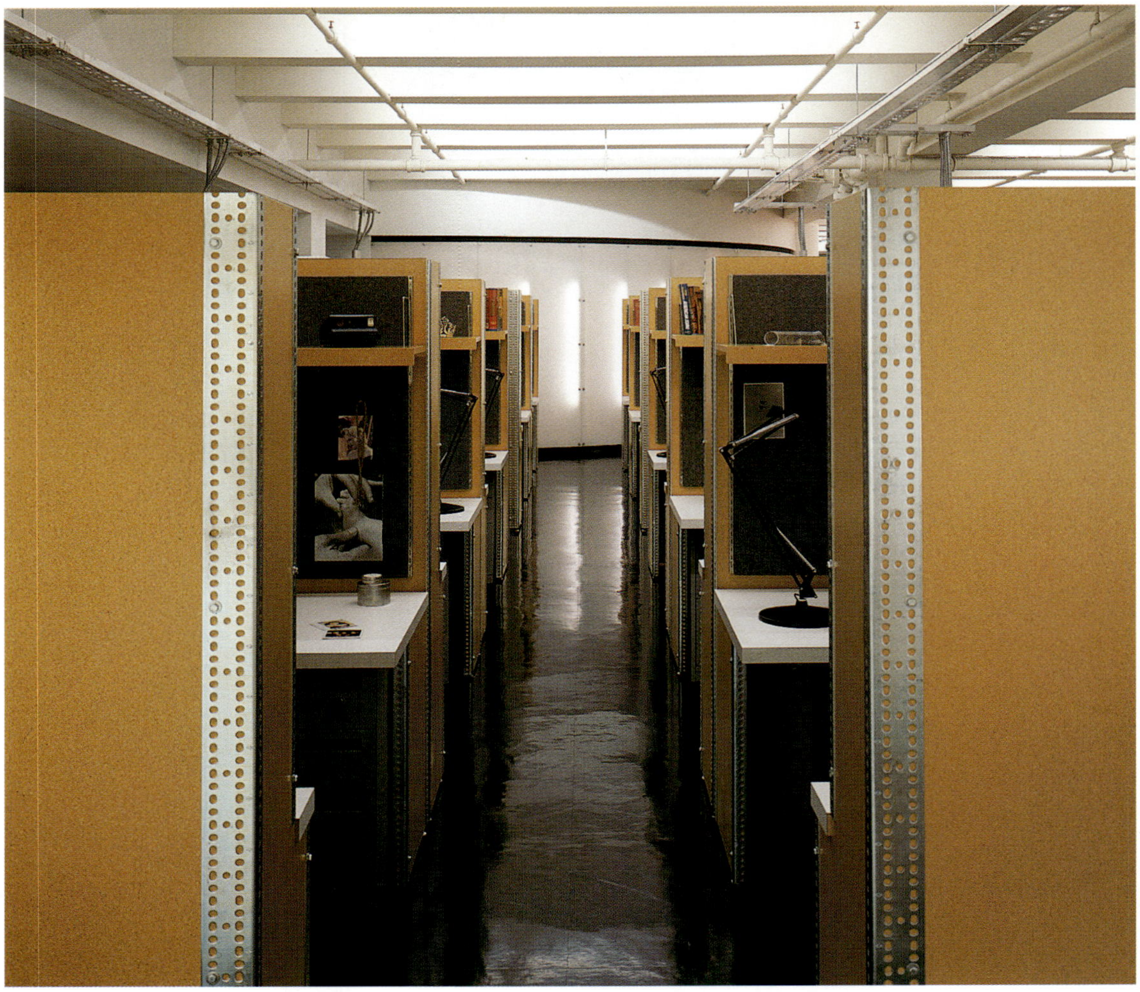

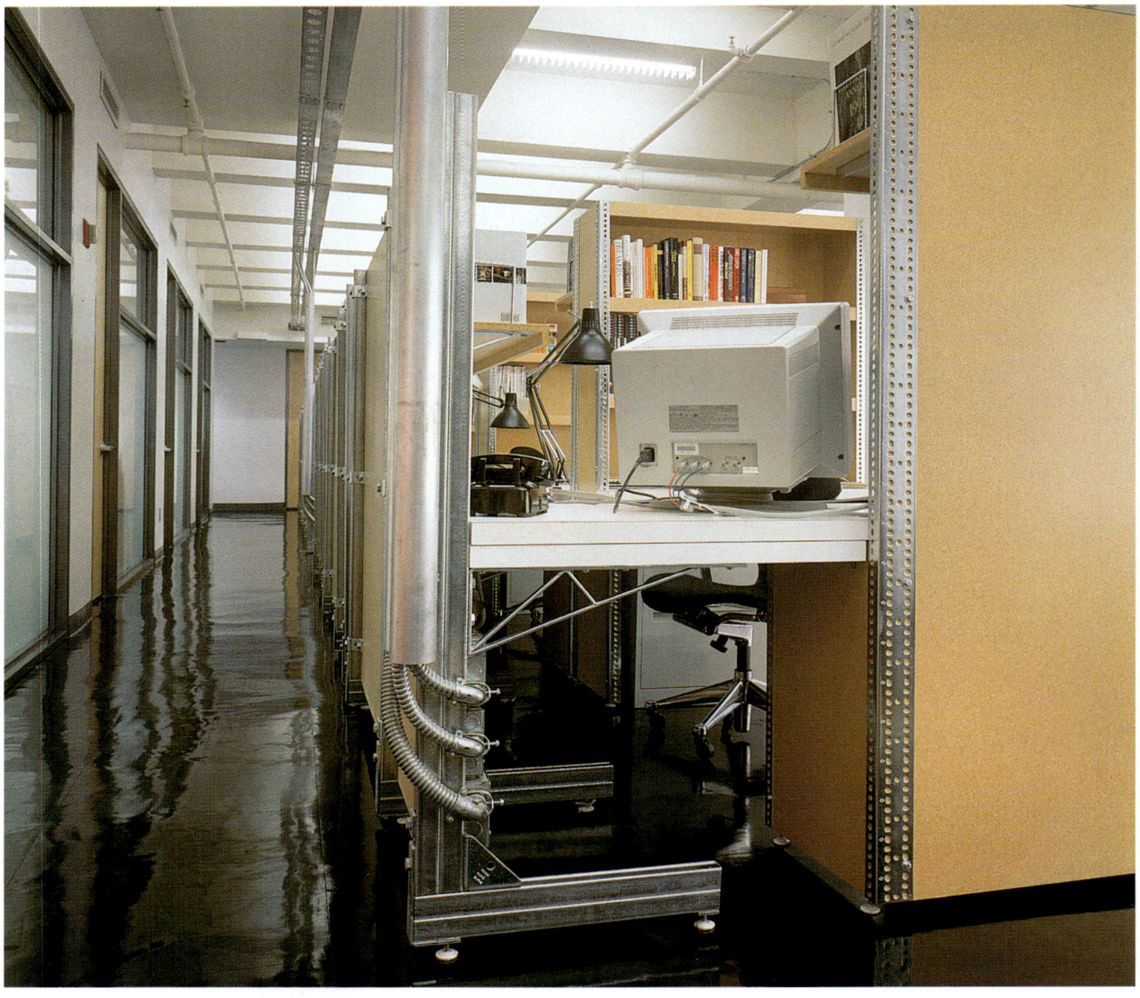

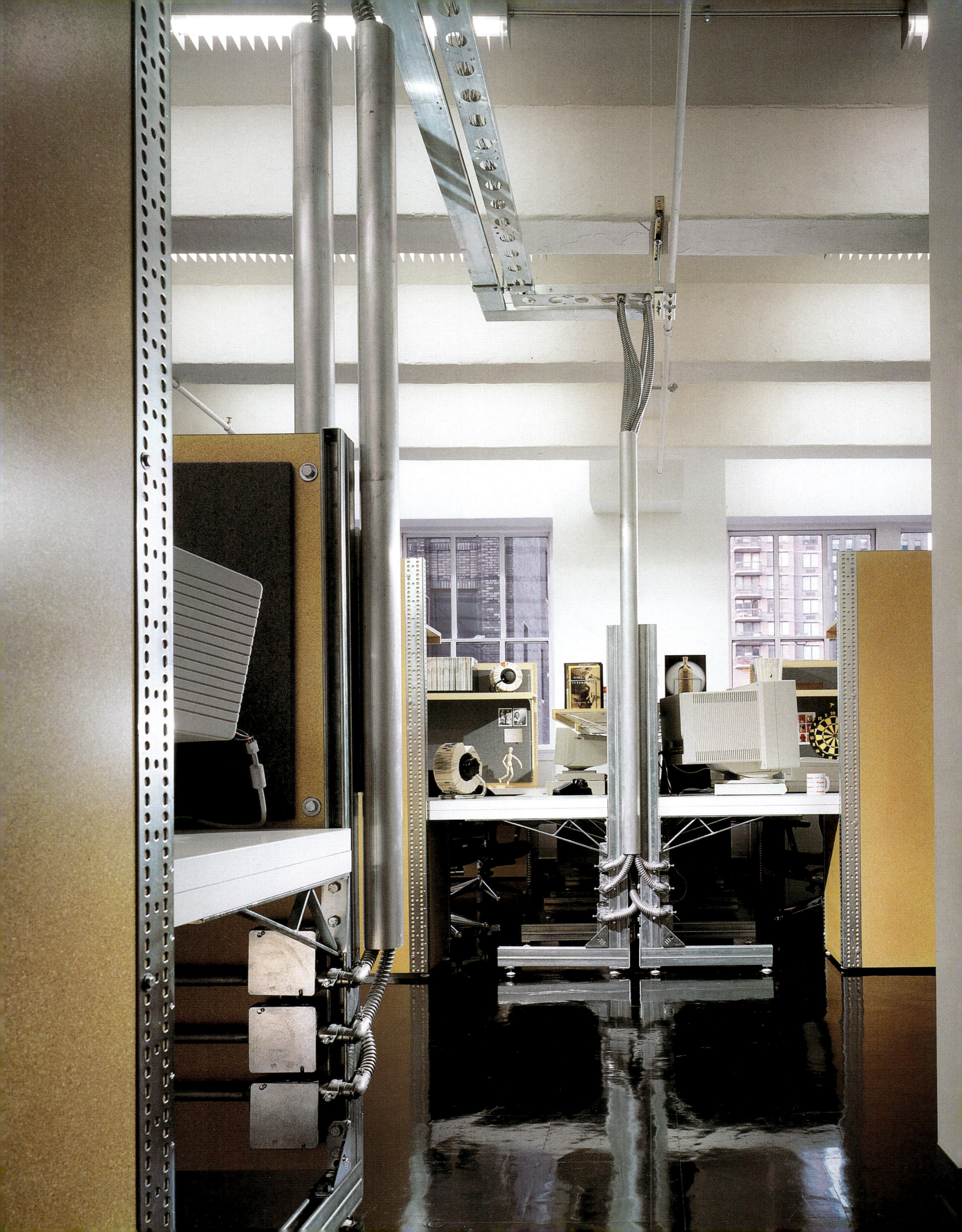

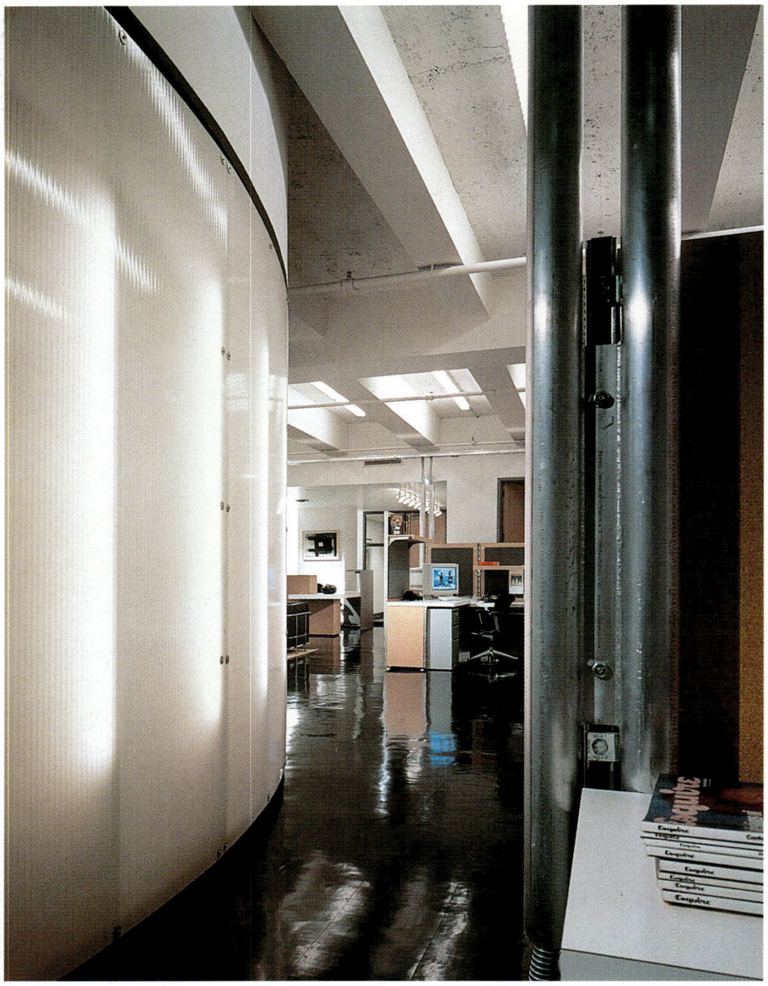
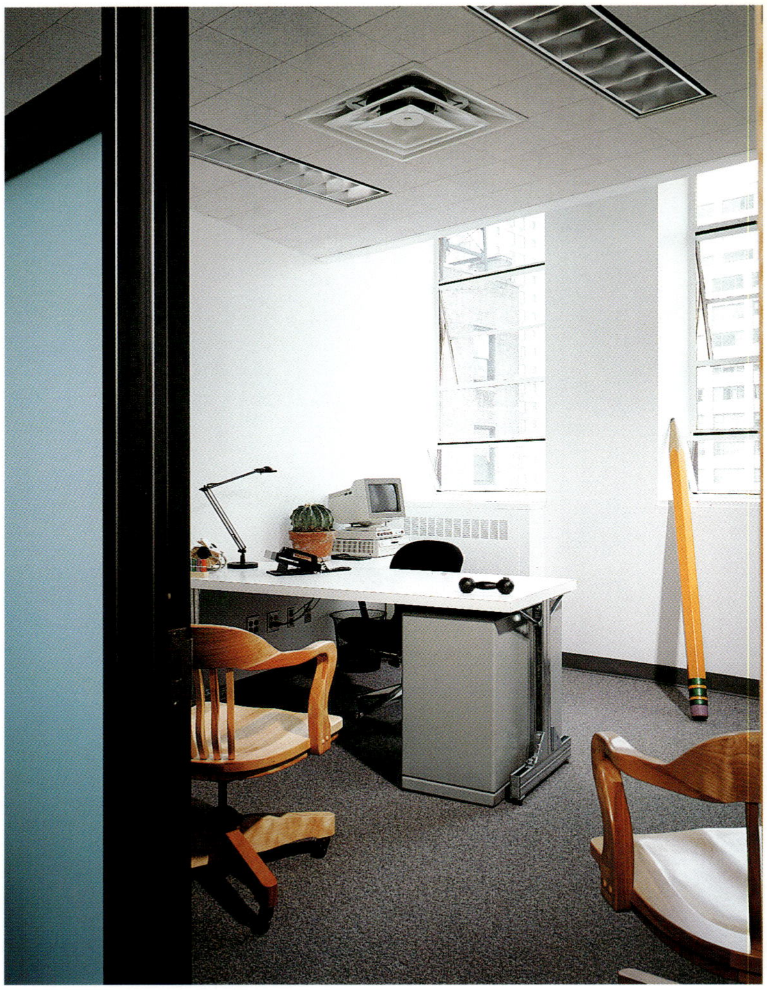

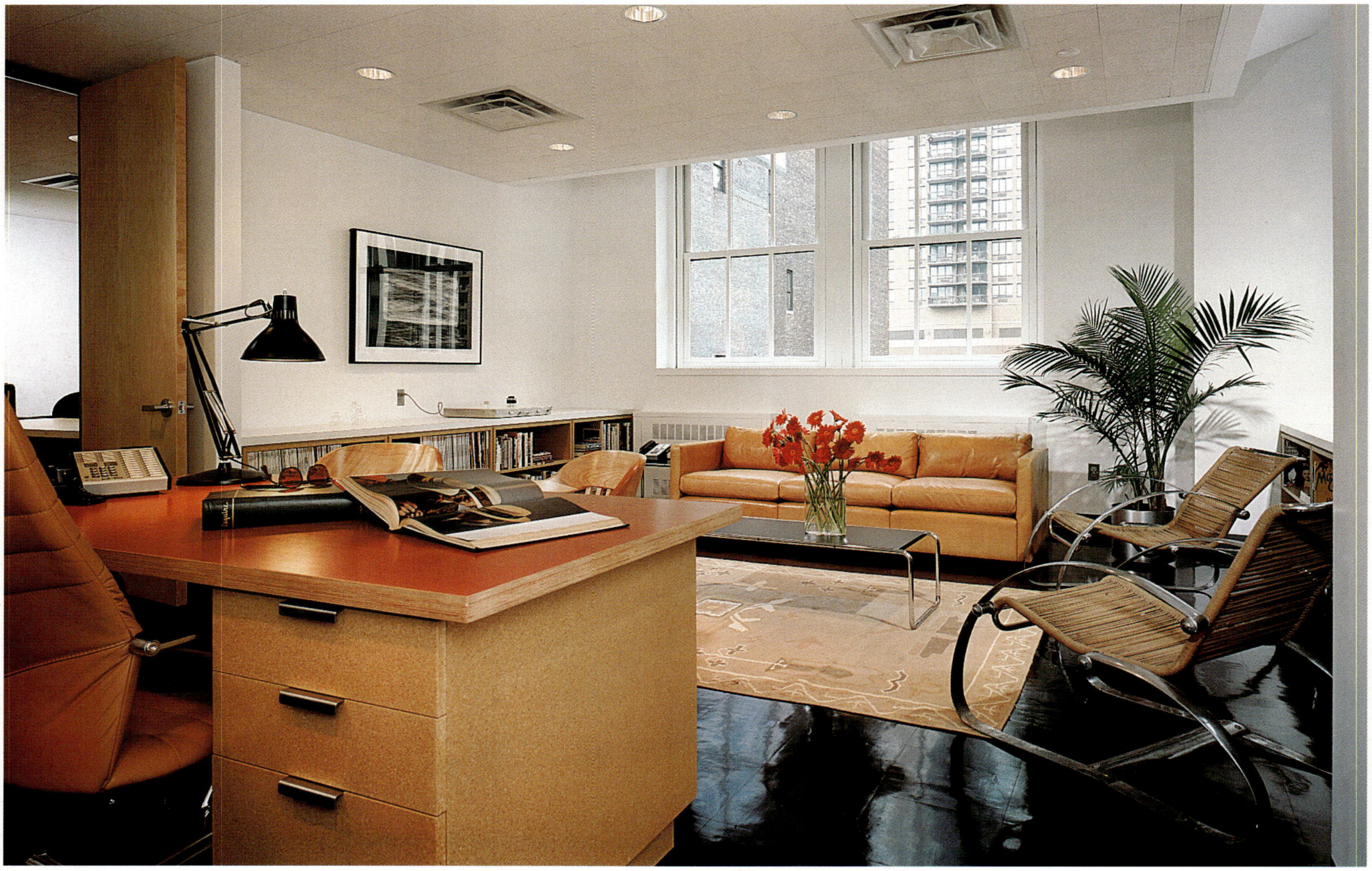

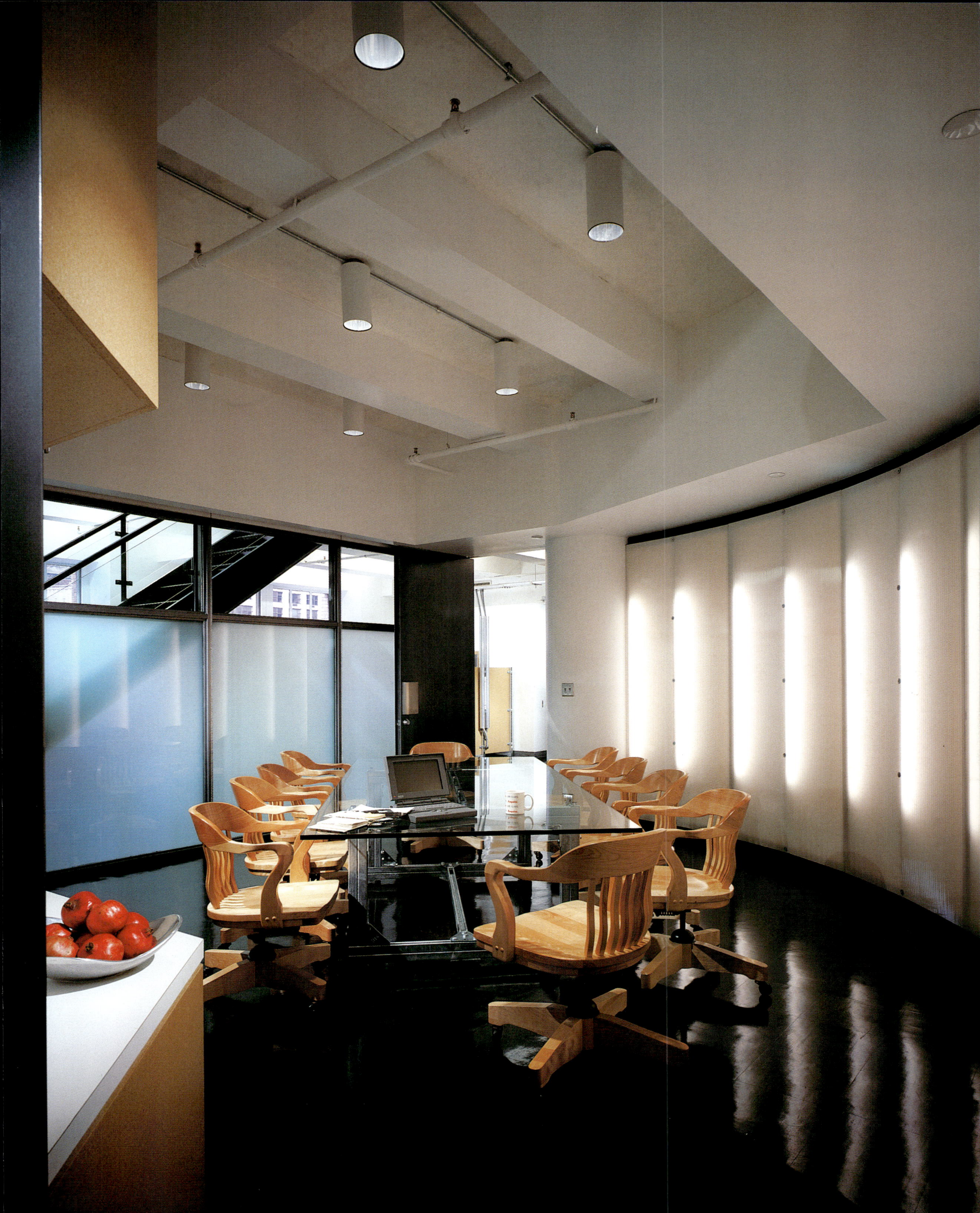

FISCHER, FRANCIS, TREES, WATTS

Linda Jacobs - Jon Nathanson Architects. New York, NY, 1995

As if floating amid the skyscrapers of Manhattan, the headquarters of this financial services firm makes the best use of the natural light flooding in from the continuous perimeter glazing, which is slightly set back from the facade to make room for a balcony running the full circuit of the building. The client's brief stipulated that there was to be no hierarchical distribution of workspaces, but rather a large open working area modulated with islands of varying type, and a set of conference rooms that could be modified for the purpose of privacy. The new design brilliantly addresses the client's specifications, creating an internal landscape that boasts a refined and functional image geared to ensuring maximum enjoyment of the commanding views of Manhattan, while carefully calibrating the main work floors with well-defined circulation access that provides a varied pattern of compositions. Greeting visitors in the elevator lobby entrance is a large glazed partition set in a wooden frame marking the entrance to the reception and offices beyond. The reception is visually linked to the arrival area via a blade-like unit in plasterboard creating a fluid horizontal volume that supersedes the glazing of the entrance and interrupts the continuity in a clever dovetailing of construction materials. The floating ceilings change dramatically in the interior; here the solid entrance units give way to a fascinating system of fabric tensile structures strung from a metal framework through which one can catch sight of the rough cement ceilings and unconcealed ducting. The ingenious lighting fixtures throw their light up onto the white fabric above, creating a diffuse wash of light over the tent-like sculpture of taut material. The airy lightness of this feature of the new design is complemented by the customized wooden fittings and furniture: long tables and functional workstations alternate with more enclosed offices, and the five conference rooms placed on axis with the entrance like a set of discreet, self-sufficient volumes. Distributed along the access corridor leading to the main work area, these are composed of glazed walls framed in geometrica wooden surrounds. The transparency of these five units means that visual continuity is not interrupted, though operable screens are built into the design to allow users to adjust the level of privacy.

Come sospesa tra il panorama dei grattacieli di Manhattan la sede di questa società di servizi finanziari sfrutta al meglio l'illuminazione naturale delle grandi vetrate continue perimetrali arretrate dal filo di facciata per ottenere un lungo balcone continuo. La richiesta della committenza era anzitutto quella di non avere una distribuzione gerarchica degli spazi di lavoro, ma piuttosto un grande open space scandito da isole operative diversificate e da una serie di sale riunione passibili di isolamento per la necessaria garanzia di privacy. Le scelte progettuali hanno risposto brillantemente agli input iniziali definendo un paesaggio interno caratterizzato da un'immagine raffinata e funzionale, tutta rivolta verso la valorizzazione della vista sulla città, ma attenta a scandire l'open space con figure e percorsi ben definiti e giocati su una ricercata leggerezza compositiva. Nel pianerottolo di arrivo degli ascensori una grande vetrata con infisso in legno segna l'ingresso agli uffici annunciando la reception. Questa è unita alla zona di arrivo con una forte lama in cartongesso che scende dal soffitto proponendosi come volume fluttuante orizzontale che supera la vetrata dell'ingresso interrompendone la continuità e creando un riuscito incastro materico. Il disegno del controsoffitto cambia radicalmente nel luminoso interno; qui ai forti volumi dell'ingresso si sostituisce un raffinato gioco di vele bianche tese su una studiata struttura metallica da cui traspare il soffitto grezzo sovrastante con gli impianti a vista. Le lampade su disegno, fissate alla struttura del controsoffitto, riflettono la luce in modo diffuso sui teli tesi in modo scultoreo nello spazio. La leggerezza e l'eleganza di questa soluzione progettuale trova riscontro negli arredi di legno su disegno. Lunghi tavoli collettivi e funzionali postazioni operative, si alternano a uffici più raccolti e alle cinque sale riunione affiancate e poste in asse all'ingresso come piccole e leggere architetture compiute. Queste, distribuite lungo il corridoio di accesso alla zona operativa, sono composte da pareti vetrate scandite dalla geometria dell'infisso ligneo. La trasparenza di questi cinque volumi permette di non interrompere la continuità visiva dello spazio, garantendo tuttavia una schermatura totale grazie a una serie di tende oscuranti meccanizzate che corrono lungo tutte le vetrate.

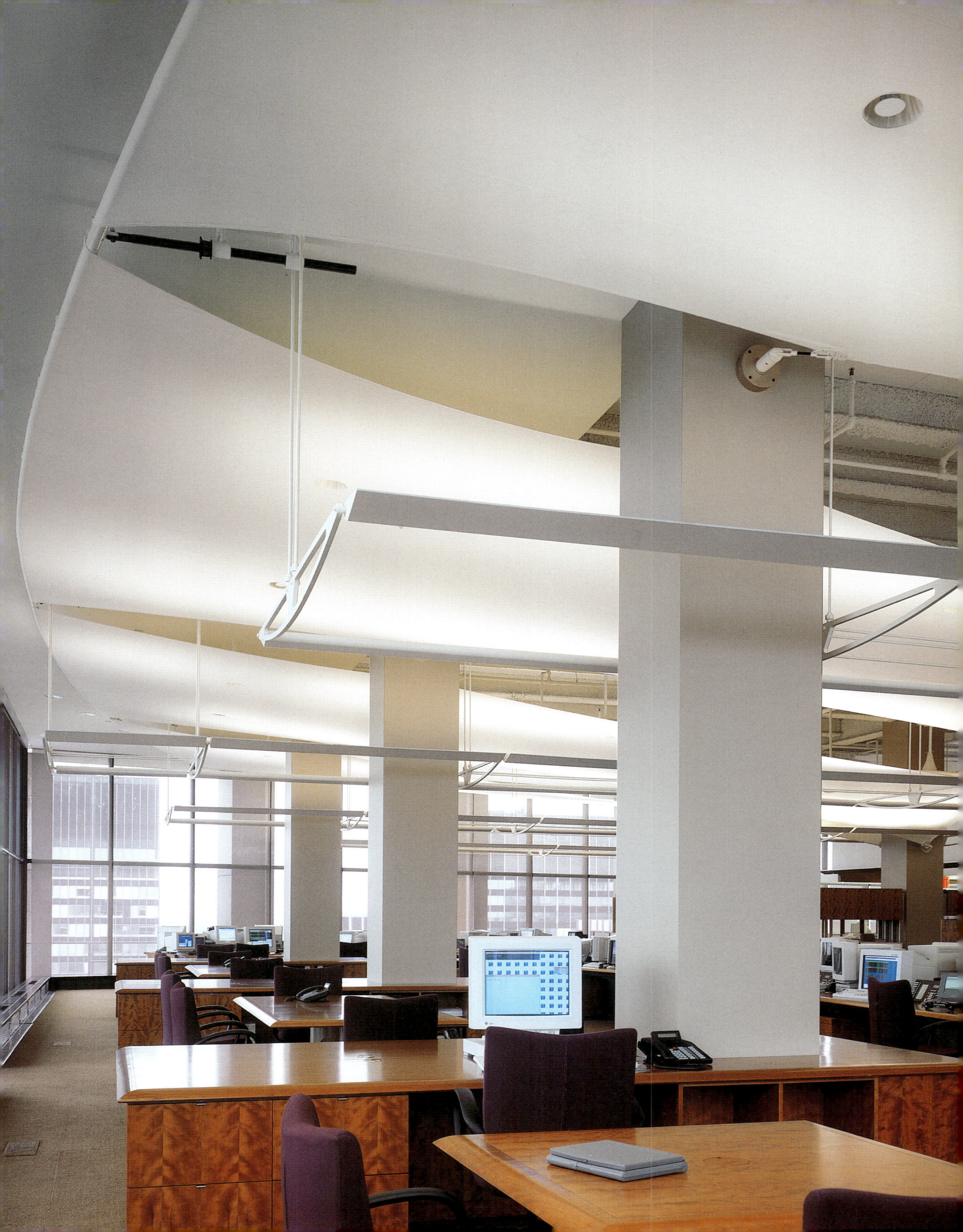

74

75

Furnishing plan / Pianta arredata.

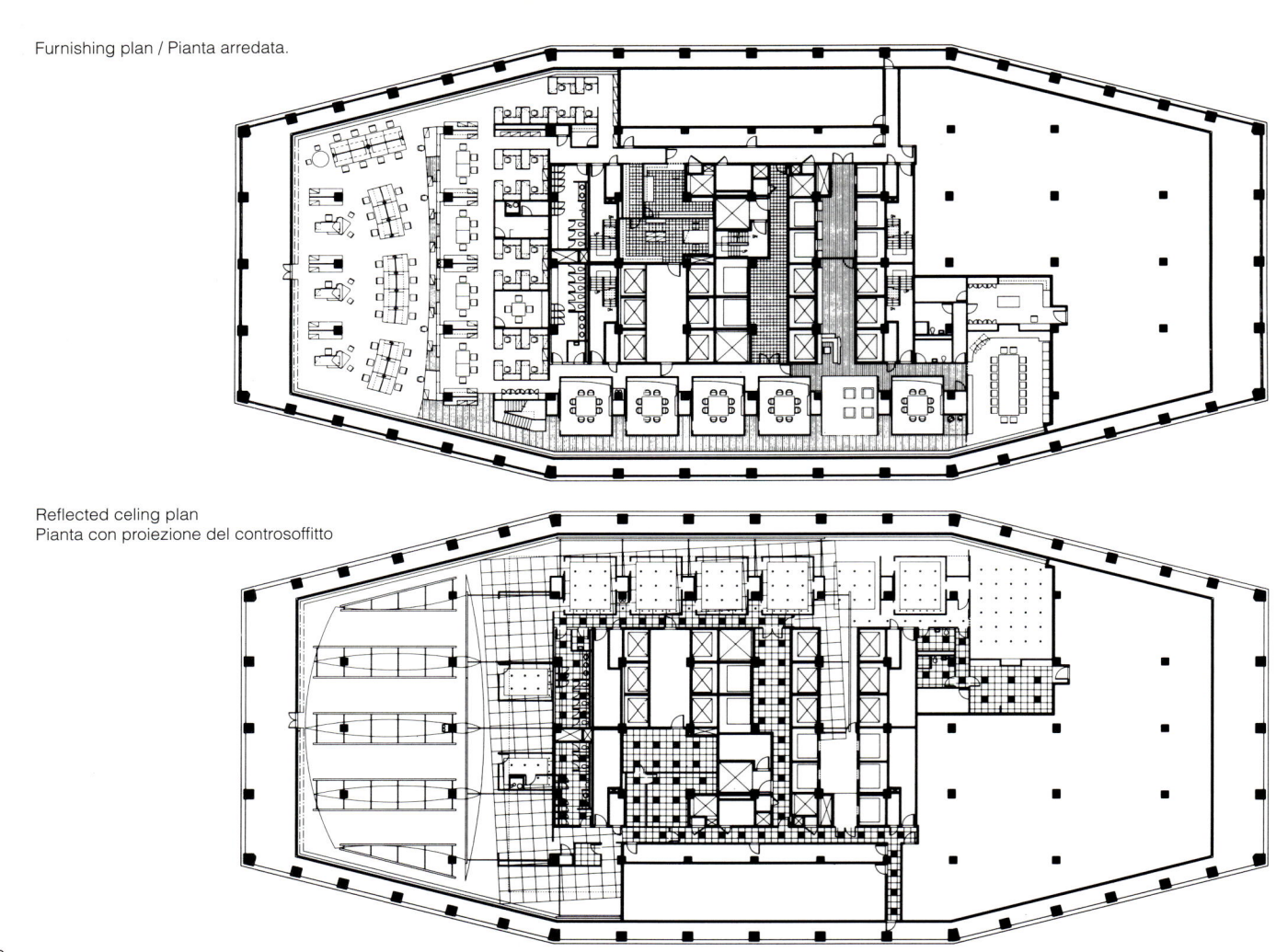

Reflected celing plan
Pianta con proiezione del controsoffitto

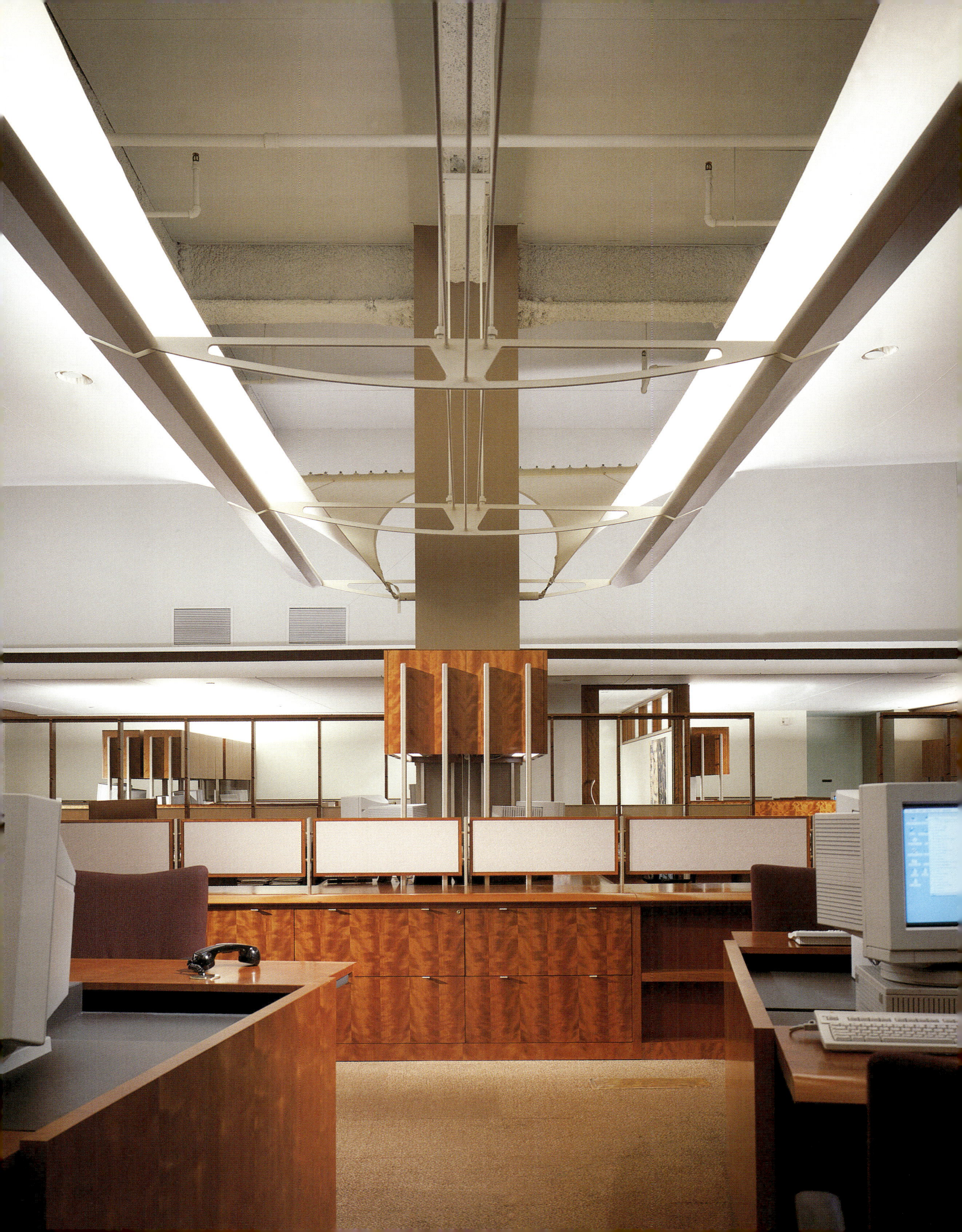

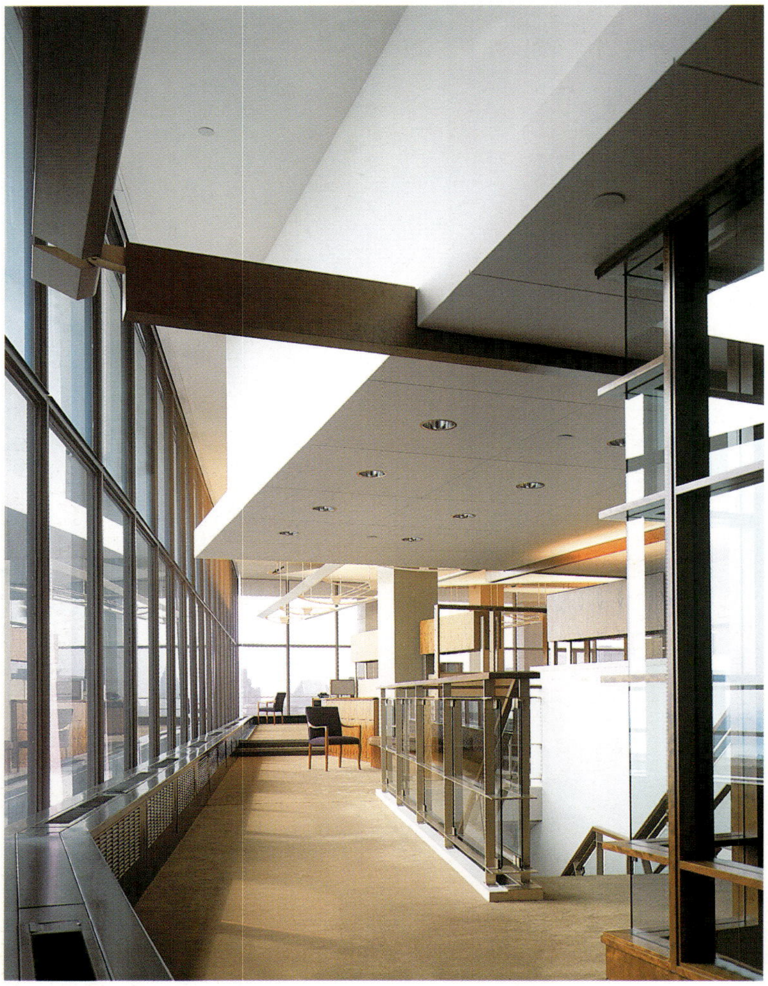

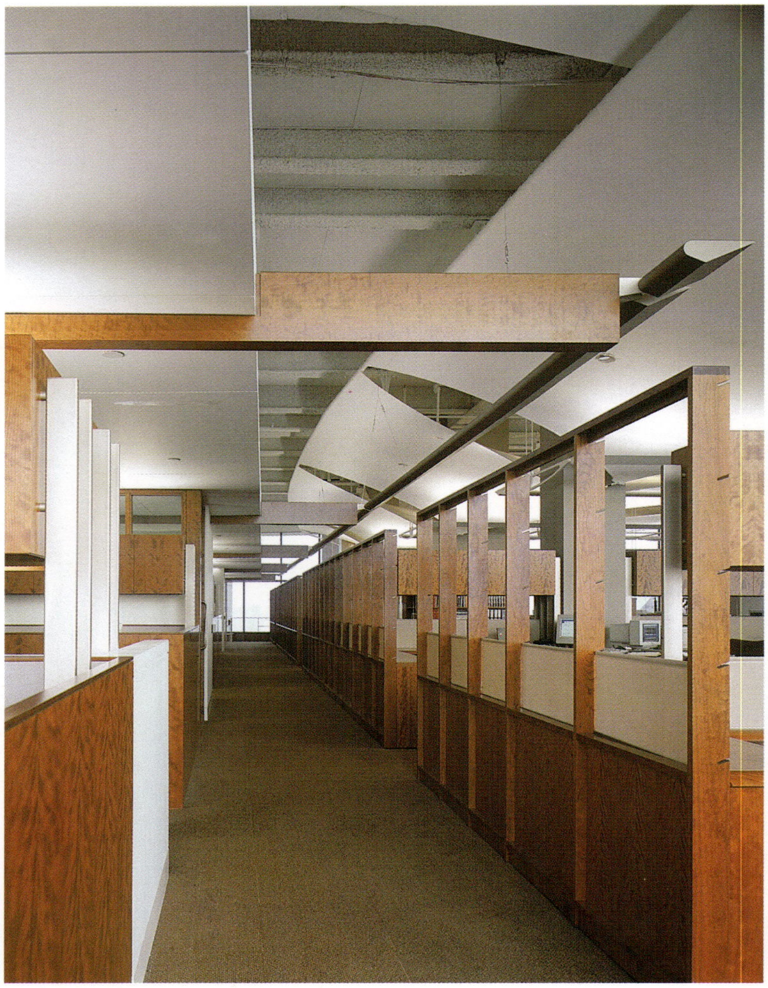

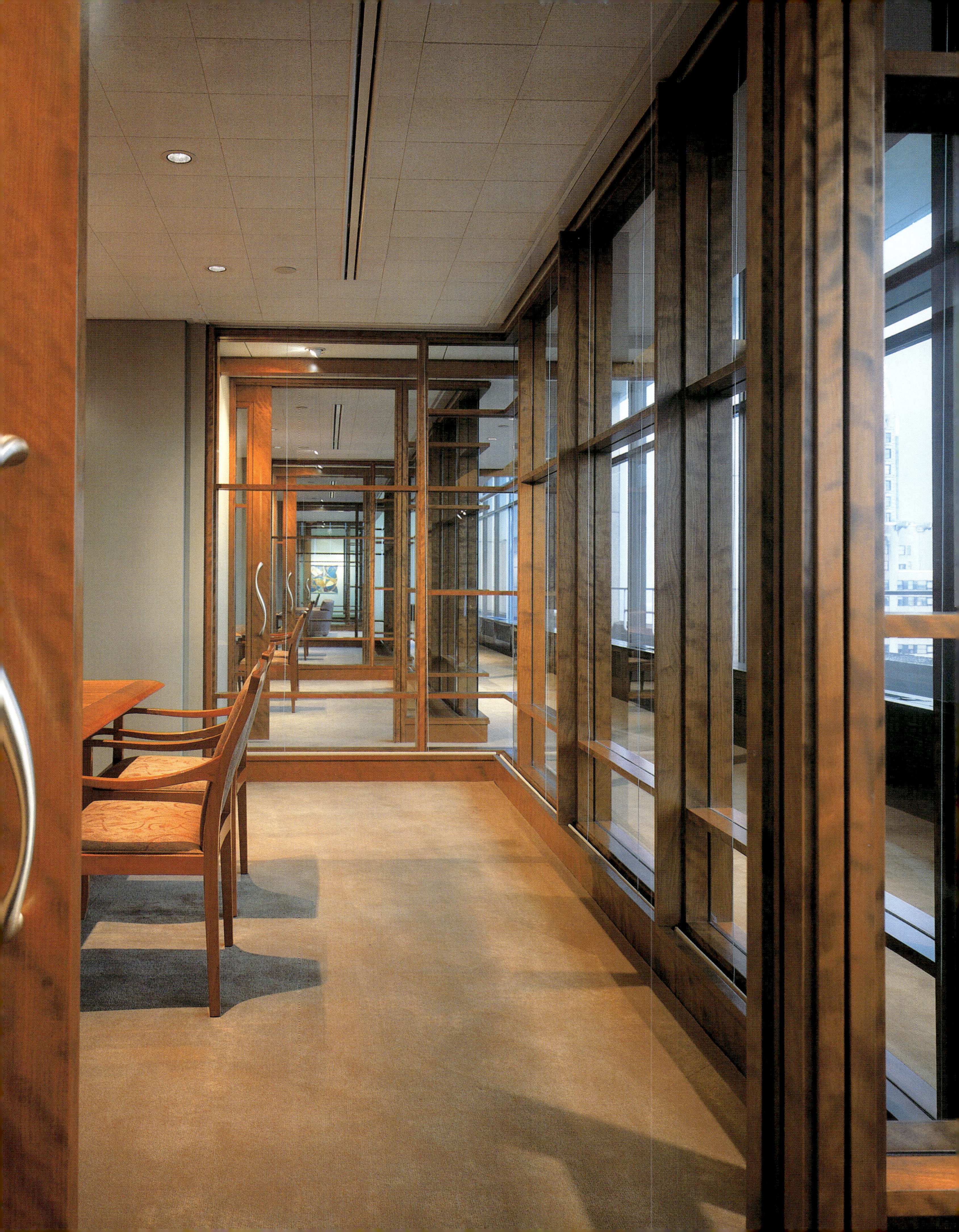

HENRI BEAUFOUR INSTITUTE
Williams & Dynerman Architects. Washington, DC, 1992

Slotted into the second and third stories of an office block built on a somewhat irregular triangular plan, the primary impression one receives of the corporate headquarters of this renowned pharmaceutical company is the extensive use of natural materials throughout the thoughtfully planned interiors in which the keynote is maximum comfort. The individual and mixed operations offices, together with those for executive use and the various conference rooms, are all distributed around the perimeter of the plan. A concave bay in one of the facades prompted the creation on both levels of a series of bowed internal walls that describe an unusual, sculptural circulation route. Sisal matting alternating with slate tiles cover most of the floors, while overhead a simple lowered ceiling of white squares flanks sections of maple, which reappears now and then as a basic reference material for the internal walls of the offices and several items of furniture (including the reception desk and the large trapezoid table of the main conference room). Together with warm natural wood, panels of glass and perforated sheeting provide an overall image of lightness and elaborate comfort. The entrance hall, which leads off from the elevator lobby, is conceived as a sort of tow-level indoor piazza, which also accommodates the reception corner. This large irregular-shaped hall affords a spacious and welcoming reception area, while providing a kind of architectural fulcrum at the center. Among its key features are a long steel railing that runs the full circuit of the perimeter, a staircase built to the same design, but with wooden treads. This is visually offset by the huge screen-wall composed of superimposed white concrete panels that develop from the floor of the entrance up to the ceiling of the story above. The direct figurative complement of his essential architectural backdrop is a sculpture by the Danish artist Per Arnoldi, which thrusts boldly into view with its strong scheme of primary colors (yellow, red, blue) and its elementary geometrical form extending the full double-height of the foyer-piazza. Resting on the slate floor, the sculpture surges up past the first-floor railing and terminates just short of the ceiling.

Ricavata al secondo e terzo livello di un palazzo per uffici dalla pianta a forma di triangolo irregolare, la sede di questa nota casa farmaceutica si caratterizza per un paesaggio d'interni che unisce a un largo impiego di materiali naturali una ricercata disposizione degli spazi e un'attenzione verso la definizione di un alto grado di comfort. Lungo i lati perimetrali sono stati disposti gli uffici operativi singoli e multipli, quelli direzionali e le sale riunioni. La rientranza circolare di un lato di facciata ha suggerito la creazione su entrambi i livelli di una serie di setti curvati in muratura che creano una successione di uffici organizzati lungo un inconsueto e scultoreo corridoio distributivo. Stuoie di sisal, alternate a piastre in ardesia, coprono gran parte dei pavimenti, mentre un semplice controsoffitto a quadrotti bianchi viene affiancato a quello in legno di acero, impiegato in alcune zone anche come materiale di riferimento per le pareti interne degli uffici e di molti arredi su disegno (tra cui il mobile reception e il grande tavolo trapezoidale della sala riunioni principale). Insieme al legno, lastre di vetro e di lamiera forata danno all'immagine complessiva un senso di leggerezza e di ricercato comfort. La zona d'ingresso, ricavata di fronte al pianerottolo ascensori, è stata pensata come sorta di piazza interna a doppio livello dove collocare anche la reception. Di forma trapezoidale irregolare, la grande hall si propone come ampio spazio di accoglienza, fulcro architettonico centrale, caratterizzato sia dal lungo ballatoio in acciaio che ne sottolinea tutto il perimetro, sia dalla scala dello stesso materiale, ma con gradini in legno, che trova il proprio sostegno visivo nella grande parete-schermo, composta da una serie di pannelli di cemento bianco sovrapposti che si sviluppano dal pavimento del piano d'ingresso sino al soffitto del piano superiore. Diretto complemento figurativo di questa essenziale quinta architettonica è la scultura, opera dell'artista danese Per Arnoldi, che riempie con la forza dei suoi colori primari (giallo, rosso e blu) e della sua elementare forma geometrica lo spazio a doppia altezza della piazza interna. La scultura poggiante sul pavimento d'ardesia si inerpica lungo il ballatoio innestandosi nella soletta, per raggiungere poi il soffitto da cui si distacca con leggerezza.

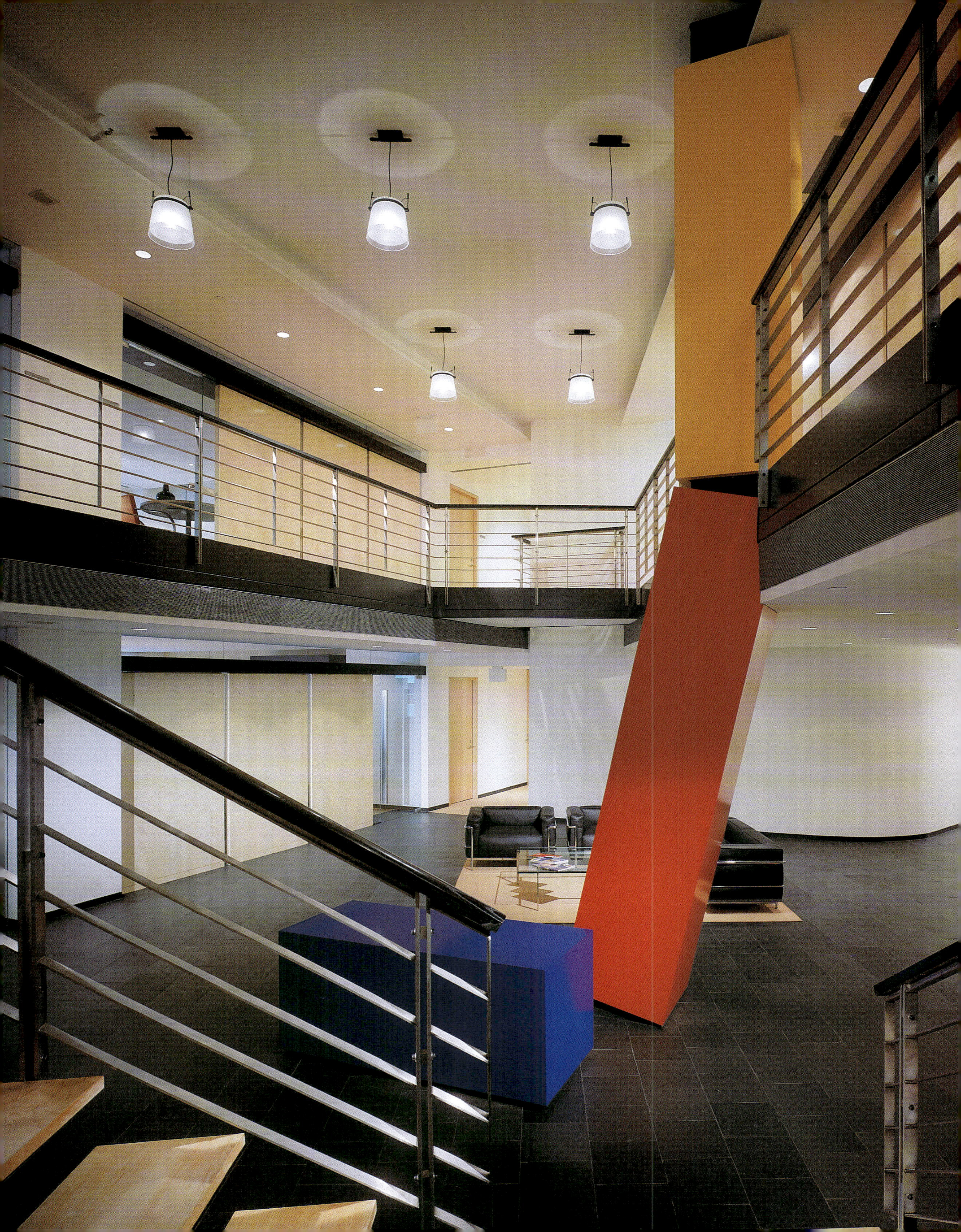

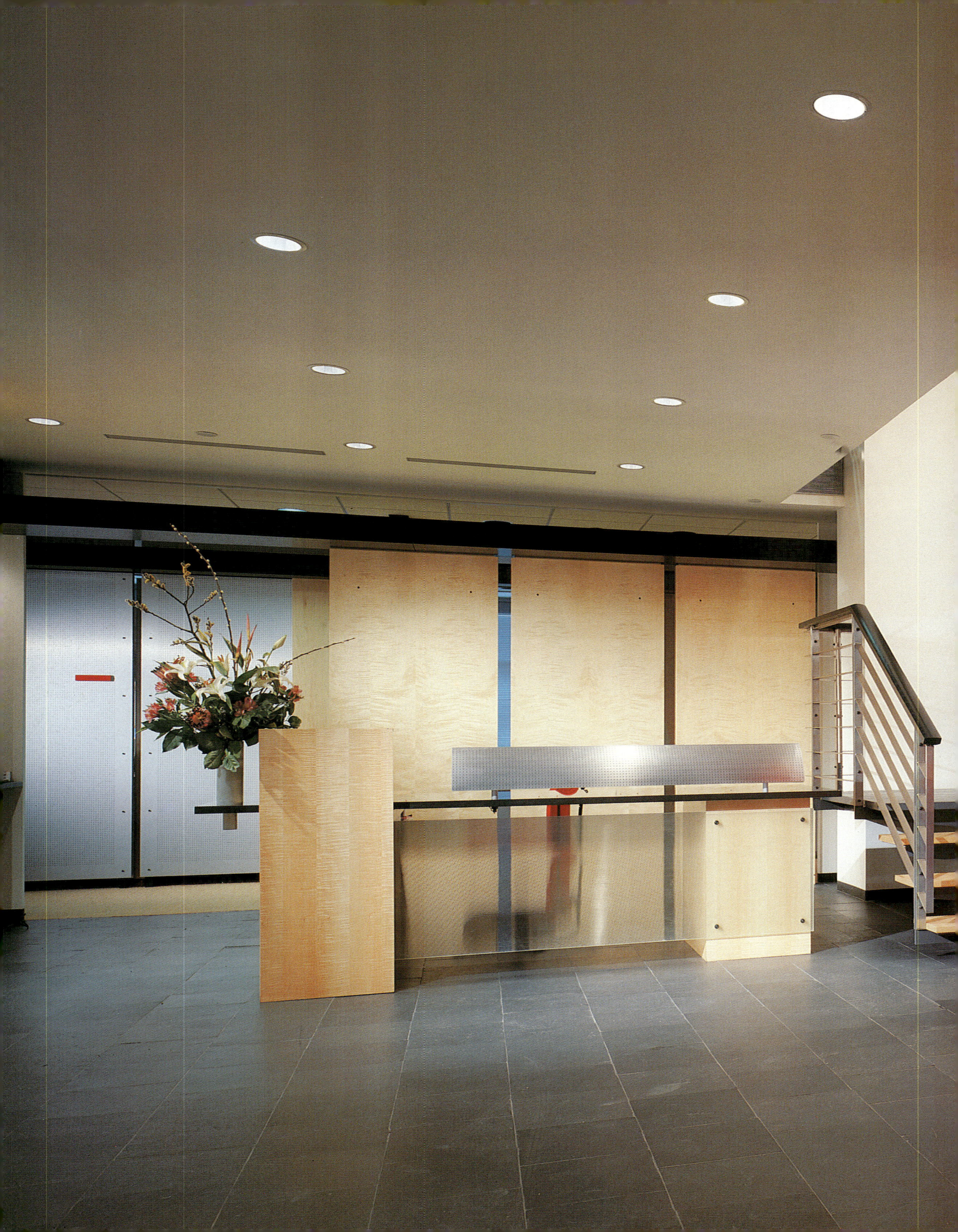

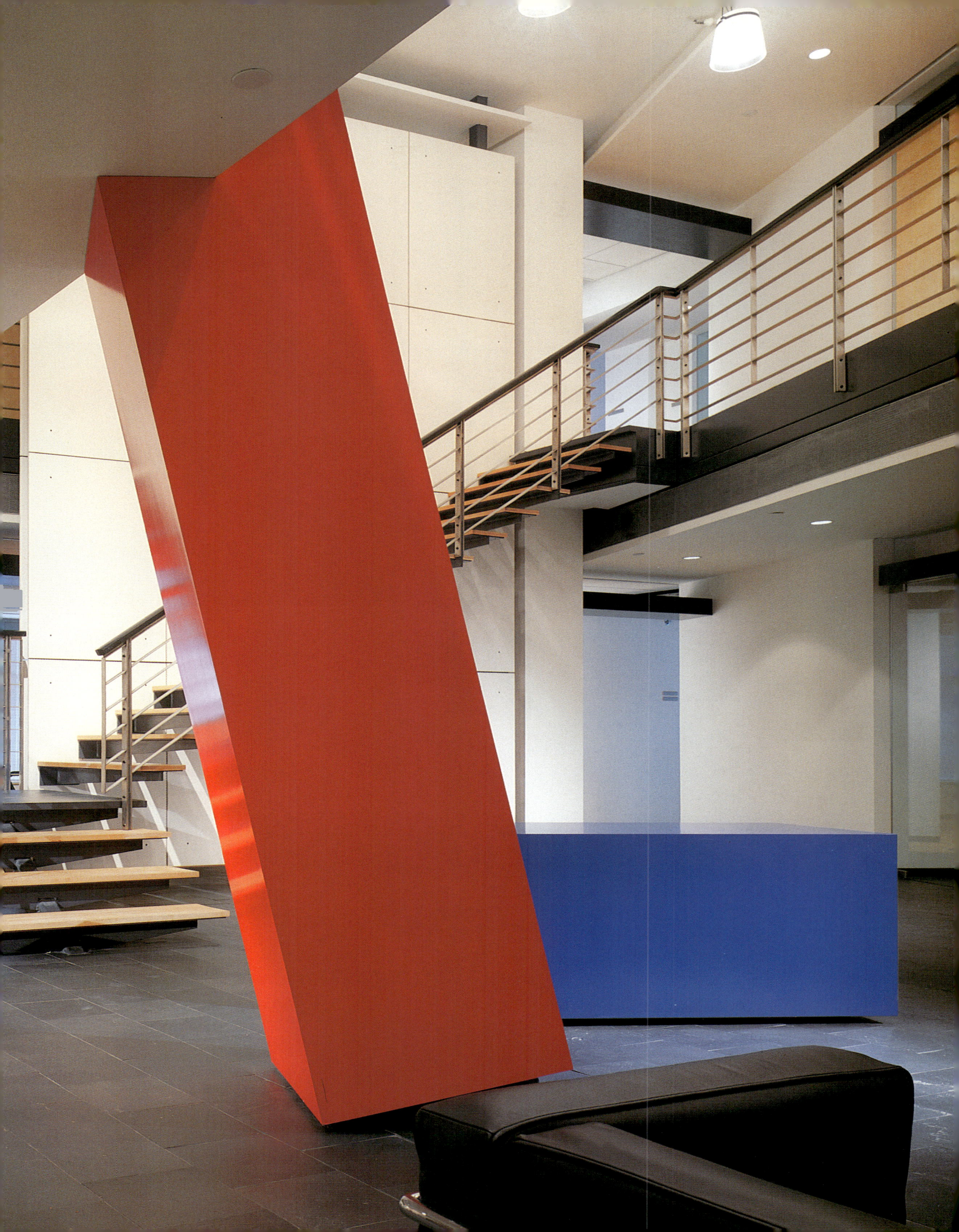

84

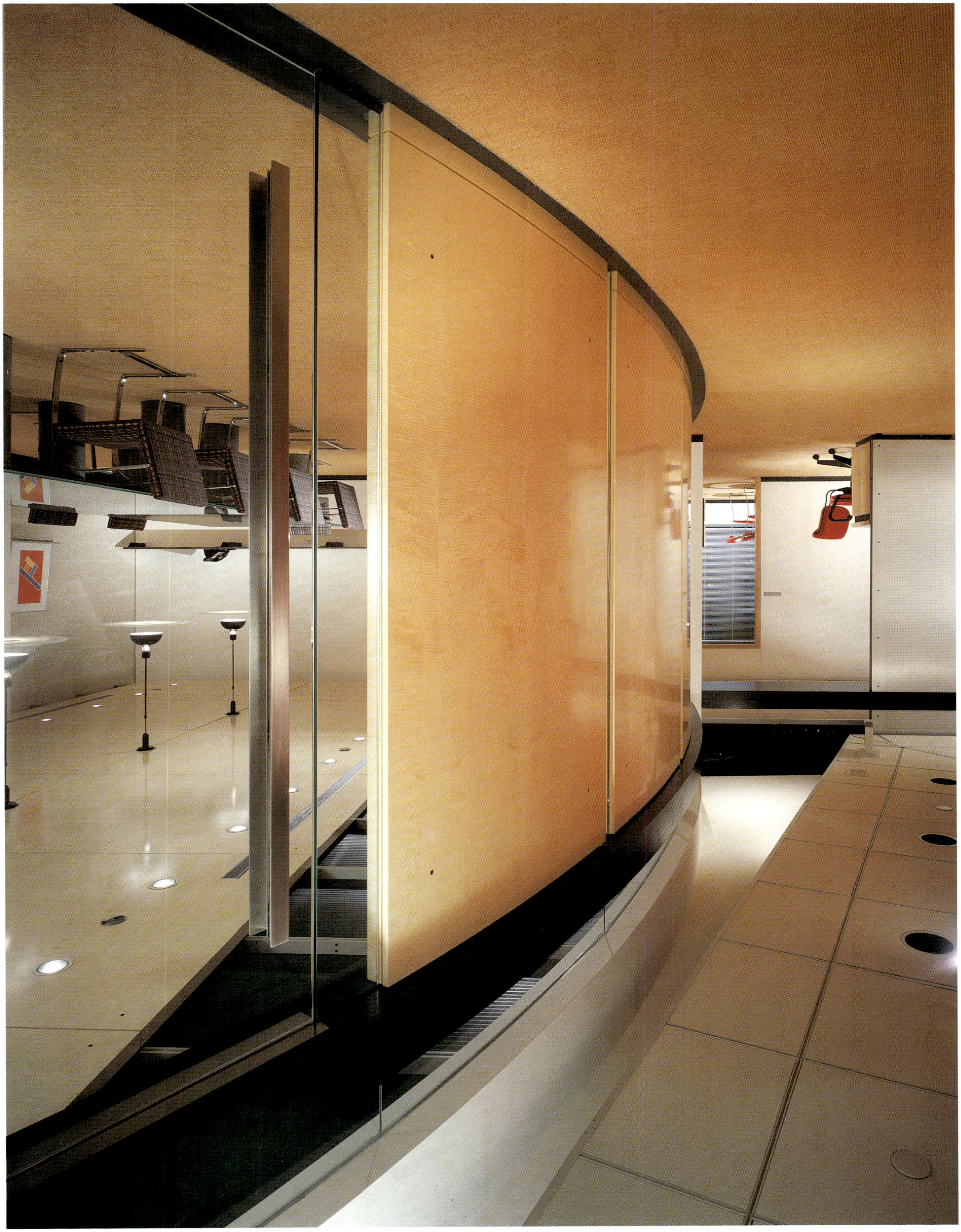

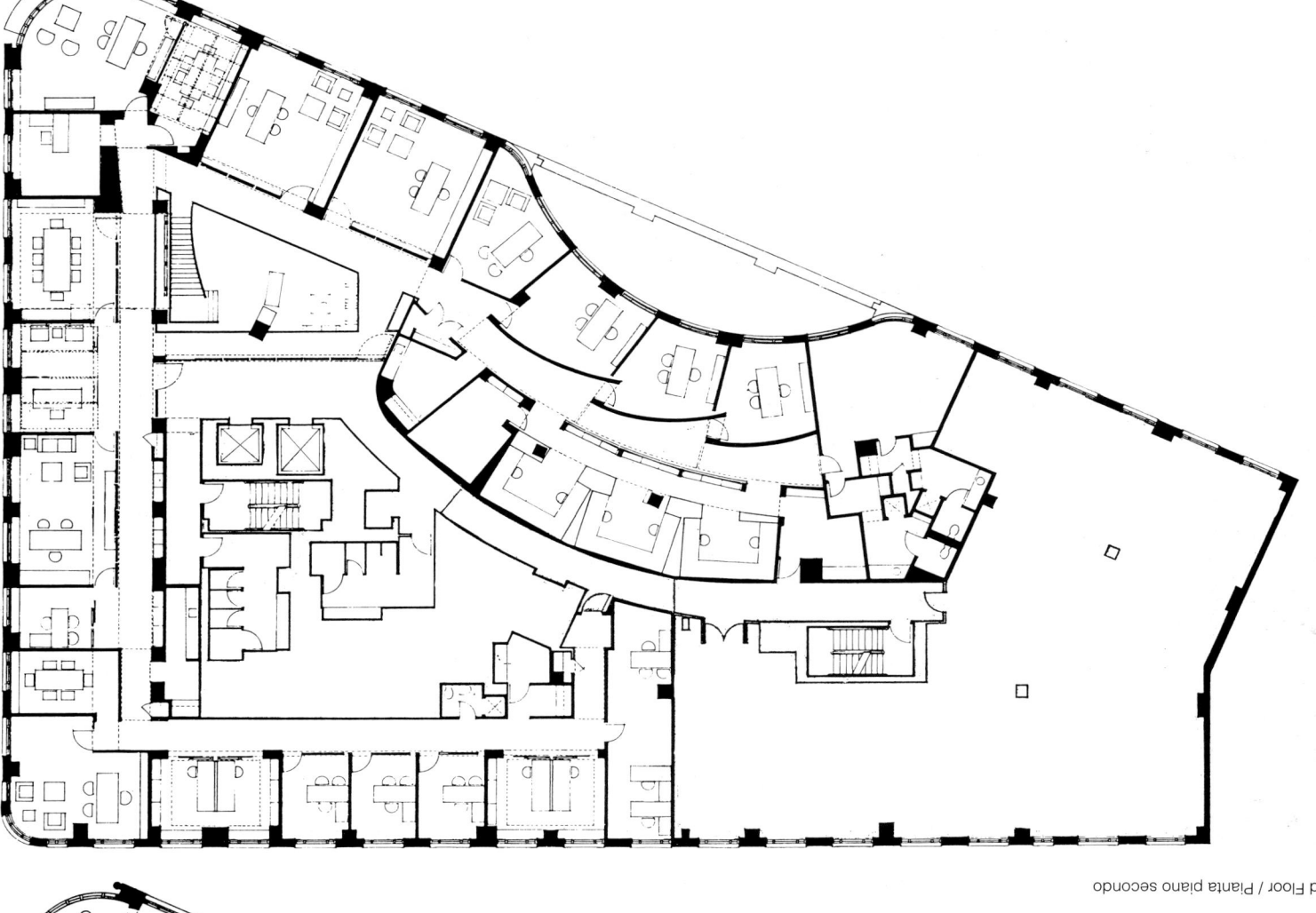

3rd Floor / Pianta piano terzo

2nd Floor / Pianta piano secondo

86

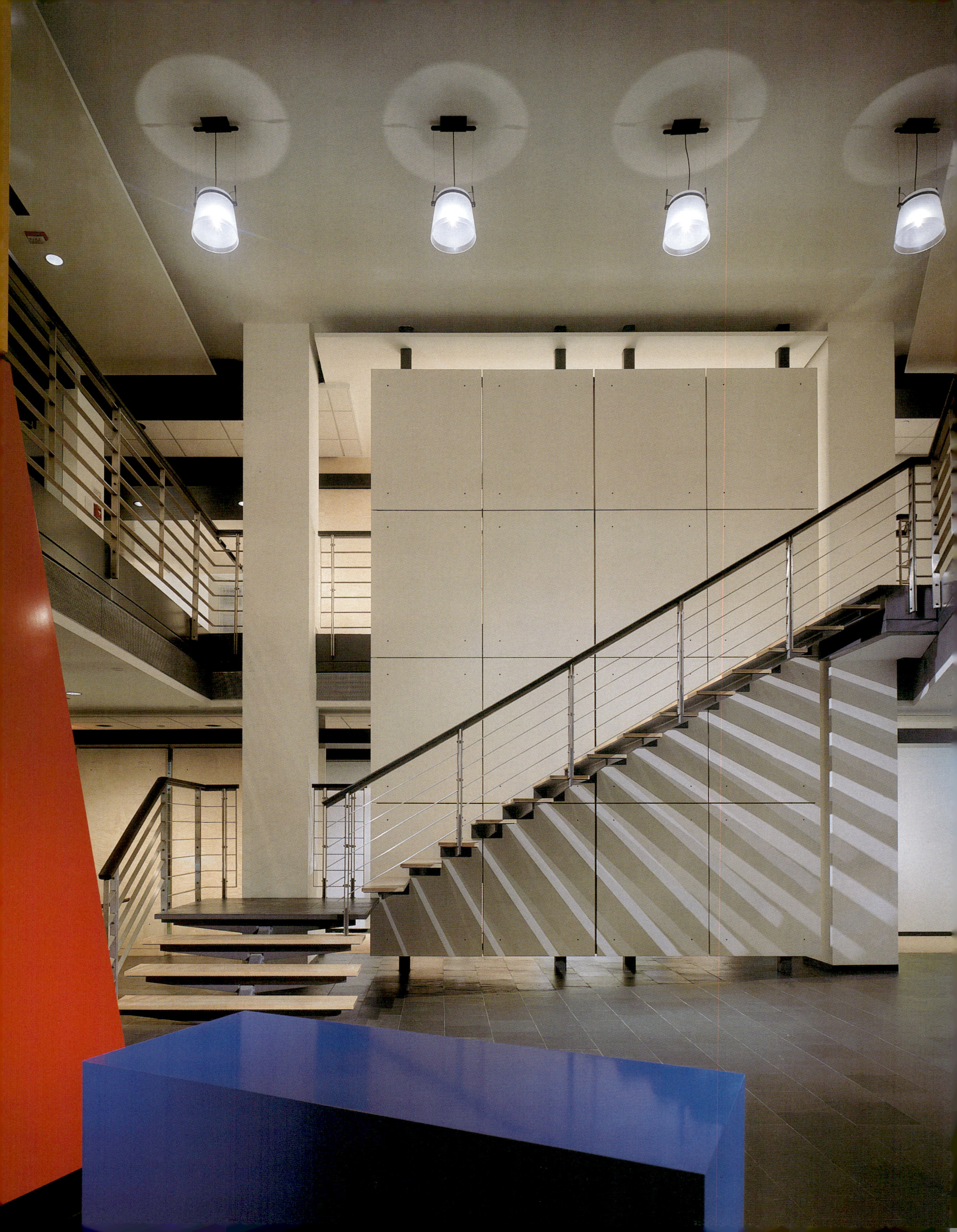

Axonometric / Assonometria dei due livelli

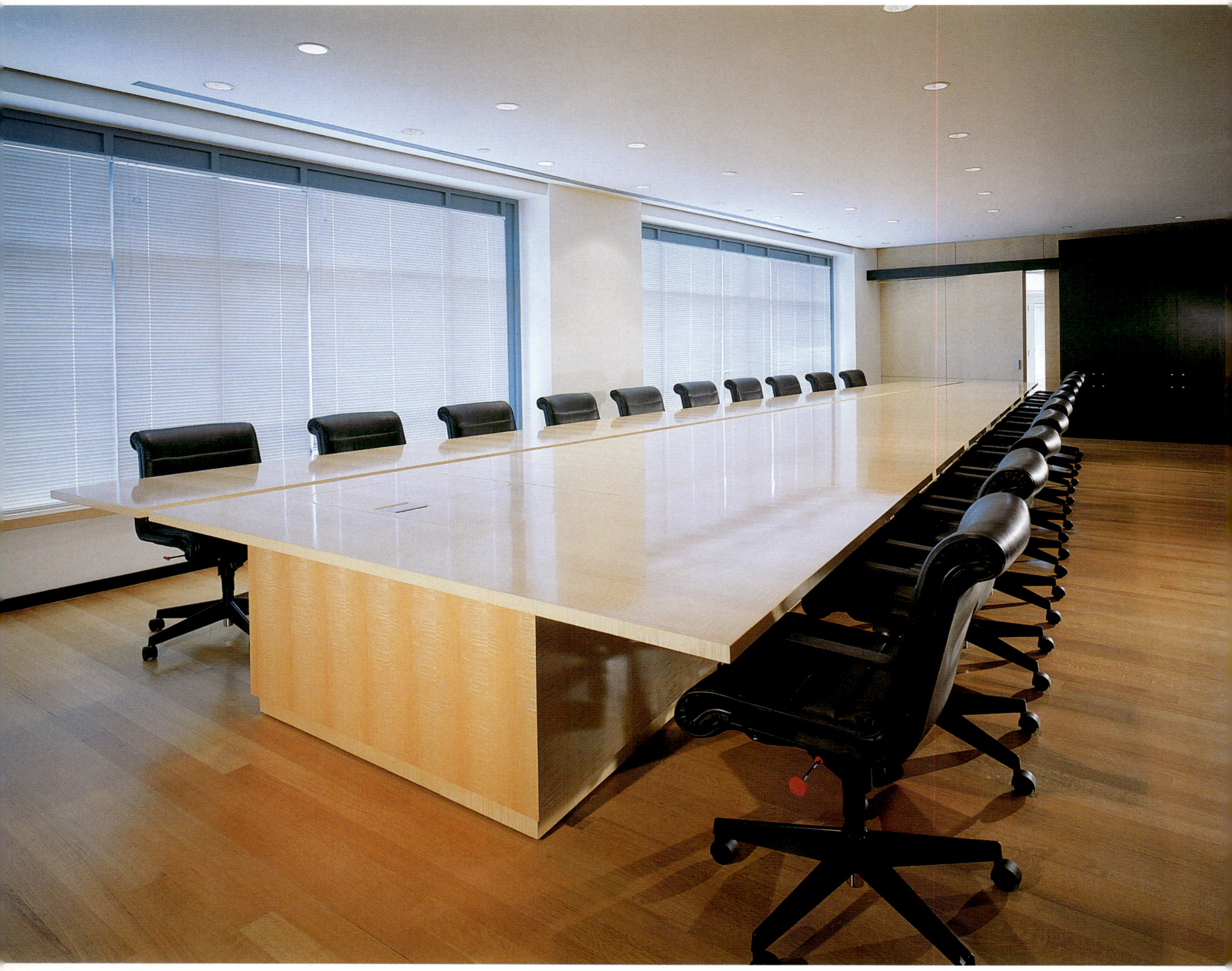

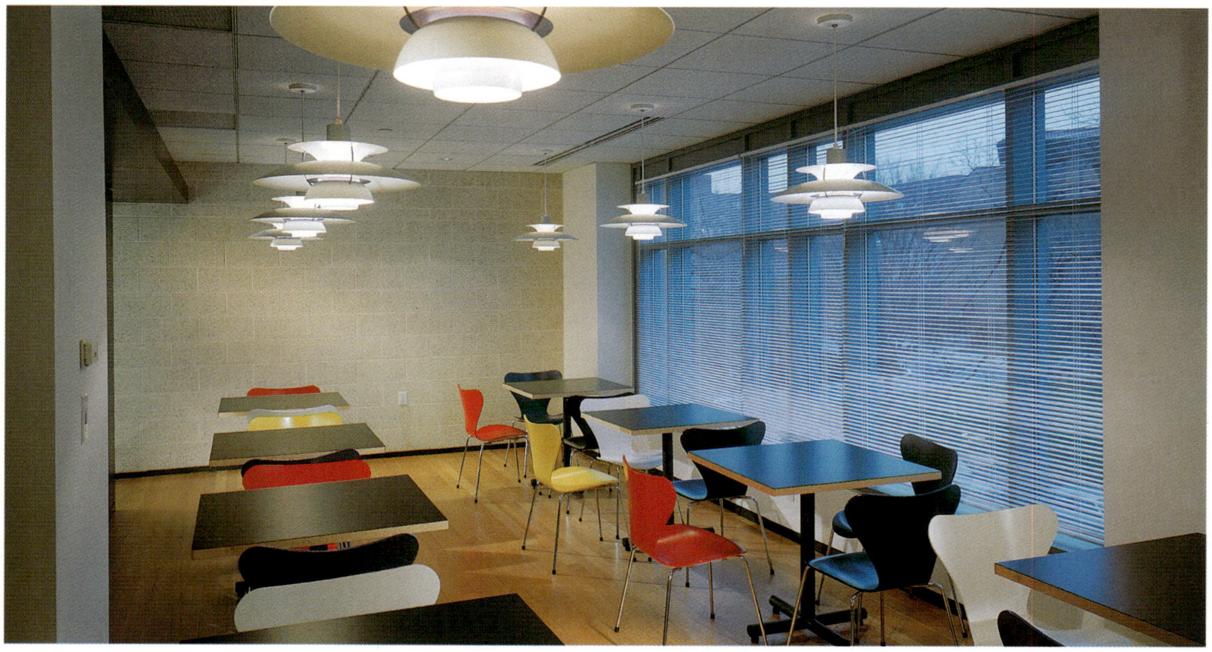

91

HUMMER WINBLAD VENTURE PARTNERS

Holey Associates Architects. San Francisco, CA, 1997

Slotted into an old warehouse loft space, these new interiors are the headquarters of a venture partnership serving software companies. The client stipulated a design in which modern ideas and functions would be favorably melded with the original warehouse-type environment of the setting. The premises themselves follow a regular oblong plan, with only two windowed facades and a striking load-bearing structure in brick (the facade walls) plus an extensive employment of timber (a dense network of roof beams for the soffit, sustained by three rows of six timber columns). The redesign of the space has successfully reconciled the existing figurative presences and materials, grafting the rehabilitated structural gridwork with a functionally revised layout of office spaces. The new scheme is cleverly modulated with a measured compound of open spaces with workstations in pairs, conference rooms, and individual offices lining the two windowed perimeter walls. The existing structure to some extent both inspired and restricted the new interior plan, obliging it to comply with the rhythm of timber beams that run lengthwise through the building, dividing it into long parallel bands. The sturdy pillars in rough timber, joined to the ceiling beams with metal brackets and burnished bolts, give further emphasis to the feel and character of the original warehouse loft, which has been figuratively and functionally revamped. The elevator and stair lobby leads out directly across the renovated wood-plank flooring to the gently concave reception desk, whose shape is echoed by the elegant curved partition behind, which screens off the entrance to the offices and is surmounted by a complex dropped ceiling that nicely underscores the composition. This is the only visible element of plasticity, a complete and self-sufficient feature that is played off against the otherwise unyielding orthogonal scheme of the interiors. A wall composed of a fascia of white plasterboard incorporating a succession of sanded glass panels in aluminum frames alternates with unobstructed areas that define the central open working zone, delimited by the two angled walls that mark the access to the corner offices. As with all the other offices along the perimeter, these are screened by walls that rehearse the design and materials of the central offices, channeling the natural light captured by the perimeter windows and filtering it through large partitions fitted with panes of sanded glass.

All'interno di un vecchio magazzino è stata ricavata la sede di una società di servizi. La committenza esprimeva il desiderio di una nuova immagine in grado di unire figure moderne e funzionali all'atmosfera del loft originario. Questo, di forma rettangolare regolare, con soli due lati finestrati, si caratterizzava per la particolare struttura portante in mattone a vista (i muri di facciata) unita ad un largo impiego del legno (fitte travi per il solaio sostenute da tre file di sei colonne affiancate). Il nuovo intervento ha saputo conservare tali forti presenze figurative e materiche inserendo nella maglia strutturale la nuova distribuzione funzionale dell'ufficio scandito da una calibrata miscela composta da spazi aperti con postazioni operative affiancate a due a due, da sale riunione e da uffici singoli posizionati lungo i due lati finestrati. La struttura preesistente ha in qualche modo suggerito e vincolato la soluzione interna che ha rispettato l'andamento delle le travi in legno che corrono in modo longitudinale nello spazio dividendolo in lunghe fasce parallele. I forti pilastri in legno massiccio, inchiavardati con piastre in ferro e bulloni bruniti alle travi che sostengono, segnano ulteriormente il carattere dello spazio originario che ritroviamo in una riuscita rivisitazione figurativa e funzionale nella soluzione di progetto. La reception è posizionata di fronte all'ascensore e alla scala; sul pavimento di legno a listoni presistente è posto un essenziale banco leggermente curvato per seguire l'andamento dell'elegante quinta che separa l'ingresso dagli uffici ponendosi, insieme al controsoffitto che la sormonta sottolineandone la soluzione compositiva, come unico elemento plastico, compiuto e indipendente, che si discosta dalla rigorosa maglia ortogonale dell'impianto complessivo. Una parete composta da una fascia in cartongesso bianco che sostiene una serie di sottili infissi di alluminio con vetro sabbiato è alternata a zone libere per definire l'open space centrale delimitato nelle testate da due pareti inclinate che evidenziano l'accesso agli uffici d'angolo. Questi sono schermati, come tutti quelli posizionati lungo il perimetro finestrato, da pareti che riprendono disegno e materiali di quella centrale, portando così all'interno la luce naturale catturata dalle aperture di facciata e filtrata dai grandi vetri sabbiati.

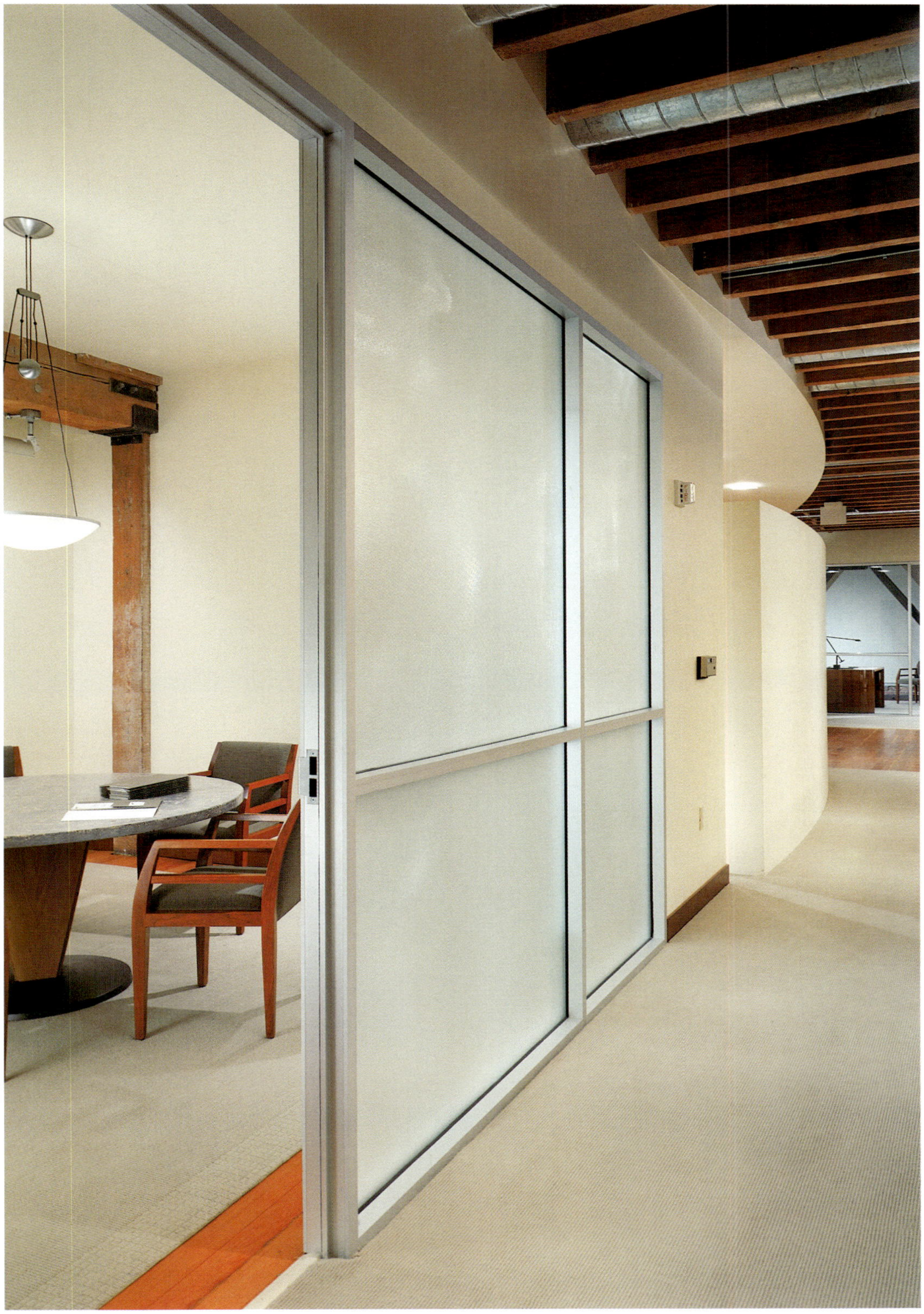

Plan / Pianta

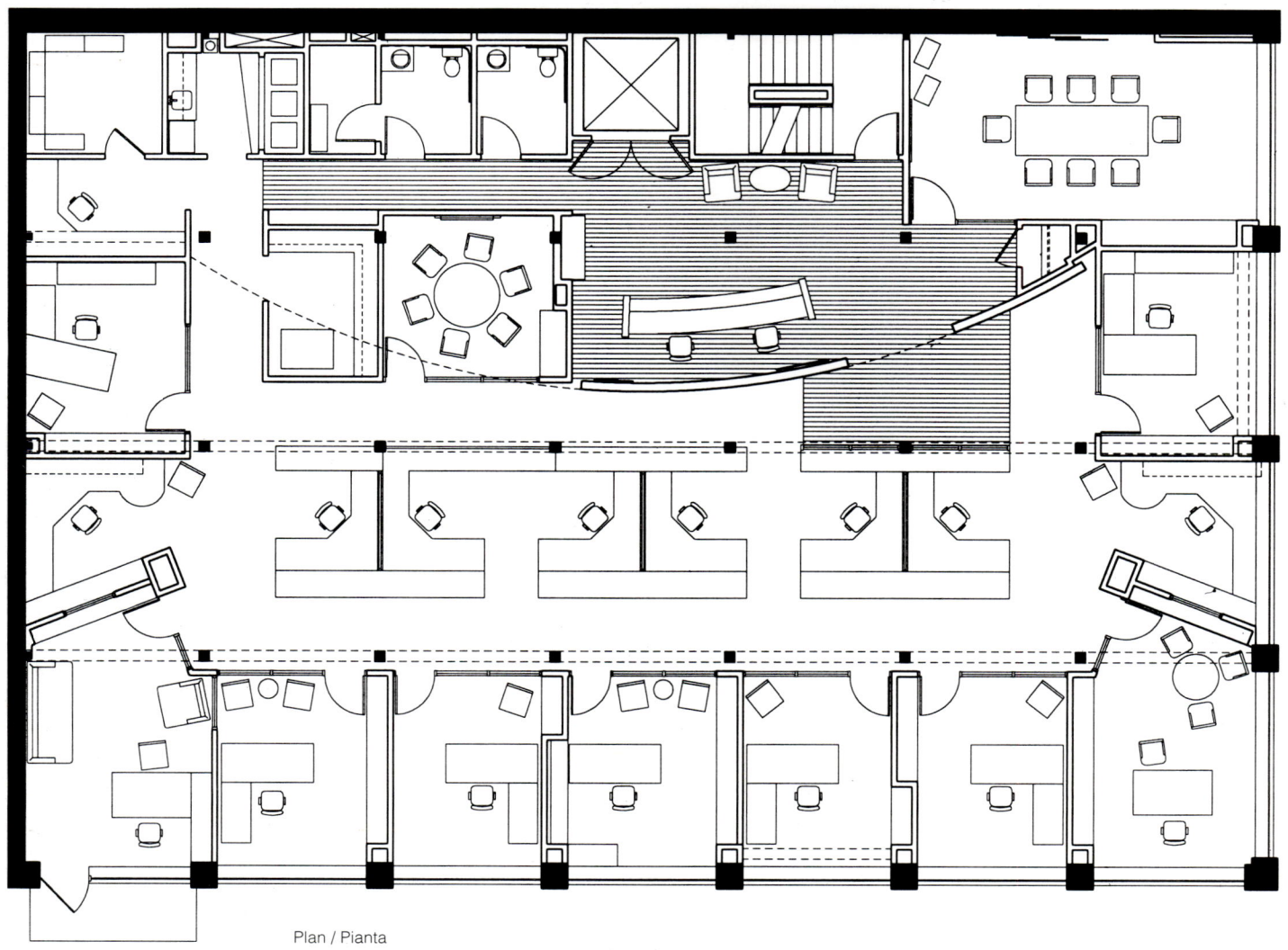

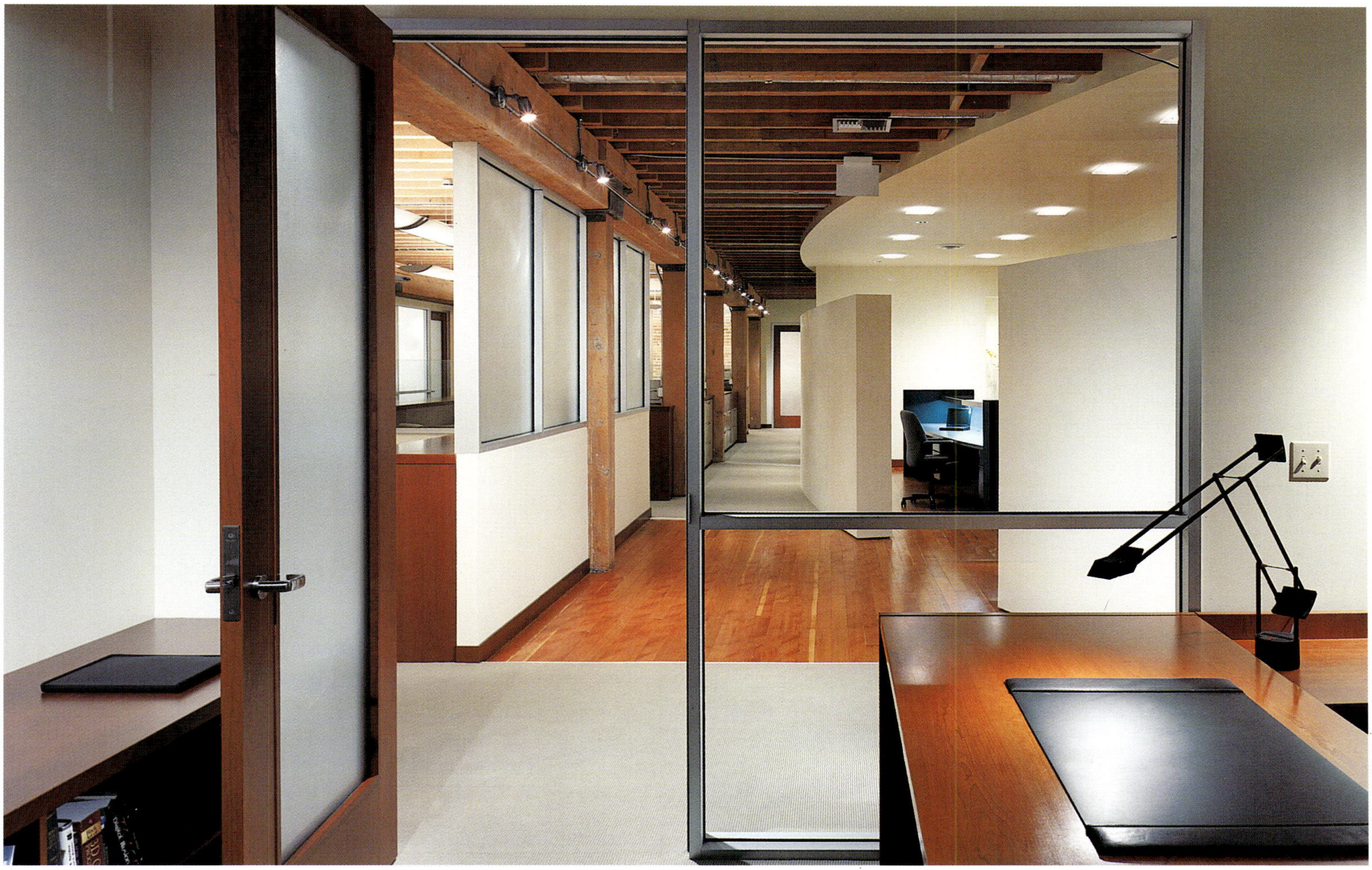

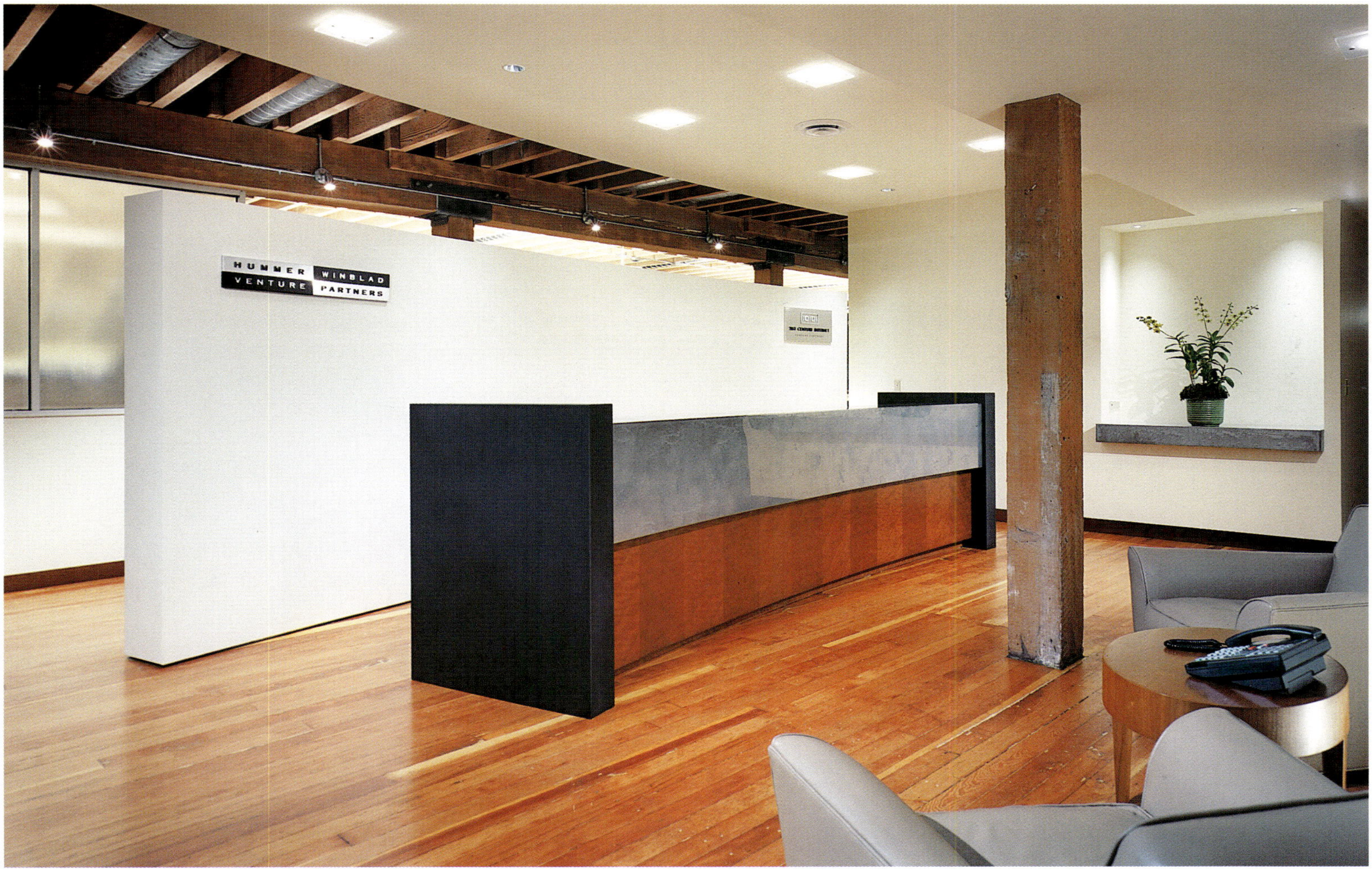
HUMMER WINBLAD
VENTURE PARTNERS

KIRSHENBAUM BOND & PARTNERS
Asfour & Guzy Associates Architects. New York, NY, 1996

Installed on the four stories of a stacked loft space in the heart of Soho, New York, the design of this advertising agency's headquarters reflects the innovatory nature of the firm's corporate philosophy. The project is basically an enlargement of the previous headquarters owing to the sharp rise in business. Two new stories were built on the original two, which were meanwhile completely remodeled and rebuilt to meet the new functional and distributive needs, while taking advantage of the three-story loft design united vertically by a new "totemic" internal stairway. This sculptural feature dominates the foyer as a functional and striking visual device, thrusting upward through the architecture to great effect. The firm's logo is carved into the wall at the entrance; an unusual "Welcome" doormat hails visitors on the threshold, a wry reminder of an old American tradition. A large, bare space provides the entrance hall, onto which looks the large meeting room, the reception desk (in lino-clad metal, behind which hangs a large compilation of Polaroid portraits of the staff), and a russet-colored stairway with metal railing that climbs in a zigzag from floor to floor. A slender illuminated tube follows the stairwell from the ground right to the ceiling of the top story. The unitary nature of these former manufacturing spaces has been maintained by using mobile partitions: meetings rooms, executive and individual offices, are always fashioned from panels treated with stucco finish in soft hues, framed in burnished metal, the upper section with glazed panels to convey the natural light into the heart of the building. For the open-plan workshops, other elegant glazed sections, transparent or sanded, are screened by partitions composed of large wooden frames containing panels of translucid material that offer a sense of light and luminosity to the work spaces. The loft look has been maintained by carefully restoring the square timber pillars, together with the brackets anchoring them to the ceiling girders, which have all been left exposed to view as they were originally.

Sviluppata su quattro livelli di un edificio a loft sovrapposti nel cuore di Soho, la sede di questa agenzia pubblicitaria riflette nell'immagine complessiva il carattere innovativo della filosofia aziendale. Il progetto si pone come ampliamento della sede precedente, dovuto alla veloce crescita del volume di affari complessivo. Ai due piani iniziali se ne sono aggiunti altrettanti, in un progetto di revisione e ricostruzione dell'architettura interna. Questa è stata pensata sia per rispondere alle nuove esigenze funzionali e distributive, sia per valorizzare gli spazi dei loft originari uniti in verticale per tre livelli da una nuova scala totemica interna, forte e riuscita presenza architettonica e scultorea che troneggia nello spazio d'ingresso come elemento di riferimento funzionale e visivo, per proiettarsi in verticale con grande slancio figurativo. Il logo dell'agenzia è proposto in negativo sulla parete dell'entrata; un inconsueto tappetino-lapide segna la soglia d'ingresso con la scritta welcome (ironica ripresa della tradizione di ogni casa americana). Un ampio spazio vuoto si propone come hall d'ingresso dove si affacciano la grande sala riunione, la reception (in metallo e linoleum ha alle spalle un pannello composto da decine di polaroid, originale ritratto collettivo dei dipendenti) e la scala rossa in metallo pensata come forte nastro a zig-zag di salita. Un sottile cilindro luminoso ne valorizza l'intero sviluppo verticale, dal pavimento di partenza al soffitto dell'ultimo livello. Il carattere unitario dei loft viene mantenuto dalla soluzione delle pareti divisorie: siano per sale riunione, uffici direzionali o singoli, sono sempre composte da pannelli trattati a stucco in tinte morbide, contenuti da profilati di metallo brunito, con parte superiore vetrata in modo da portare la luce naturale del perimetro nella zona centrale. Per le zone operative a open space, alte eleganti vetrate, trasparenti o sabbiate, sono schermate da quinte composte da grandi cornici di legno contenenti pannelli di materiale traslucido che offrono un senso di leggerezza e di grande luminosità agli ambienti di lavoro. Infine il carattere architettonico dei loft è stato mantenuto nel restauro dei pilastri in legno e nelle strutture di ancoraggio alle travi del soffitto, lasciate a vista nella loro figura originaria.

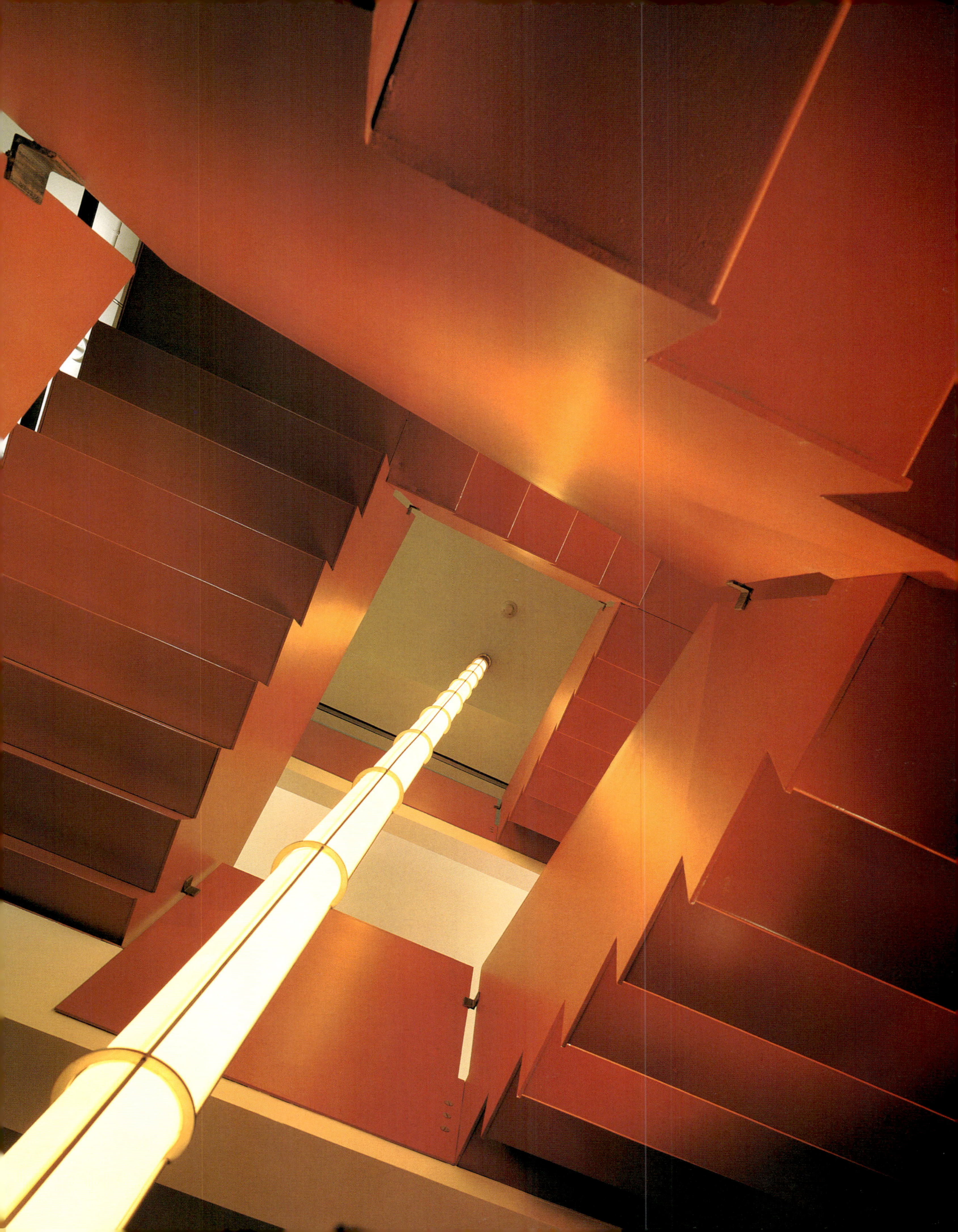

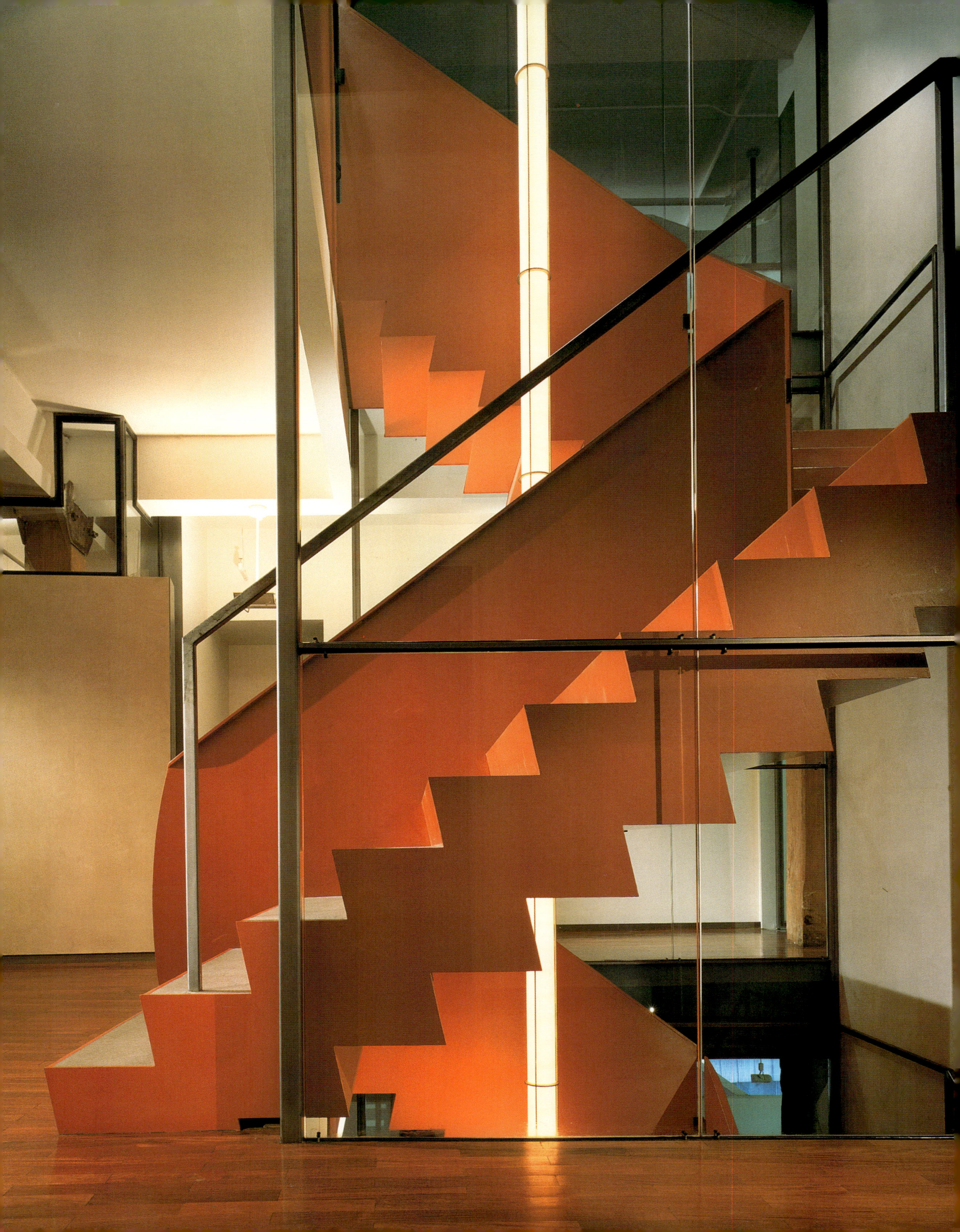

99

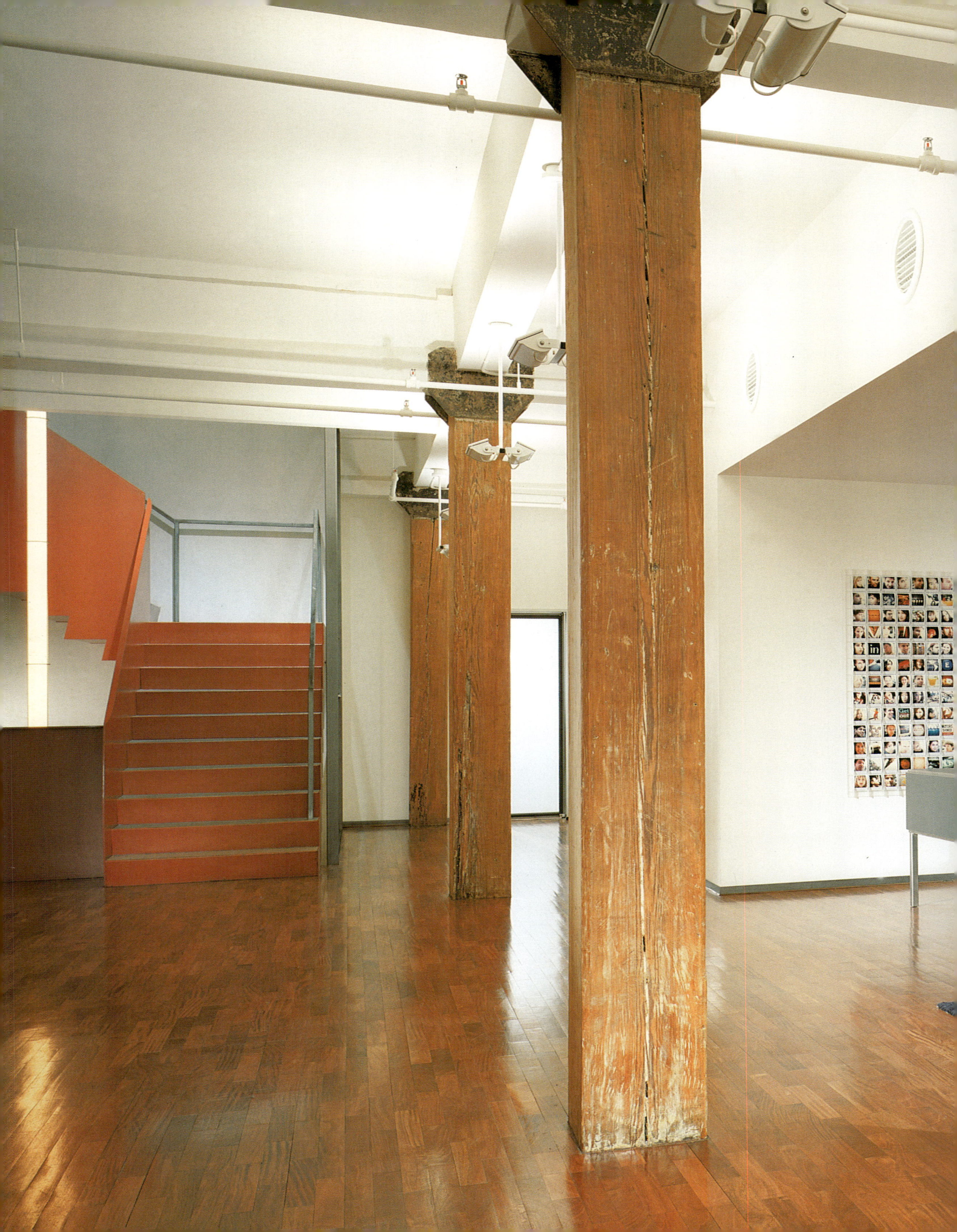

GREAT CREATIVE SHOULD FEEL LIKE A FRIEND TALKING TO YOU · "IDEAOCRACY" IS WHERE PEOPLE MAKE
RICHARD KIRSHENBAUM

Fourth Floor Plan / Pianta piano 4°

1. Entry / Entrata
2. Reception / Reception
3. Conference / Sala riunioni
4. Principal's office / Ufficio direzionale
5. Brand room / Brand room
6. Open work space / Open space

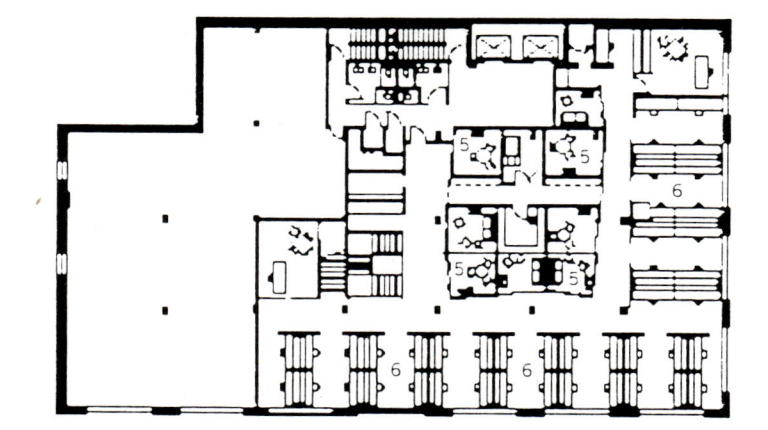

Fifth Floor Plan / Pianta piano 5°

103

LANCASTER GROUP WORLDWIDE INC.

Quantrell Mullins & Associates Inc. New York, NY, 1994

Spread over three stories, the hallmarks of the design of the Lancaster Group headquarters is flexibility, a great variety of individual office types, and the clever used of natural light, which is harnessed from the building facades and channeled into the work spaces to the very core of the building. The classic open-plan configuration prompted the designers to create an initial operations area directly illuminated by the facade openings and distributed around the four sides of the building's perimeter. The independent spaces thus obtained from this initial work zone are individual offices strategically alternated with meeting rooms. These spaces look onto the second, internal work zone, which boasts an open plan with elegant custom-built workstations in maple flanked by neatly designed reception desks. As a means of bringing light to the internal work zone, the inner walls of the perimeter offices are entirely glazed, affording a succession of transparent partitions decorated with wave motifs and sanded stars, an echo of the group's wave-and-star logo, which is reiterated in the reception areas. The liberal use of glass as a key architectural feature enhances the sense of lightness and elegance of the overall concept of the design, which is characterized by a rigorous and measured combination of materials, visual devices, and colors. The architectural tone of the offices is advertised in the arrival landing, where a strip of black marble flooring is offset by the geometrical bulkhead above, passing by a series of assertive doorways and surrounds in the same black stone for each of the elevator entrances, set between wall sections of fine maple paneling. The black pathway is framed by a band of veined white marble interrupted at the elevator doors, like an invitation. White marble is also used for the reception and corridors, where sets of steel columns enclose the cabling. A cobalt blue carpet gives comfort and class to the separate offices and meeting rooms, and open spaces, a color that is reiterated in some of the custom-built fittings (as in the waiting lounge, and product presentation rooms), which form a direct complement.

Sviluppata su tre livelli la sede della Lancaster Group si caratterizza anzitutto per flessibilità e vasta scelta tipologica degli uffici e per l'impiego della luce naturale, catturata dai fronti dell'edificio e portata all'interno degli spazi lavoro sino al nocciolo tecnologico centrale. La classica pianta libera ha suggerito ai progettisti di creare una prima fascia operativa direttamente illuminata dalle aperture di facciata e distribuita lungo i quattro lati perimetrali. Gli spazi indipendenti così ottenuti formano la prima zona di lavoro, composta da uffici singoli alternati a sale riunioni posizionate strategicamente. Questi spazi si affacciano sulla seconda zona lavoro interna, organizzata secondo un ordinato open space con eleganti postazioni su disegno dai piani in legno d'acero affiancate da studiate reception. Per illuminare in modo naturale la zona open space, le pareti interne degli uffici perimetrali sono interamente in vetro, una successione di lastre trasparenti decorate con motivi a onda e con stelline sabbiate che reinterpretano liberamente il logo del Gruppo, ripreso anche nella soluzione compositiva delle reception. L'ampio uso del vetro quale elemento architettonico di riferimento sottolinea la leggerezza e l'eleganza delle scelte complessive di un intervento caratterizzato da una rigorosa e calibrata miscela di materiali, figure e colori. L'immagine architettonica degli uffici è già annunciata dal pianerottolo di arrivo, dove un tappeto di marmo nero si affianca, sotto un controsoffitto a cassettoni geometrico, alla serie di riusciti portali dello stesso materiale, cornici architettoniche ripetute per tutti gli ascensori separati tra loro da superfici rivestite in legno d'acero. Il tappeto di marmo nero è incorniciato da una fascia di marmo bianco venato interrotta da strisce nere di invito alle porte degli ascensori. Lo stesso marmo bianco è impiegato nell'interno della pavimentazione di reception e corridoi, dove una serie di colonne in acciaio ospitano i cavi delle reti telematiche. Una moquette blu cobalto scandisce uffici singoli, sale riunioni e open space, per trovare in alcuni mobili e pareti/armadio su disegno dello stesso colore (nelle zone di attesa e nelle sale di presentazione dei prodotti) il diretto elemento complementare.

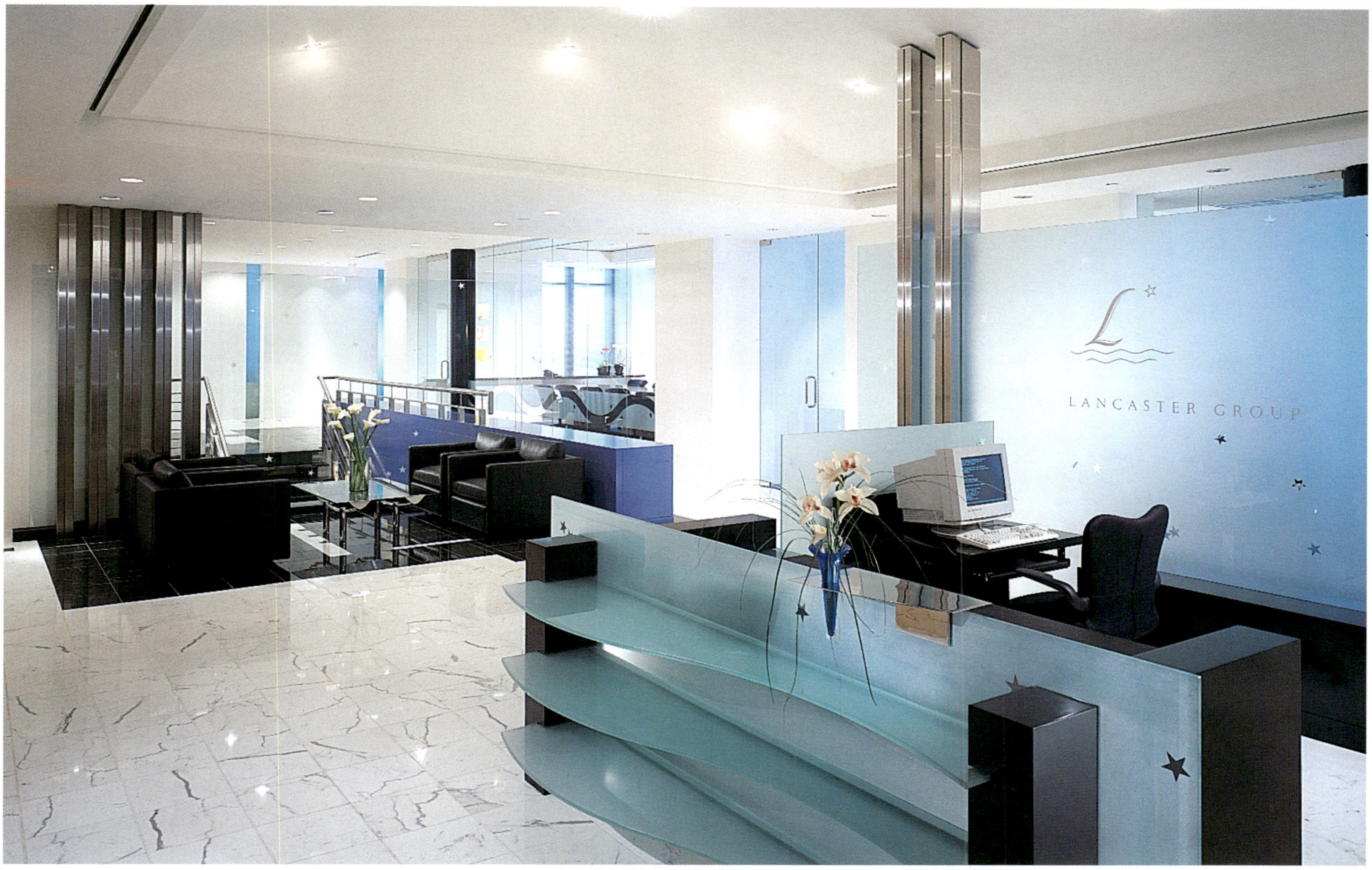
LANCASTER GROUP

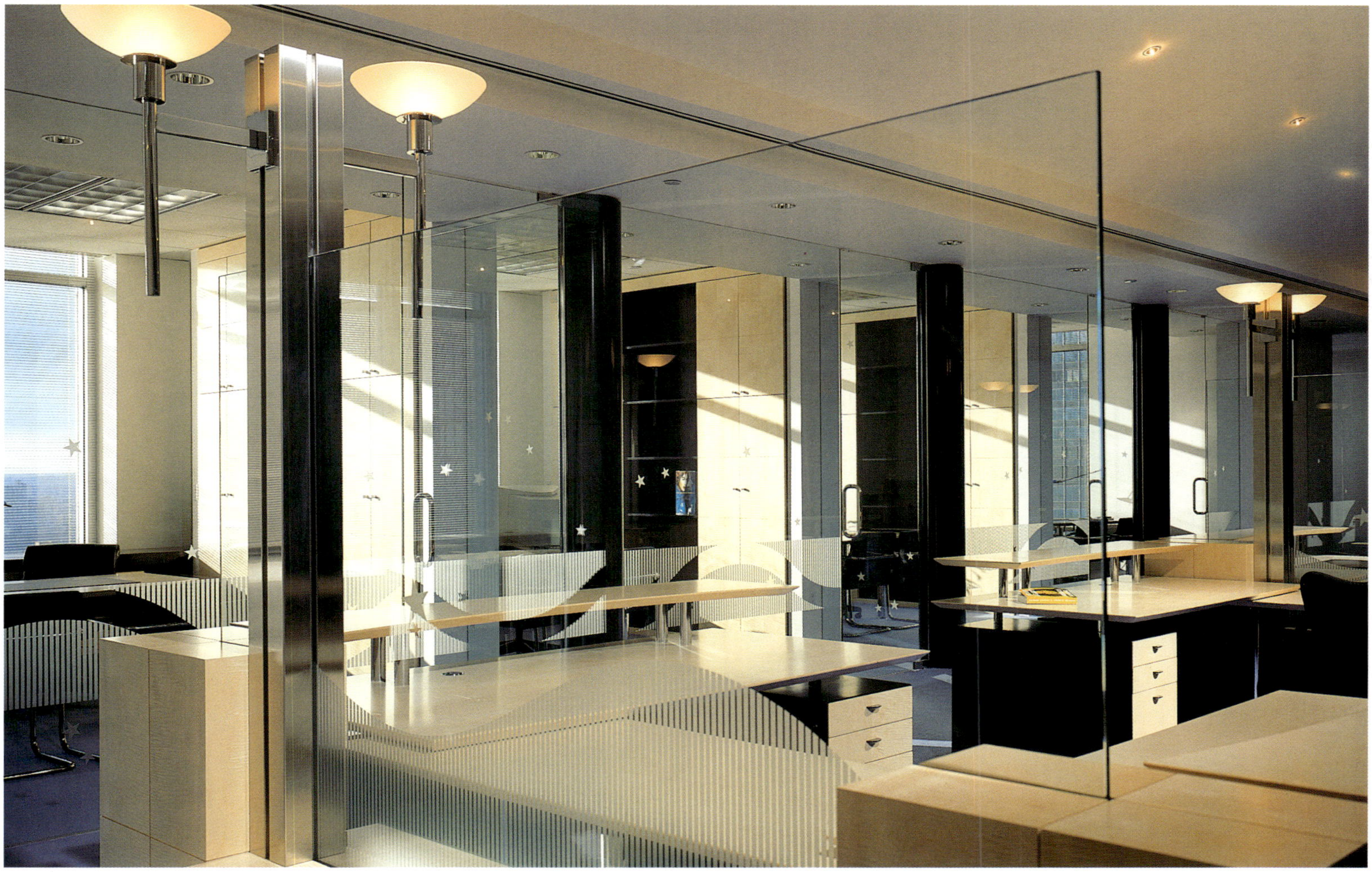

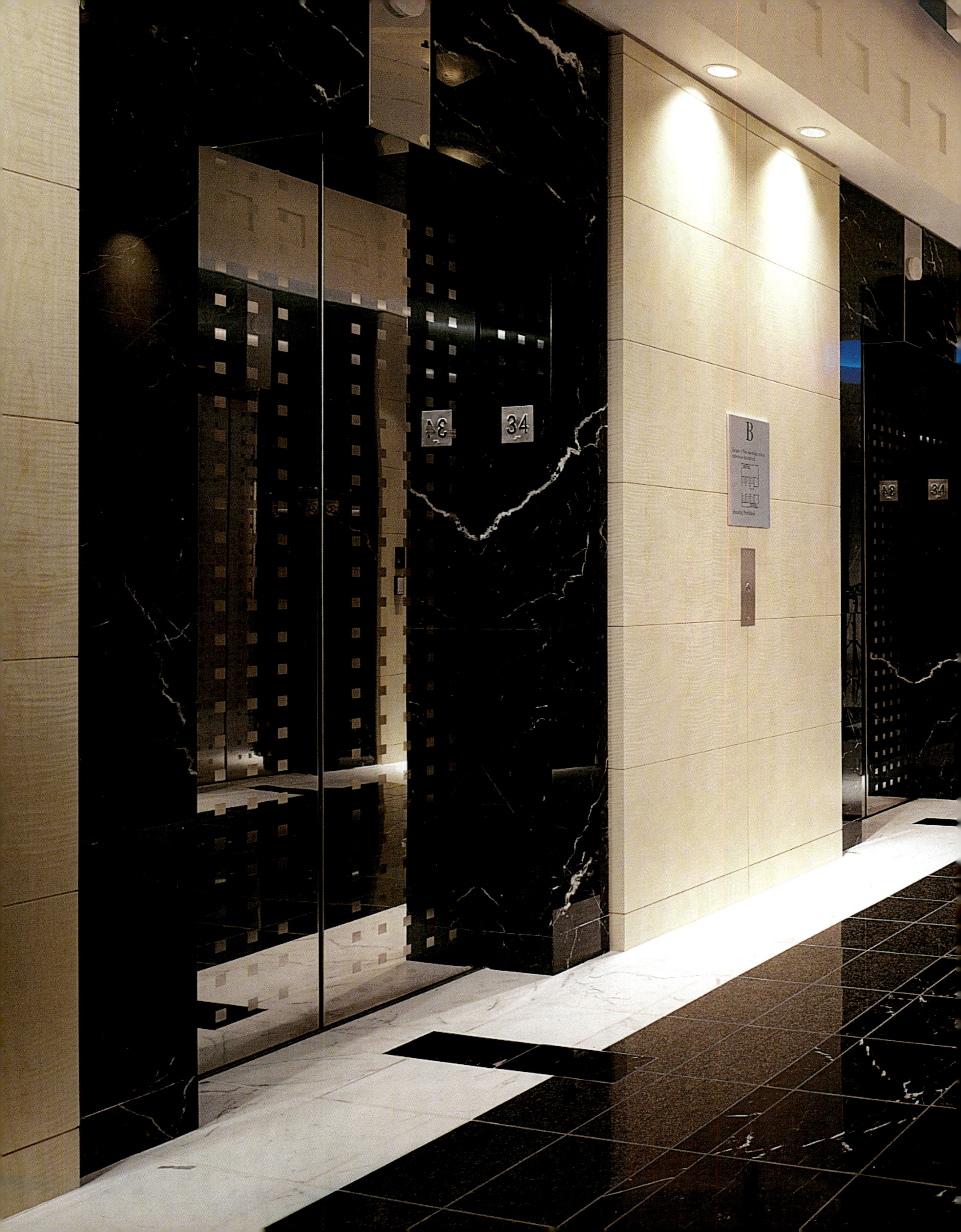
34
B

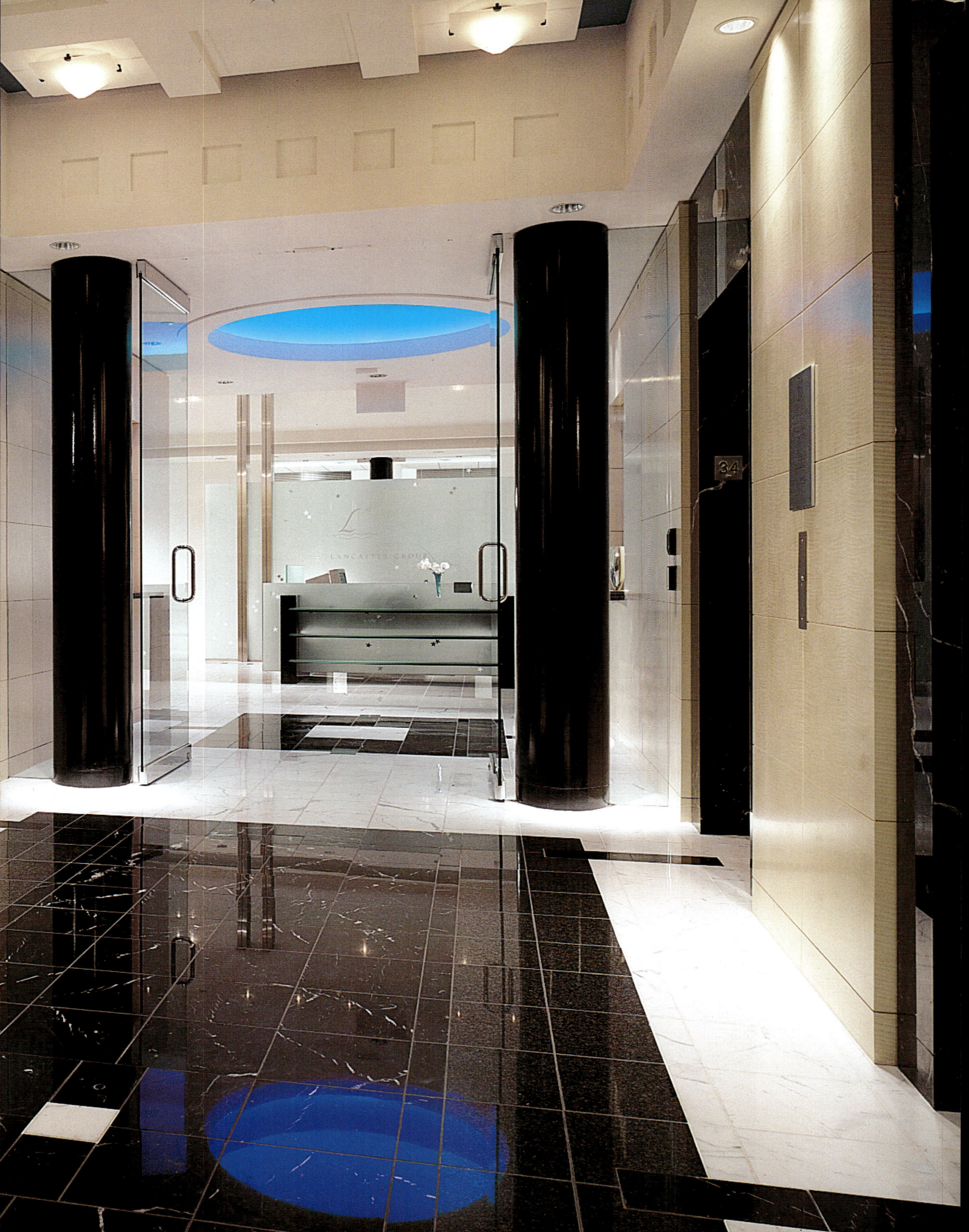
34

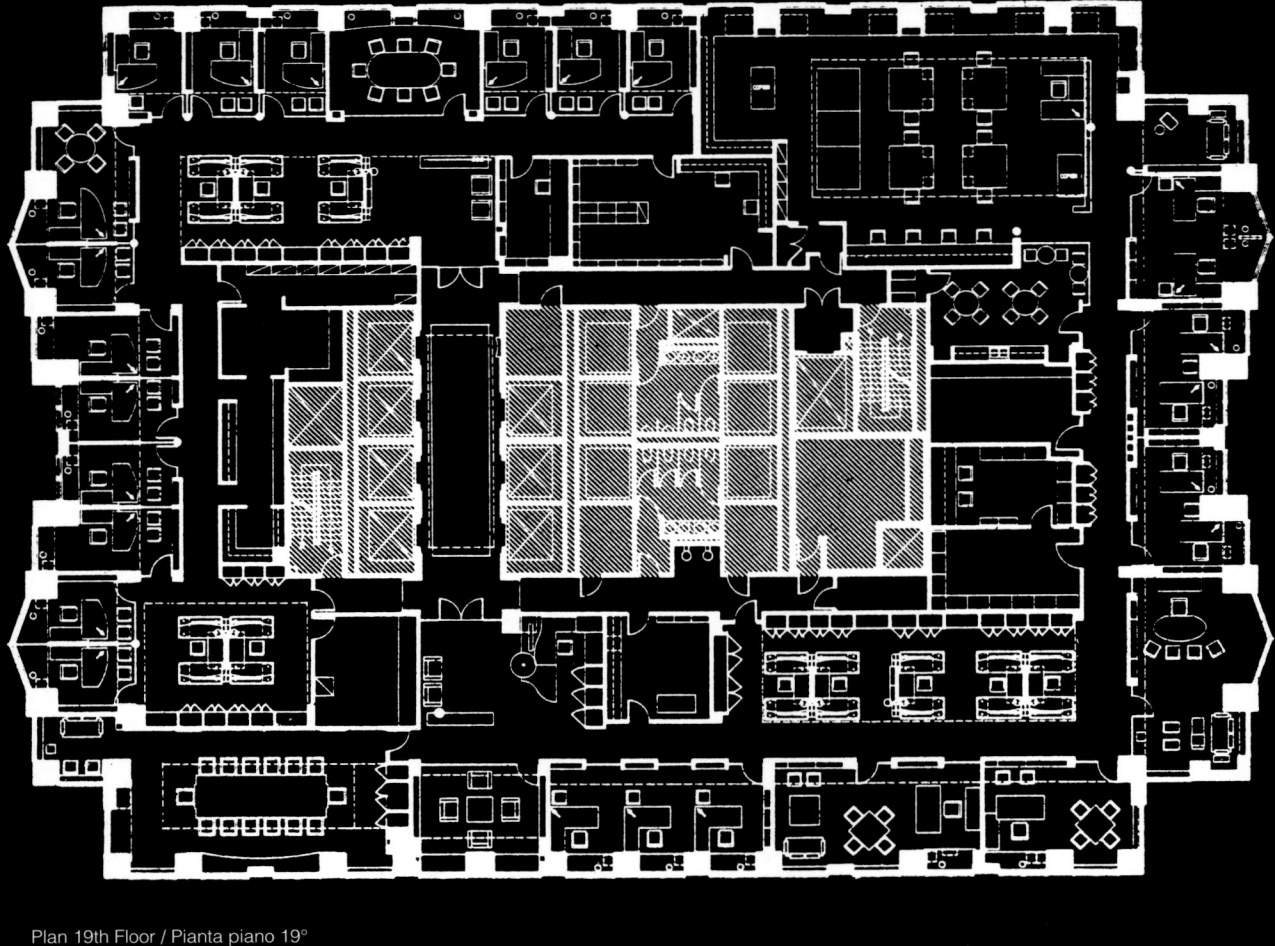

Plan 19th Floor / Pianta piano 19°

Plan 33rd Floor / Pianta piano 33°

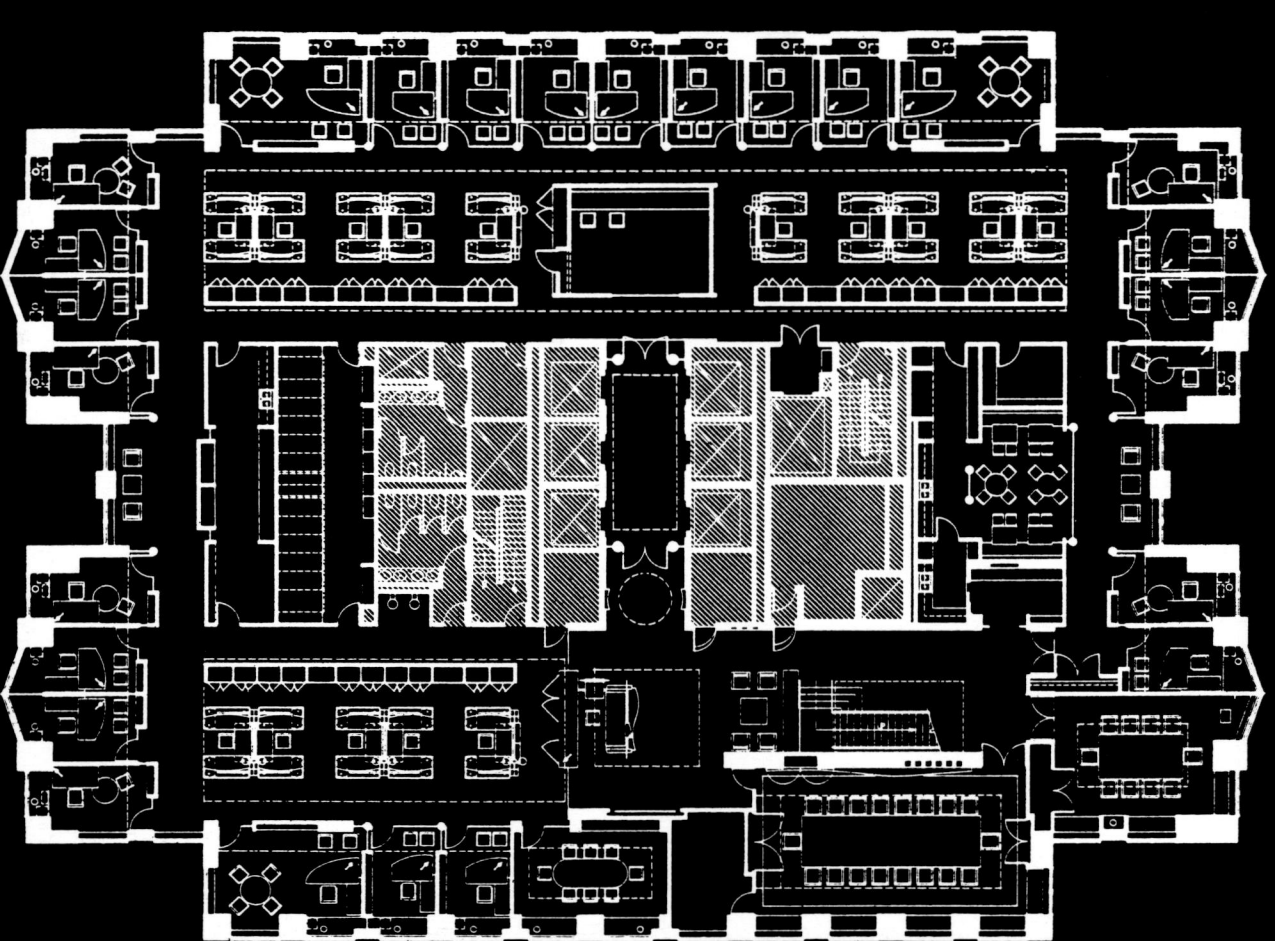

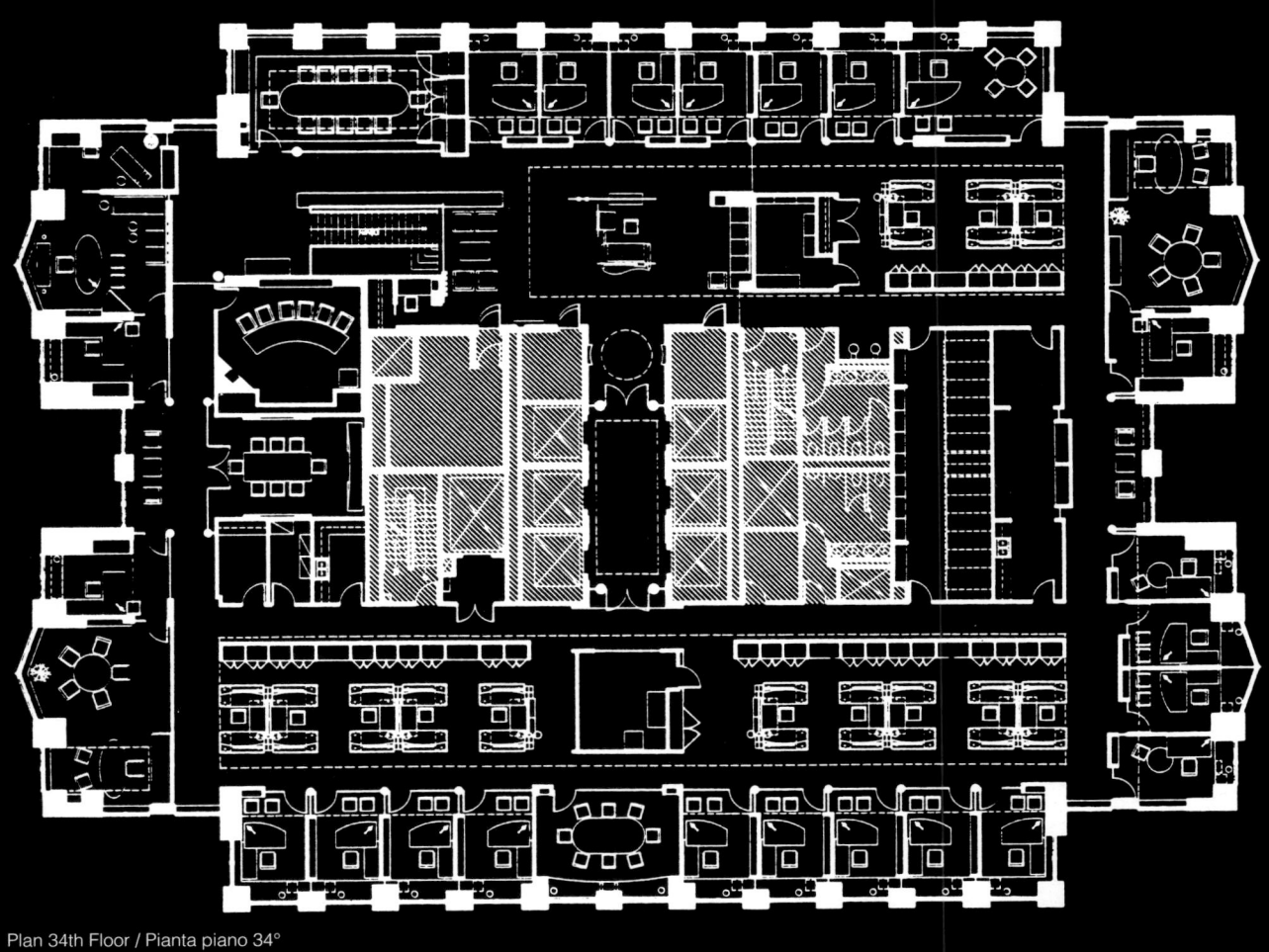

Plan 34th Floor / Pianta piano 34°

109

Prospectic view of reception area of 34th Floor
Vista prospettica della zona Reception al 34° piano

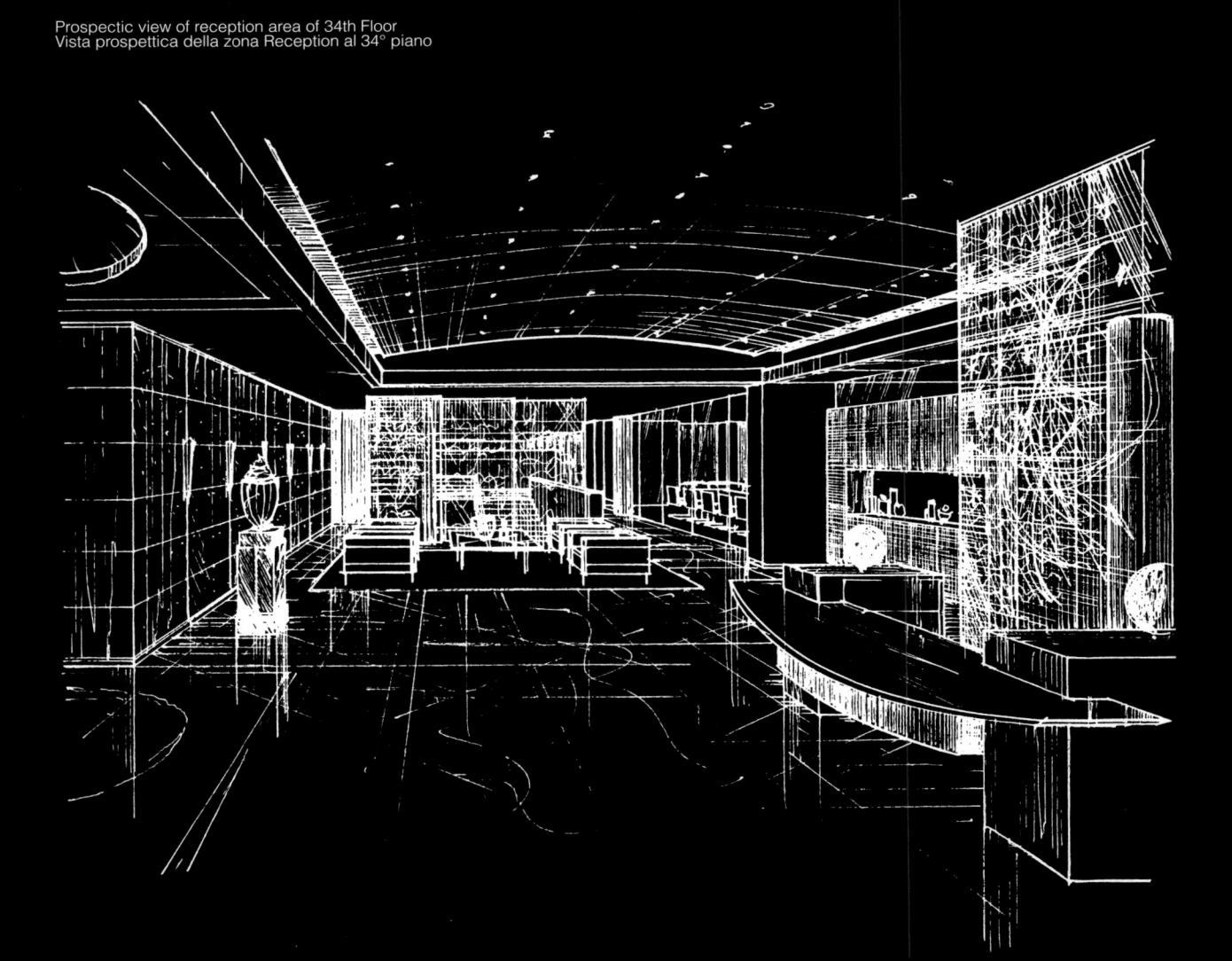

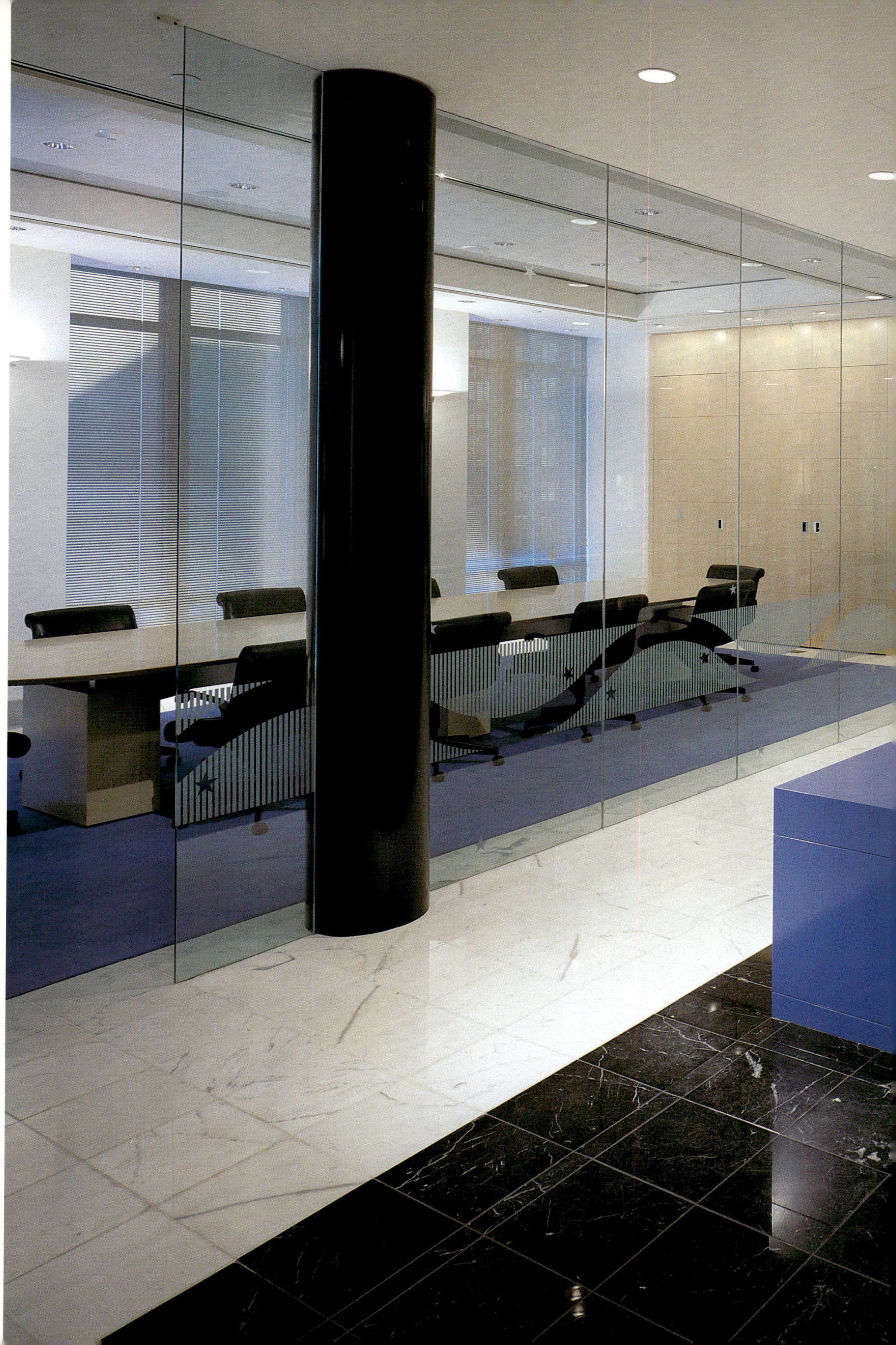

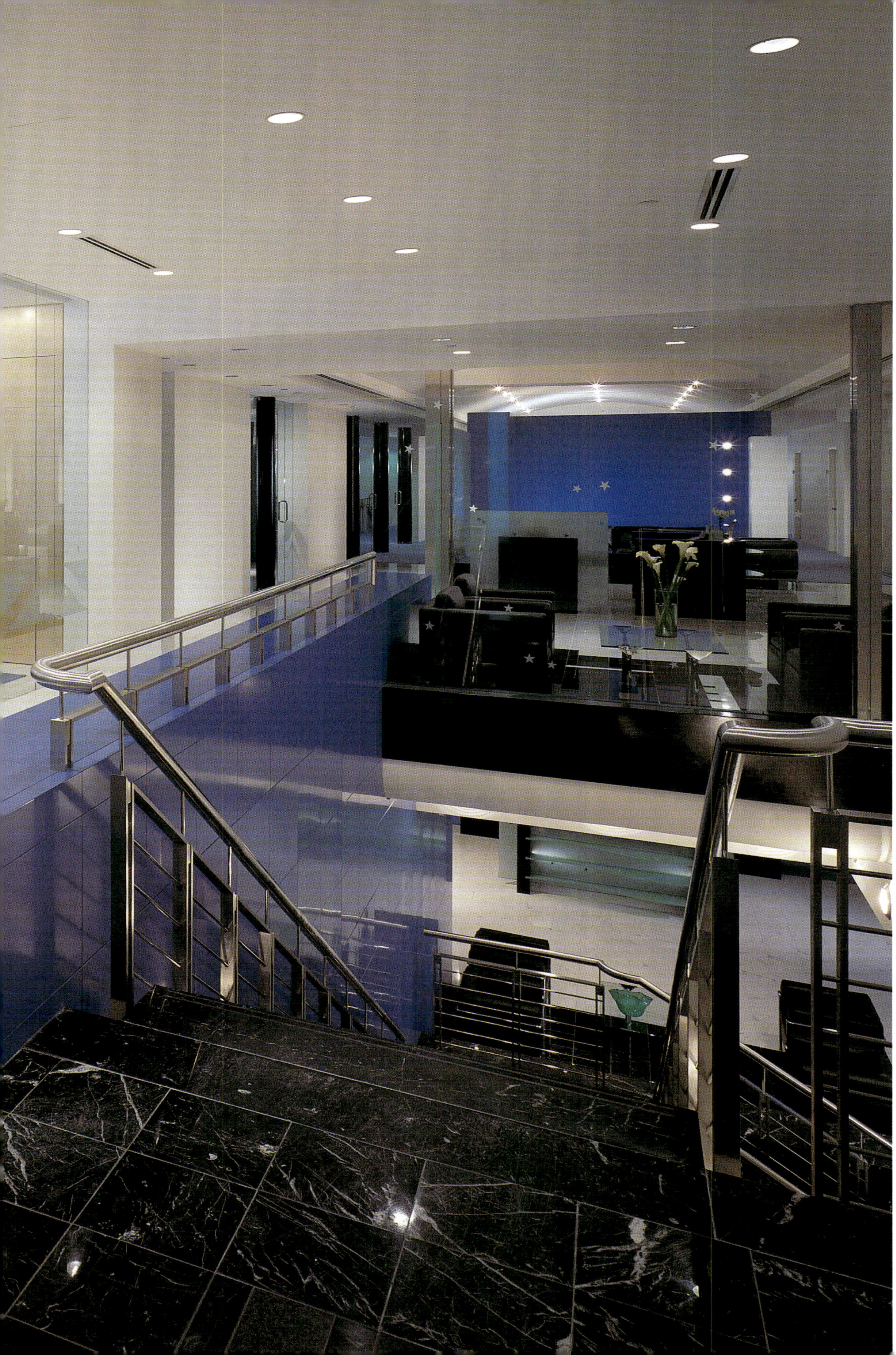

112

113

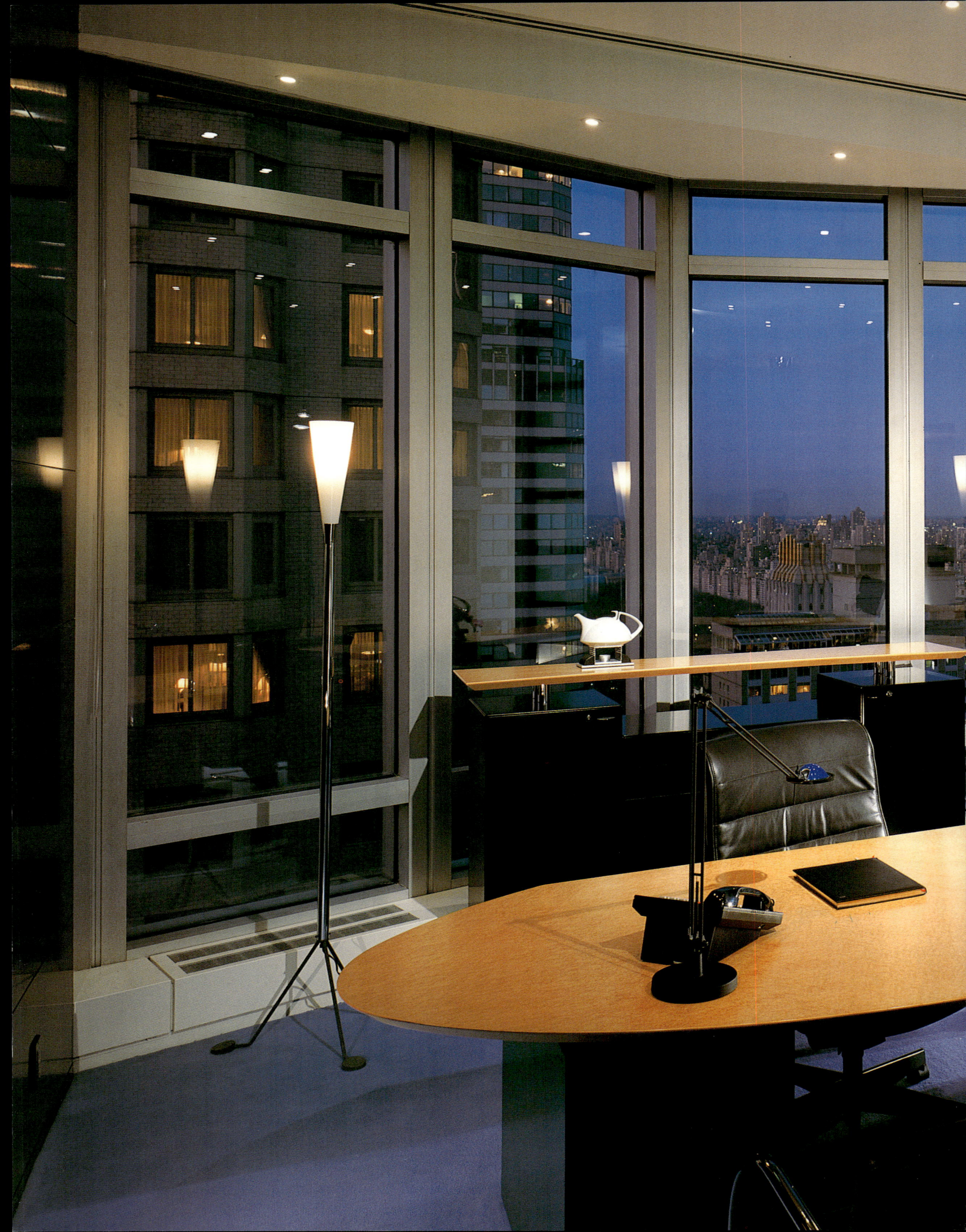

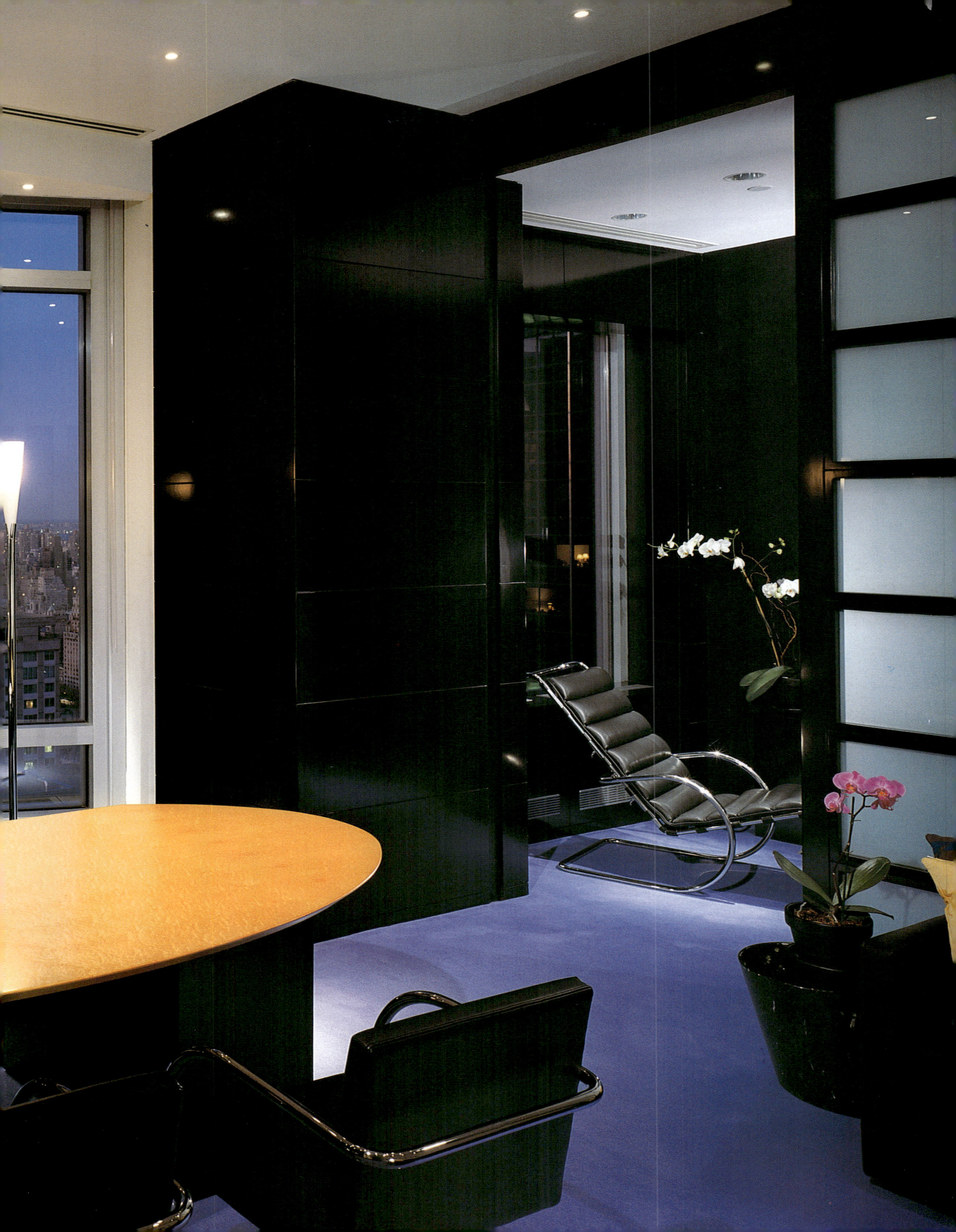

NEW LINE CINEMA - EAST
Smith Miller + Hawkinson Architects. New York, NY, 1992

Situated on two contiguous upper floors of Manhattan south of Central Park, with splendid views over the park, Seventh Avenue, and the Hudson, this suite of offices for a film production company boasts an intriguing L-shaped plan that was dictated by the building shape itself. The stair and elevator block is positioned in one partially windowless corner of the L. The structural specifics of the plan provided the designers with a point of departure around which to construct a set of interiors devised to take advantage of the views of the city, and offer new and unusual spatial conditions and points of view. For their reworking of the floor plan, the architects have assembled a string of perimeter offices on the lower floor, separated by plasterboard partitions set into wooden surrounds, along the top of which run a series of transparent panels. These openings, a visual hallmark of the composition, allow daylight to flow from the perimeter glazing into the inner office area. The 18th floor is linked to the one above via a neat steel and glass staircase, set obliquely, which extends through the new, narrow free section with its exposed roof beams, and a peculiar section of floor in clear glass. This calibrated double-height feature has been cut out around the main conference room, leaving a gap in the floor, which thereby takes on the appearance of a compact, self-sufficient space, suspended, as it were, between the two floors of the suite. On the 19th floor stands the reception area, integrated with the elevator lobby with its rough metal doors repeating the design concept of the emergency exit. At the back of the lobby a tall, narrow mirror reflects the perimeter windows, giving added depth to the slate-floor arrival area. The reception desk proper is a stark geometrical composition that announces the general philosophy of the redesign: it is composed of a clever combination of vertical and horizontal planes, profiles and surrounds of varying thickness and materials (wood, plasterboard, metal, or glass) carefully matched with the composition of oblique volumes of the false ceilings and the floor plan, which is underlined by circulation routes and walls skewed against the building facade, giving emphasis to the new internal perspectives.

Agli ultimi piani di un edificio per uffici affacciato sul lato sud di Central Park, sulla Settima Avenue e sul fiume Hudson, è stata ricavata questa sede per una società cinematografica. La pianta a 'L' dell'edificio, con blocco scala e servizi posizionati nell'angolo privo in parte di aperture, è stata assunta dai progettisti come sorta di scatola edilizia di semplice riferimento planimetrico in cui costruire percorsi e figure d'interni in grado di valorizzare alcune viste panoramiche della città e di offrire nuove e inconsuete dimensioni spaziali e studiati punti di vista. A livello planimetrico si è operato organizzando nel livello inferiore una serie di uffici perimetrali separati tra loro con pareti in cartongesso contenute da modanature in legno che alla quota sopra le porte sostengono una serie di lastre in vetro trasparente. Queste aperture, elemento compositivo di riferimento, portano negli spazi di lavoro più interni la luce naturale catturata dalle finestre di facciata. Il diciottesimo piano è unito al livello superiore con una studiata scala in acciaio e vetro che in posizione angolare si sviluppa nel nuovo stretto vano libero da cui emergono le travi strutturali e dove è creato anche un inconsueto piano calpestabile in vetro. Questo calibrato taglio a doppia altezza è stato ricavato intorno alla sala riunione principale che assume così il senso di volume sospeso, piccola e compiuta essenziale architettura posta tra i due piani degli uffici. Al diciannovesimo piano è organizzata la zona reception integrata al pianerottolo ascensori caratterizzati dalle porte di lamiera grezza, che ripetono la soluzione di quella limitrofa dell'uscita di sicurezza. Sul fondo uno specchio alto e stretto riflette le aperture di facciata sviluppando virtualmente la prospettiva della zona d'arrivo. Dal pavimento di ardesia emerge il mobile reception in legno, essenziale forma geometrica che annuncia la generale filosofia dell'intervento. Questo appare come un ricercato assemblaggio di superfici verticali e orizzontali, di modanature e profilati di diverso spessore e vari materiali (legno, cartongesso, metallo e vetro) rapportati con attenzione al gioco compositivo dei volumi obliqui del controsoffitto e alla soluzione planimetrica sottolineata da percorsi e pareti ruotati rispetto ai riferimenti del filo facciata, per enfatizzare le nuove prospettive interne.

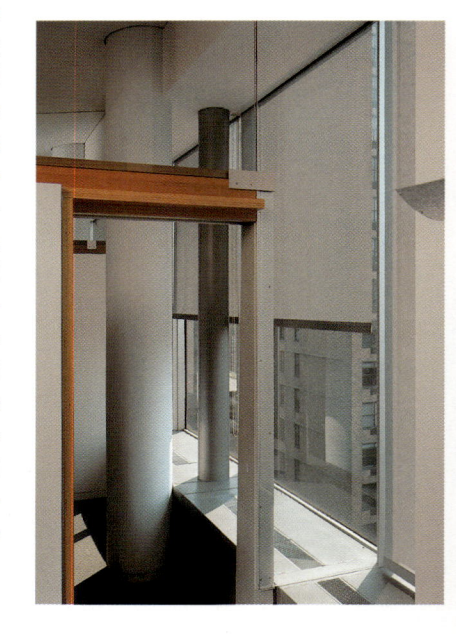

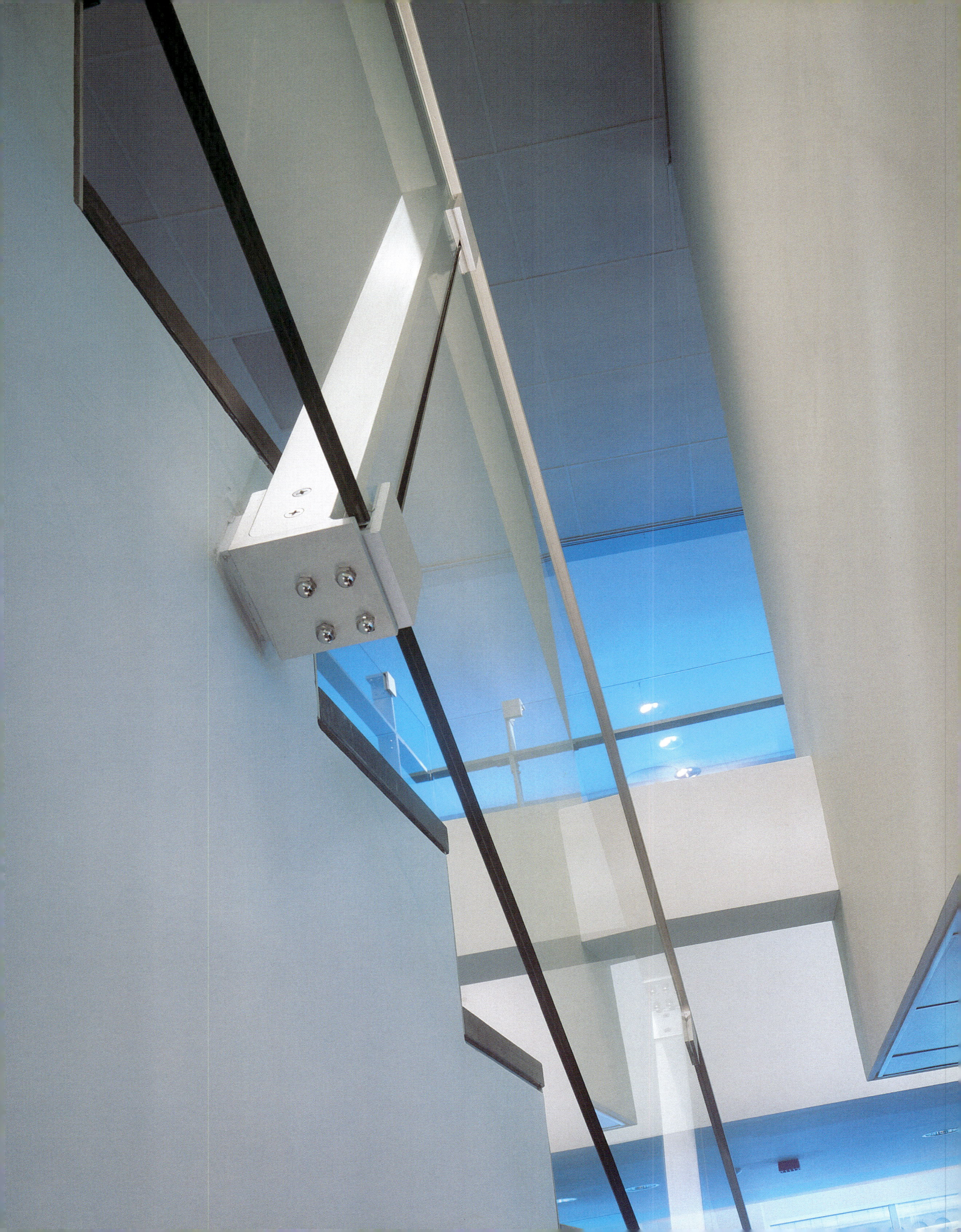

EXIT
EVERYTHING YOU'VE HEARD IS TRUE!
TIM ROBBINS
GRETA SCACCHI
FRED WARD
WHOOPI GOLDBERG
PETER GALLAGHER
A ROBERT ALTMAN FILM
The Player

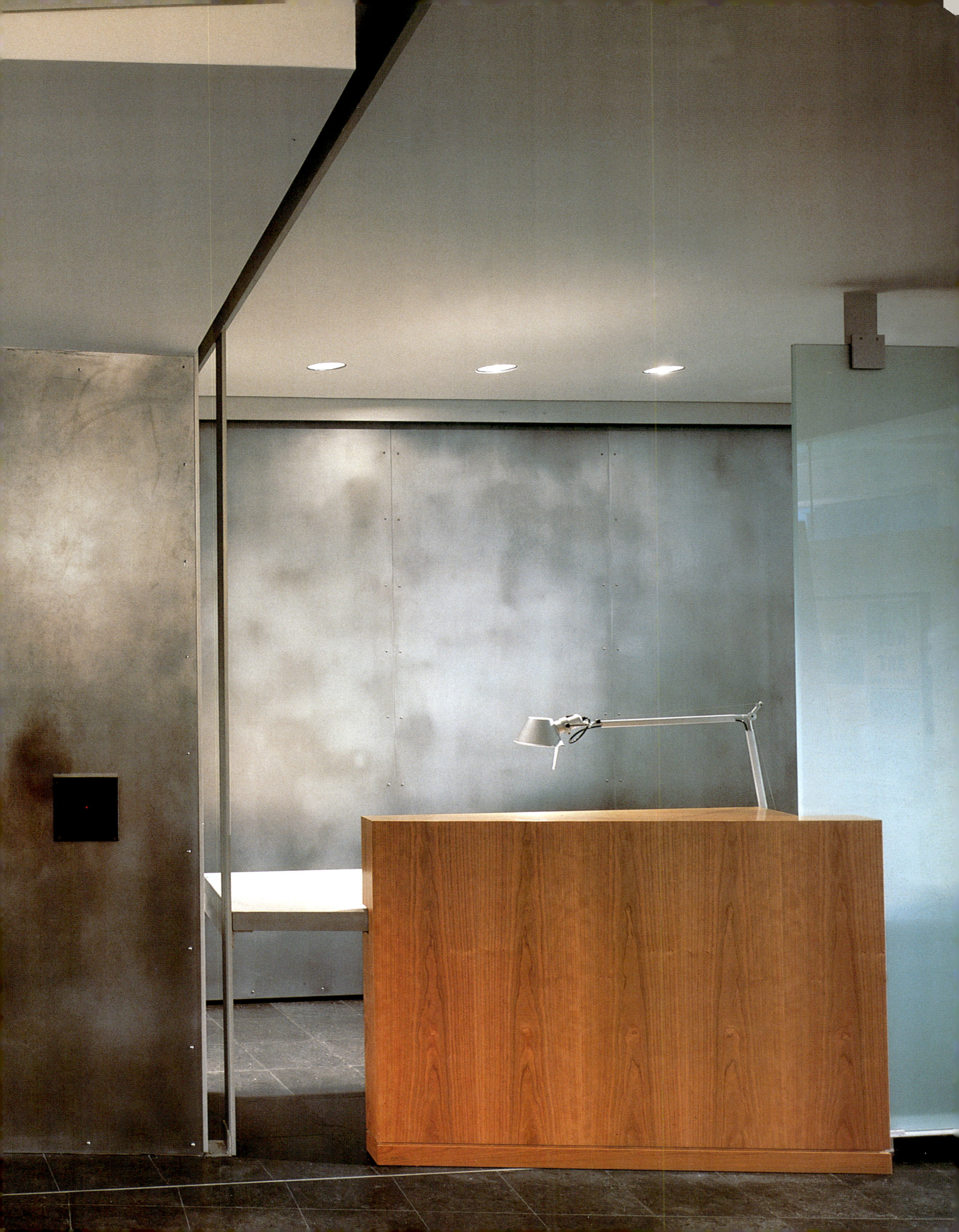

120

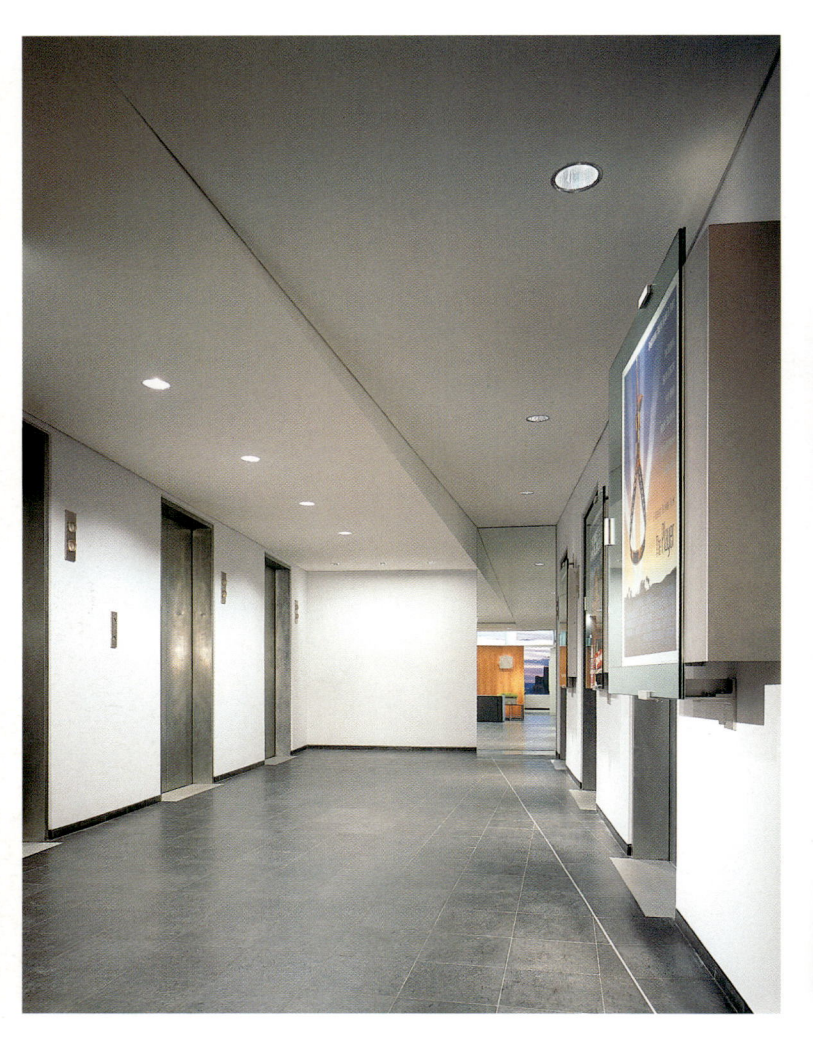

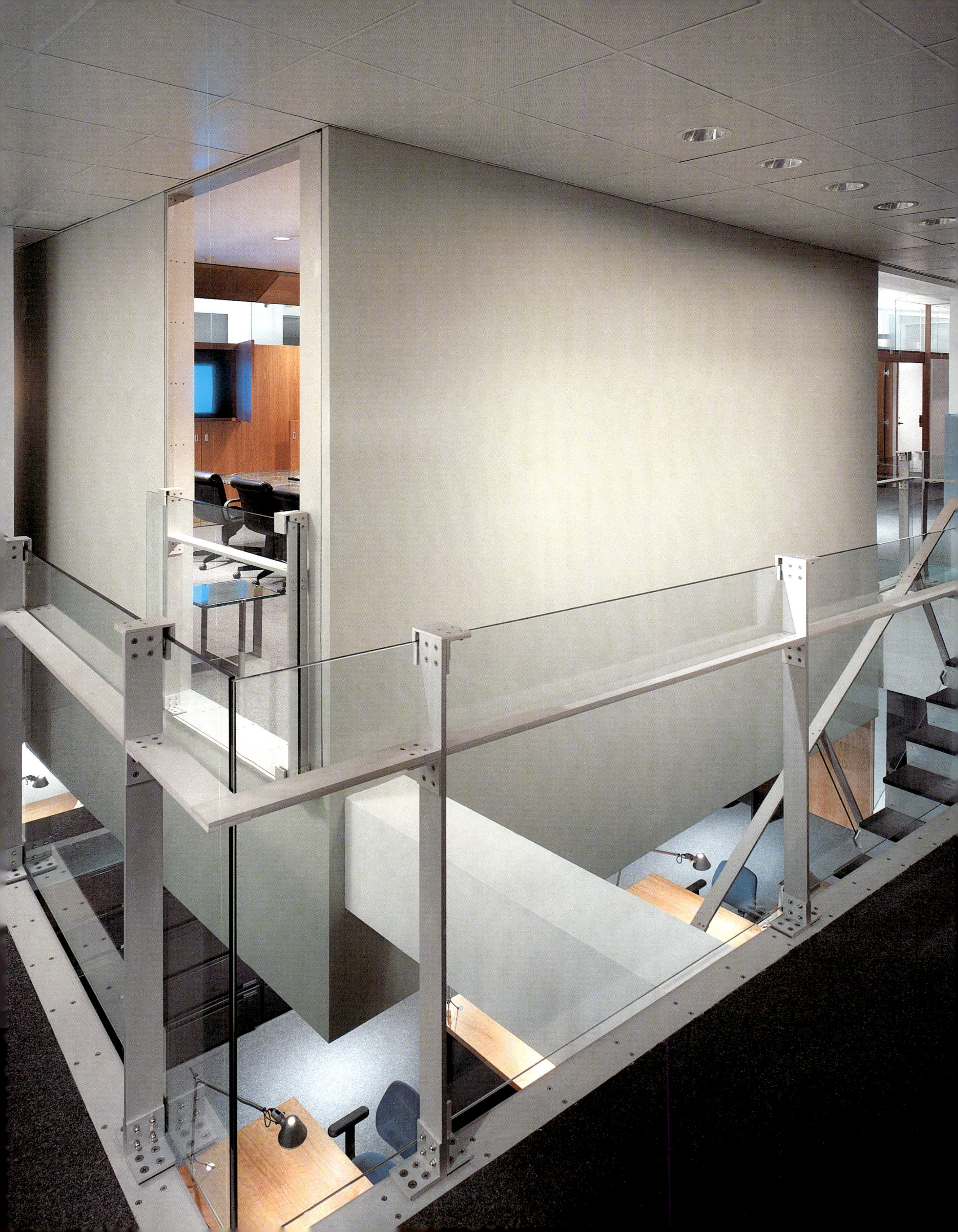

Axonometric of office type / Assonometria di un ufficio tipo

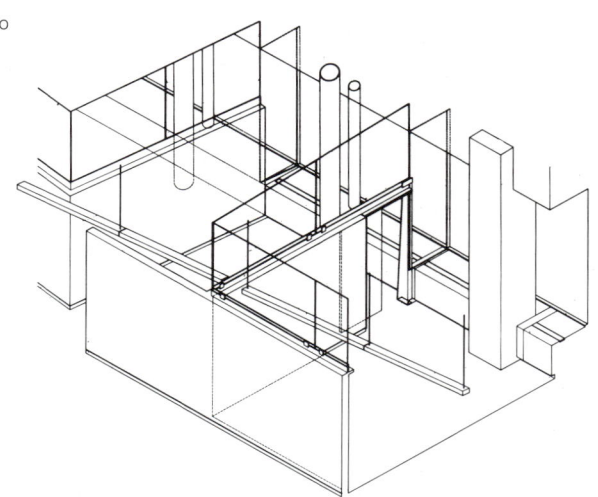

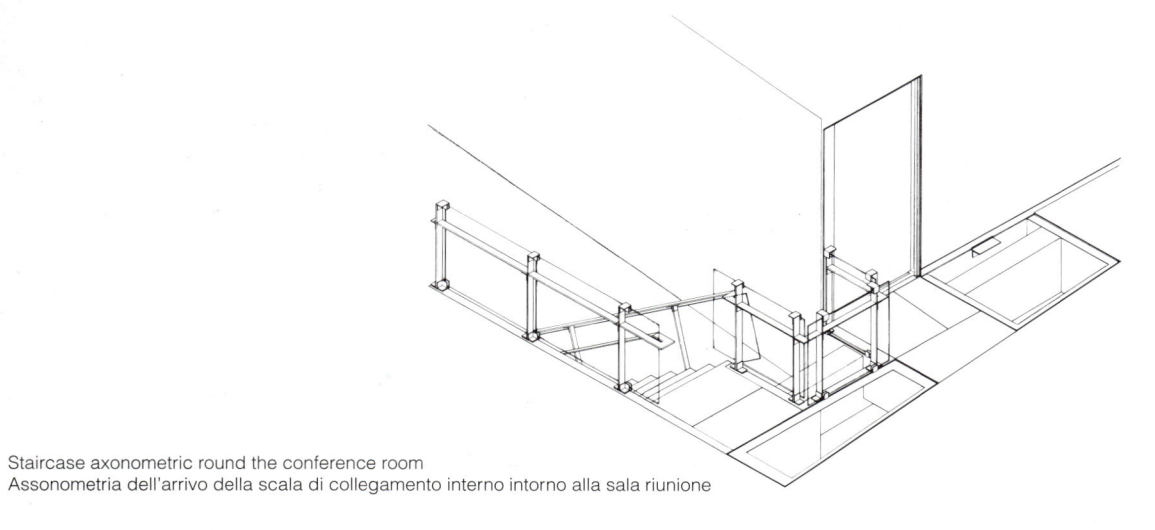

Staircase axonometric round the conference room
Assonometria dell'arrivo della scala di collegamento interno intorno alla sala riunione

Furnishing plan of reception area and office / Pianta arredata della zona reception e di parte degli uffici

Nineteenth floor plan / Pianta del 19° piano

124

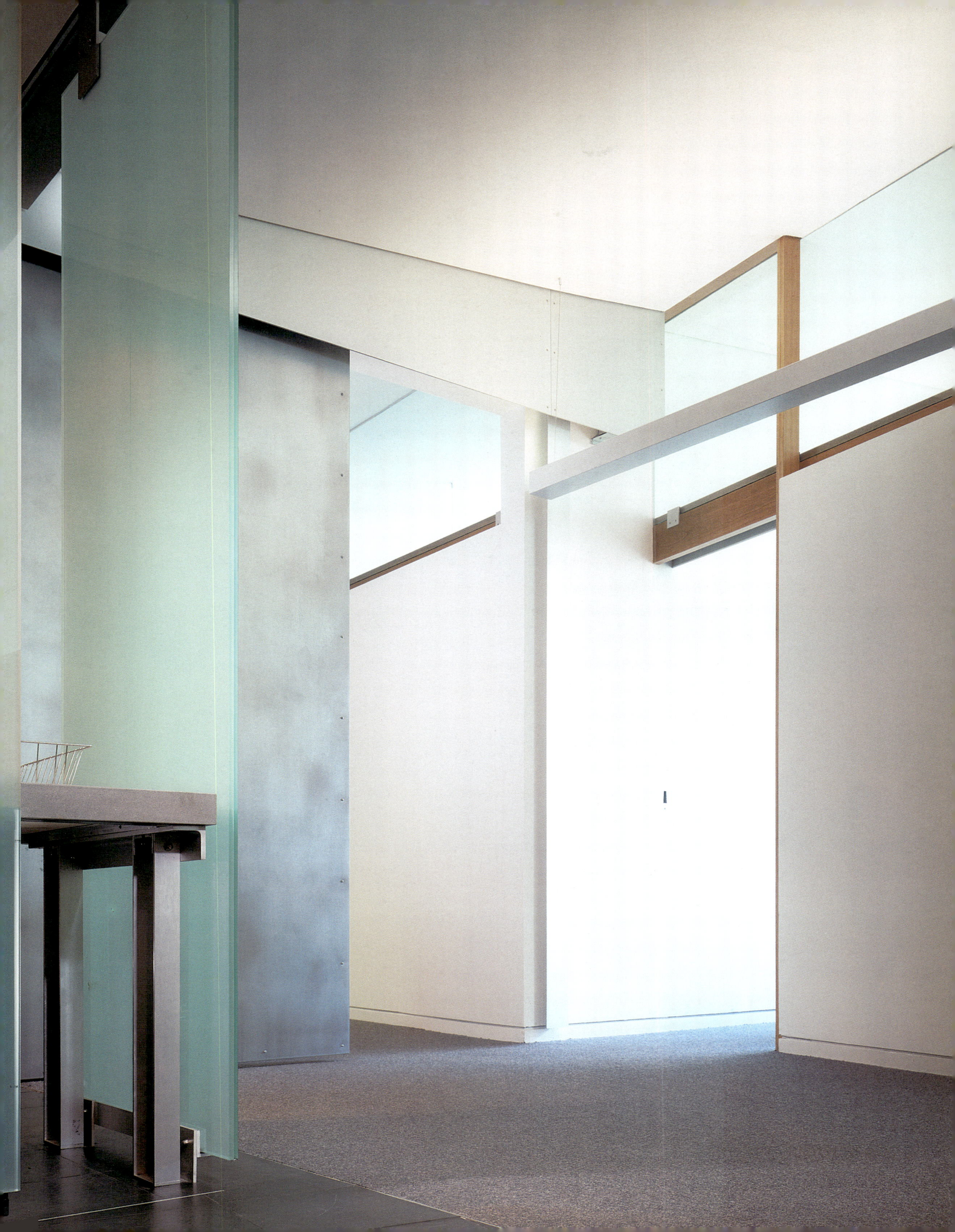

OFFICE HEADQUARTERS
TsAO & McKown Architects. New York, NY, 1992

As if suspended among the skyscrapers of Manhattan, the new management headquarters of this manufacturer of household articles created by architects and designers boasts unusual compositional verve, a meticulous choice of furnishings, materials, and an overall visual impact that make it appear to waver between an exclusive domestic setting and a strikingly original service environment. Sited on the 57th floor of the Carnegie Hall Tower in the heart of New York, the offices sprawl over all the available floor space, making good use of the facade glazing. The singular location of the building, in the center of the city, and the outstanding vistas - particularly those on the north and south sides - seem to have determined the way the interiors are distributed, to take advantage of the surrounding cityscape. In this way, the main executive office occupies a self-sufficient space with private restroom and separated from the vast reception area by means of a corridor, the entire north frontage, which is set with continuous window sections that frame the breathtaking panorama of Central Park below. Here the customized ceiling light with its large oval of sanded glass overhangs the desk (a collector's piece by Emile Ruhlmann, 1927), complemented by a long, pale gray service desk running the length of the window. The south side of the building, facing the midtown Manhattan skyscrapers and the Hudson, is occupied by two offices and a meeting room characterized by a false ceiling fitted with built-in strip lighting and perimetral downlighters, by a wall composed of rectangular panels clad in capitonnée material, by upholstered chairs by Gilbert Rohde (1930) around a black lacquered table of the same period. A long service corridor equipped with rows of tall custom-built cabinets in English maple that terminate in a back-lit section, joins the office area with that of the reception, a large, uncluttered space with an almost metaphysical mood that boasts a checkerboard floor, an intriguing ceiling arrangement, and several ingeniously shaped partitions.

Come sospesa tra i grattacieli di Manhattan, la sede direzionale di una ditta produttrice di oggetti per la casa creati da architetti e designer, sembra oscillare -per grande qualità compositiva, accurata selezione di arredi, scelta dei materiali e immagine complessiva- tra esclusiva dimensione domestica e inconsueta quanto accurata tipologia terziaria. Ubicati al 57° piano della Carnegie Hall Tower, nel cuore di New York, gli uffici sono distribuiti su tutto il piano disponibile sfruttando al meglio le aperture di facciata. La particolare collocazione dell'edificio, in posizione centrale rispetto alla pianta della città, e l'eccezionale vista offerta soprattutto dalle finestre dei lati nord e sud ha in qualche modo suggerito la soluzione distributiva, tesa a valorizzare il panorama urbano all'intorno. Così l'ufficio direzionale principale occupa, come sorta di spazio a sé corredato di bagno privato e separato dalla vasta area reception con un corridoio, tutto il fronte nord segnato da una apertura centrale a nastro continuo che incornicia in modo insuperabile la vista prospettica del Central Park sottostante. Qui una lampada ovale in vetro sabbiato, su disegno, scende dal soffitto per sottolineare la scrivania (un pezzo originale di Emile Ruhlmann del 1927) che ha alle spalle un ampio piano attrezzato sottofinestra, grigio chiaro. Il lato sud, rivolto verso i grattacieli della *midtown* e il fiume Hudson, è invece occupato da due uffici e dalla sala riunione, caratterizzata da un controsoffitto a strisce luminose, da una parete composta da pannelli rettangolari rivestiti in capitonnée, dall'arredo che vede una serie di sedie imbottite del 1930 disegnate da Gilbert Rohde intorno a un tavolo laccato nero dello stesso periodo. Un lungo corridoio attrezzato con una serie di eleganti mobili contenitore a tutt'altezza su disegno, in legno d'acero inglese, conclusi da una fascia luminosa interna, unisce la zona uffici con l'area reception. Questa si popone come ampio spazio vuoto, quasi metafisico, in cui un pavimento in marmo a scacchi grigi e bianchi si unisce a un sapiente gioco compositivo di slittamenti del soffitto e di leggere quinte architettoniche su disegno.

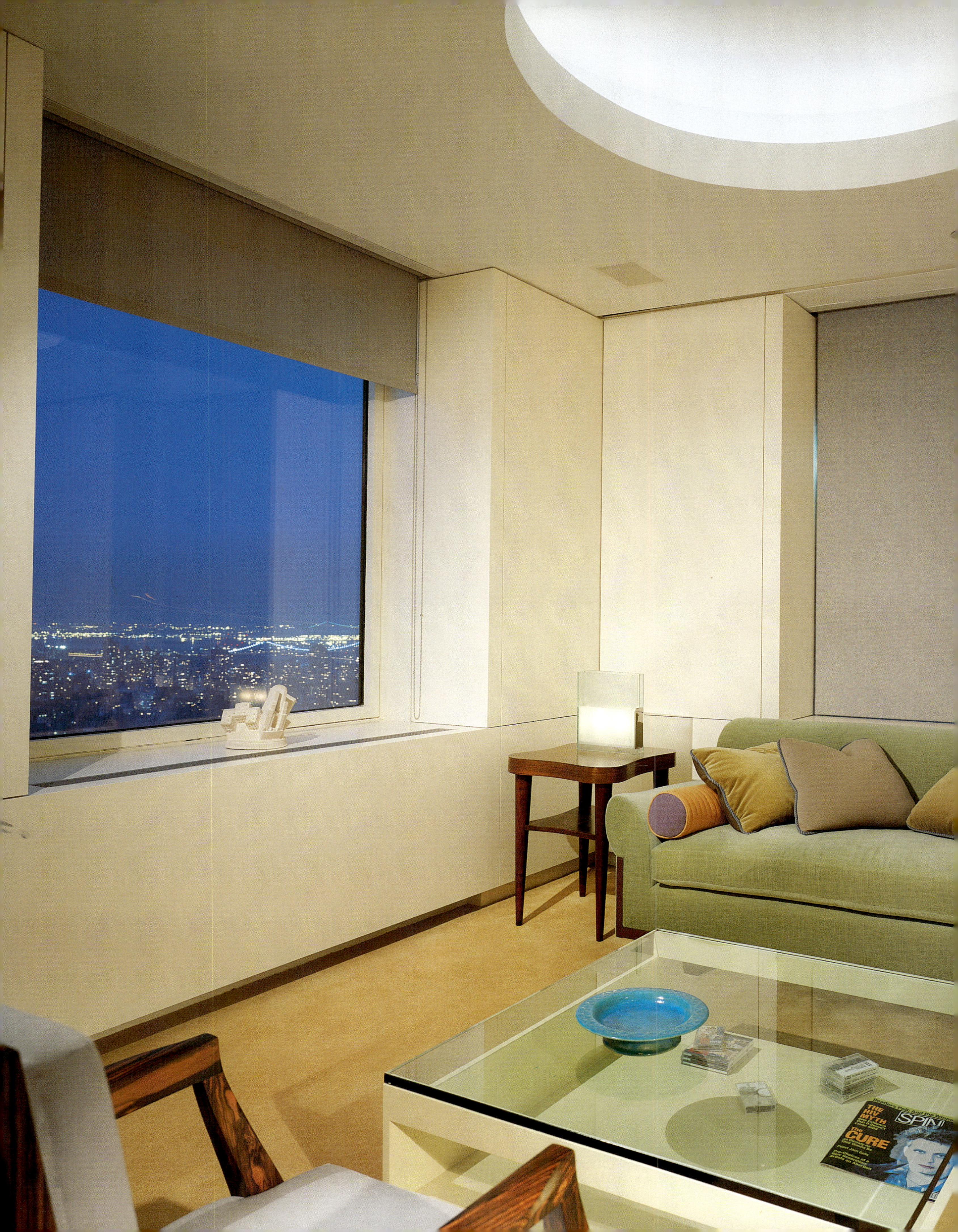
SPIN
THE HIV MYTH
The CURE

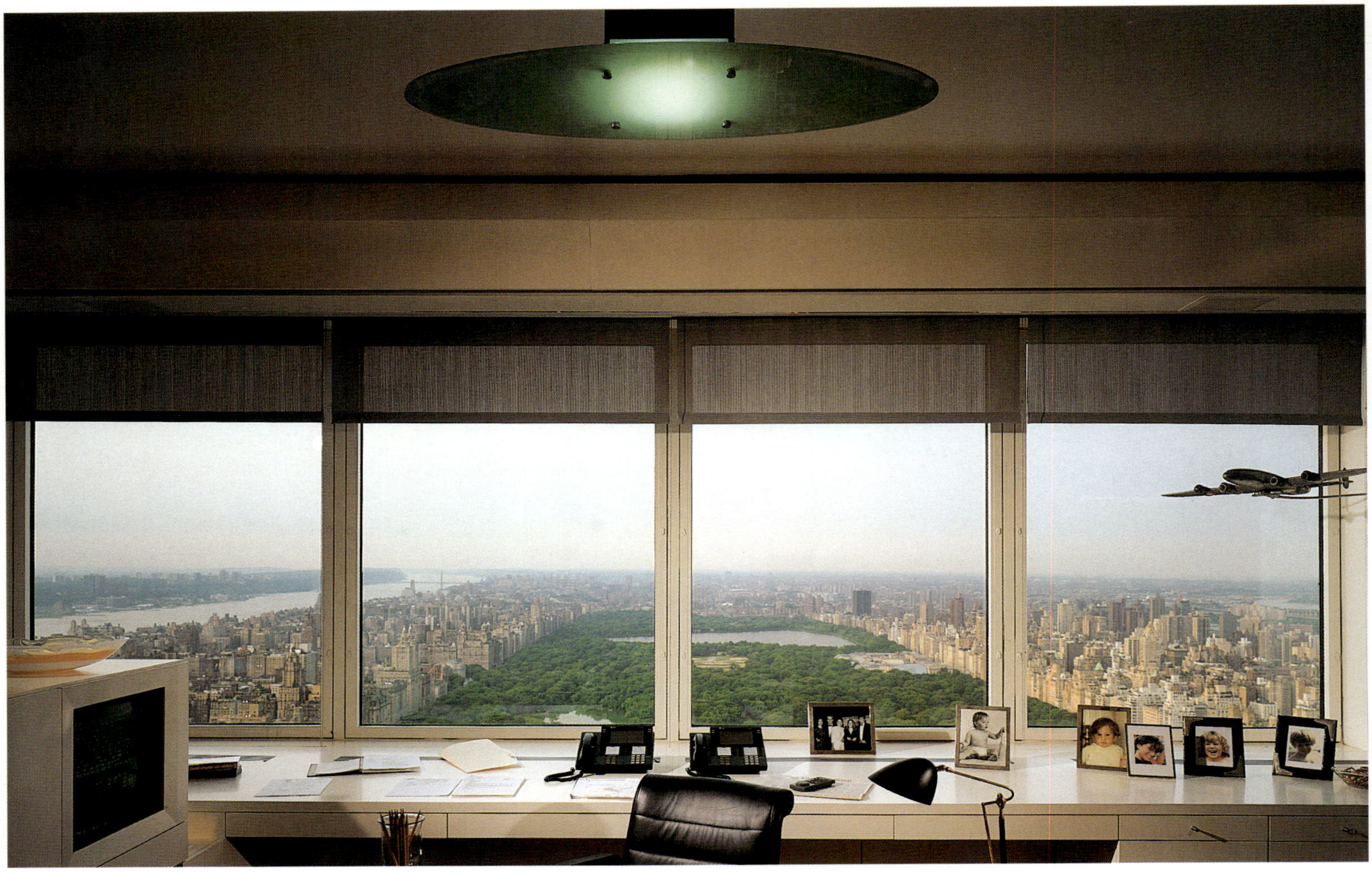

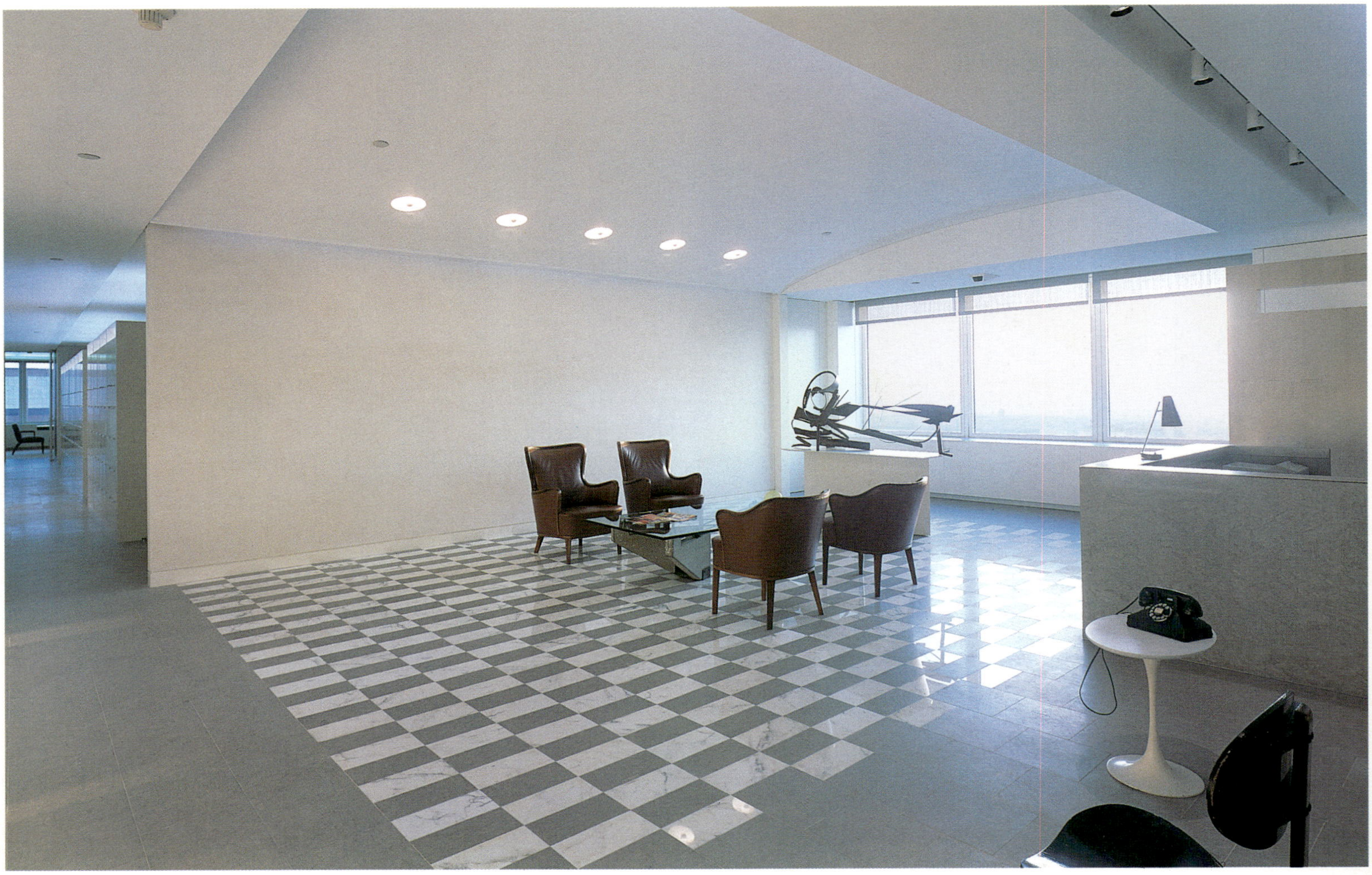

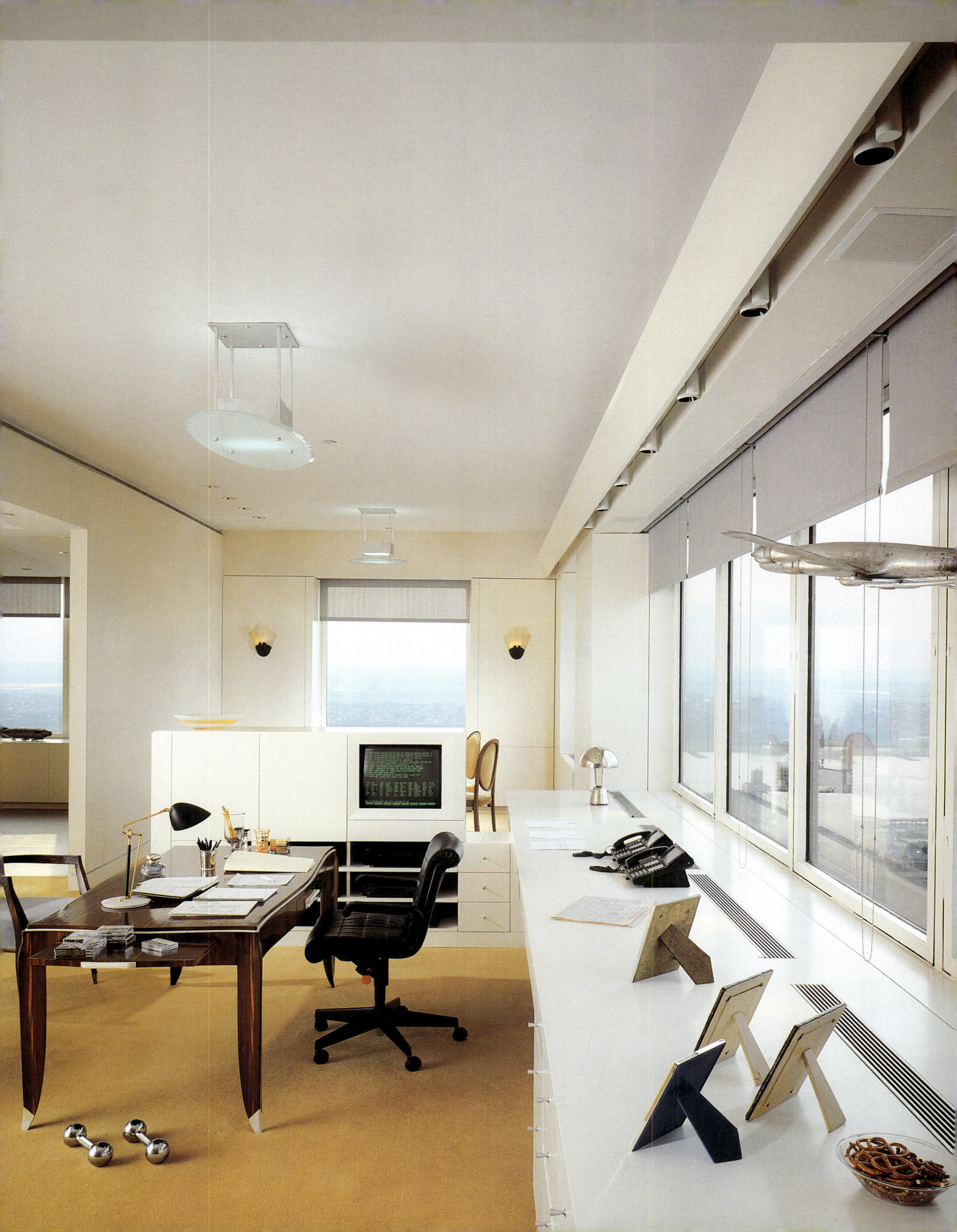

130

131

Plan / Pianta:

1. Office / Ufficio
2. Conference room / Sala riunioni
3. Pantry / Dispensa
4. Copy room / Stanza fotocopie

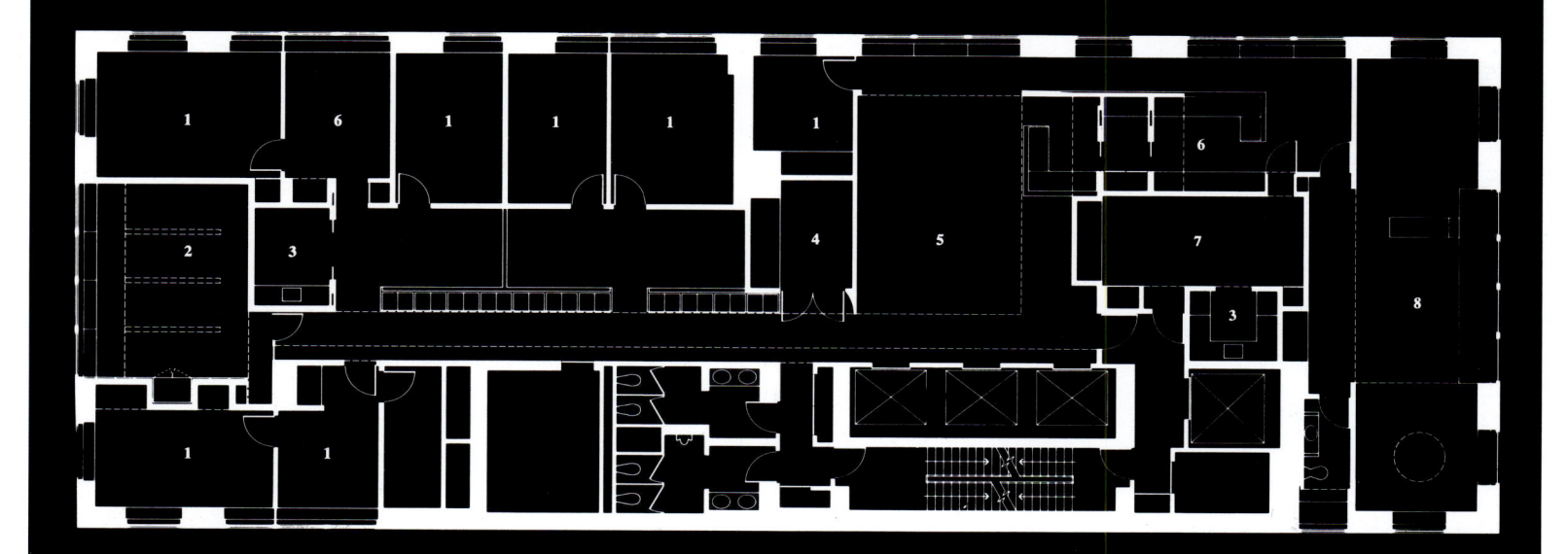

5. Reception
6. Executive reception / Reception esecutiva
7. Mailroom / Stanza spedizioni
8. Executive office / Uffici esecutivi

132

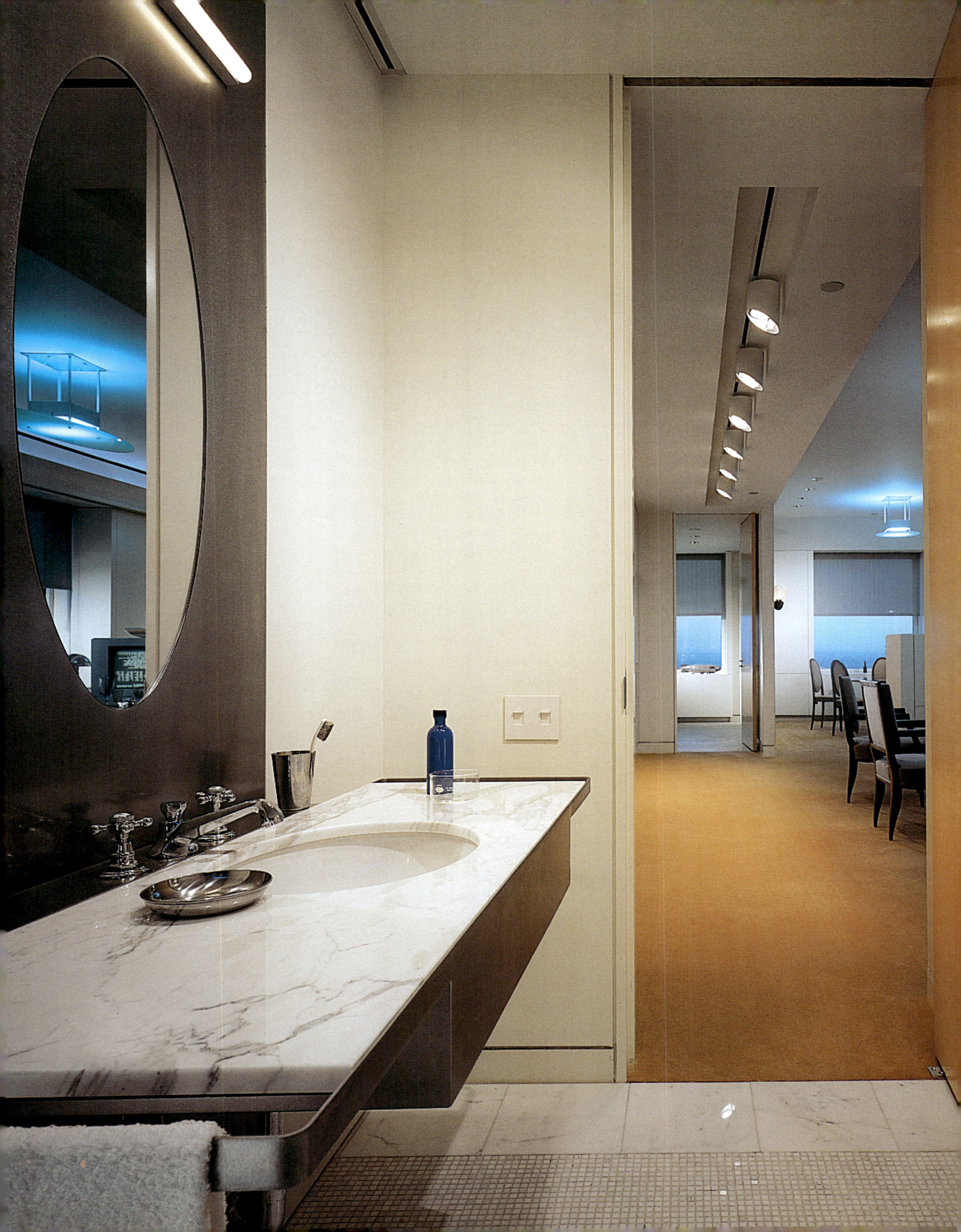

PUTNAM, LOVELL, DEGUARDIOLA & THORNTON

Architecture + Light. San Francisco, CA, 1996

Section South / Sezione Sud

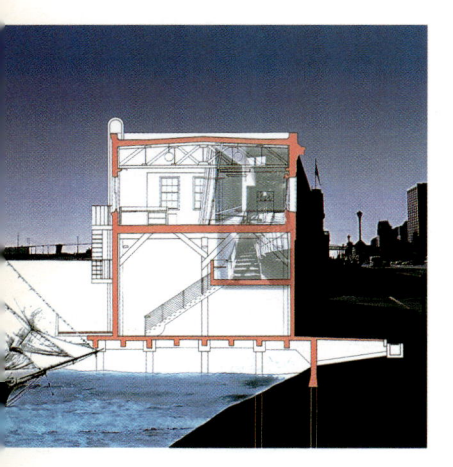

Slotted inside one of the key historical landmarks of the Embarcadero zone in San Francisco, built in the 1920s to receive goods and travelers docking from the Pacific seaways, this successful reworking of a series of abandoned public spaces has managed to conserve the historical features of the building, its stylistic motifs, and in part, reminders of the original structural and material elements. The interiors have been restructured with the addition of a few extra stories in order to boost the floorspace available for the new offices. Besides this scheme of enlargement, the new design has taken advantage of the building's morphology, particularly the section over the original monumental entrance portal, now fully glazed to afford a magnificent view of the bay and city beyond. Here a large double-height reception area has been created, equipped with metal stairways and landings in pierced industrial sheeting alluding to the shapes and materials of the former seafront wharves. On the upper story, which accommodates the offices and conference rooms, the original network of timber trusses has been carefully restored, reinforcing the image of the spatial subdivision and deliberately offset by the style of the offices themselves. To take further advantage of this reticular timber setting, the office walls consist of an alternation of inclined, curved glazing that terminates below the trussed ceiling so as not to interrupt the sense of spatial continuity. The ingenious concept of slotting architectural units within the original framework is expressed by an alternation of enclosed work areas and open plan, geared to valorizing the history of one of the city's landmark buildings. A further homage to the historical context can be seen in the sand-blasted glass table of the conference room, on which is drawn a map of the waterfront as it was in the 1920s.

All'interno di uno degli edifici storici più importanti della zona dell'Embarcardero della città, costruito negli anni '20 per accogliere le navi al molo n°5 e fungere da simbolico portale architettonico per le merci e i viaggiatori provenienti dall'Oceano Pacifico, questo progetto ha saputo reinventare una serie di spazi abbandonati preservando l'aspetto storico dell'edificio, le sue testimonianze stilistiche e in parte le tracce strutturali e materiche originarie. L'interno è stato ristrutturato aggiungendo alcune solette e aumentando così la superficie utilizzabile per la distribuzione dei nuovi uffici. Accanto a un ampliamento degli spazi disponibili, l'intervento ha saputo valorizzare la morfologia dell'edificio, anzitutto nella parte in corrispondenza del grande arco originariamente d'ingresso e oggi chiuso da una nuova ampia vetrata rivolta verso l'eccezionale vista della Baia. Qui si è creato uno spazio aperto a doppia altezza in cui sono state organizzate le scale metalliche e i pianerottoli in lamiera industriale forata che vogliono rivisitare figure e materiali dei magazzini portuali. Al piano superiore, dove sono organizzati uffici di rappresentanza e sale riunioni, sono state mantenute le imponenti travature di legno inchiavardate che, restaurate con cura, emergono con forza nello spazio architettonico suddiviso e ricomposto secondo soluzioni che volutamente si staccano dalla forte presenza lignea delle travi reticolari. Per valorizzare questa scenografica presenza strutturale le pareti dei nuovi uffici, costruite con vetrate in curva inclinate o con felici composizioni in cartongesso, si fermano alla quota sottotrave per non interromperne il compiuto disegno e la successione nello spazio. Il riuscito scopo progettuale di costruire nuove piccole architetture all'interno di quella dell'edificio originario si è concretizzato nell'alternarsi di spazi di lavoro chiusi e a open space, tesi alla valorizzazione della storia di una significativa architettura di uno dei luoghi-simbolo della città. Un ulteriore omaggio al contesto storico consiste nella decorazione sabbiata del grande piano di cristallo del tavolo riunioni ottenuta disegnandovi la planimetria del *waterfront* urbano risalente al 1920.

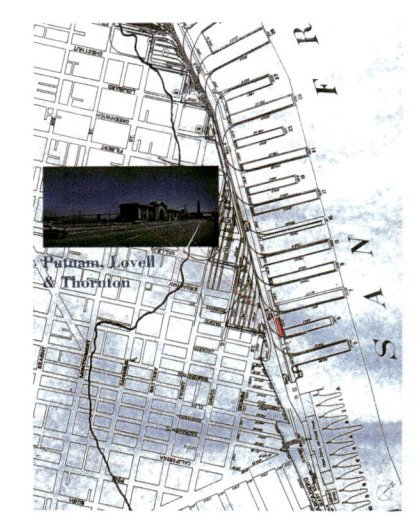

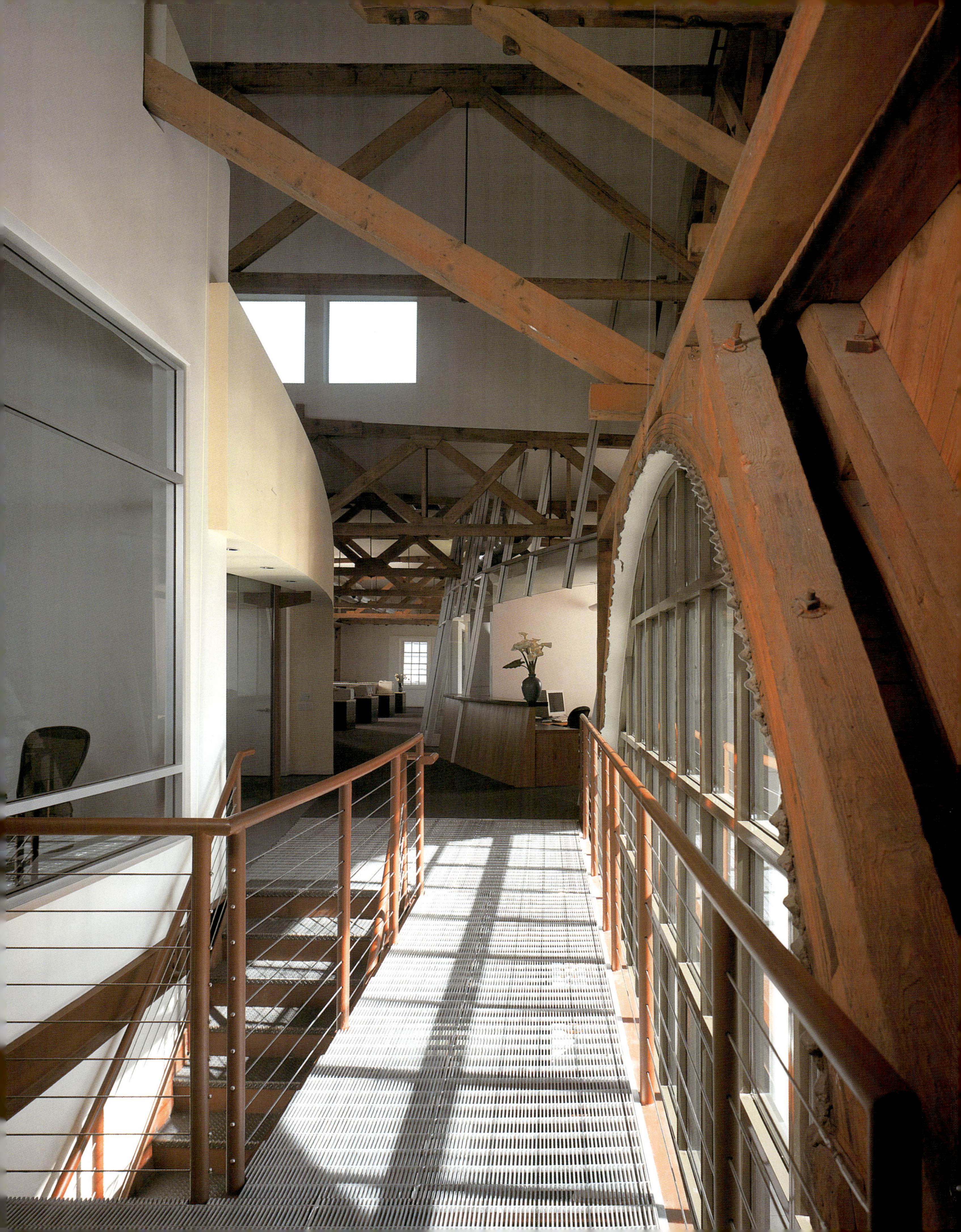

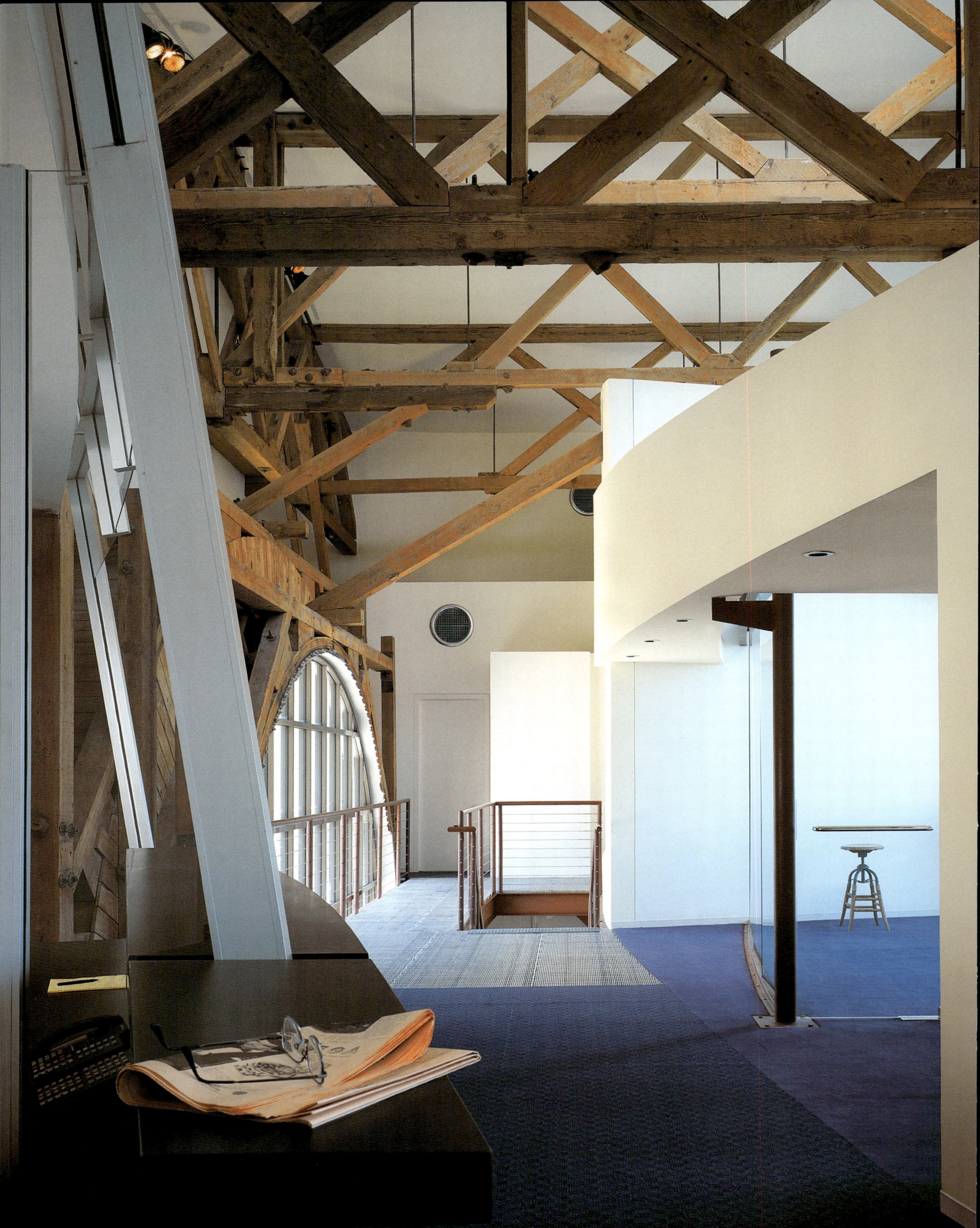

137

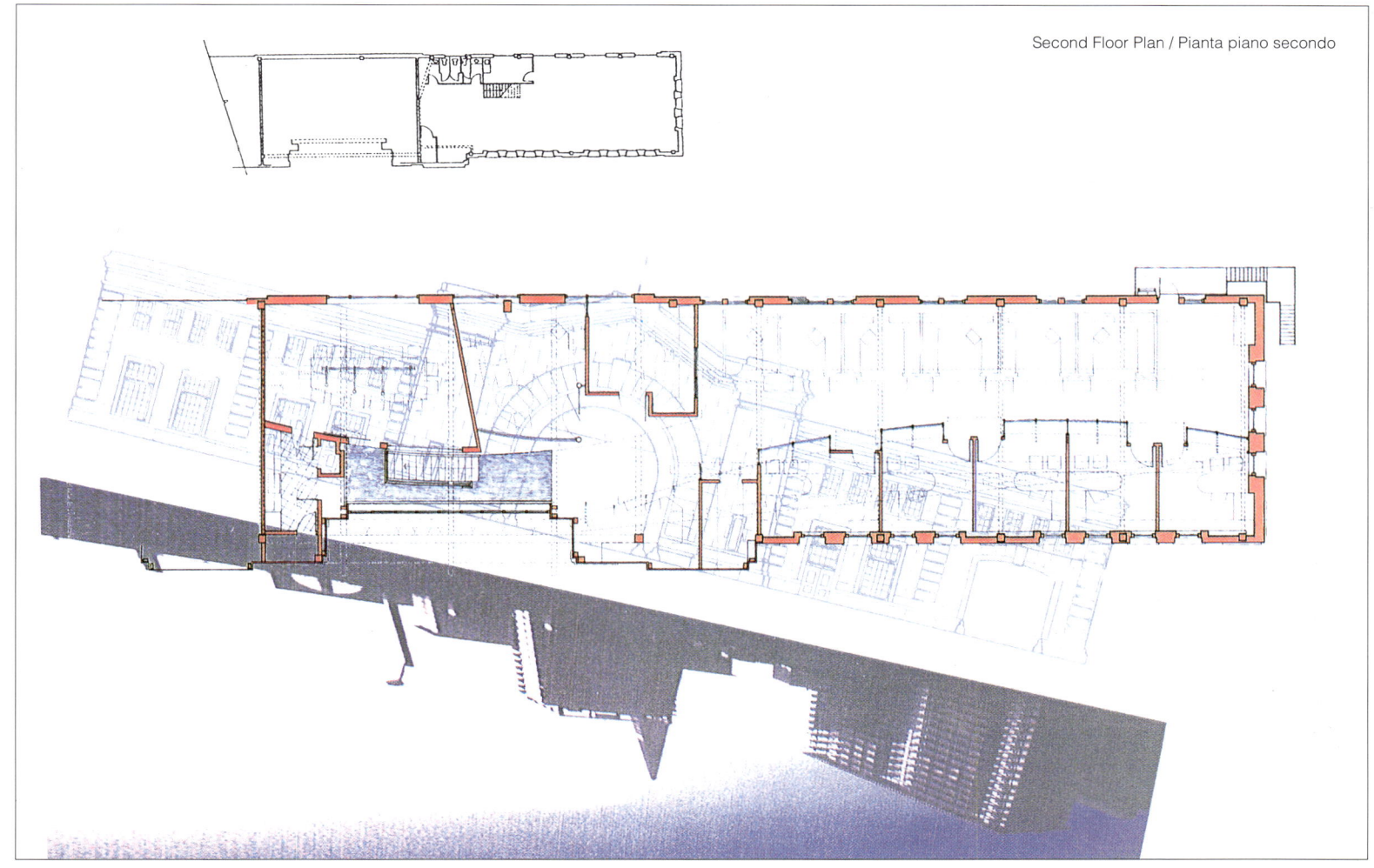

Second Floor Plan / Pianta piano secondo

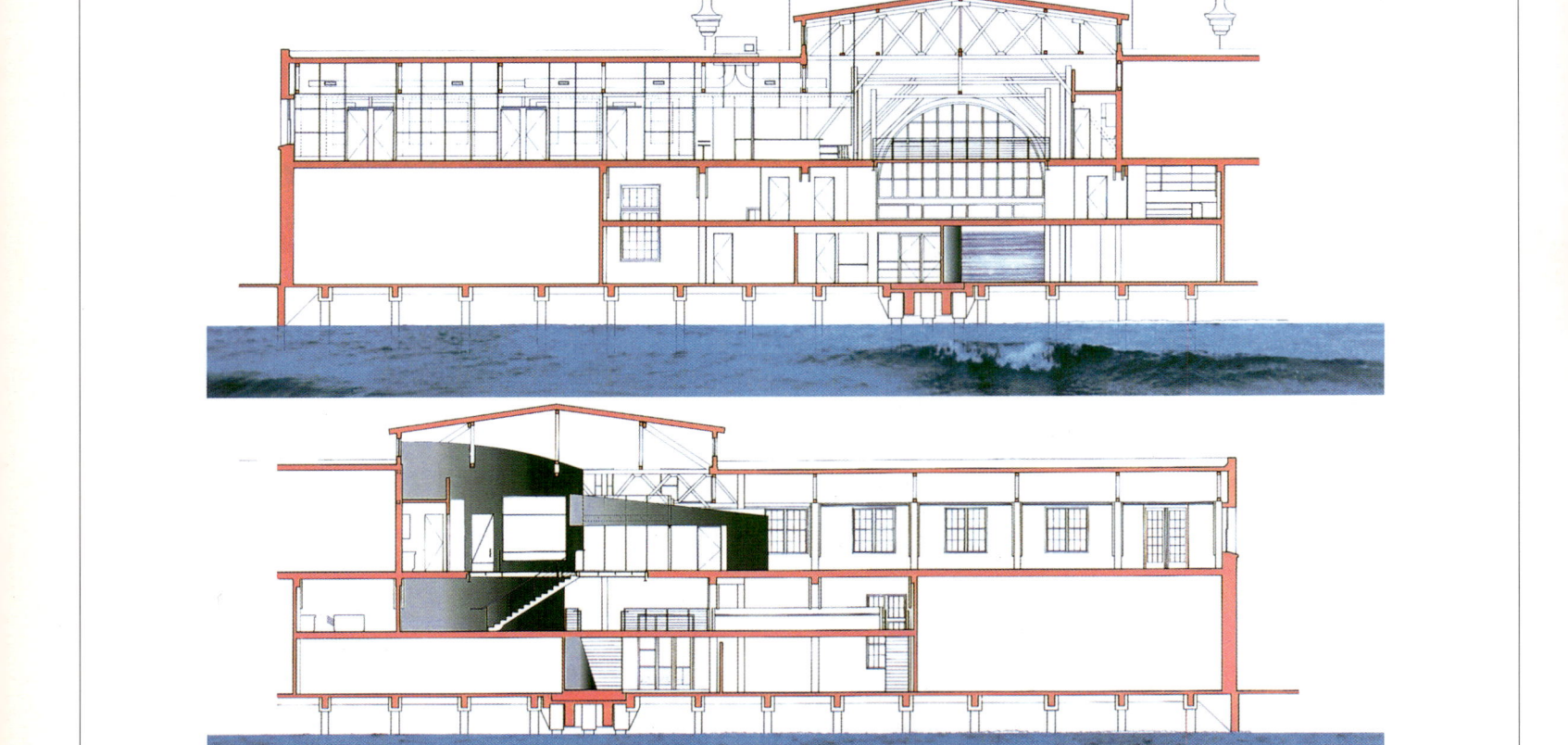

Sections West and East / Sezioni Ovest e Est

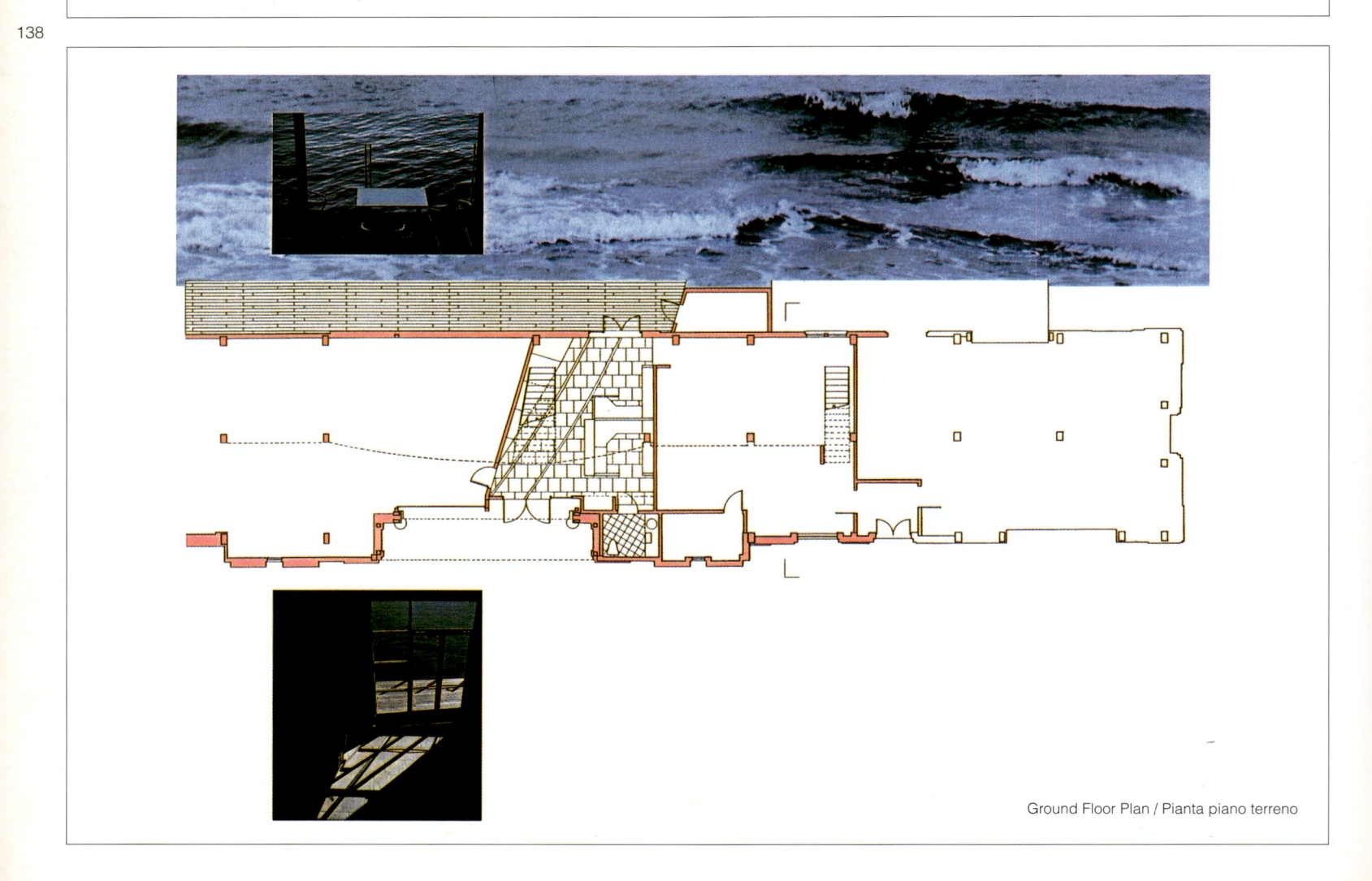

Ground Floor Plan / Pianta piano terreno

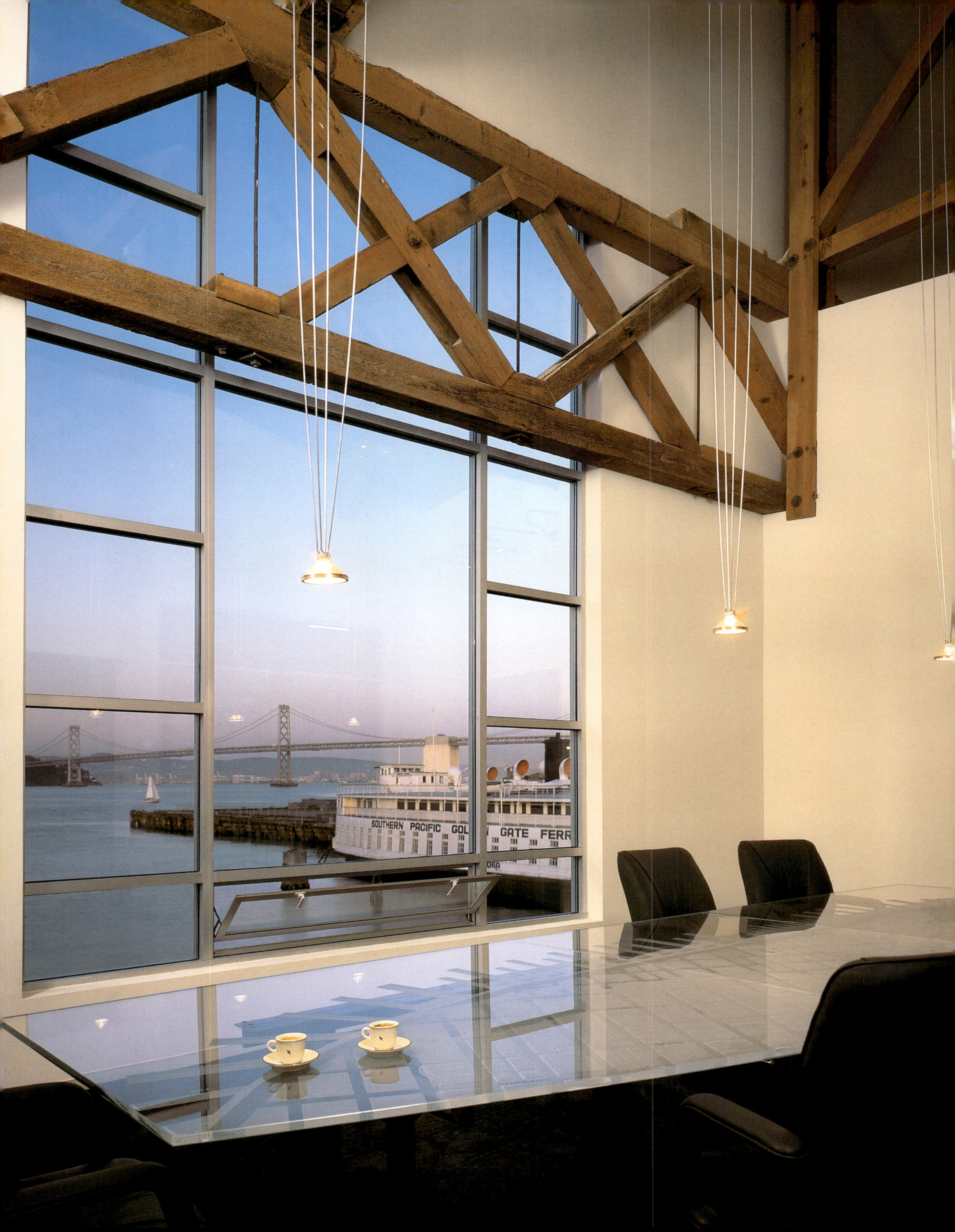
SOUTHERN PACIFIC GOL
GATE FERR

SILICON GRAPHICS COMPUTER SYSTEMS
STUDIOS Architecture. Mountain View, CA, 1992

Conveniently slotted into the midst of the headquarters of Silicon Graphics, the world's leading producer of digital 3-D animation software and hardware, is a comprehensive product demonstration center. Extending through a two-story space, the new demo center is closely linked to the neighboring offices, thereby ensuring a good mix of production activity with those relative to the illustration of the products themselves, with additional areas for gatherings and meetings with clients. The visuals of the demo center's interiors match the distinctly high-tech identity of the host building, which opts for uninhibitedly expressed metal structures and exposed ductwork projecting from a ceiling of corrugated metal sheeting painted white. The spare, factory-style slant to this new shed-laboratory design is enhanced through a fetching choice of colors and materials, the furnishings, and the overall compositional features, endowing the whole with a sense of warmth and welcome that is openly declared from the ground-floor entrance, which gives onto a set of operations zones and a large demonstration hall with curved walls that are mirrored in the design of the low bulkhead above, and repeated in the conference table beneath. At the entrance, a tiled floor of pale stone bordered with a dark blue carpet is overshadowed by a hefty pink beam that demarcates the transition from reception area to waiting lounge, where unassuming padded armchairs colored violet and fuchsia are dotted around a broad, skeletal metal staircase that ascends to the first floor of the double-height atrium. The stair winds around a bright yellow pylon-type trellis which towers up into the cupola-like opening in the roof above. Meanwhile, monitors transmit demos of computer graphics as visitors ascend the stairs. Along one side of the double-height room stands an array of demonstration stations enclosed in white geometrical units. From a suspended ceiling in metal mesh overhead hang custom-designed light fittings which create a unobtrusive vaulted canopy composed of wrinkled copper sheeting, suspended in the void. Other more traditional viewing stations are arranged in the open space, which is flanked by two large conference rooms, and a large area set aside for offices.

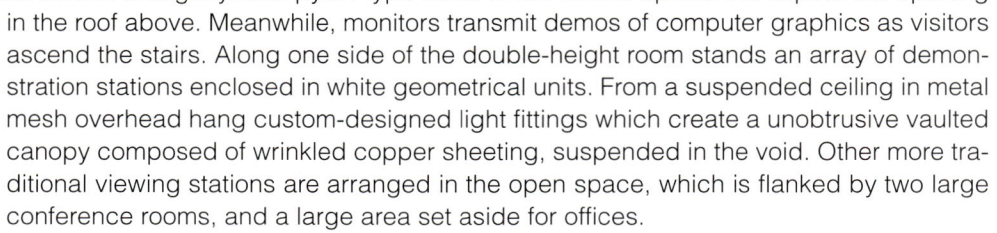

All'interno della sede generale della Silicon Graphics, leader nel mercato della produzione di software e computer relativi all'animazione grafica tridimensionale, è stato ricavato un centro di dimostrazione dei prodotti. Sviluppato in uno spazio distribuito su due livelli, il centro è strettamente connesso ai laboratori e agli uffici limitrofi miscelando quindi le attività di produzione con quelle relative all'esposizione dei prodotti e a zone dedicate agli incontri e alle riunioni. L'immagine del progetto si riconduce a quella high-tech dell'edificio complessivo: con struttura in ferro a vista e condotti degli impianti colorati che risaltano sotto la copertura in lamiera ondulata coibentata, verniciata di bianco. Tuttavia all'immagine industriale ed essenziale del capannone-laboratorio si aggiunge, tramite la scelta dei colori e dei materiali, degli arredi e delle soluzioni compositive generali, un senso di calore e di accoglienza volutamente denunciato già al piano terreno. Qui sono disposte delle zone operative e un'ampia sala dimostrativa, caratterizzata dalle pareti in curva riprese nella forma del forte volume che scende dal soffitto per sottolineare lo stesso disegno, ripetuto per il tavolo riunioni in legno sottostante. Nell'ingresso, un pavimento in piastrelle di pietra chiara è incorniciato da una moquette azzurro scuro disposta sotto una grande trave rosa che separa la reception da una zona attesa. Qui delle essenziali poltroncine imbottite, color viola e fucsia, sono disposte intorno alla grande e leggera scala in ferro che, ubicata nel vano a doppia altezza, conduce al primo piano. La scala si sviluppa intorno ad un traliccio giallo che, raggiungendo la grande apertura circolare nel soffitto del piano superiore, sostiene dei monitor che proiettano immagini di grafica computerizzata proposte al visitatore durante la salita. Nel livello superiore, sotto un controsoffitto in rete metallica e lungo un lato del vano a doppia altezza, sono organizzate tre postazioni dimostrative contenute in bianchi box geometrici, cui corrispondono delle lampade su disegno, pensate come leggere coperture a volta, realizzate con sottili fogli di rame fluttuanti nel vuoto. Altre postazioni più tradizionali sono disposte nell' open space affiancato da due grandi sale per conferenze e da una vasta zona per uffici.

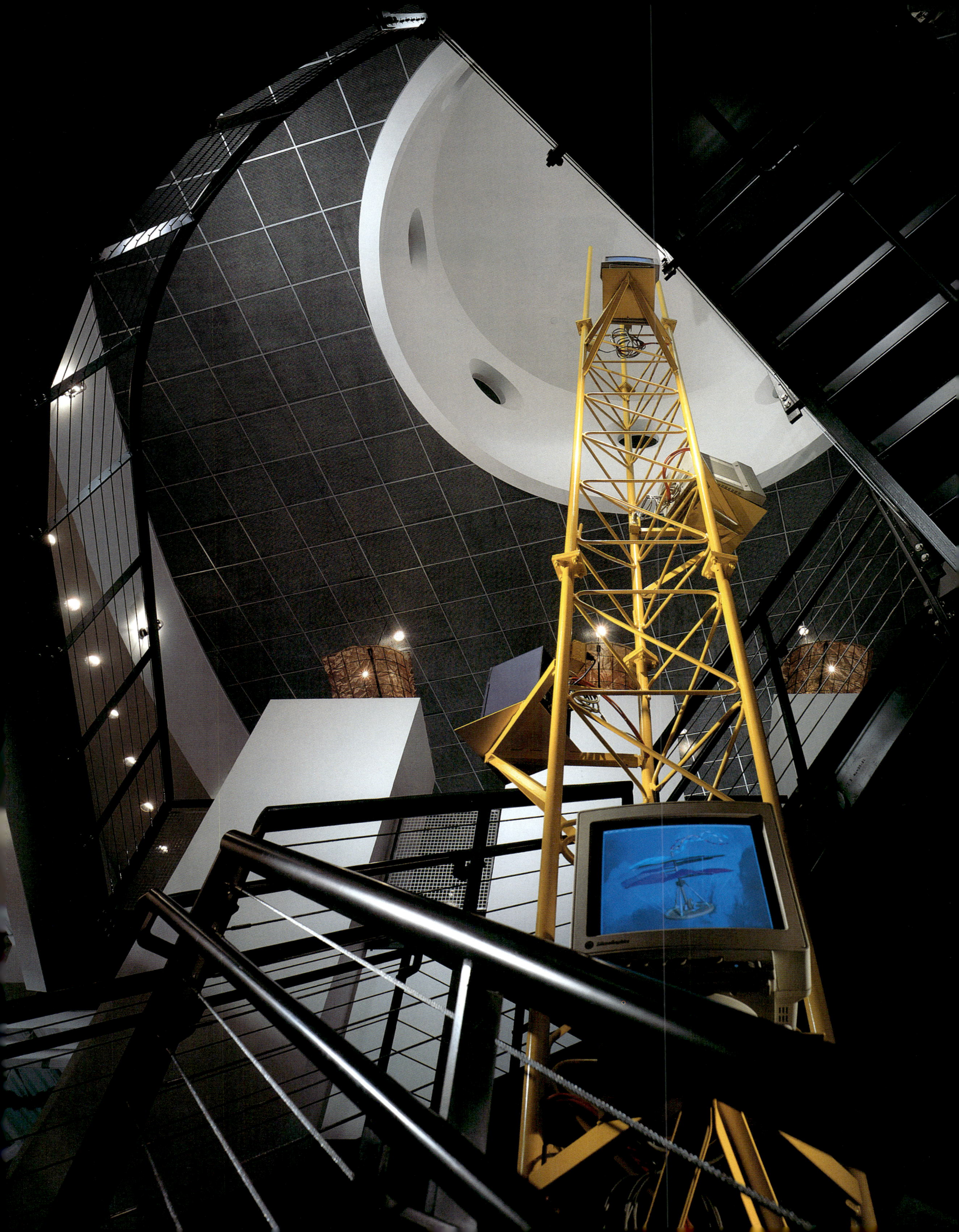

142

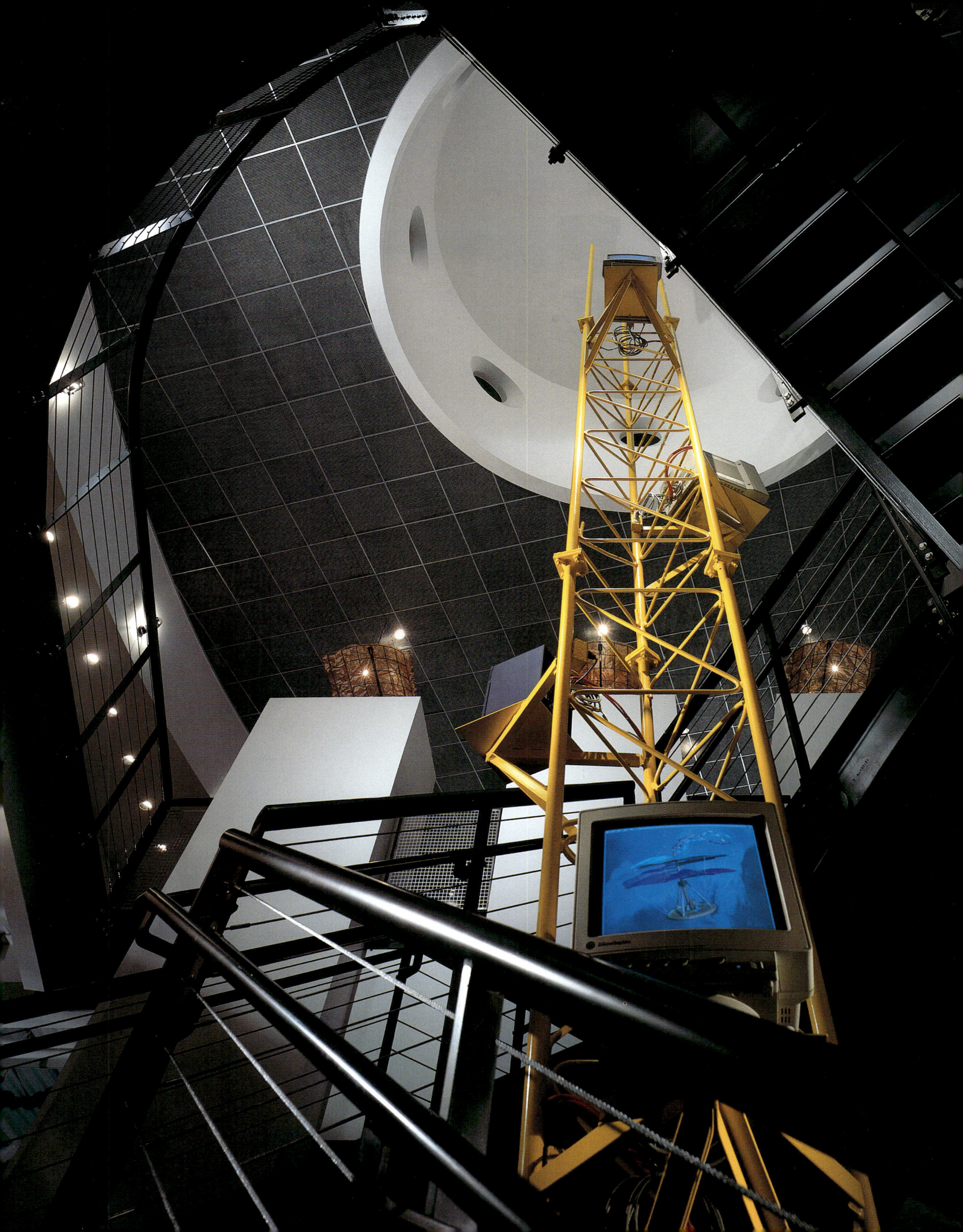

142

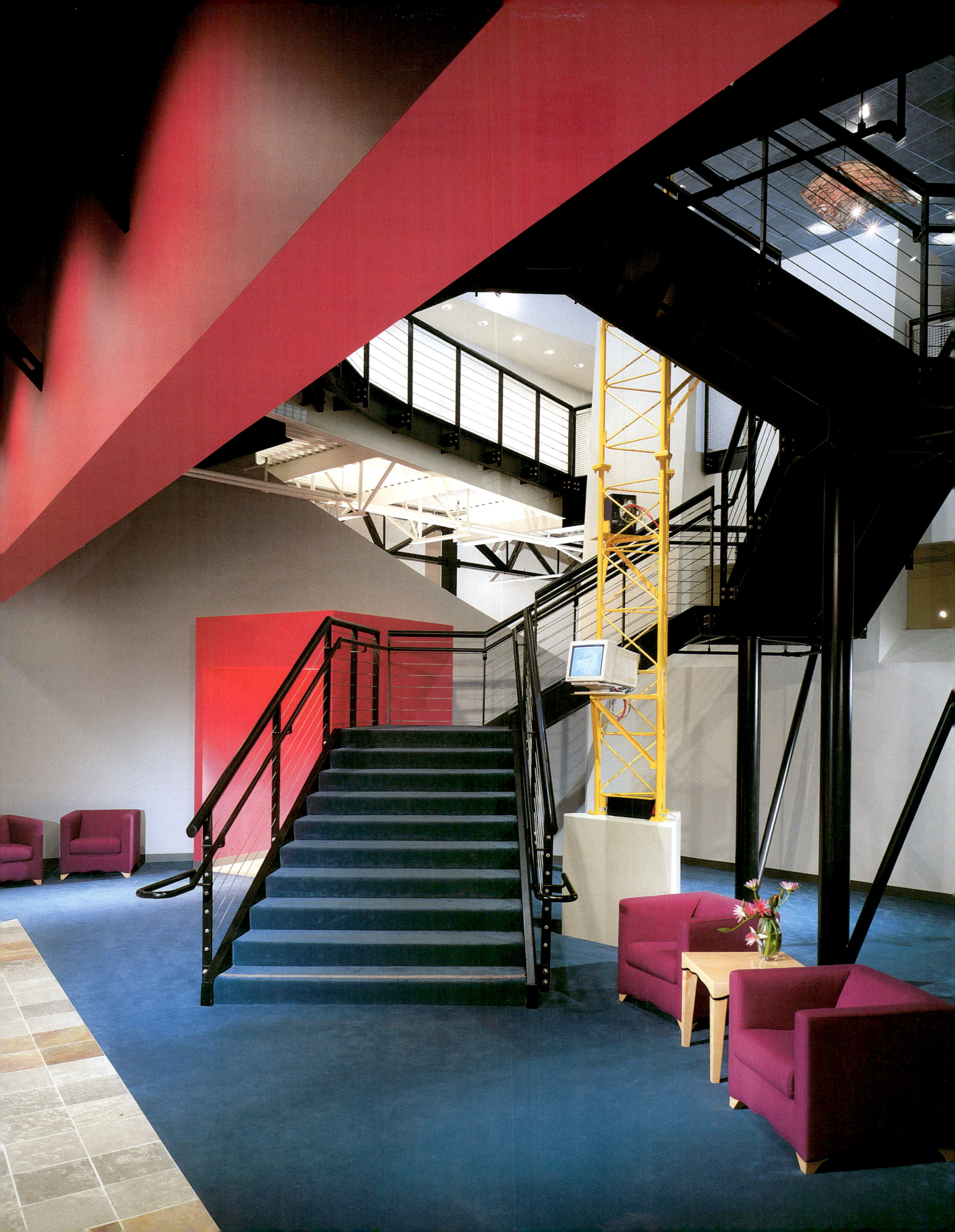

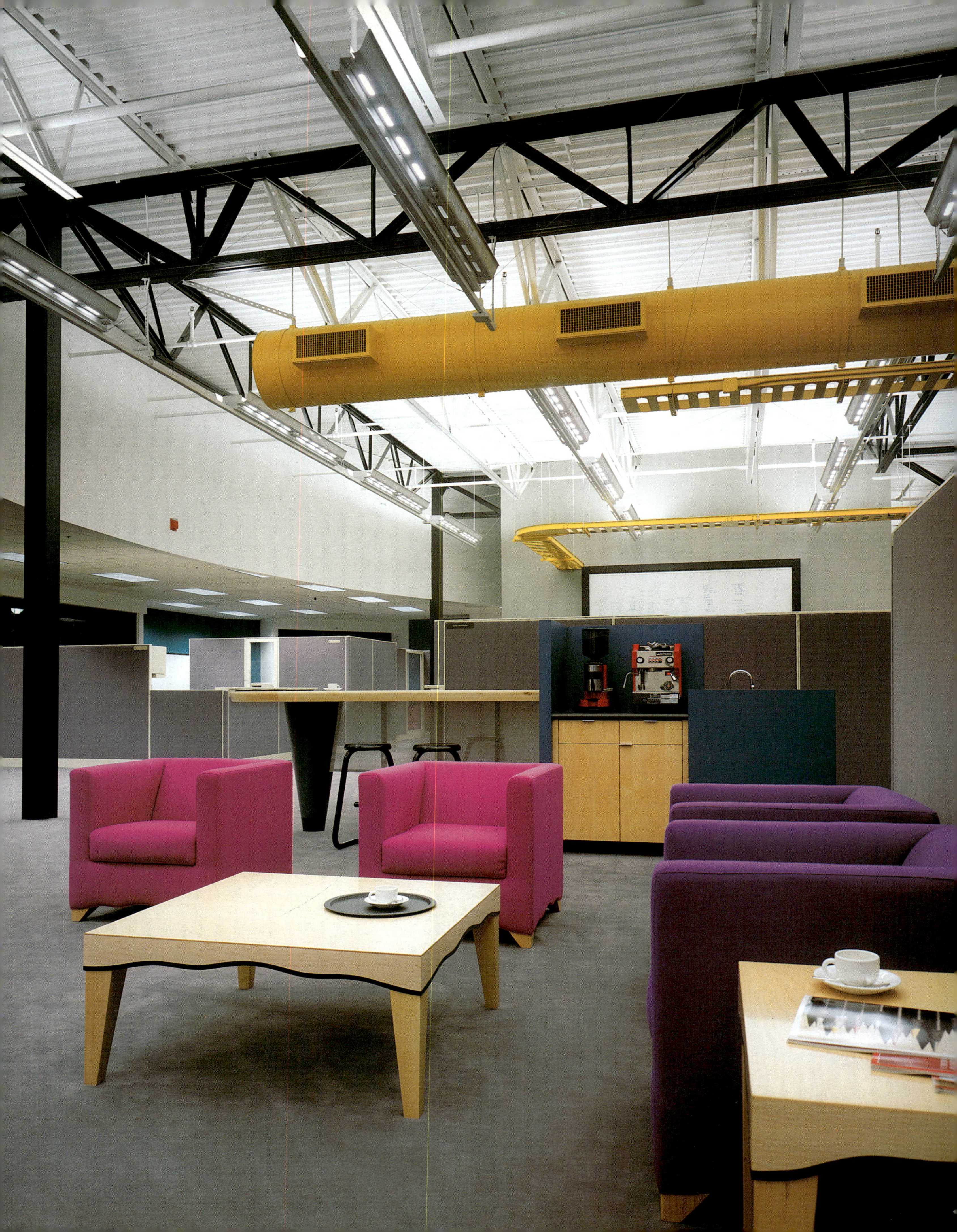

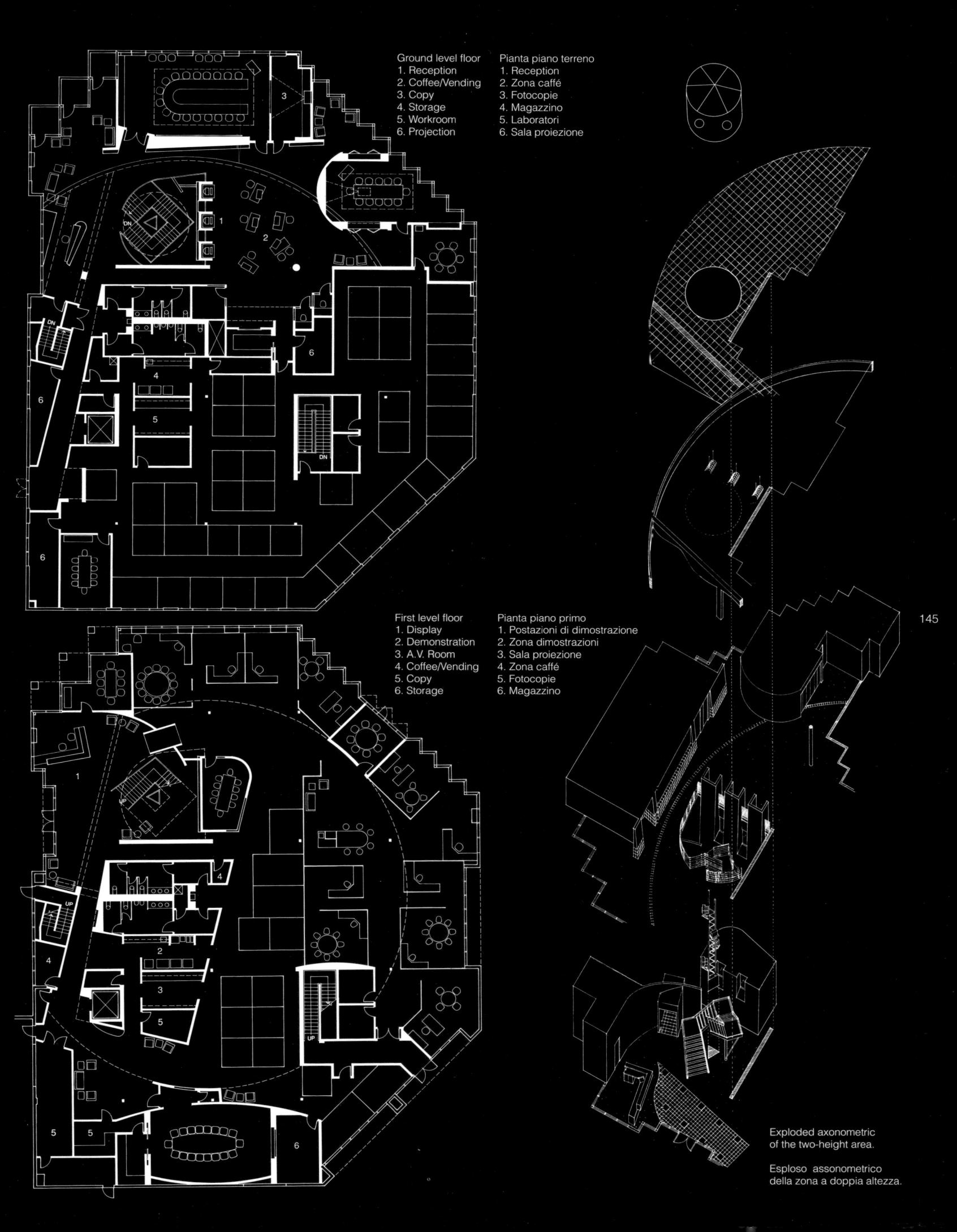

Ground level floor
1. Reception
2. Coffee/Vending
3. Copy
4. Storage
5. Workroom
6. Projection

Pianta piano terreno
1. Reception
2. Zona caffé
3. Fotocopie
4. Magazzino
5. Laboratori
6. Sala proiezione

First level floor
1. Display
2. Demonstration
3. A.V. Room
4. Coffee/Vending
5. Copy
6. Storage

Pianta piano primo
1. Postazioni di dimostrazione
2. Zona dimostrazioni
3. Sala proiezione
4. Zona caffé
5. Fotocopie
6. Magazzino

Exploded axonometric of the two-height area.

Esploso assonometrico della zona a doppia altezza.

SONY MUSIC INTERNATIONAL
TAS Design. Miami Beach, FL, 1995

Distributed on the last two stories of an Art Deco monument built in 1933 along the Lincoln Road, the design of the Sony Music headquarters is nicely tuned to the mood of the Deco district and the nearby Lincoln Road Mall, a 1950s prototype of today's shopping center. Taking its cue from the idea of the commercial promenade wending its way among various architectural forms, the new project involves the distribution of the offices on two stories creating a double-height section below the skylights, a device which, besides offering a flood of overhead illumination, creates a connective area that provides a central, piazza-like architectural hub to the entire scheme, around which the rest of the routes circulate with annular logic. The idea of situating offices and conference rooms around the windowed building perimeter and locating the functional zones in an open-plan hub around the internal stairway may at first sight appear a somewhat conventional approach; actually it is part of the architects' intention to construct a series of quite different design episodes within the original building shell. Features that the designers have highlighted are the exposed floors in reinforced concrete, which are nicely interplayed with a ceiling bulkheads that offer a clever variety of levels, partitions, and geometries. Here and there the ceiling design seems to prompt the other architectural features, as in the wood-paneled sections near the reception, and the open-plan operations workstations. The ample use of horizontal glazing together with graceful aluminum grillwork creating lightweight, transparent partition walls between the perimeter offices and the central area, allows plenty of natural light to filter through, while emphasizing the contrasts between the original ceilings and those of the new design. Complementing the flat surfaces of the new ceilings, with their recessed downlighters and incisive geometrical profiles, are various large suspended discs which float above the square concrete pillars, creating a series of marquee-like canopies, as if to stress the urban analogy between work spaces and the outside world.

Ubicata agli ultimi due livelli di un edificio Art Déco costruito nel 1933 lungo la Lincoln Road, la sede della Sony Music riflette nelle soluzioni architettoniche adottate l'atmosfera del famoso Déco District e della Lincoln Road Mall, prototipo degli anni '50 di isola pedonale destinata allo shopping. L'idea di passeggiata pedonale, di percorso tra varie architetture è stato lo spunto di partenza del progetto che ha distribuito su due livelli gli uffici creando in corrispondenza di un lucernario uno spazio a doppio livello che, oltre a catturare la luce zenitale dall'alto, crea una zona connettiva configurandosi come cerniera architettonica centrale, sorta di riuscita piazza interna attorno cui sviluppare un percorso distributivo ad anello. La soluzione di collocare uffici amministrativi e sale riunioni lungo le pareti finestrate perimetrali e distribuire le zone funzionali a open space nella fascia interna, attorno alla scala di collegamento interna agli uffici, se può apparire in un primo tempo come scelta di tipo convenzionale in realtà denuncia le proprie ragioni di progetto nel riuscito tentativo di costruire una serie di differenti episodi architettonici all'interno dell'edificio originario. Di quest'ultimo è denunciata la struttura dei solai in cemento armato a vista che viene valorizzata dal ricercato gioco del controsoffitto, disegnato su diversi livelli secondo studiate partizioni e geometrie. Il progetto del controsoffitto assume un valore compositivo primario che guida in un certo senso le altre soluzioni architettoniche: dalle pareti rivestite in legno nei pressi della reception alla distribuzione delle isole operative open space. L'ampio uso di vetrate a fasce orizzontali e di una sottile rete d'alluminio, impiegate come leggere e trasparenti pareti divisorie tra uffici perimetrali e zona centrale, permette di portare la luce naturale nell'interno valorizzando il contrasto tra i soffitti originari e di progetto. Alle superfici piane del nuovo controsoffitto, segnate da faretti a incasso e da decisi tagli geometrici, si affiancano i grandi dischi sospesi che, collocati in corrispondenza di alcuni pilastri, si configurano come essenziali padiglioni interni, sottolineando il carattere di analogia urbana tra spazi di lavoro e ambiente esterno.

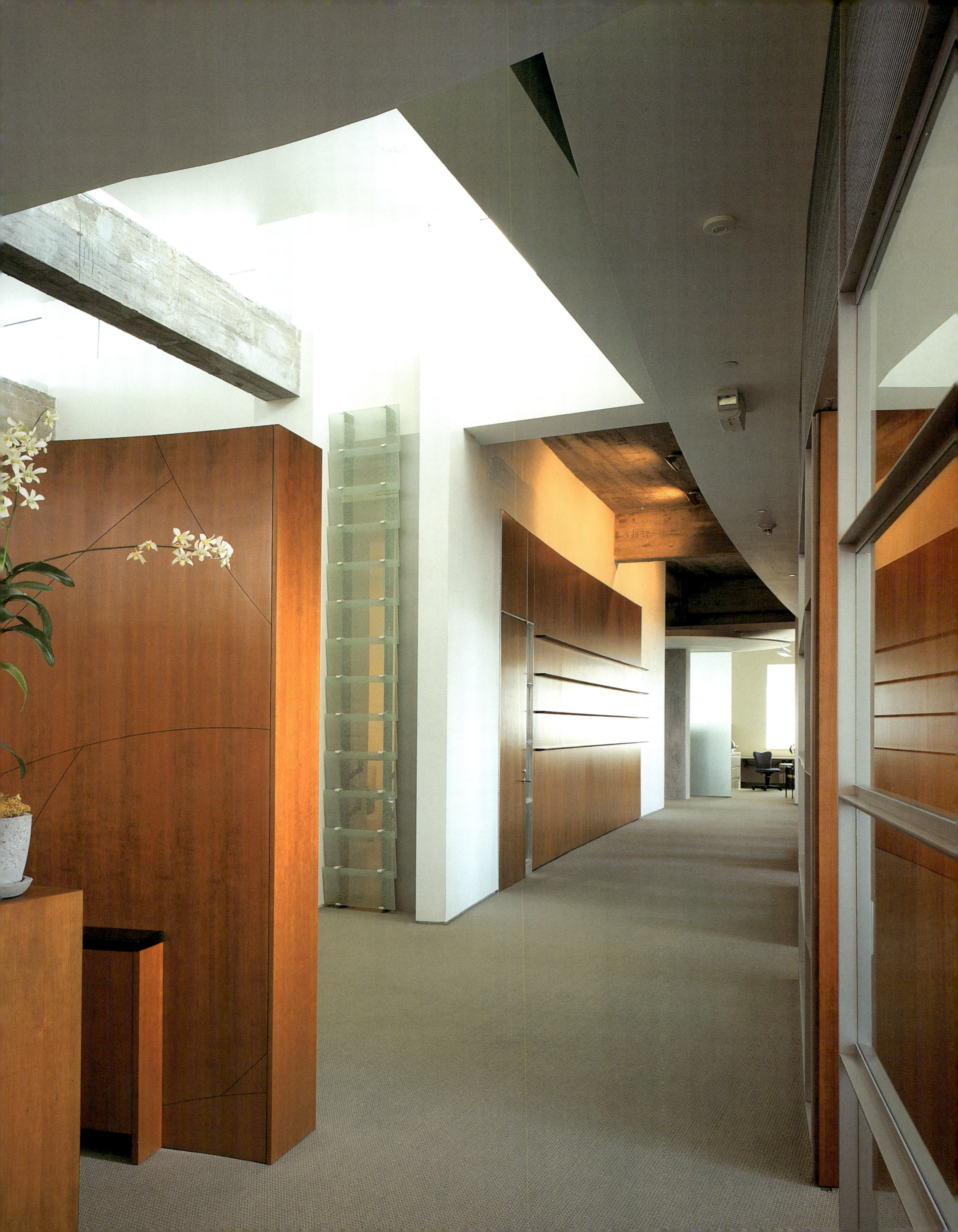

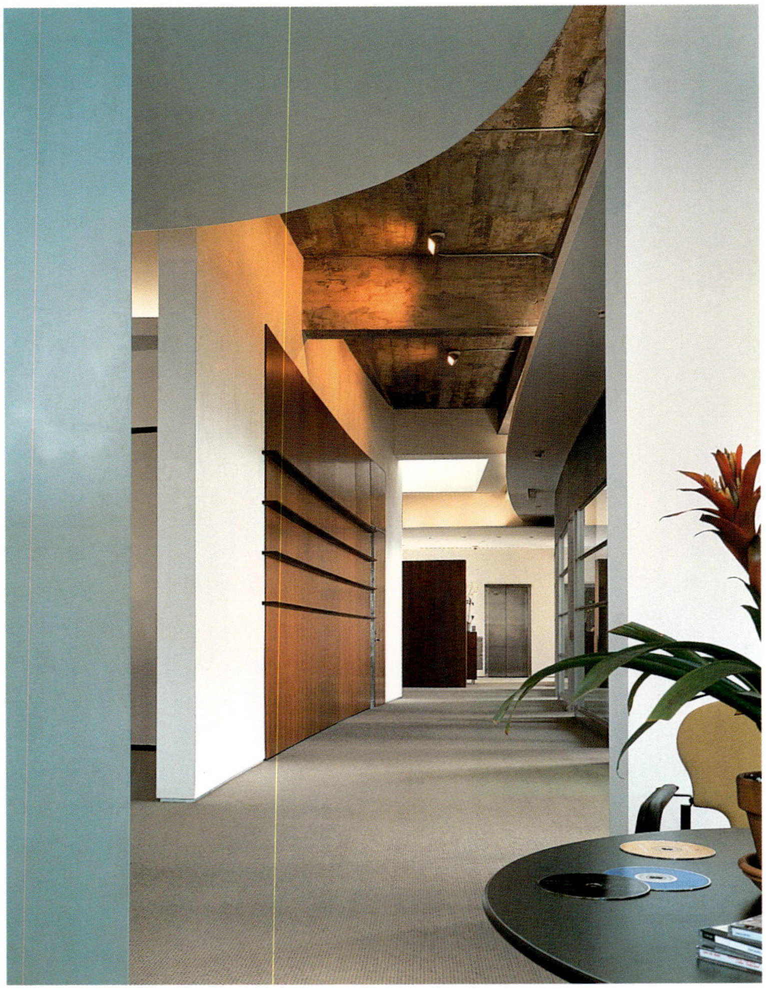

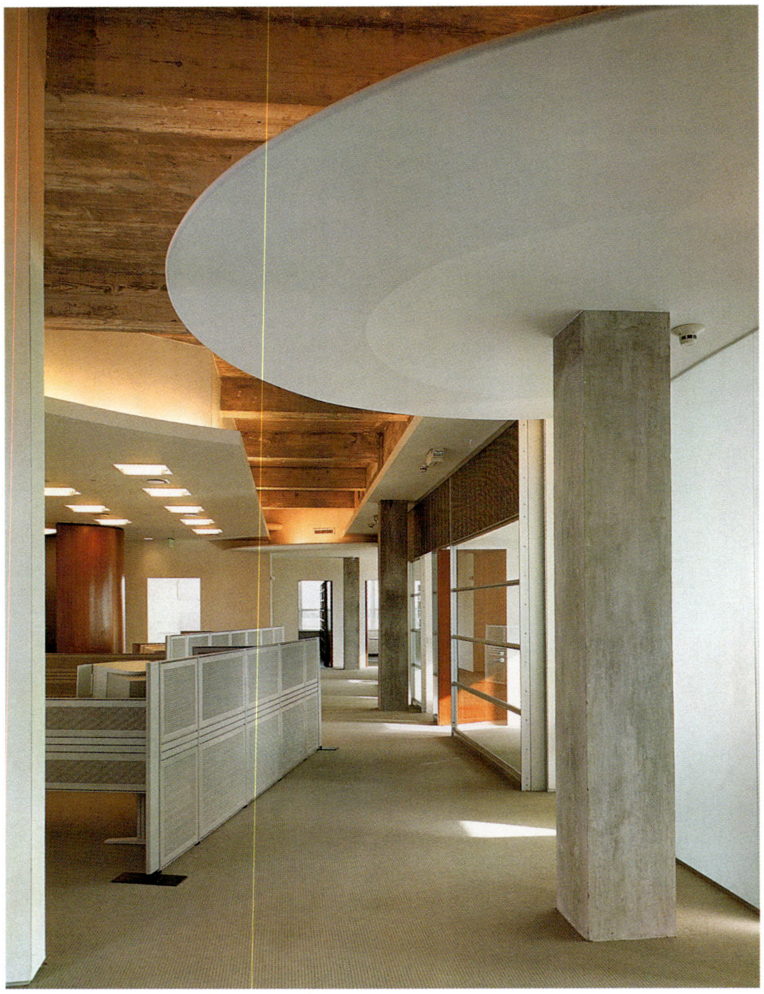

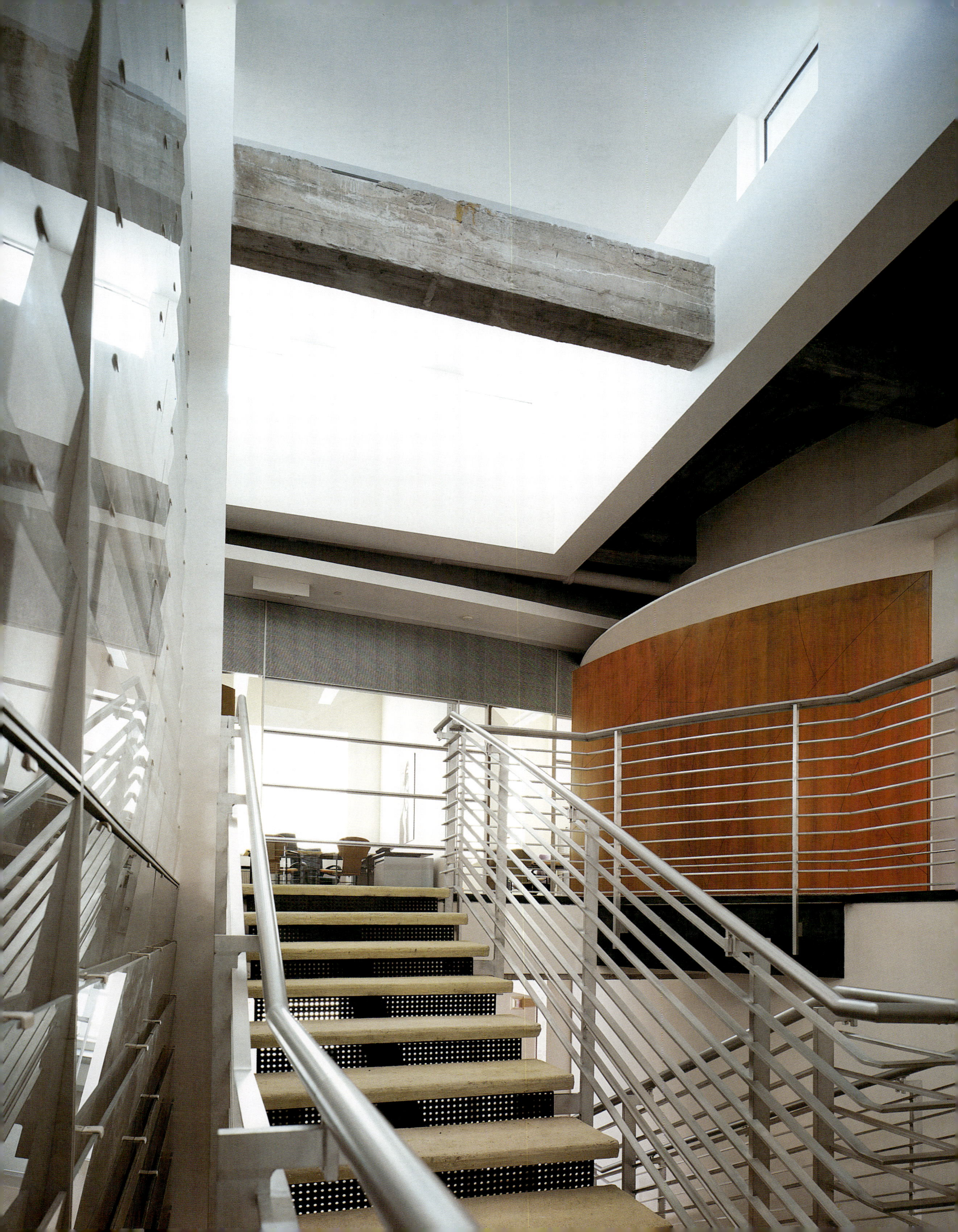

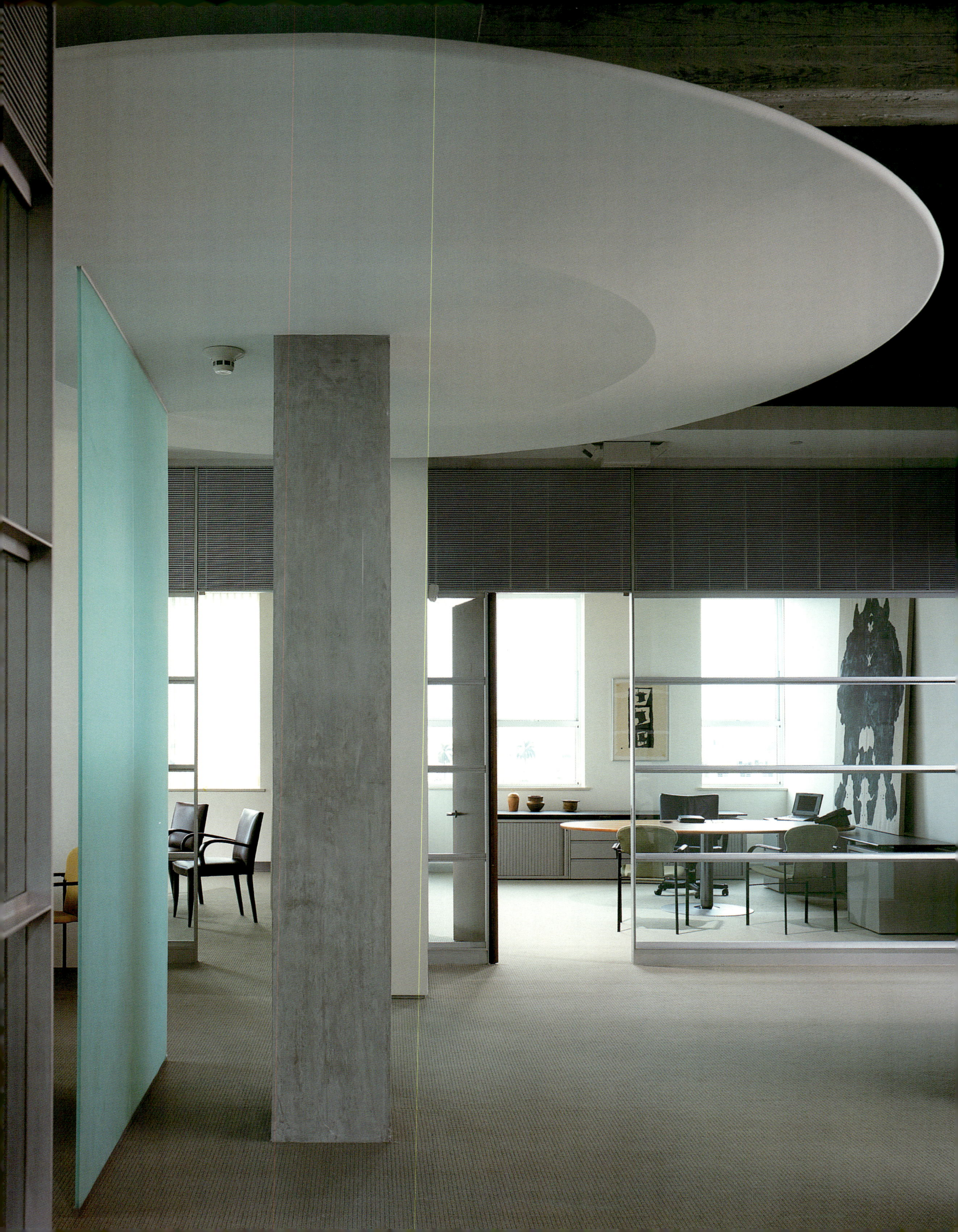

151

152

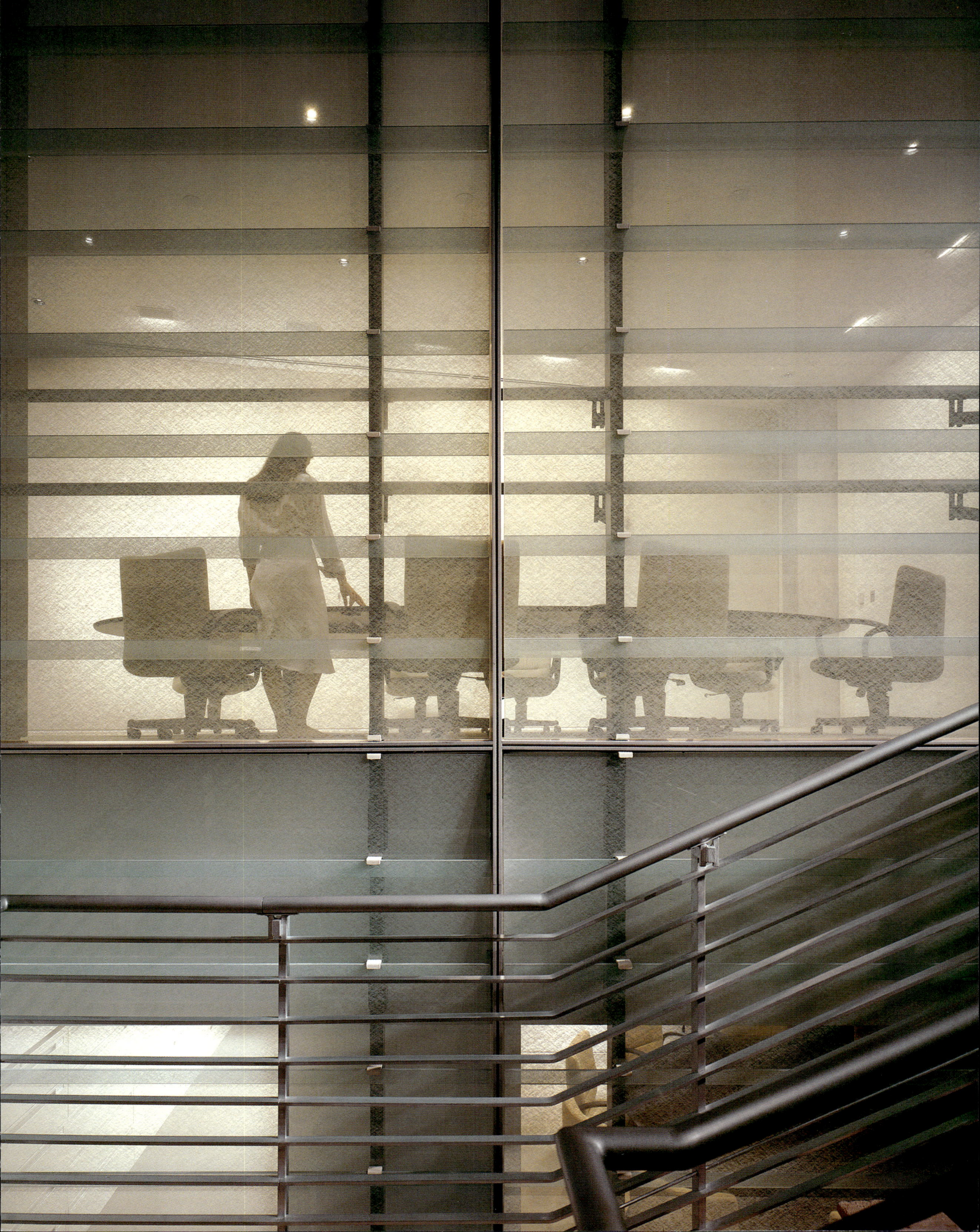

154

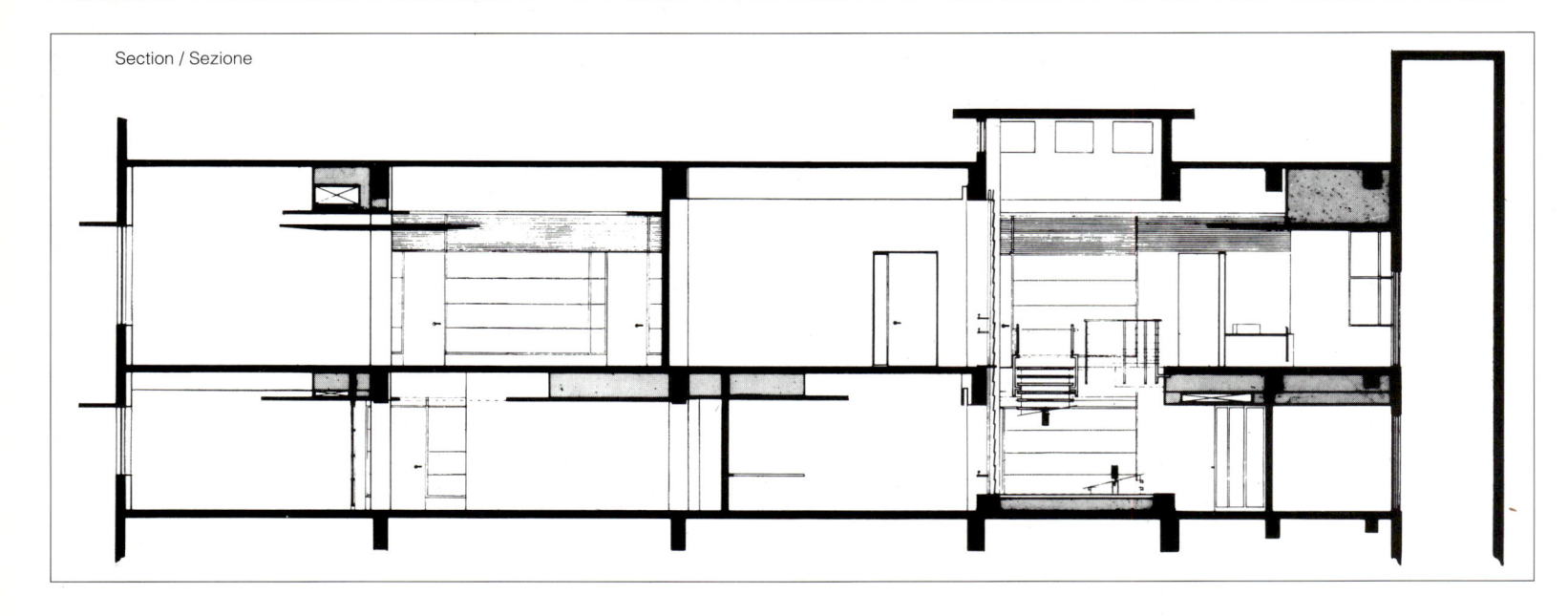

Section / Sezione

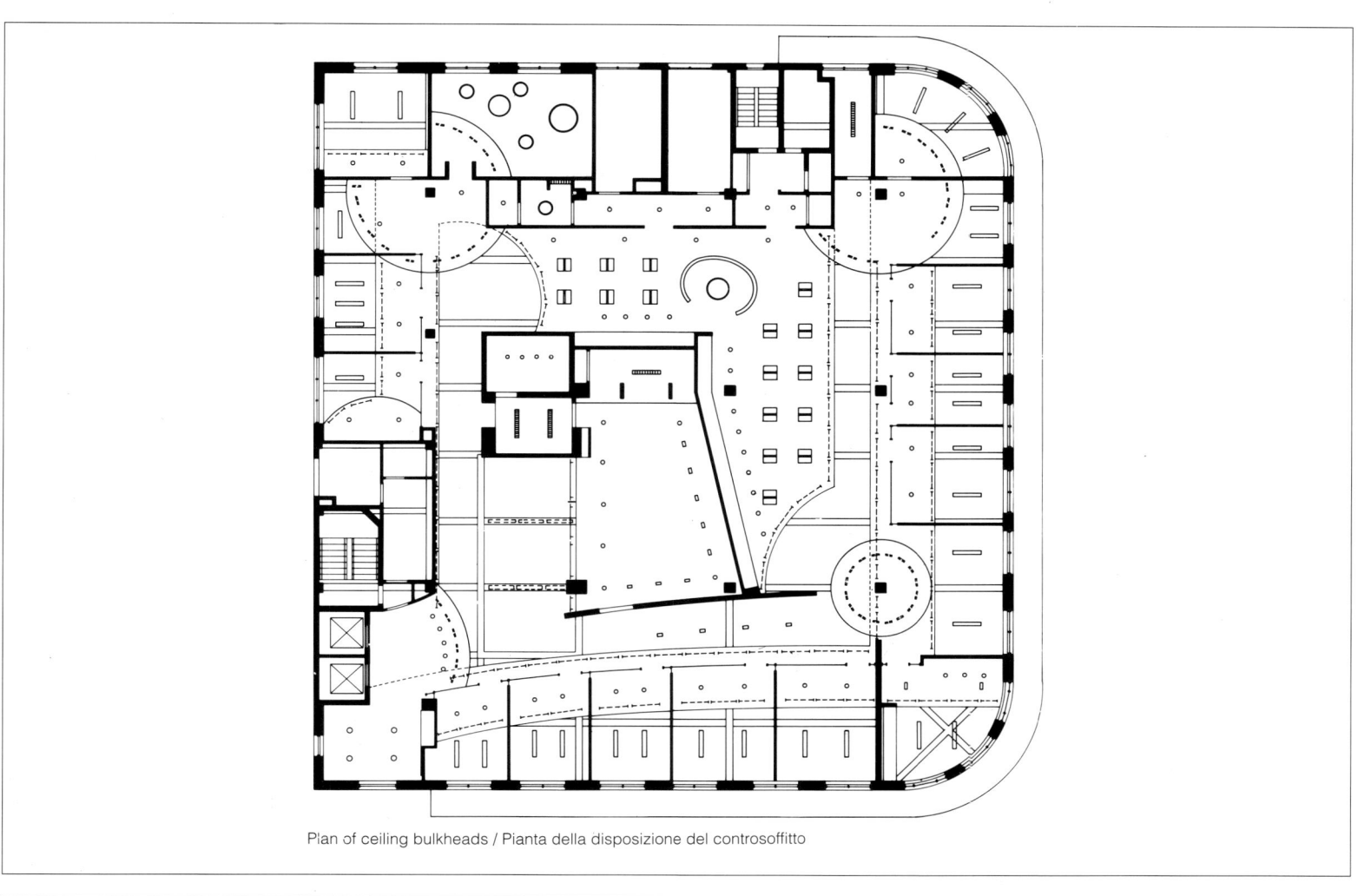

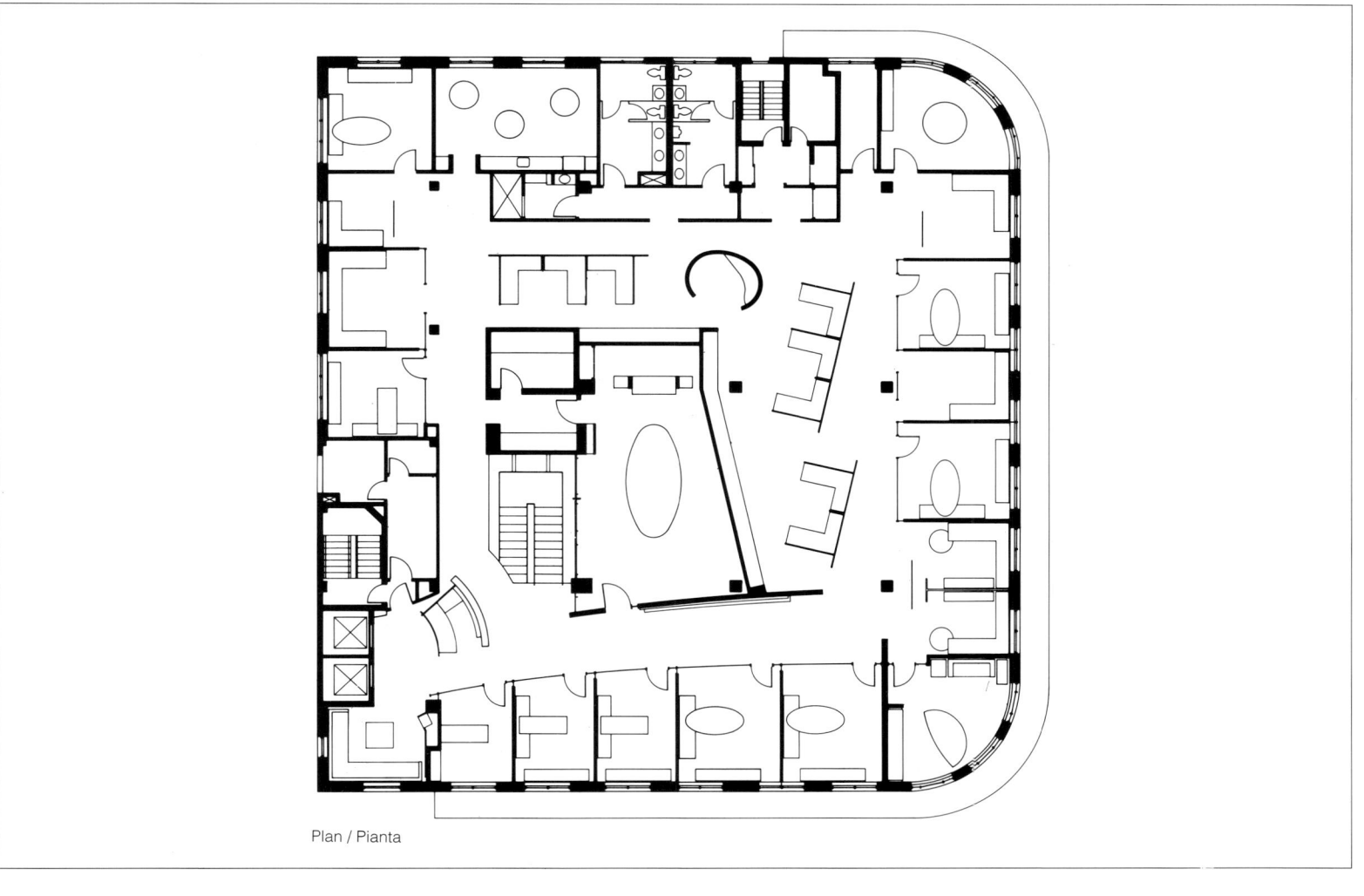

Plan of ceiling bulkheads / Pianta della disposizione del controsoffitto

Plan / Pianta

SQUIRE, SANDERS & DEMPSEY
STUDIOS Architecture. Cleveland, OH, 1992

Generously distributed over eight stories of a large office building, the headquarters of this leading attorneys partnership, which was established some one hundred years ago, in addition to addressing the necessary distribution criteria for the different working environments, comprises a choice of materials and composition that does justice to the studio's corporate image. Each story of the building follows an open-plan scheme structured around a central hub containing the staircases, elevators, and restroom facilities. As regards the standard floor layout, the architects have given precedence to harvesting all the natural light possible, arranging the attorneys' offices around the building's perimeter, separated from the rest by means of a second operations zone with large glazed doorways and neat curved partition walls of sanded glass panes in a wooden lattice. This effective compositional feature gives tone to the overall design, allowing the light to filter through to the inner areas, giving a sense of airy harmony to the long corridors that provide access to the small meeting rooms, workstations, and open-plan areas. On the floor housing the library department, functional reading posts are ranged along the facade perimeter, which is occupied on one side by offices that follow the standard floor layout, repeated in two operative zones flanked by the central service core. On the office level devoted entirely to conference rooms, a dark Australian wood is used on various occasions as wall-cladding, flanked by other types of wood for the geometrical inserts of all the custom-designed meeting-room tables. In correspondence with the brightly lit reception area, with its large windows on the surrounding panorama, a double-height space offers a large main entrance hallway, where a staircase for the exclusive use of the firm leads up to the administration floor. The entrance is prefaced by the strong architectural treatment of the elevator lobby with walls faced in African slate in a variety of shades. Meeting rooms of assorted dimensions are arranged around the perimeter of the building, together with another office zone. Along the entire border climbs the overscaled staircase, with a customized thirty-seater table, whose tapered design is repeated in the elegant false ceiling overhead, from which a foldaway monitor screen hangs.

Distribuita su otto livelli di un grande palazzo per uffici, la sede di questo studio legale, che vanta ben cento anni di attività, oltre a rispondere alle esigenze distributive e a ottimizzare il funzionamento dei diversi ambienti di lavoro, ben rappresenta nelle scelte compositive e materiche l'immagine professionale dello studio. Ogni livello dell'edificio era caratterizzato da una pianta libera distribuita intorno a un nucleo centrale dove sono collocati vani scala, ascensori e servizi. Per quanto riguarda il 'piano tipo', le scelte progettuali hanno valorizzato l'uso della luce naturale distribuendo lungo il perimetro di facciata gli uffici degli avvocati, separati da una seconda zona operativa interna con ampie porte vetrate e con riuscite pareti in curva, costruite in legno e vetro sabbiato. Elementi compositivi che concorrono a costruire la ricercata immagine architettonica complessiva, queste quinte traslucide portano la luce nelle zone interne dando un senso di leggerezza e di armonia ai lunghi corridoi distributivi, su cui si affacciano piccole sale riunioni, postazioni di lavoro e zone open space. Al piano occupato dalla biblioteca, funzionali postazioni di consultazione sono posizionate lungo il perimetro di facciata, occupato per un lato da uffici che seguono la soluzione del piano tipo, ripetuta in due zone operative affiancate al nocciolo servizi centrale. Nel livello dedicato interamente alle sale riunioni, un legno scuro australiano è impiegato in varie occasioni quale elemento di rivestimento parietale, affiancato da altre essenze per gli inserti geometrici di tutti i tavoli riunione su disegno. Qui, in corrispondenza con la luminosa reception, aperta con ampie vetrate verso il panorama all'intorno, una hall a doppia altezza si propone come grande spazio d'ingresso principale, dove una scala ad esclusivo uso dello studio conduce al piano amministrativo. L'ingresso è anticipato dal forte trattamento architettonico del pianerottolo ascensori con pareti rivestite in lastre d'ardesia africana a diverse tonalità. Sale riunioni di varie dimensioni sono collocate lungo il perimetro dell'edificio insieme a una zona uffici. Lungo un intero lato si sviluppa la sala di dimensioni maggiori, con un tavolo su disegno per trenta persone la cui forma affusolata è ripetuta nell'elegante disegno del controsoffitto, dove è posizionato il proiettore televisivo a scomparsa.

157

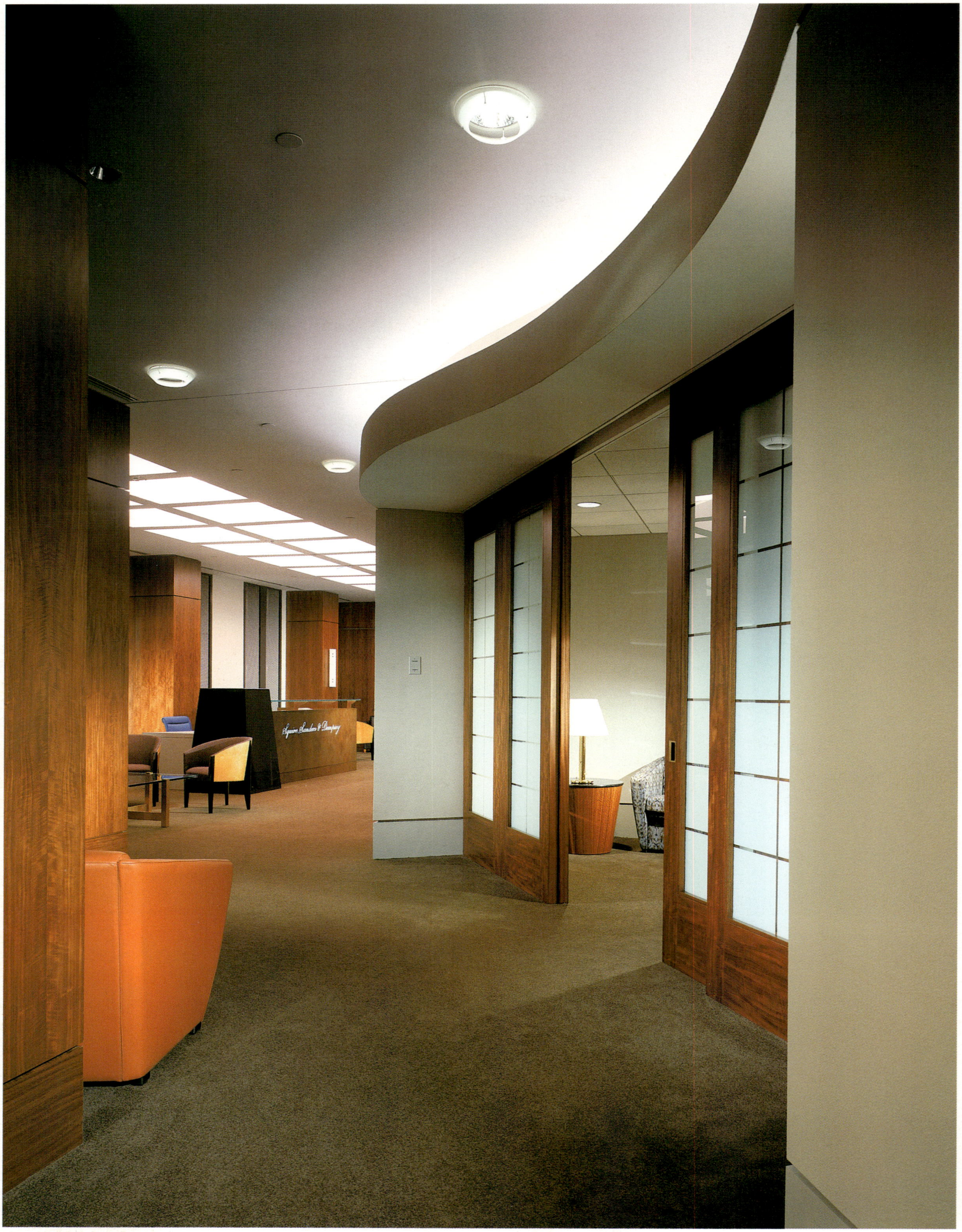
Squire, Sanders & Dempsey

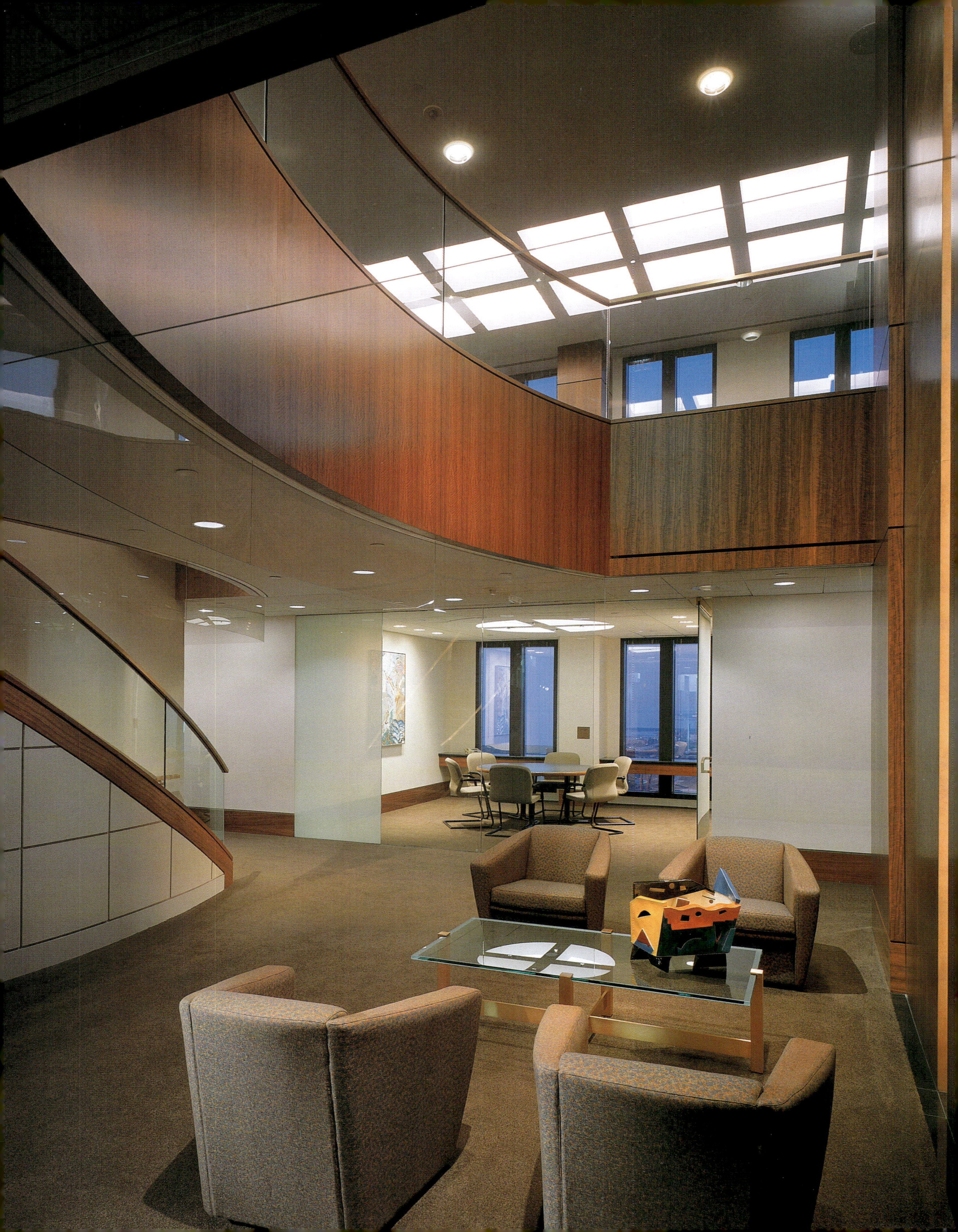

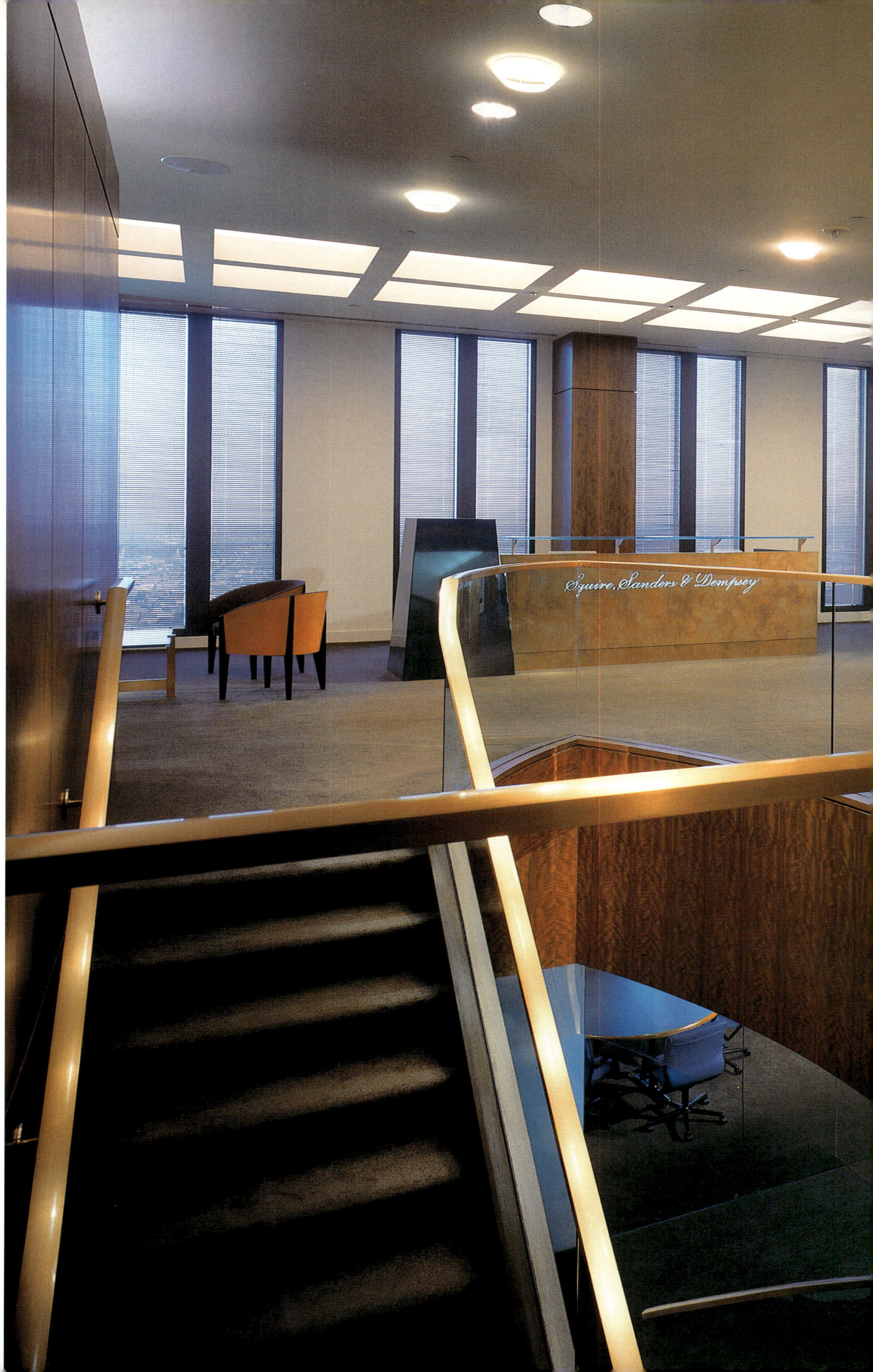
Squire, Sanders & Dempsey

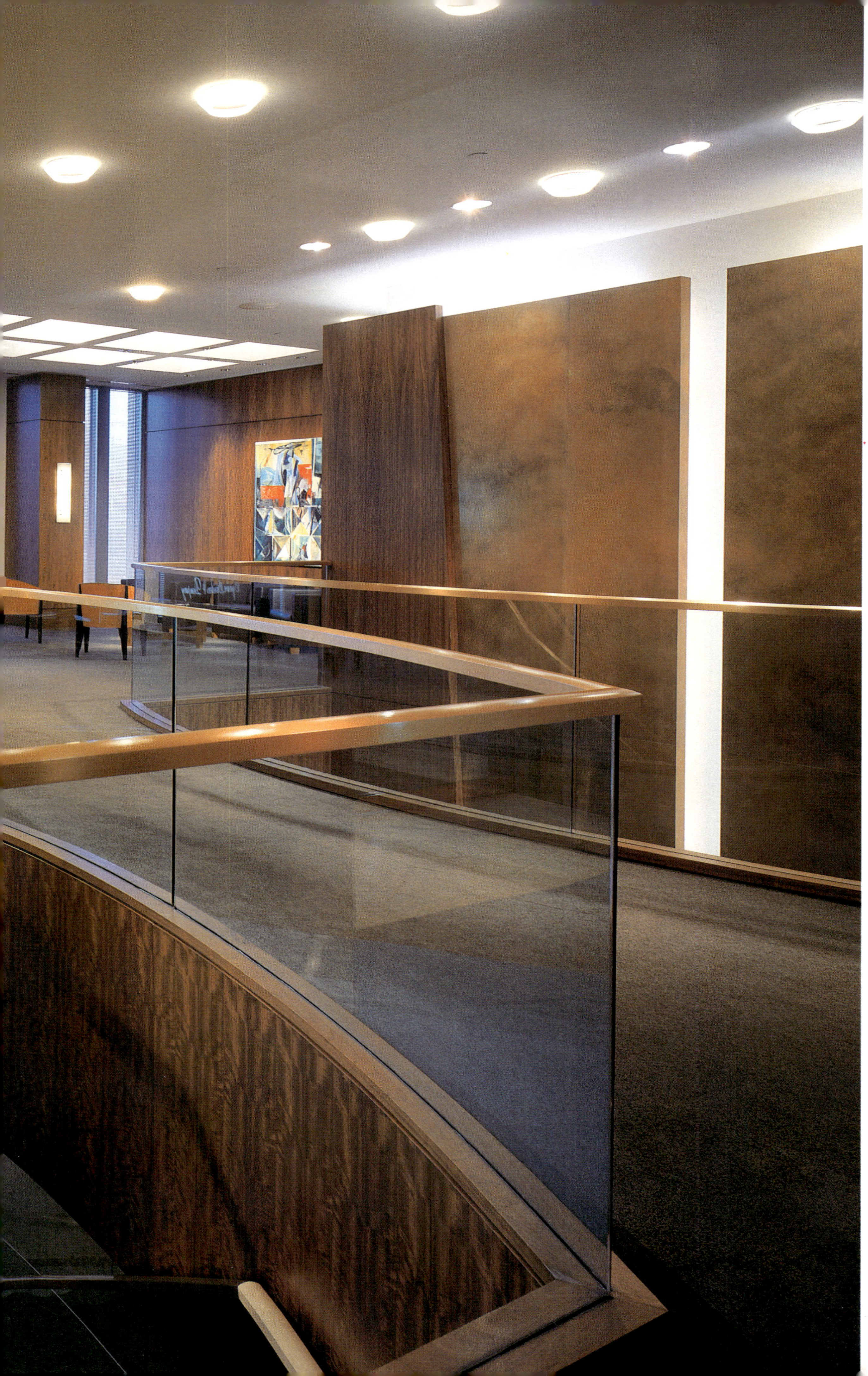

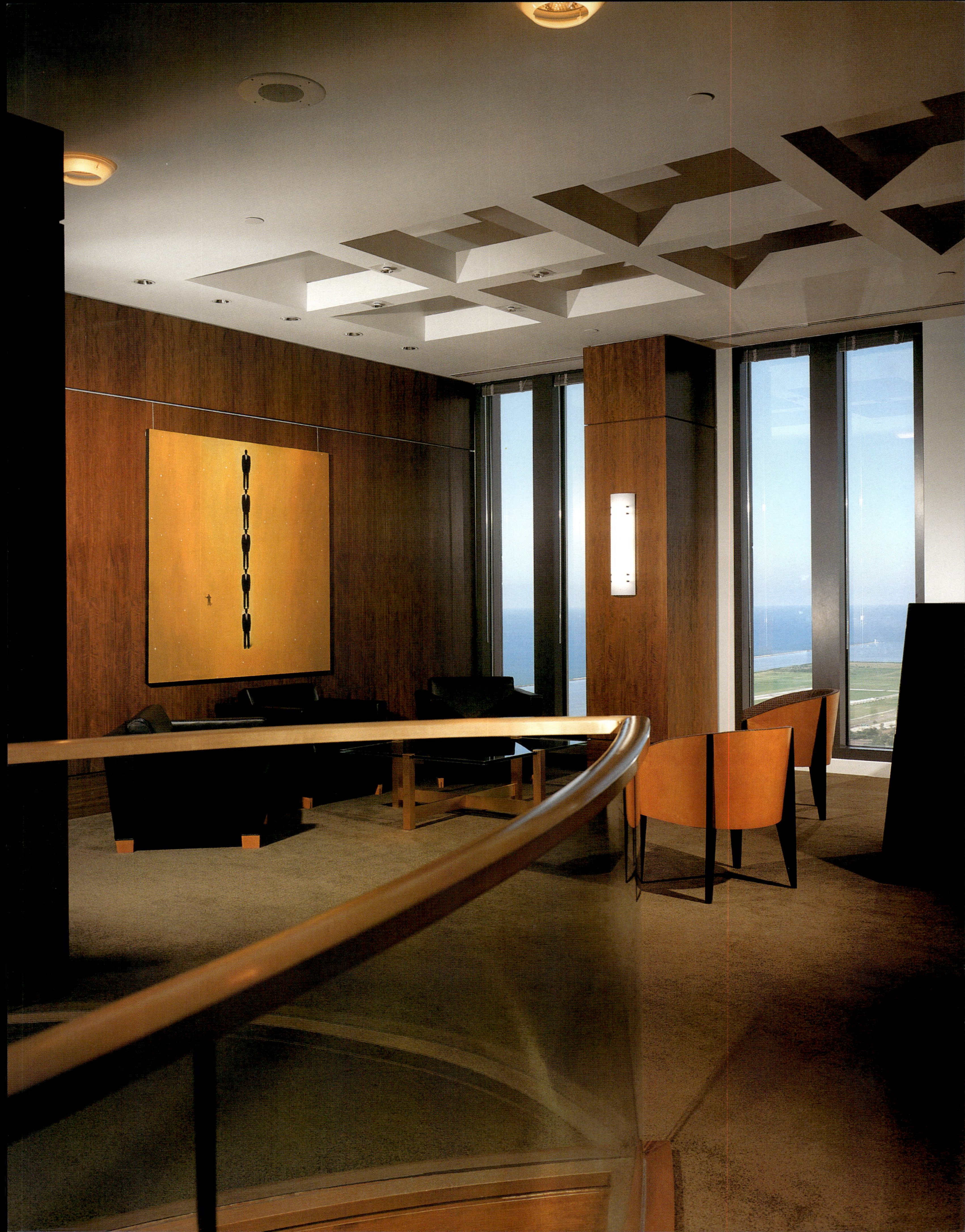

163

164

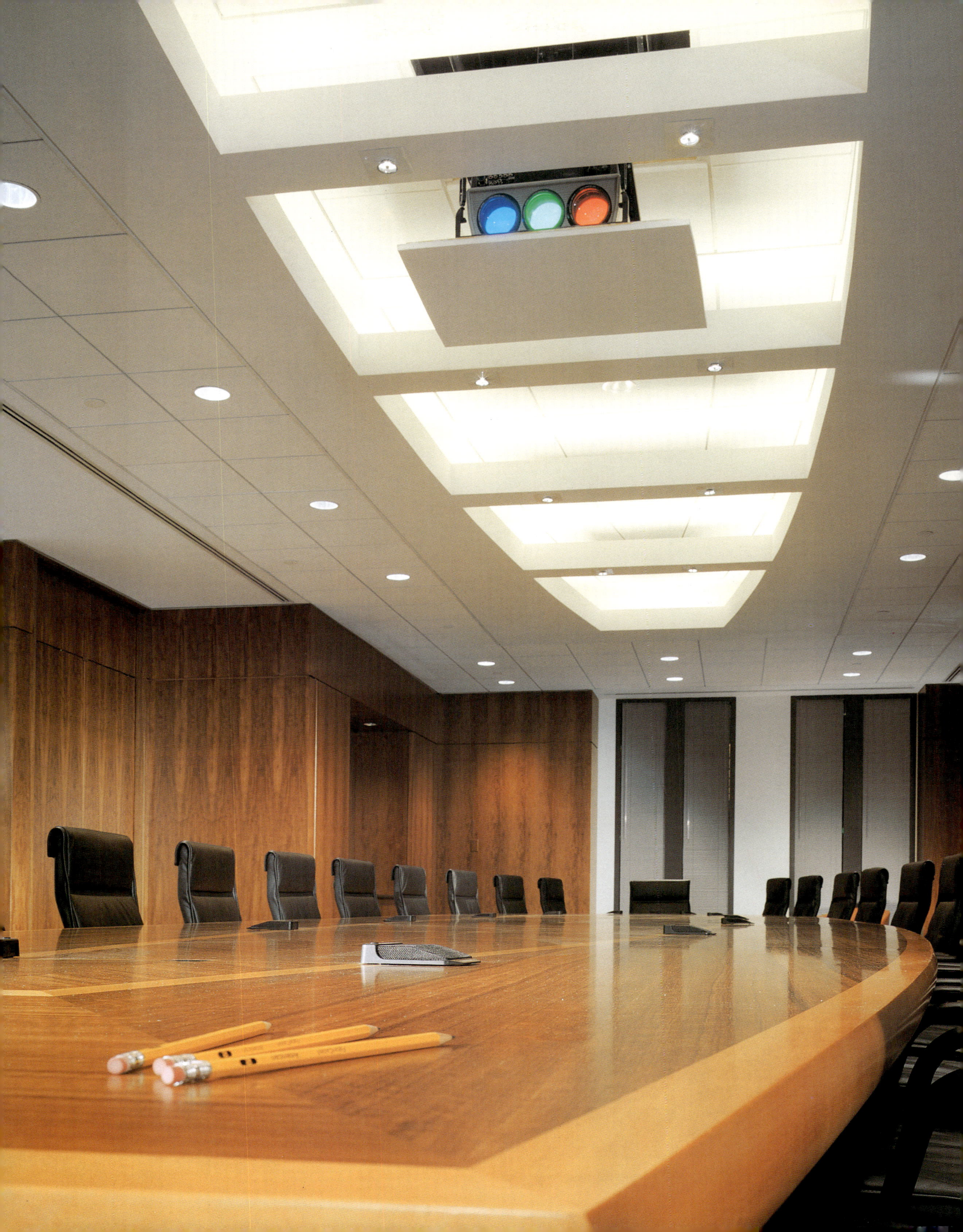

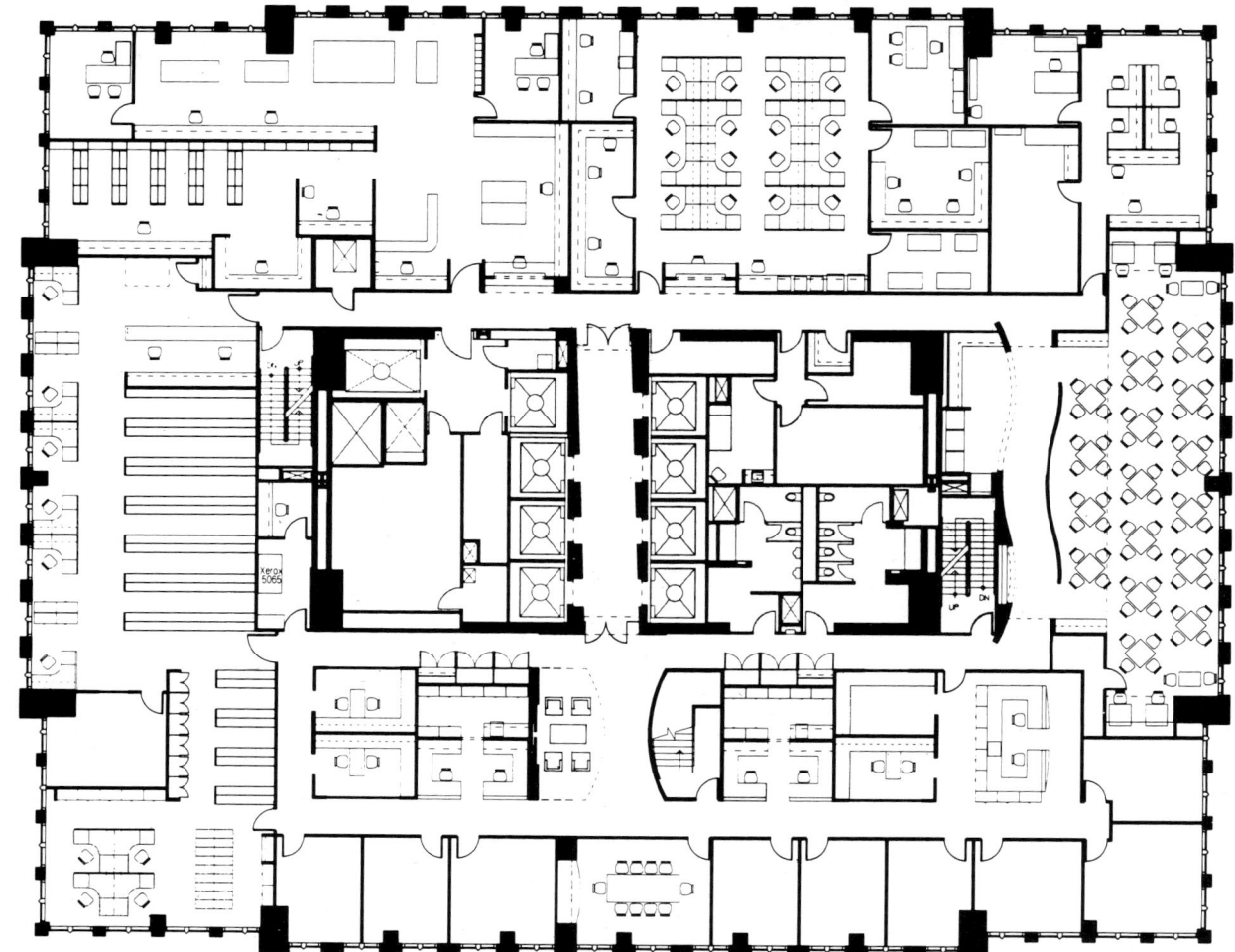

Administrative floor / Piano Amministrazione

Typical attorney floor / Piano Tipo Uffici dei procuratori

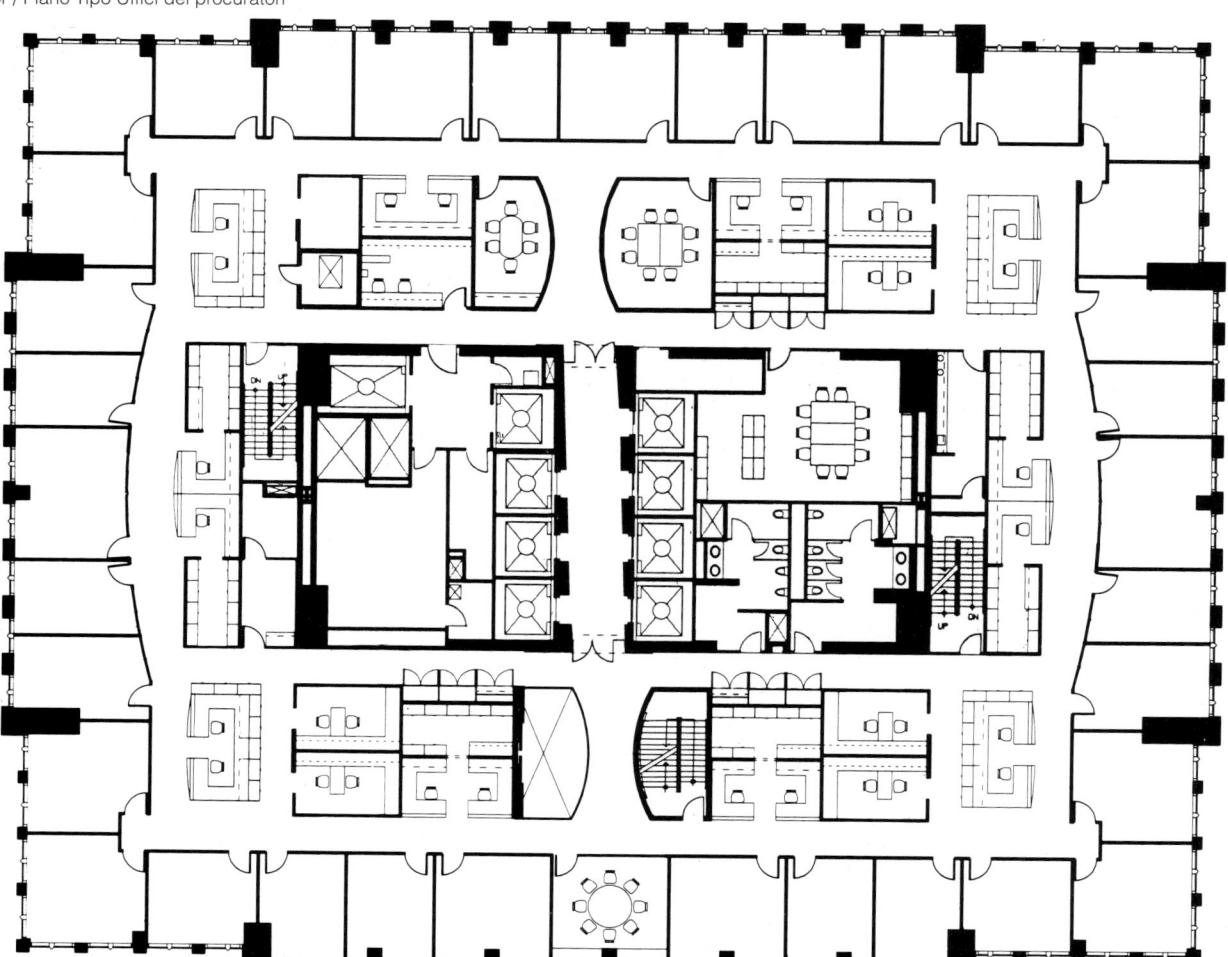

Conference center / Piano Sale Riunioni

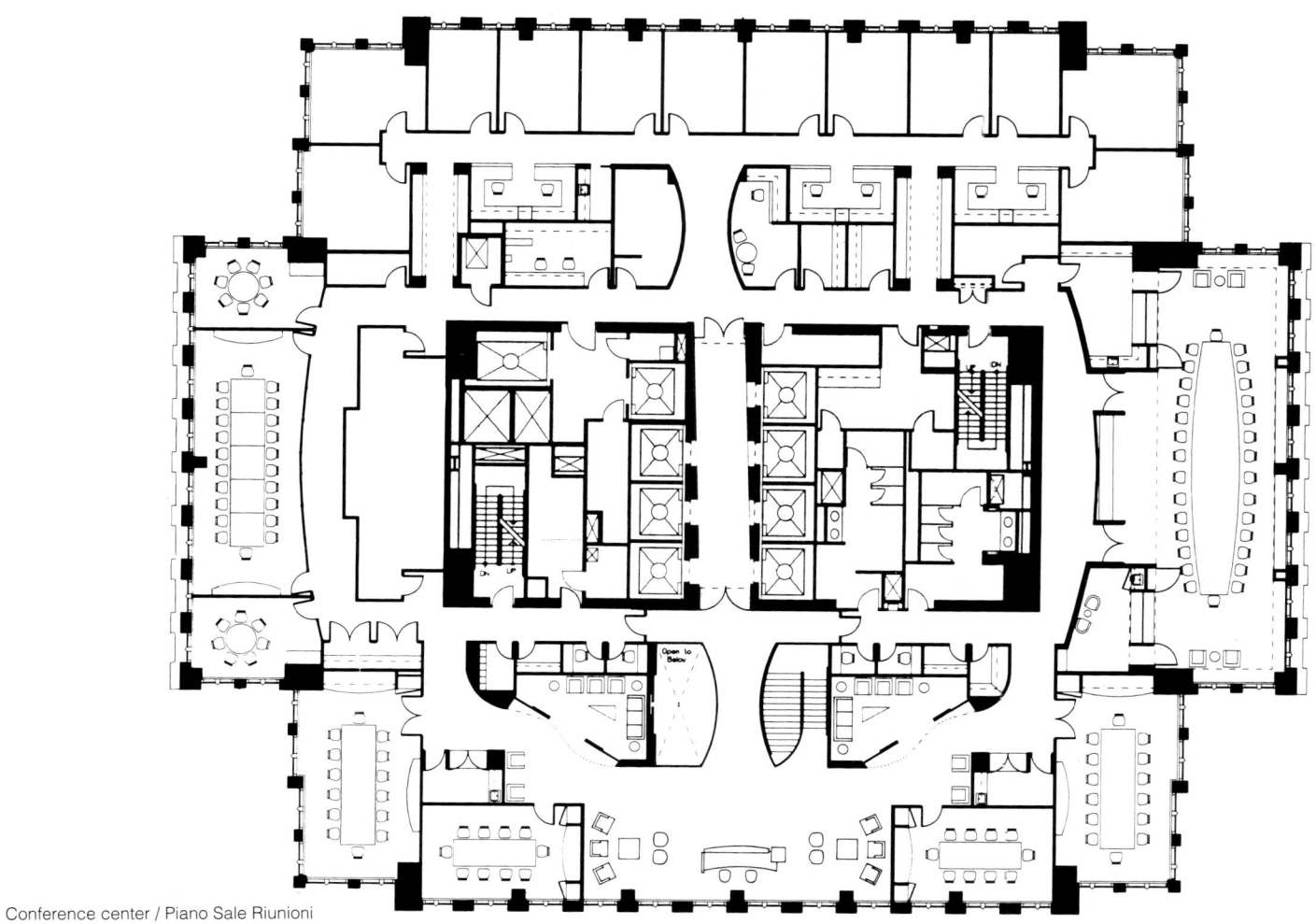

Library floor / Piano Biblioteca

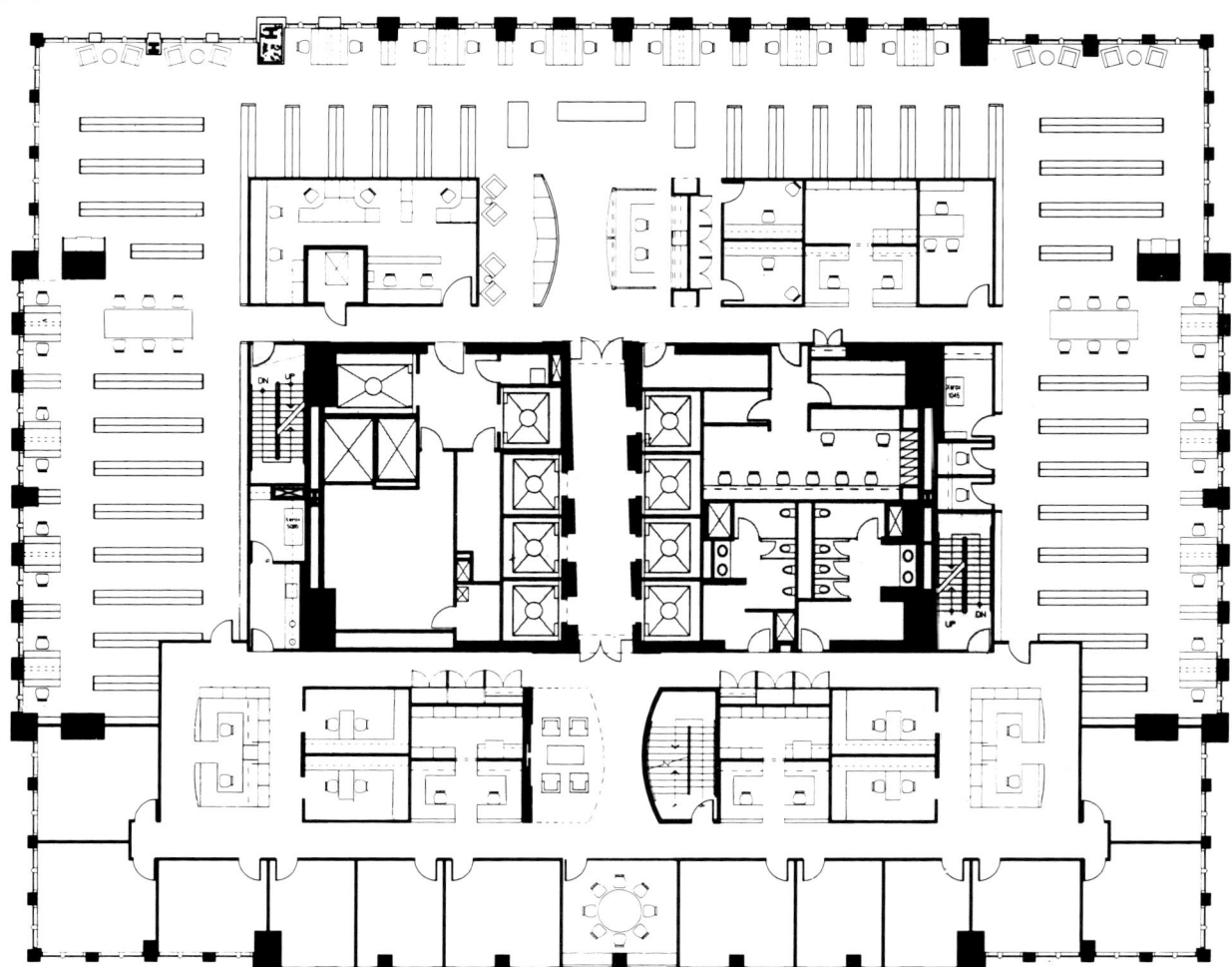

STEVE GOLD PRODUCTIONS
Carl D'Aquino Interiors, Inc. New York, NY, 1995

This new design for the headquarters of a film and video production company offered the architects a great opportunity to experiment combining industrial and unconventional materials in a highly effective compositional and functional synthesis. The somewhat tight budget obviously posed certain limits to what materials could be employed, but this seems to have contributed to the winning overall effect of the new interiors. The editing and production area, together with those for the executive offices and conference room, are situated along the windowed perimeter so as to take advantage of natural light; the central zone, meanwhile, is taken up with the reception, the workstations, and an assistants' room. All these are distributed through an airy, carefully organized open space. The entire interior has been freed of the pre-existing false ceilings, thereby exploiting the full height of the space, organizing a series of divider walls finished in light gray stucco, interrupted in geometrical fashion by tall maple doors that perform like sculptures (with cementer's trowels for handles) and by small apertures with sanded, horizontally striped glazing that allows natural light to filter into the central area while conserving the necessary privacy of the perimeter offices. The same idea has been employed to separate the workstations in the open space, harnessing the available natural light. Handsome traditional wooden seats and benches (in Bank of England style) are stationed here and there, and the large reception desk emerges boldly in a sweeping curve. This last has been appointed the role of pivotal architectural feature of the interiors; with its natural Lumasite top and base in backlit translucent material, a further striking element is the corner element in red lacquer that vies nicely with the color of the duct enclosures overhead, which traverse the entire suite of offices in strong yellow and blue, offsetting the uniform white of the ceilings, modeling it into a series of running prisms punctuated by bulbous air vents (of the type used in Japanese factories), and by a series of track-mounted downlighters complementing the garage-type light fittings on the walls.

Il progetto della sede di una società di produzione di film e video è stata occasione per sperimentare l'uso di materiali industriali e non convenzionali all'interno di una brillante sintesi compositiva e funzionale. Il basso budget disponibile ha in un certo modo imposto le scelte materiche, che hanno però determinato una riuscita immagine dello spazio complessivo. Gli uffici operativi (editing e produzione), insieme a quelli direzionali e alla sala riunione, sono stati collocati lungo le facciate finestrate per fruire della luce naturale, mentre la zona centrale è stata occupata dalla reception, dalle postazioni di lavoro e da un ufficio per gli assistenti, tutti collegati tra loro in un grande open space attentamente calibrato. Liberato l'intero spazio disponibile dai controsoffitti presistenti, si è valorizzata tutta l'altezza disponibile organizzando una serie di pareti divisorie trattate a stucco spatolato grigio chiaro e interrotte, secondo studiate partizioni geometriche, da alte porte in legno d'acero pensate come superfici scultoree mobili (con cazzuole da lavoro usate come inconsuete maniglie) e da piccole vetrate decorate a sottili strisce orizzontali sabbiate che portano luce nella zona centrale, garantendo allo stesso tempo la necessaria privacy degli uffici perimetrali. La medesima soluzione è stata adottata anche per separare tra loro le postazioni di lavoro nell'open space, valorizzando l'impiego della luce. Sedie e panche tradizionali in legno (il modello che si trova nella Bank of England) emergono nello spazio insieme al grande banco reception centrale in curva. Questo è stato assunto come elemento architettonico interno di riferimento, caratterizzato dalla struttura in Lumasite naturale con base in materiale traslucido retroilluminato, cui si aggiunge un forte elemento angolare laccato di rosso che ben si rapporta ai colori del rivestimento dei condotti dell'aria condizionata soprastanti. Questi si sviluppano colorando in giallo e blu la bianca superficie del soffitto modellandola secondo dei prismi regolari segnati da essenziali bocchettoni sferici impiegati nelle fabbriche giapponesi e da una serie di faretti sospesi che si affiancano a quelli a muro utilizzati di solito nei garages.

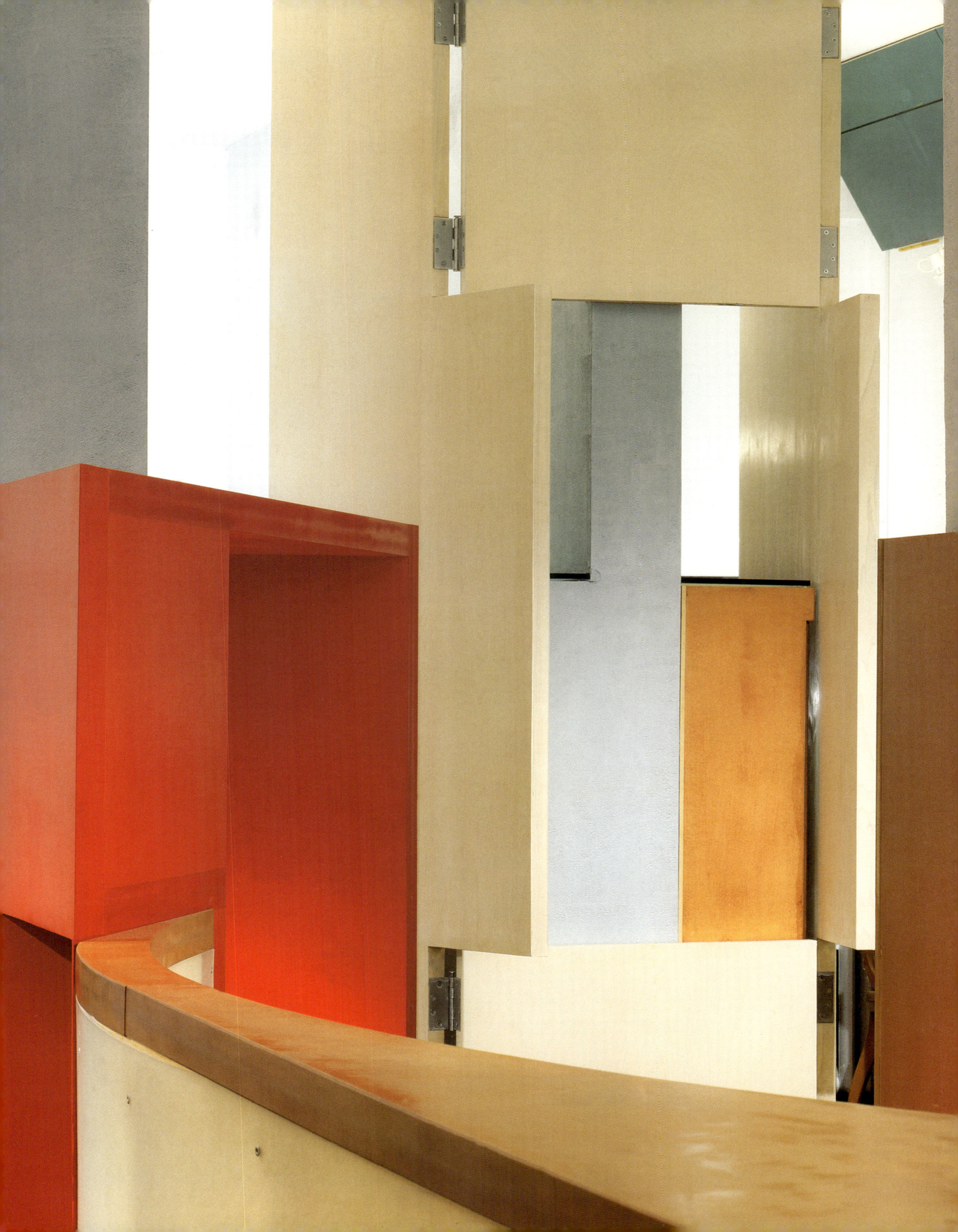

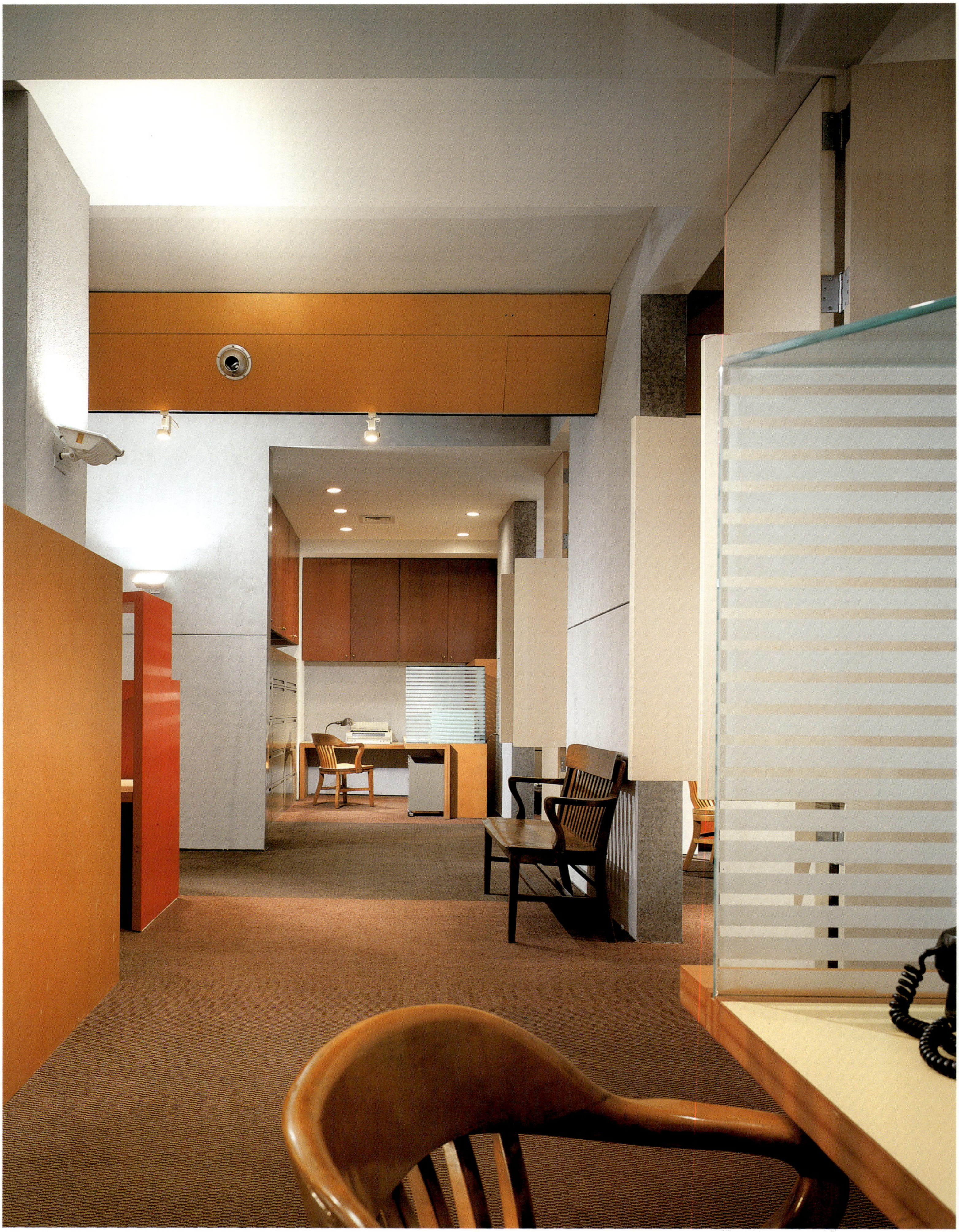

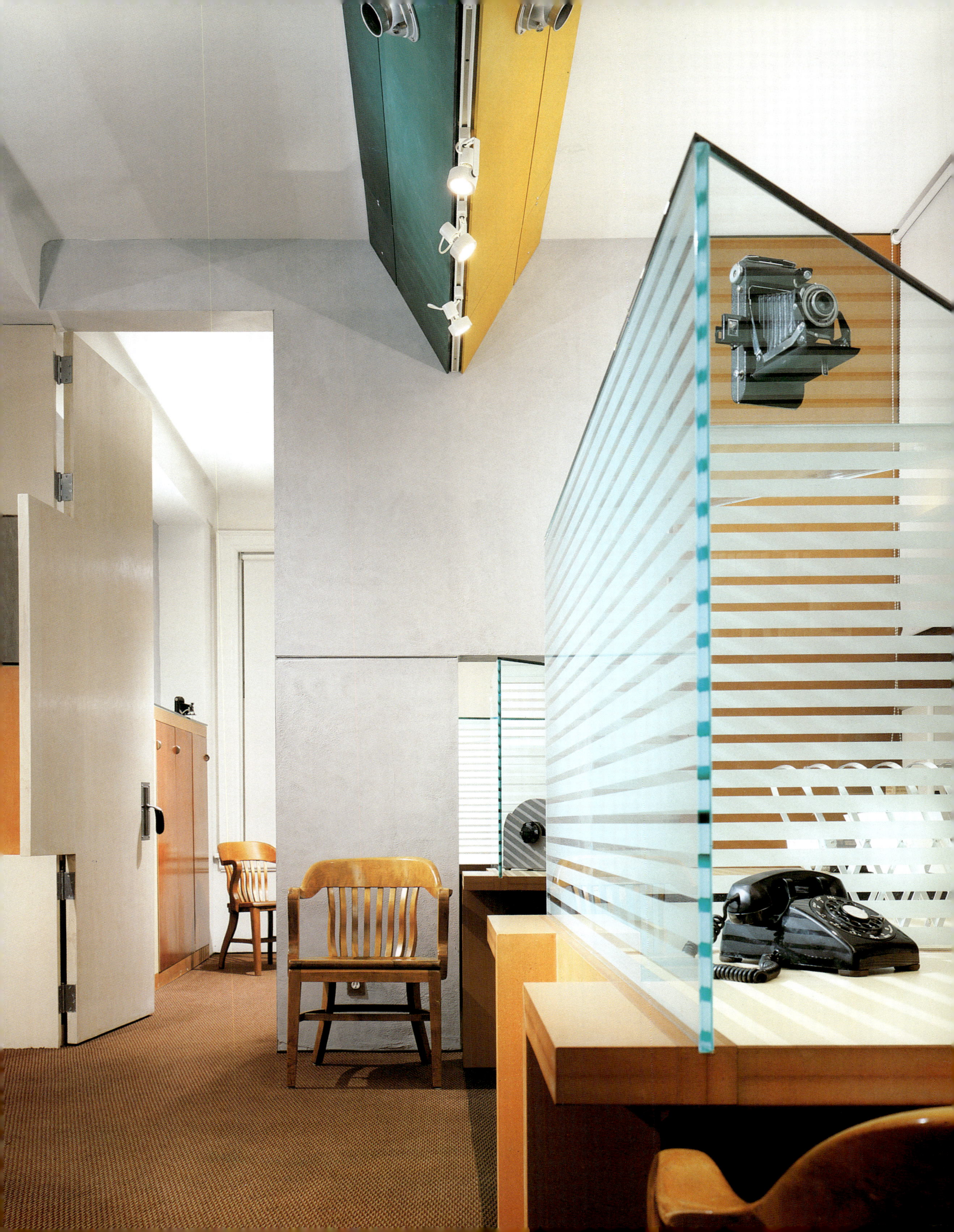

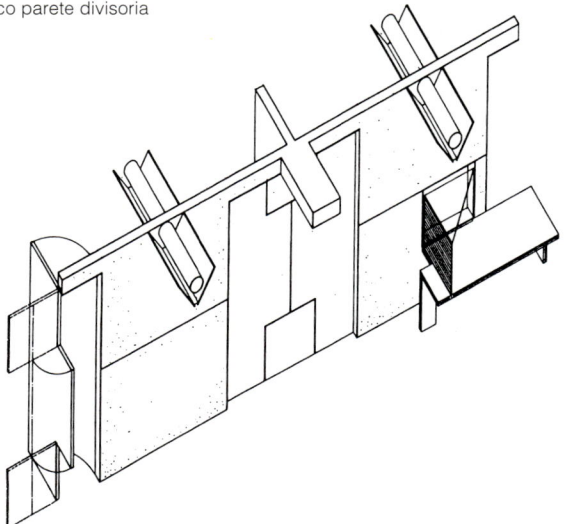

Axonometric detail of partition wall / Particolare assonometrico parete divisoria

172

Interior front / Fronte interno

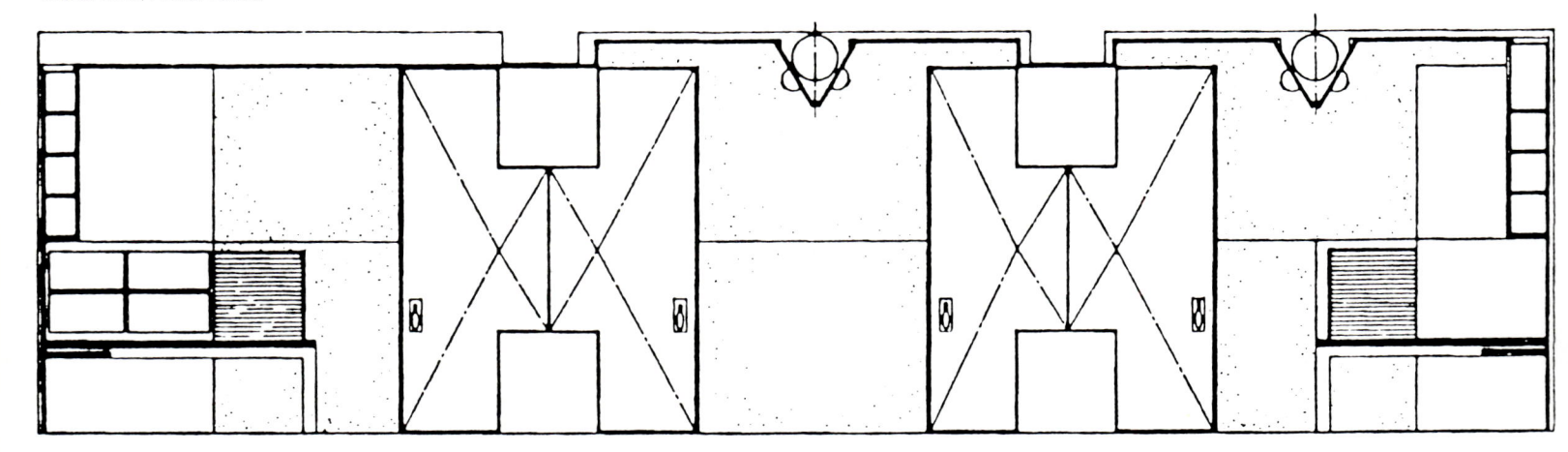

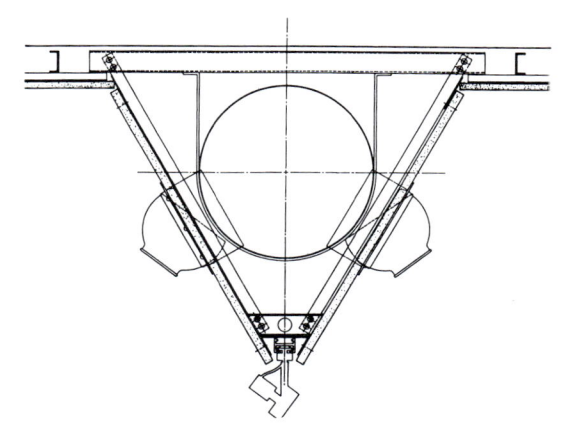

Duct enclosures traverse the entire length of the office
Particolare condotto aria condizionata

Plan / Pianta

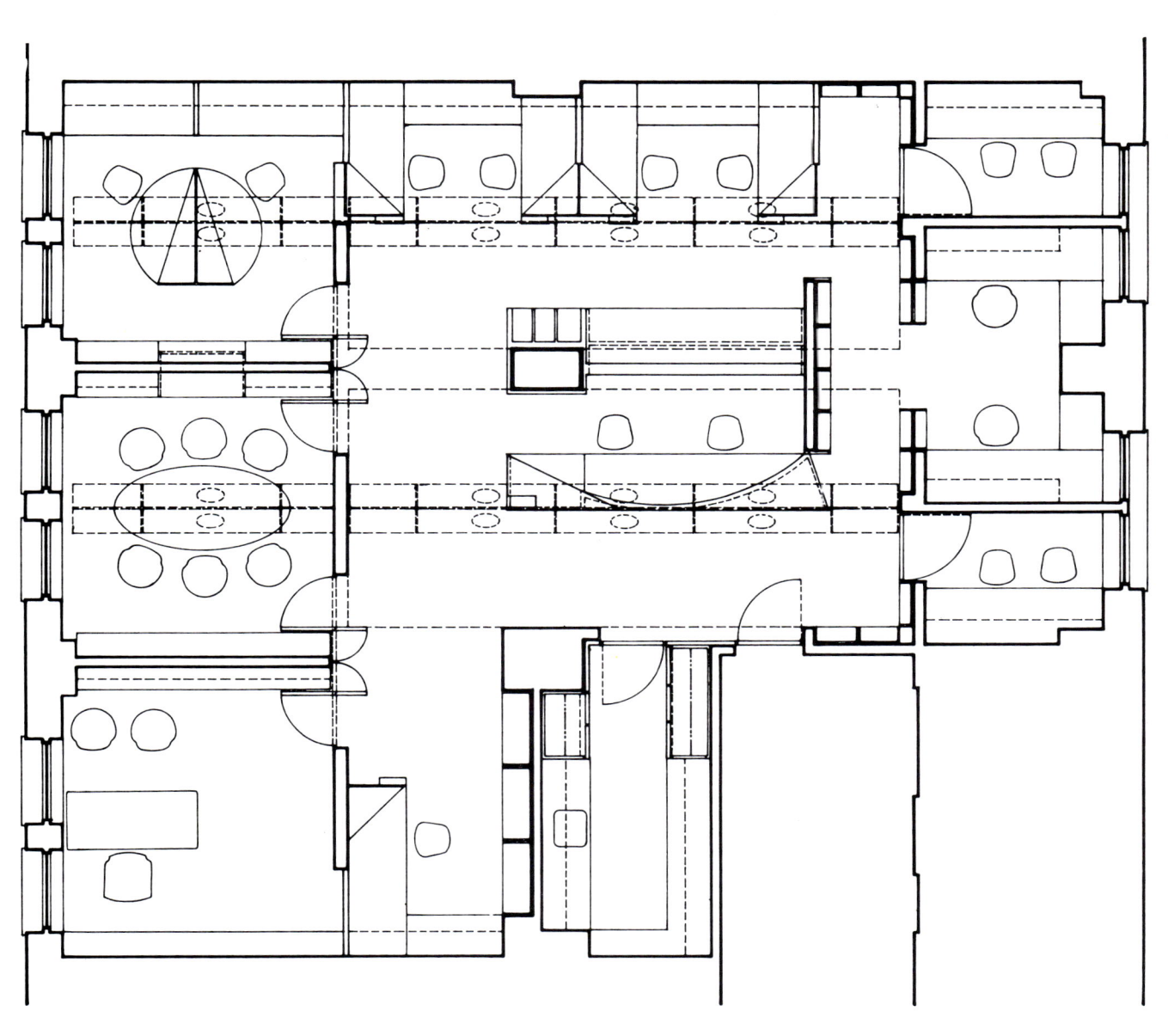

173

TIME OUT

Margaret Helfand Architects. New York, NY, 1996

Slotted into an ample loft-type space orchestrated with traditional iron columns and timber floor, the offices of the New York edition of *Time Out* reflect the innovatory and informal style of the magazine itself, a weekly journal that gives a detailed breakdown of news, events, exhibitions, and other cultural happenings taking place in the city. The limited budget steered the architect toward the use of economic materials of the kind used in industrial settings, and to creating walls and partitions normally destined to be finished in finer materials. Nonetheless, the creative application of so-called poor materials, whose functional features and inherent roughness are unabashedly left in full view, united with a mindfully designed distributive solution and the design of the furnishings, has in this case entailed the transformation of the interiors with a convincing architectural solution that works in terms of overall impact and its ergonomic and functional aspects. The loft is conceived as a unitary container. The interiors have therefore maintained their regular elongated layout, patterned by the white central columns flanked by the new wedge-shaped duct enclosures that house all the cabling and the air-conditioning systems, nicely emphasizing the dimensions of the existing space. The internal divisions are created with partitions of translucent corrugated fiberglass set in bronze and aluminum surrounds anchored to the floor and ceiling. These lightweight, unobtrusive walls are complemented by lower panels in strand board, a rough-patterned material that oddly resembles marble; these screen off the conference room from the seventy-odd individual workstations, which are made of the same material. The workstations are arranged through the space, structuring it architecturally into a network of operative units composed of ingeniously dovetailed elements without any metal joints. Around the workstation area are various separate offices and meeting rooms equipped with tables (also in strand board) and some very elementary-looking chairs in hammered metal.

Ricavati in un ampio loft scandito dalle tradizionali colonne in ghisa e caratterizzato da un vecchio pavimento di legno, gli uffici del settimanale "Time Out" rispecchiano il carattere innovativo e informale della rivista che riporta con attenzione la selezione degli appuntamenti d'arte, culturali e del mondo dello spettacolo che avvengono in città. Il ristretto budget a disposizione ha indirizzato le scelte progettuali verso materiali economici, impiegati normalmente a livello industriale o per formare le strutture di muri e pannelli da rivestire con altre finiture. Tuttavia l'impiego creativo di materiali poveri, denunciati apertamente nel loro aspetto funzionale e nella loro finitura originaria, uniti a uno studio accurato della soluzione distributiva e del disegno degli arredi, si trasforma in questo caso in una soluzione architettonica convincente sia dal punto di vista dell'immagine complessiva, sia per quanto riguarda l'aspetto ergonomico e funzionale. Il loft è stato assunto come scatola architettonica unitaria; lo spazio interno mantiene così l'aspetto di spazio regolare stretto e lungo scandito dalla serie di colonne centrali verniciate di bianco affiancate dal nuovo condotto a sezione triangolare che ospita gli impianti telematici e i condotti dell'aria condizionata, sottolineando nel suo sviluppo rettilineo la dimensione dello spazio esistente. Le divisioni interne sono state costruite con pannelli divisori in materiale semitrasparente incorniciati con profili di bronzo e alluminio fissati a pavimento e a soffitto. Questa serie di pareti leggere ed evanescenti si affiancano a pannelli più bassi in medium density a trama larga, dall'inconsueto ed efficace effetto marmoreo, che separano alcune sale riunioni dalle settanta postazioni operative per i computer costruite con lo stesso materiale. Queste si propongono come arredi architettonici distribuiti nello spazio, serie di funzionali posti lavoro attrezzati, composti dall'incastro di superfici irregolari assemblate per gravità, senza l'ausilio di perni metallici. Alle postazioni distribuite secondo isole attrezzate, nel loft si affiancano alcuni uffici e sale riunioni con tavoli sempre in medium density e lineari sedie su disegno in lamiera metallica grezza.

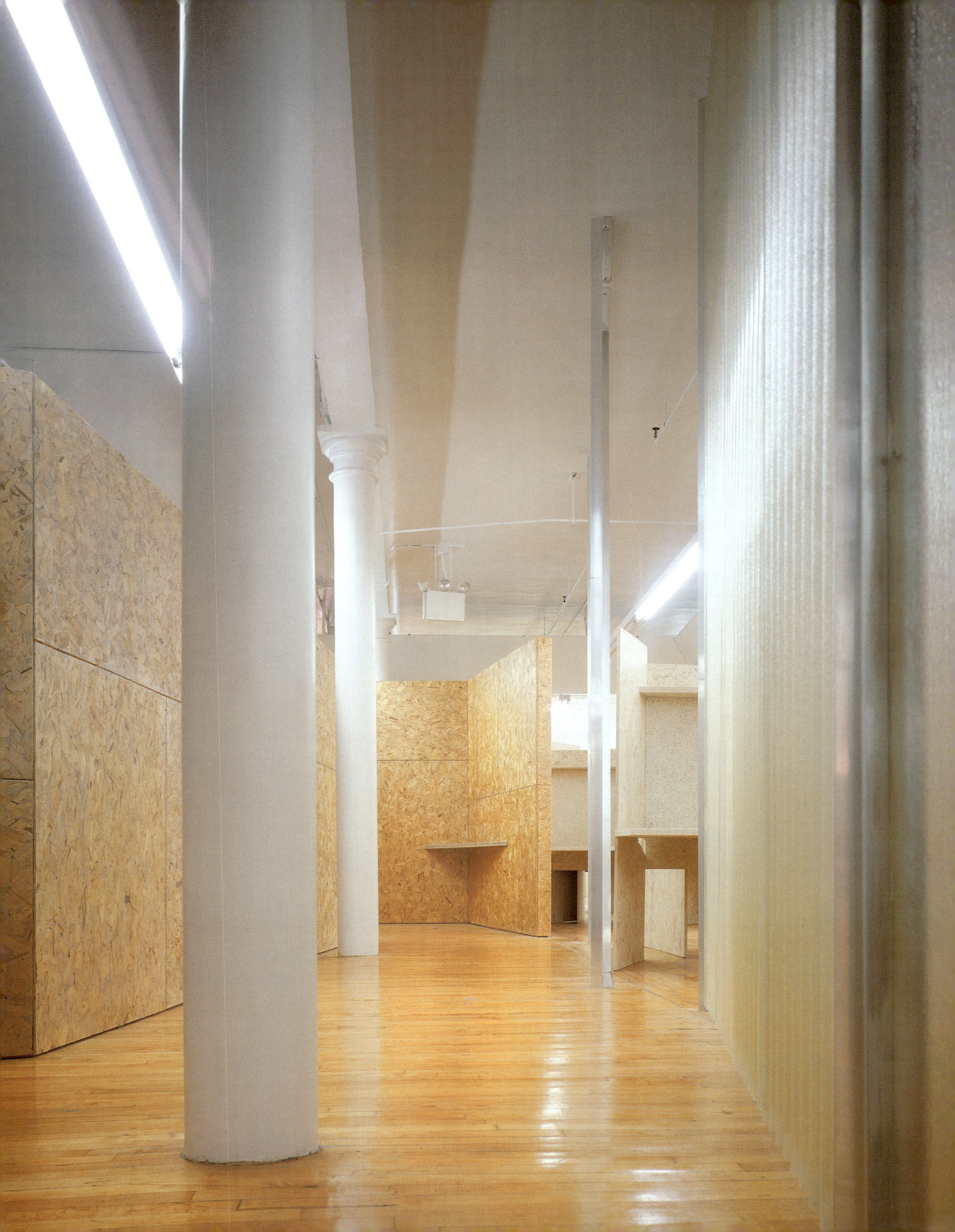

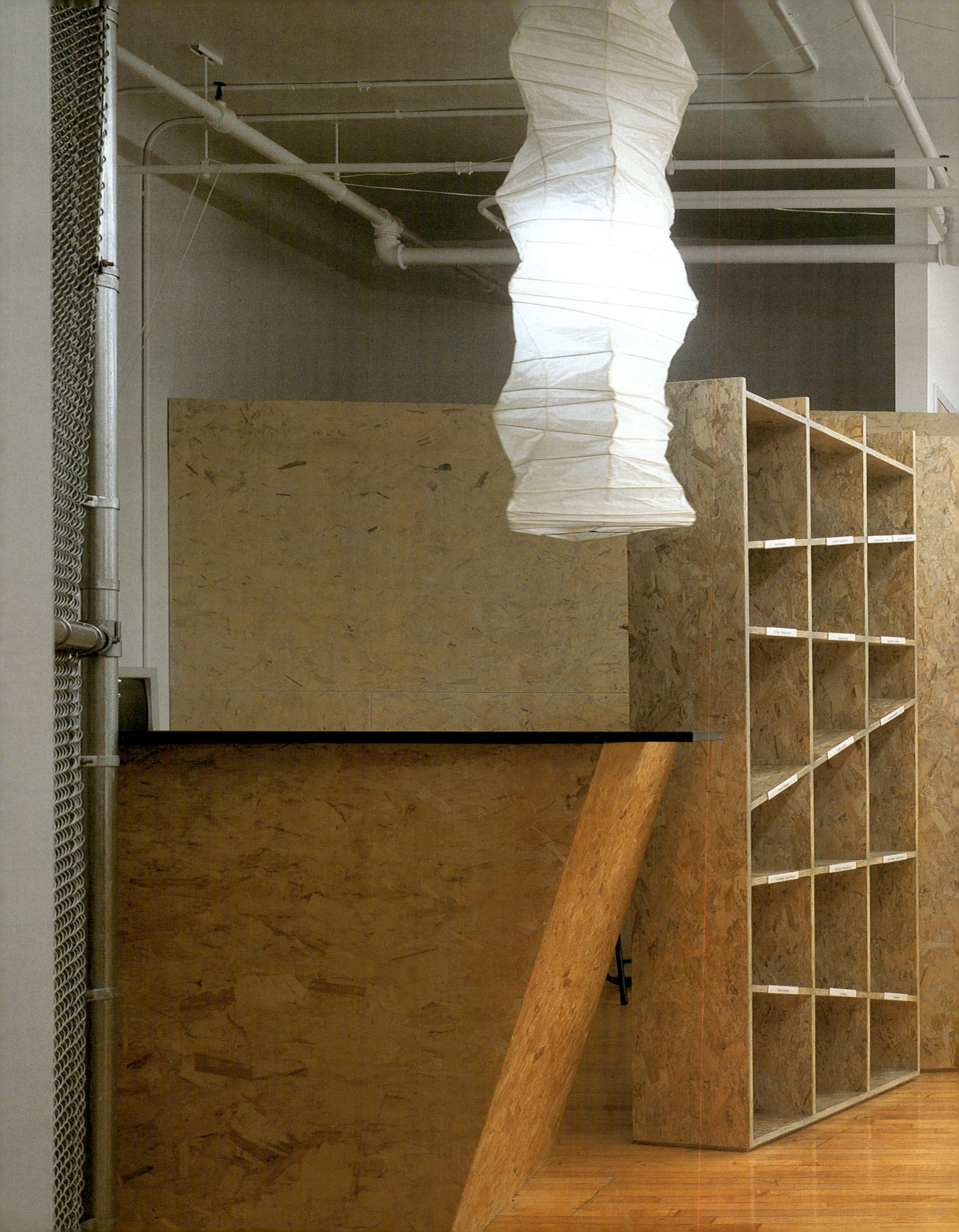

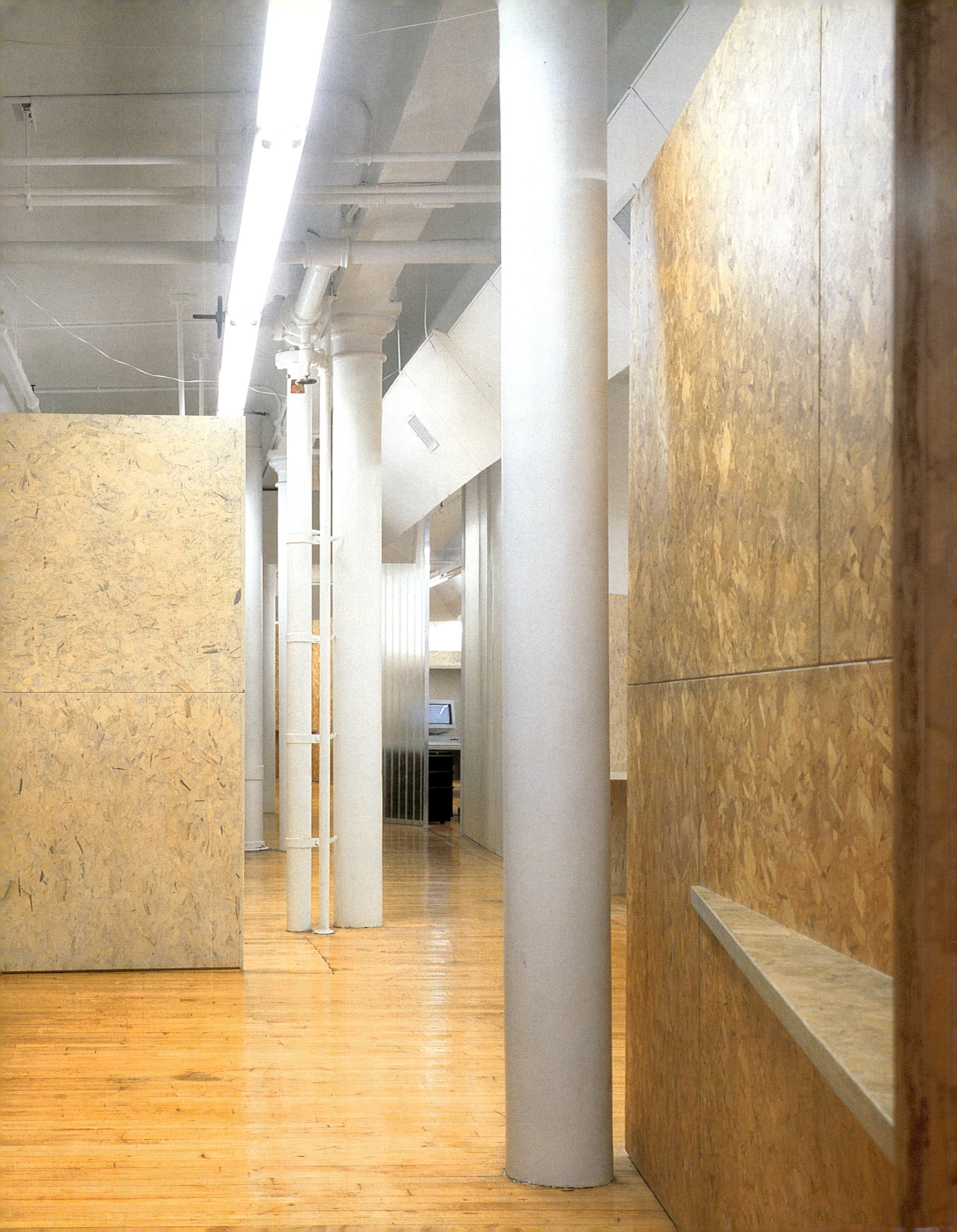

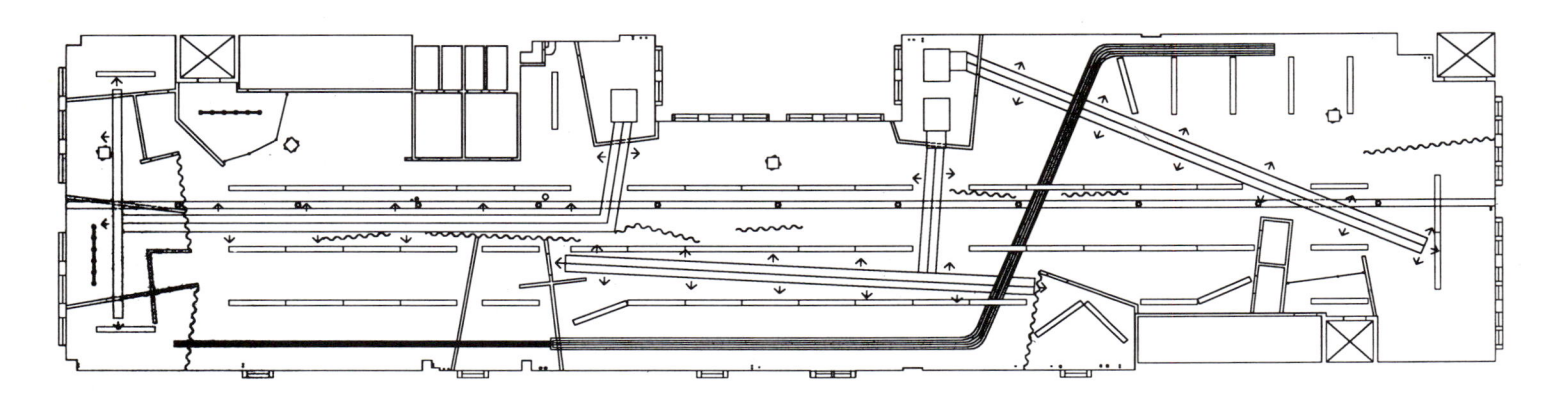

Plan / Pianta

Reflected ceiling plan / Pianta della disposizione a soffitto

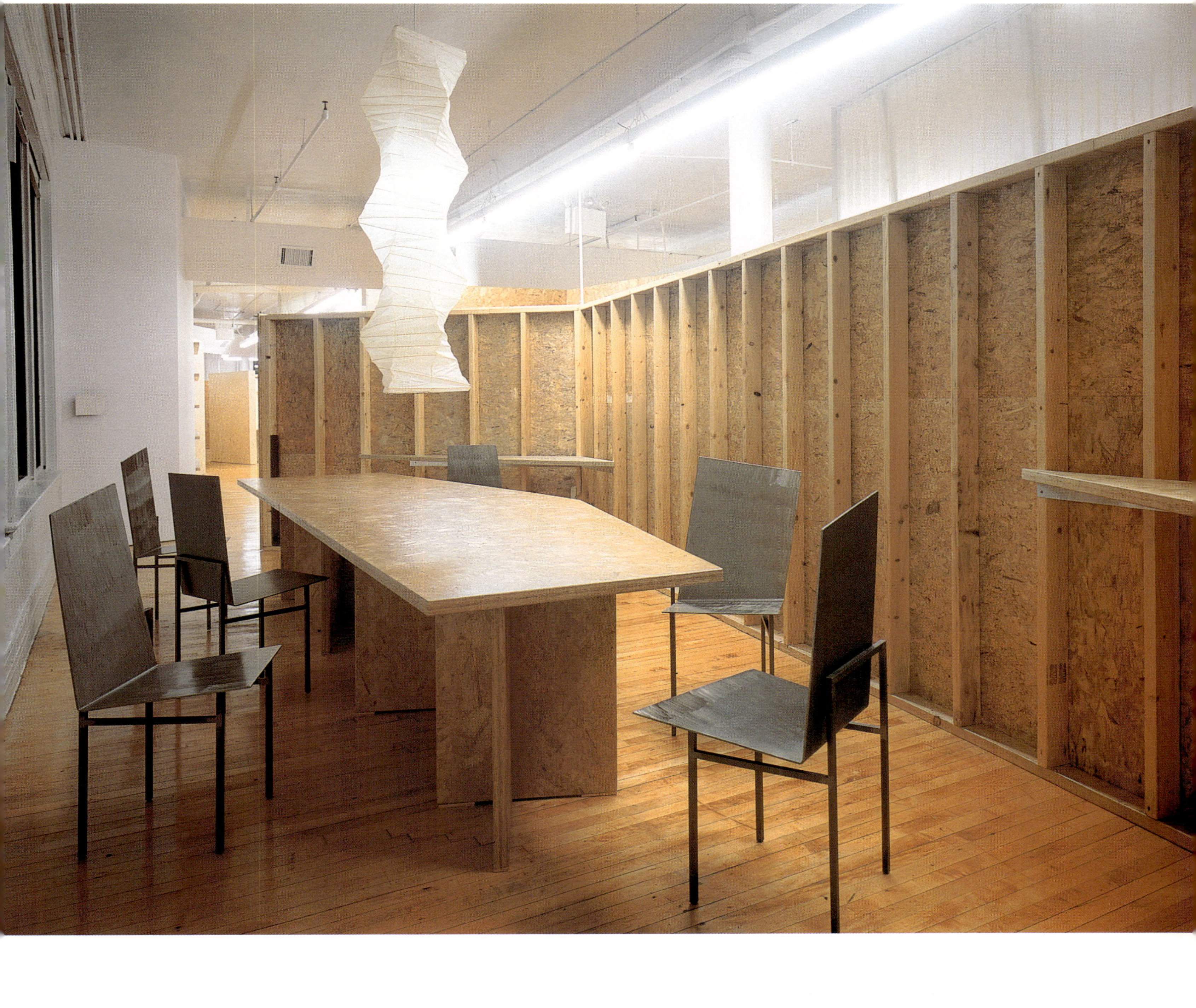

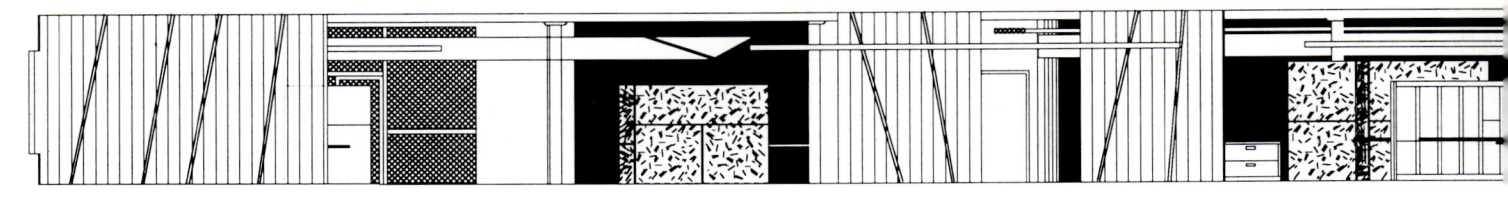

Section elevation / Sezione longitudinale

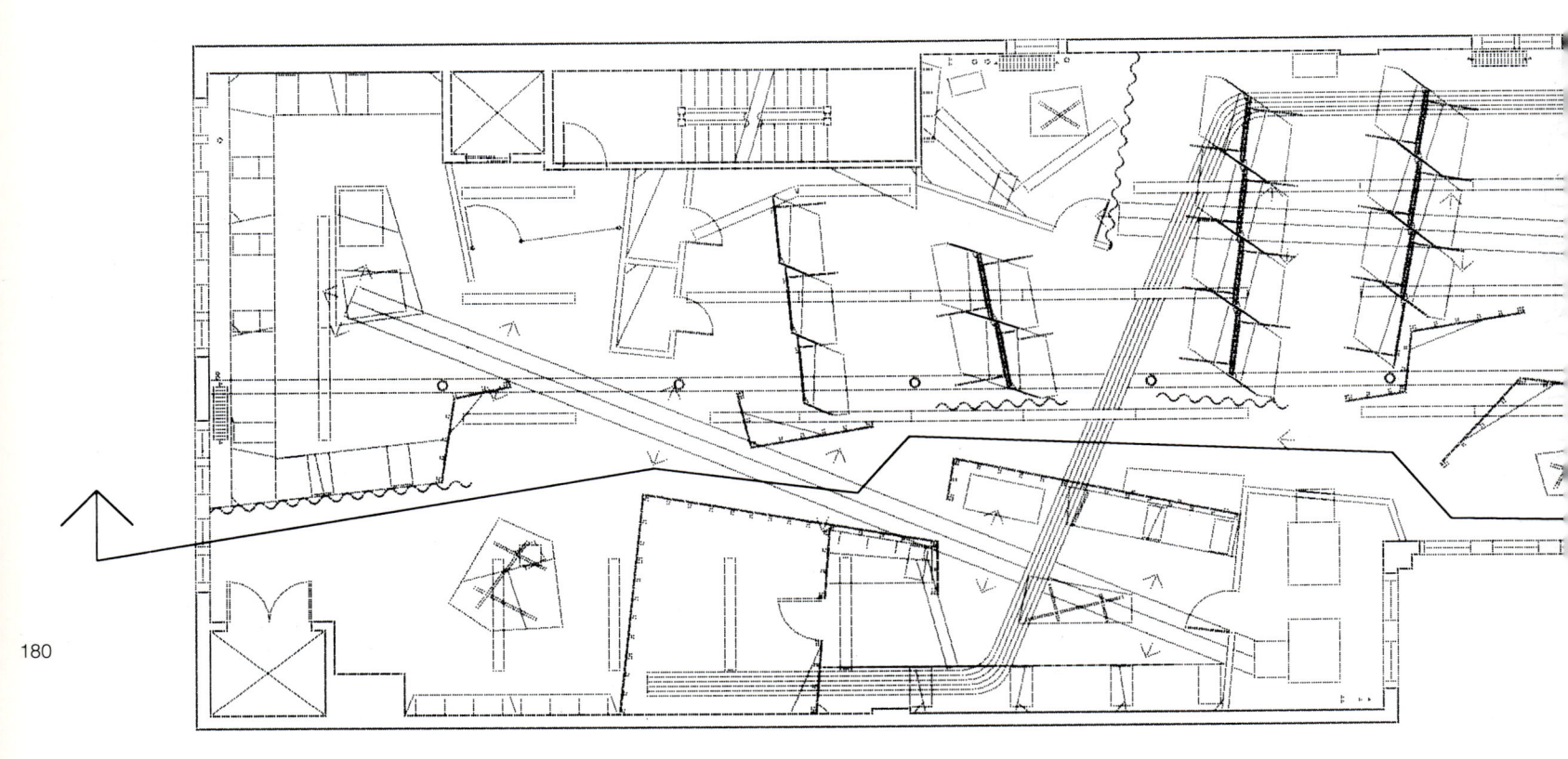

Plan / Pianta

181

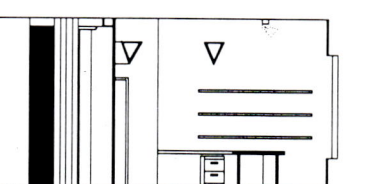

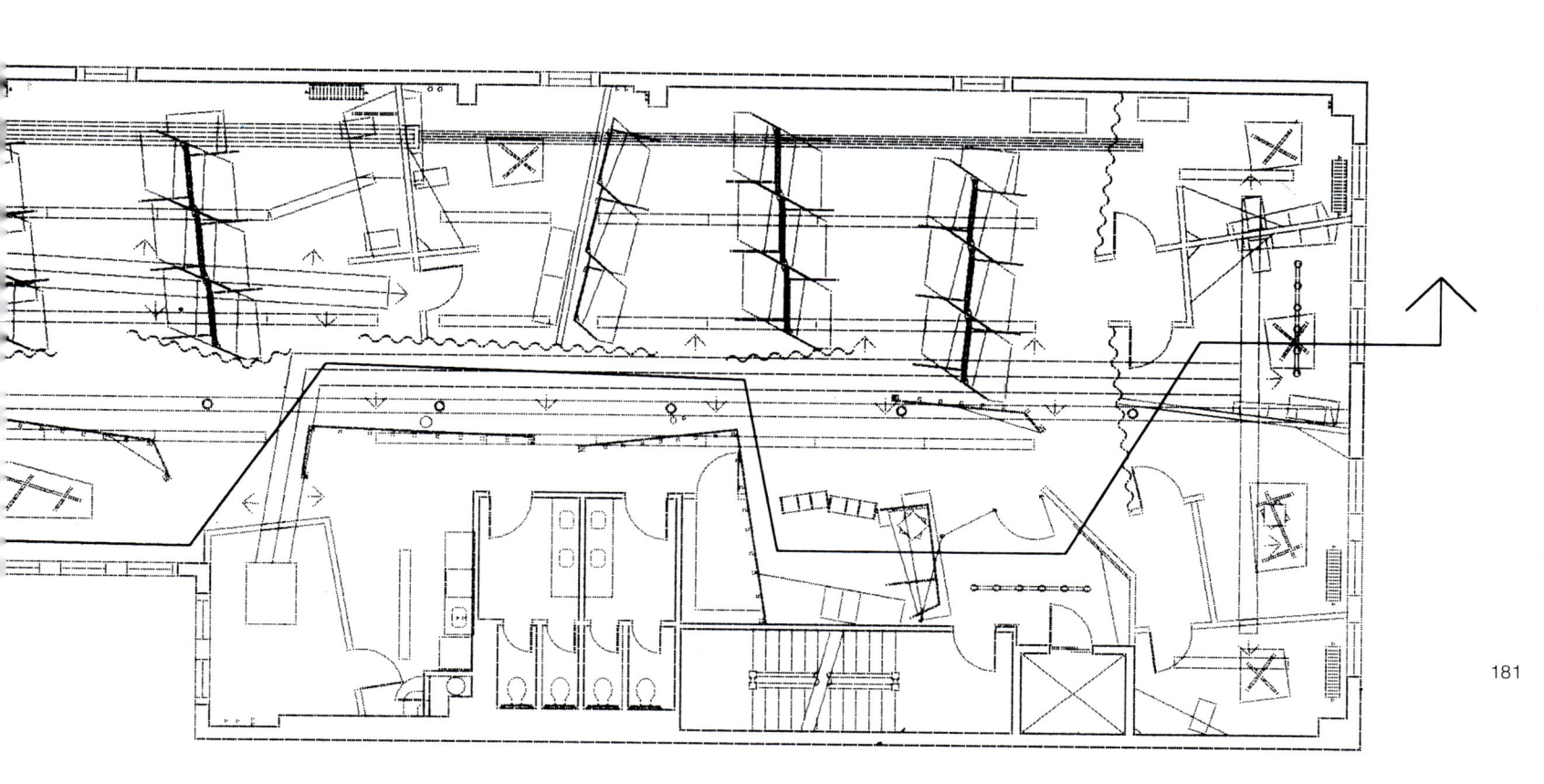

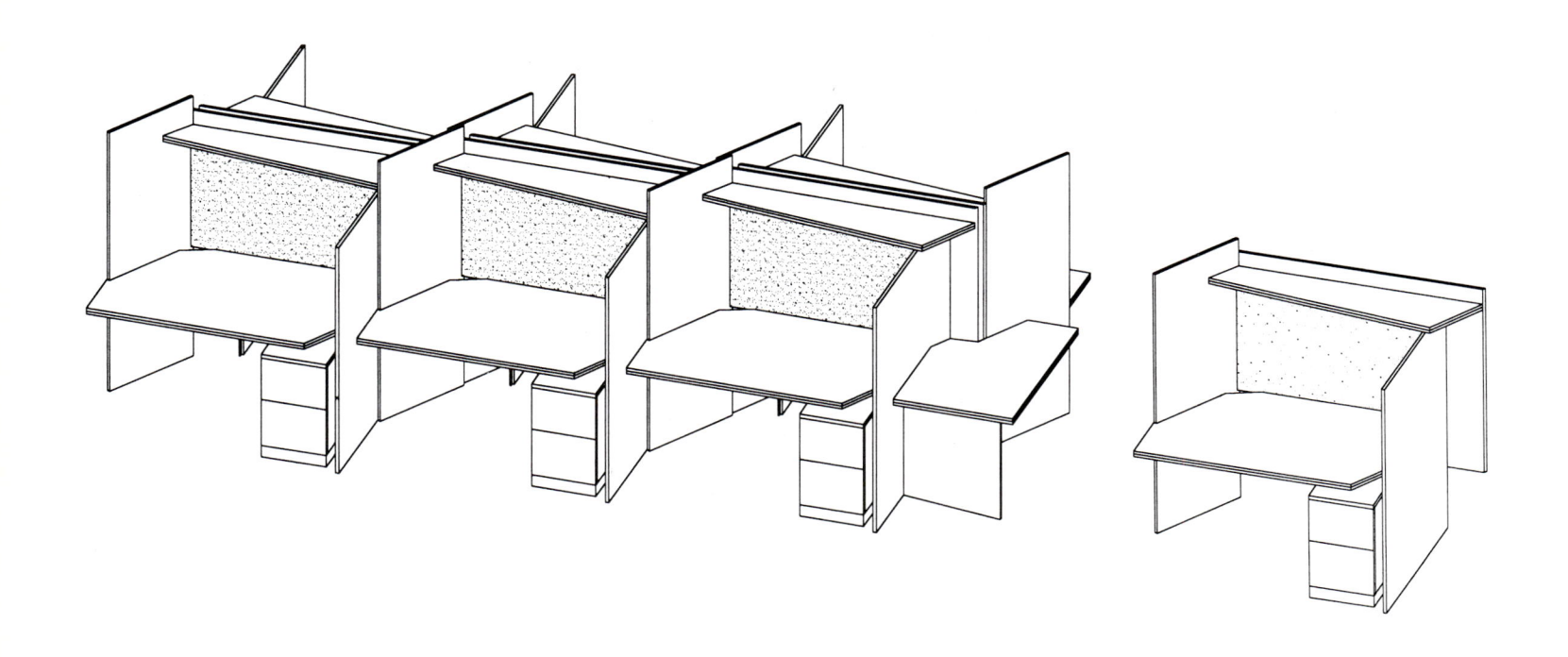

Axonometric of customized Workstations
Vista assonometrica delle postazioni di lavoro su disegno

182

183

TOMMY BOY

Turett Collaborative Architects. New York, NY, 1992–1997

Distributed on two levels of a converted factory space, the headquarters of Tommy Boy, a rap music record company, has favored a use of materials and style that is completely in tune with the informal nature of the record label. Both the original conversion scheme (1992), and the more recent enlargement on the floor below (1997), involved the use of standard materials and design solutions common to factory and commercial loft conversions. As is usual in this kind of redesign, the features of the original loft space are stressed by the exposed ductwork and other plants; but in this case the pre-existing cement floors have also been preserved, with their sporadic signs of wear and tear, sometimes quite conspicuous. The building's former destination as a factory is also hinted at by certain features typical of the creative remodeling ideas used on both levels. On the thirteenth story, a series of raw timber uprights stained pale green support beams of the same material and color, forming an architectural framework that marks off the central zone. Two long corridors lined with offices run a circuit round this wooden framework, which encloses a series of workstations arranged on an open plan and configured by low walls in unfaced cinder blocks. The corridor is lit by curious truncated neon lamps fitted to unworked metal fittings, creating a quirky luminous geometry along the distribution routes. The timber framework terminates in a curved wall of aluminum paneling and a circular meeting room finished in the same material; grafted into the outer corner of the room is a cube-shaped entryway faced in strongly veined veneer. The reception area has unquestionable visual impact: irregular-shaped black prisms of loudspeakers double up as wall and ceiling fixtures. These are upstaged by an array of brightly colored pieces of furniture that vie with the back wall mounted with photographs of the recording artists on the Tommy Boy label. The recent extension on the twelfth floor endorses the design philosophy expressed on the story above, with the addition of new ideas, such as the circular enclosure for the staircase that accesses the next floor. An assortment of uncustomary facilities are accommodated on this floor (rooms for aerobics, yoga, and weightlifting), enhancing the brightly colored environment, which is well-lit thanks particularly to the translucent ceilings and backlighting of the long corridors.

Distribuita su due livelli di un edificio industriale a loft sovrapposti, la sede della Tommy Boy, casa discografica di musica rap, appare in sintonia stilistica e materica con il carattere informale dell'etichetta. Sia il primo intervento del 1992, sia il recente ampliamento al piano sottostante hanno visto l'impiego di materiali e soluzioni standard, usati di solito nei magazzini industriali e nei loft commerciali. Il carattere dei loft originari è sottolineato anche dagli impianti a vista e dalla conservazione dei pavimenti di cemento preesistenti, che recano ancora macchie indelebili e a volte vistose, residui delle antiche lavorazioni. Tale vocazione di laboratorio industriale è poi richiamata da una serie di soluzioni che caratterizzano creativamente entrambi gli interventi. Al tredicesimo piano, una serie di setti in legno grezzo tinteggiati all'anilina a poro aperto in colore verde, su cui poggiano travi orizzontali dello stesso materiale e colore, formano una struttura architettonica compiuta che segna con forza la zona centrale. Due lunghi corridoi, su cui si affaccia una serie di uffici, corrono lungo la struttura lignea che contiene una serie di postazioni operative a open space, scandite da muretti in laterizio a vista. Delle riuscite lampade al neon, sostenute da snodi in ferro grezzo, formano un'inconsueta geometria luminosa lungo i percorsi distributivi. La struttura in legno è conclusa da una parete in curva di alluminio e da una sala riunioni circolare dello stesso materiale in cui si innesta, con felice salto compositivo e materico, un cubo-portale rivestito in legno venato. Di grande impatto la zona reception, con una serie di casse acustiche nere impiegate come rivestimento parietale a prismi irregolari. Questi sono alternati a una serie di arredi colorati che ben si rapportano alla parete luminosa con le foto degli artisti della 'Tommy Boy". Il recente ampliamento del dodicesimo piano riprende la stessa filosofia del piano superiore e alcune soluzioni, come la zona circolare interna da cui si sviluppa la nuova scala di collegamento. Una serie di inconsuete funzioni (sala aerobica, per lo Yoga, sollevamento pesi) caratterizzano il nuovo livello, incrementando il comfort dello spazio di lavoro, colorato e luminoso, anche grazie alle pareti e ai soffitti traslucidi e retroilluminati che definiscono i lunghi corridoi.

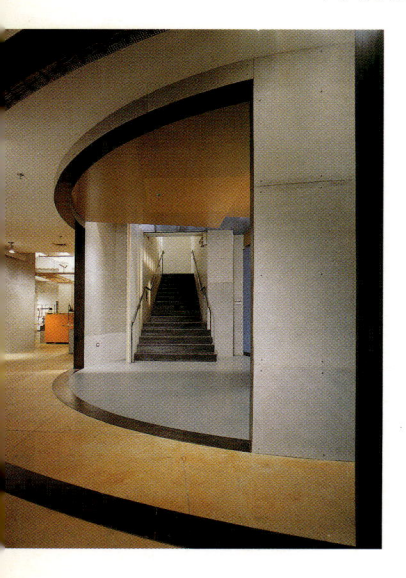

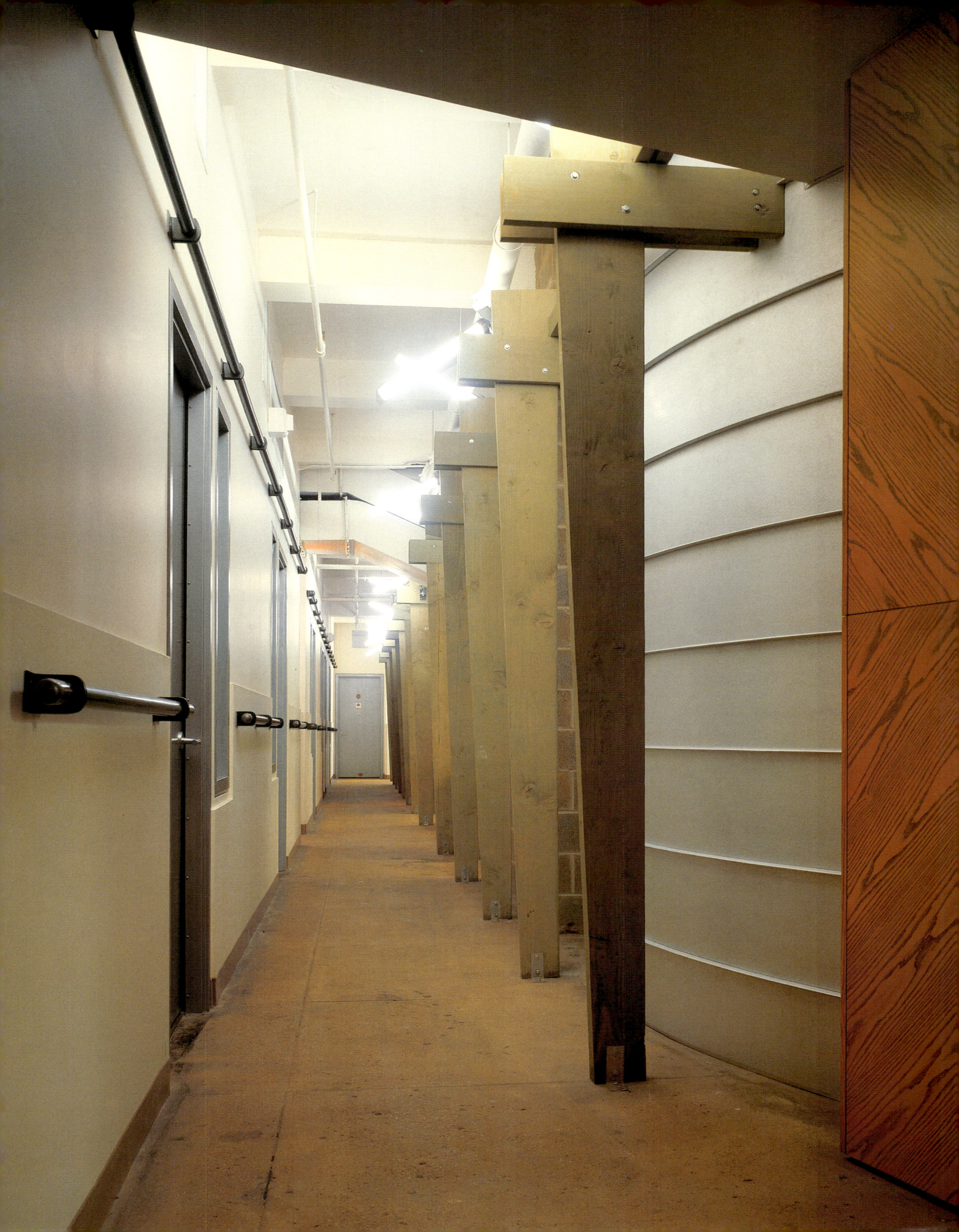

186

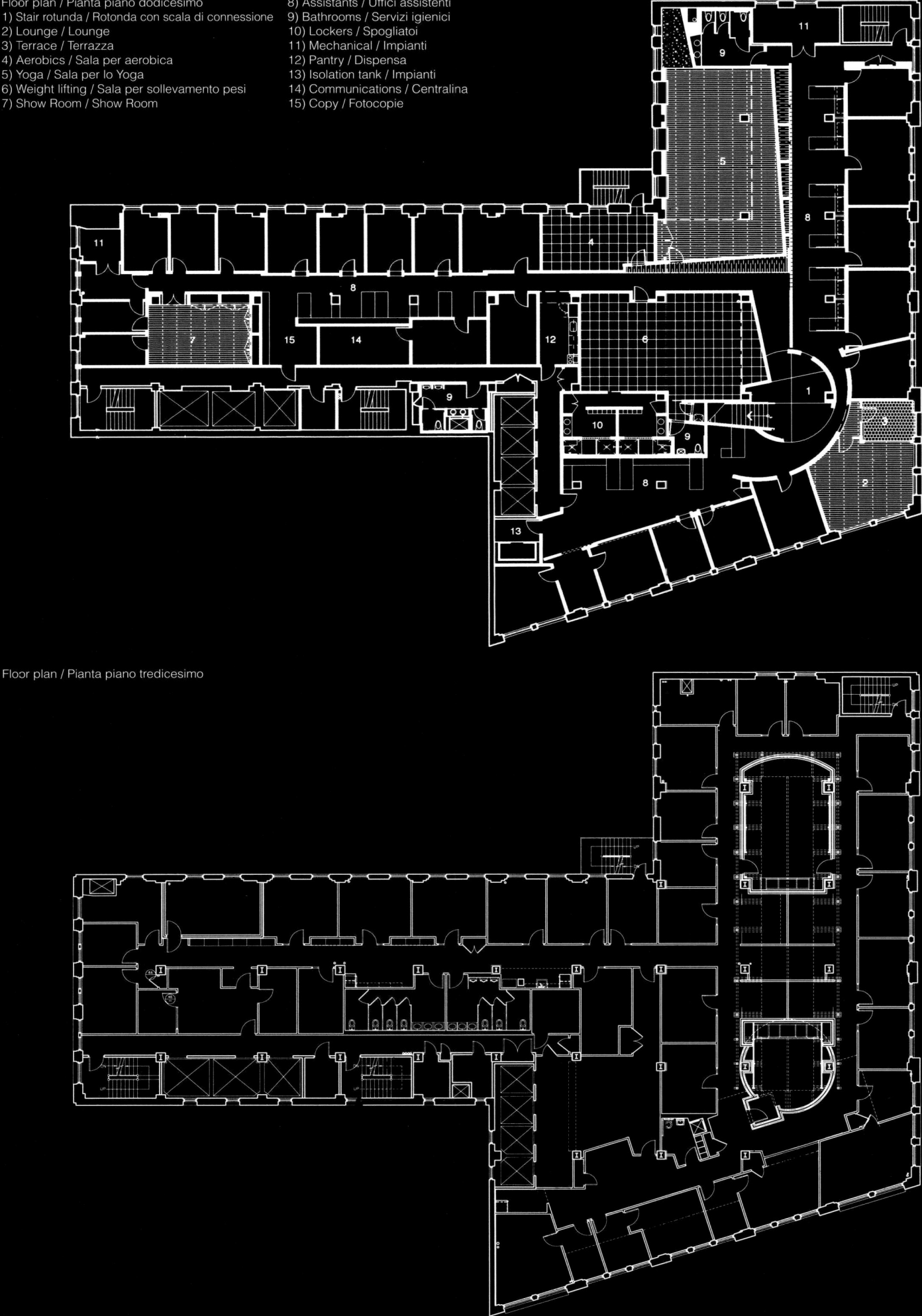

Floor plan / Pianta piano dodicesimo
1) Stair rotunda / Rotonda con scala di connessione
2) Lounge / Lounge
3) Terrace / Terrazza
4) Aerobics / Sala per aerobica
5) Yoga / Sala per lo Yoga
6) Weight lifting / Sala per sollevamento pesi
7) Show Room / Show Room
8) Assistants / Uffici assistenti
9) Bathrooms / Servizi igienici
10) Lockers / Spogliatoi
11) Mechanical / Impianti
12) Pantry / Dispensa
13) Isolation tank / Impianti
14) Communications / Centralina
15) Copy / Fotocopie

Floor plan / Pianta piano tredicesimo

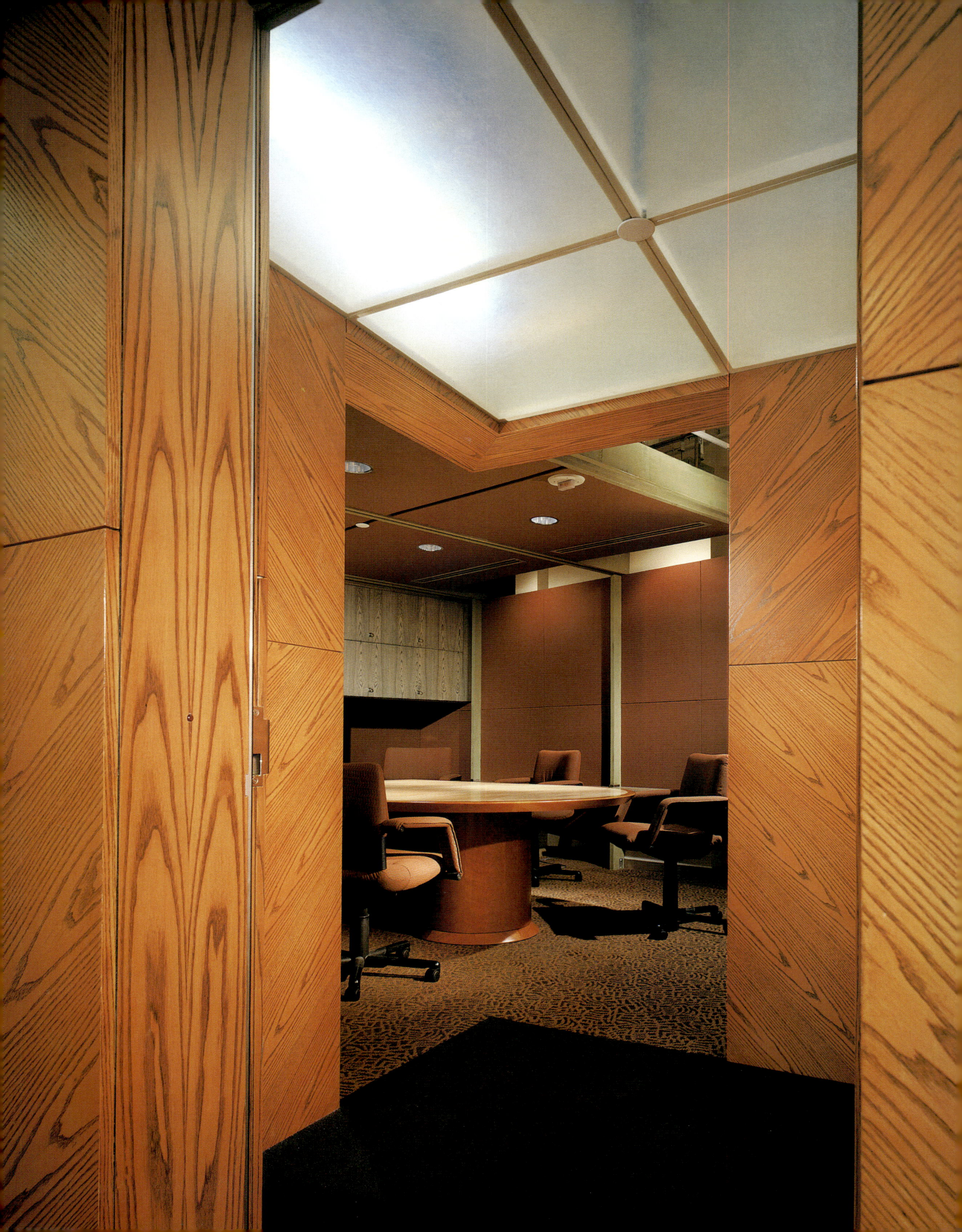

189

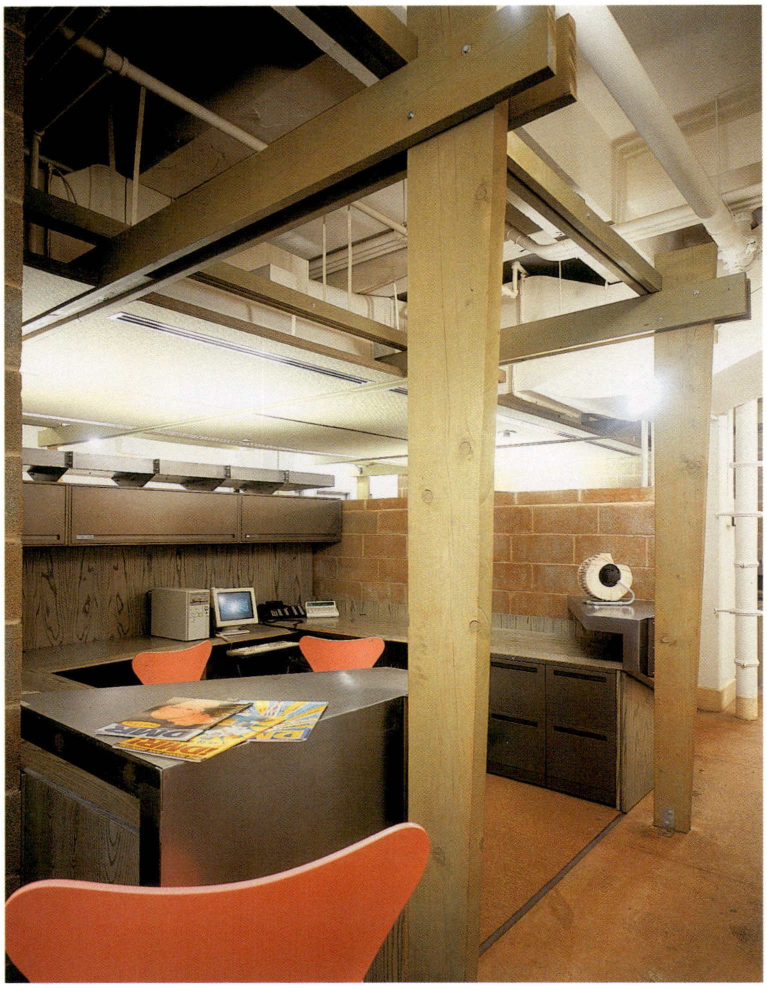

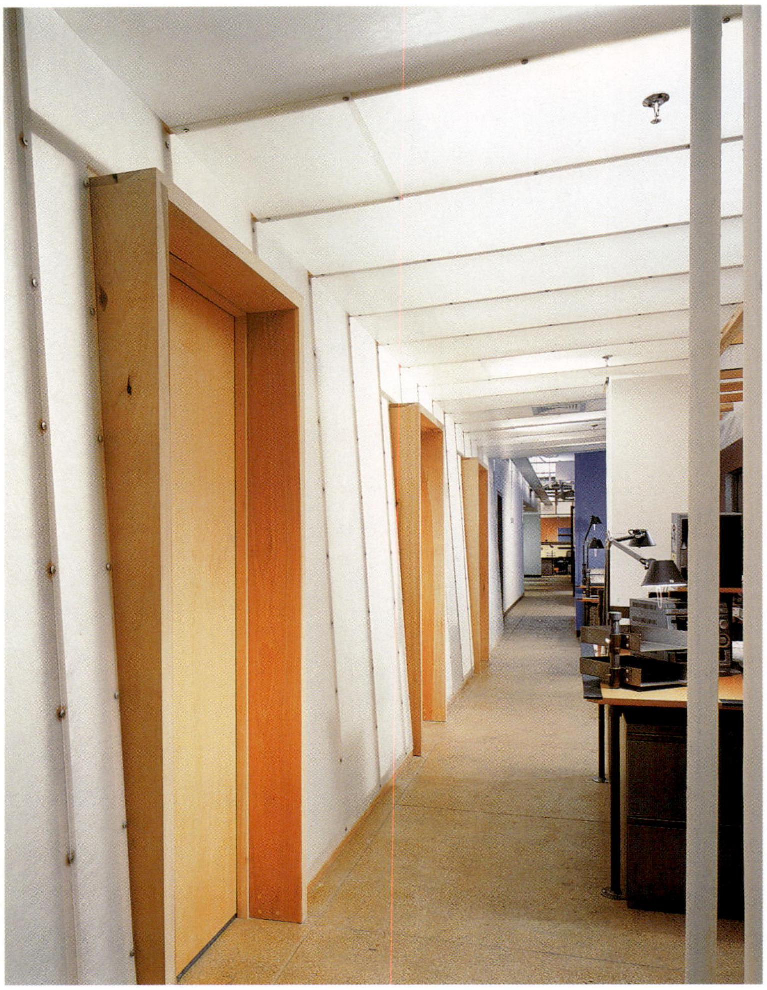

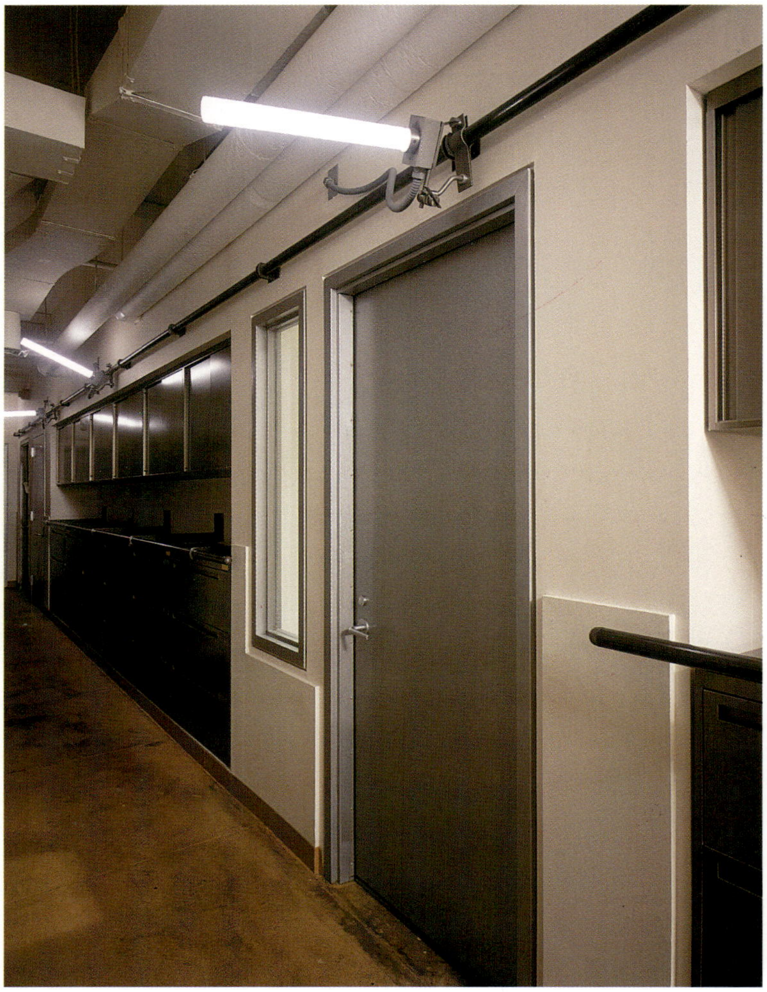

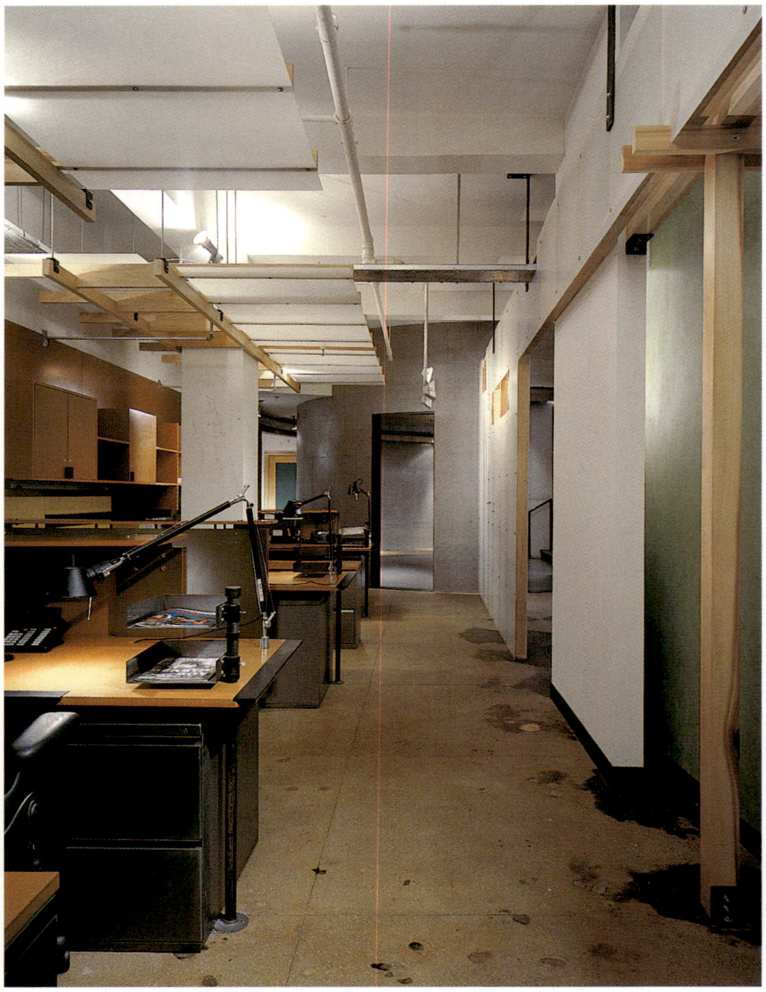

191

192

193

VARET MARCUS & FINK
STUDIOS Architecture. Washington, DC, 1992

This project for the head offices of a major legal consultancy in Washington prompted the architects to apply certain select design elements whose interaction would establish a set of distribution routes and view-lines that would endow the office suite with a memorable impression, while duly addressing the functional needs expressed in the client's brief. The entire composition of the new interiors hinges on two main circulation spines set at rightangles to each other. These axes issue from the circular reception area that gives straight onto the elevator lobby, which is animated by pilasters in sheet metal and can be screened off by an intriguing sliding partition in metal mesh trimmed with the same material. Brushed sheet metal is also used for part of the reception desk itself, which is completed by a heavy block of veined marble. The cylindrical space of the reception lobby, whose walls are finished in blue stucco, underscores the geometric design of the floor, which is paved in the same veined marble as the desk; while the orthogonal circulation routes that intersect the space interrupt the continuity, underlining the interlocking effect, an interruption that is further accentuated by the abrupt change of materials from blue stucco to pale mahogany veneer. Each of the two axes creates a prominent perspective, particularly because of the clever splaying of the walls. One axis leads off left toward the library, the other right to the meeting room beyond the elevator lobby; the other axis proceeds down past a small lounge and through a series of swiveling doors in sanded glass to the main conference room. A doorway off this lounge gives access to a smaller meeting room secluded behind a transparent wall of glass panes decorated with sanded vertical strips. In the anteroom here a structural pillar has been deftly exploited as a sculptural feature, neatly finished in pale yellow stucco. Meanwhile, through the operations halls, a succession of stout archways in blue stucco mark another architectural pathway, creating an additional perspectival vista.

Il progetto degli spazi di lavoro per uno studio legale è stata occasione per sperimentare l'impiego di una serie di elementi architettonici capaci di creare nel loro incastro compositivo una serie di precisi percorsi e scorci prospettici in grado di rispondere alle esigenze funzionali della committenza e allo stesso tempo di costruire una forte immagine di riferimento. L'intera disposizione degli uffici ruota intorno all'incastro di due percorsi distributivi principali, ortogonali, incernierati tra loro nell'incastro dello spazio cilindrico della reception d'ingresso. Questa è direttamente rivolta verso il pianerottolo degli ascensori, enfatizzati da una serie di lesene in lamiera, ma ne è schermata (come la sala riunioni che ne segna l'estremità opposta) da una forte griglia metallica contenuta in un infisso dello stesso materiale, caratterizzato da un accurato disegno geometrico. Lamiera metallica grezza spazzolata è impiegata anche per definire il forte volume irregolare del mobile reception, cui si affianca un parallelepipedo in marmo bianco venato. Lo spazio cilindrico dell'ingresso-reception, dalle superfici parietali trattate a stucco azzurro, sottolinea la sua forma geometrica elementare nel disegno della pavimentazione che riprende lo stesso materiale lapideo del banco reception, mentre i percorsi ortogonali che lo attraversano ne interrompono la continuità volumetrica sottolineandone l'incastro anche con il cambiamento materico delle pareti rivestite in mogano chiaro. I due percorsi creano delle forti prospettive (accentuate anche dalla voluta strombatura delle pareti) rispettivamente tra una sala riunioni e biblioteca, e tra reception e sala riunioni principale. Questa, con tavolo su disegno in metallo spazzolato e piano in legno, è ubicata, dopo una zona di attesa, dietro una serie di porte di cristallo sabbiato girevoli su perno centrale. Di fianco alla sala riunioni principale è organizzata una sala riunioni di dimensioni minori. Delle lastre di vetro sabbiato a strisce verticali la separano dalla sala d'attesa prospiciente, dove un pilastro strutturale è stato trasformato in elemento plastico: un cilindro decorato con stucco giallo. Una serie di forti portali, trattati a stucco azzurro, sono ripetuti nelle zone operative, definendo un ulteriore percorso architettonico, prospettiva interna che si aggiunge a quelle di riferimento principali.

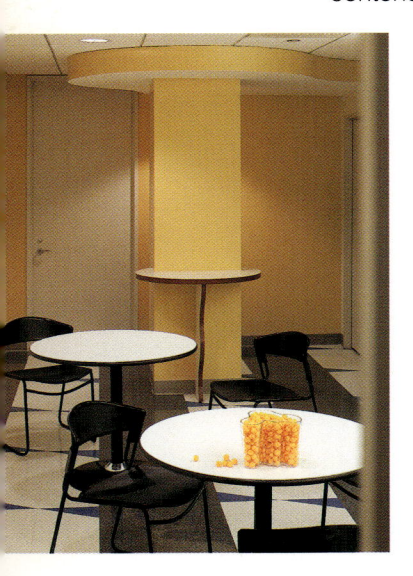

Varet
Marcus
& Fink P.C.

196

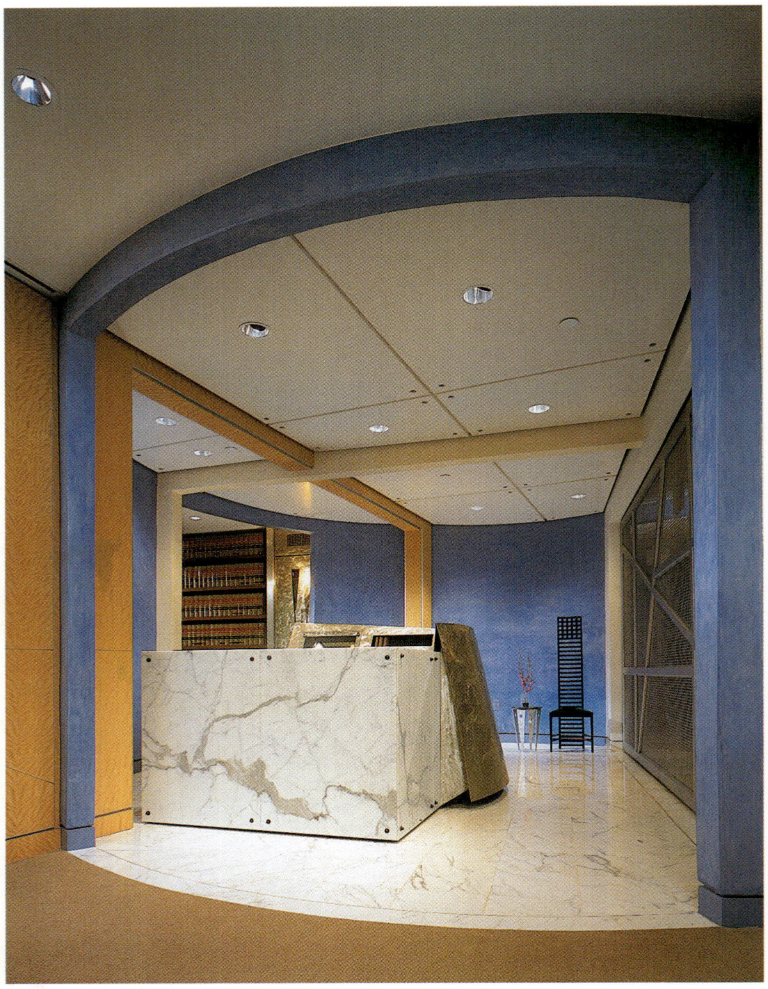

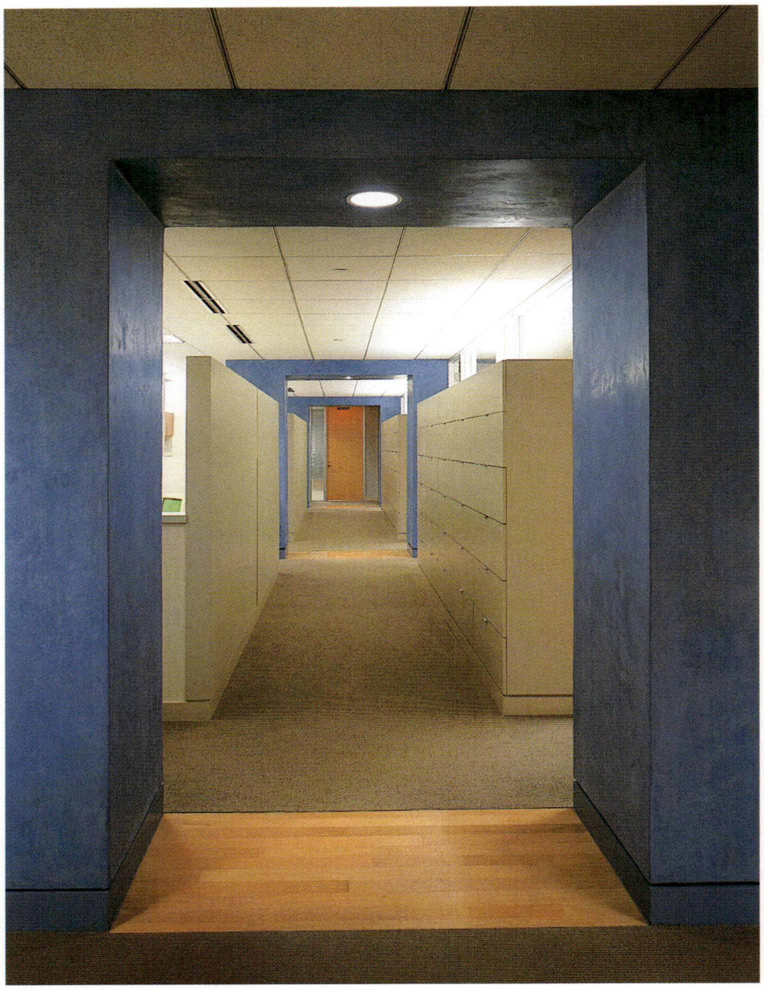

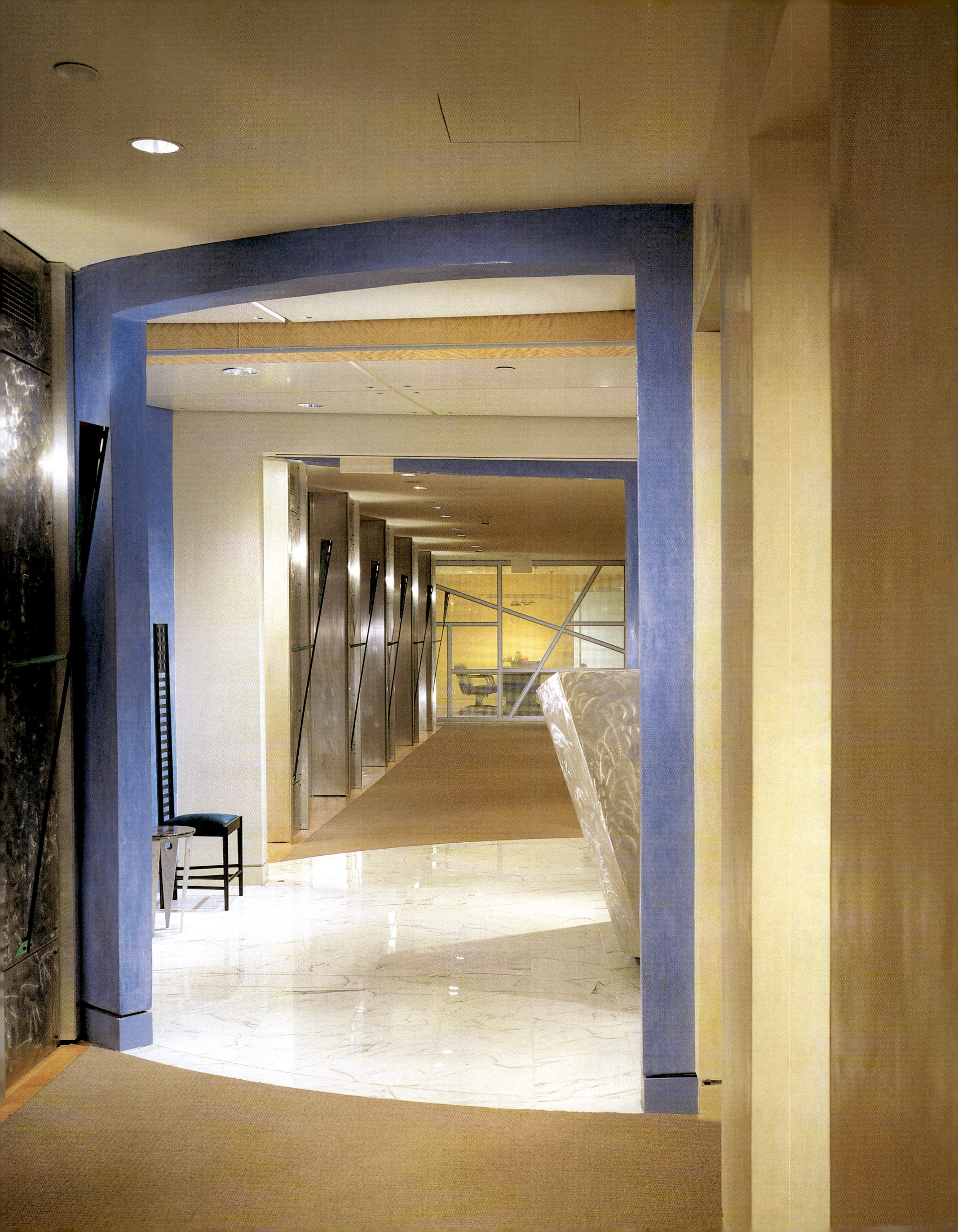

Axonometric sketch / Schizzo assonometrico

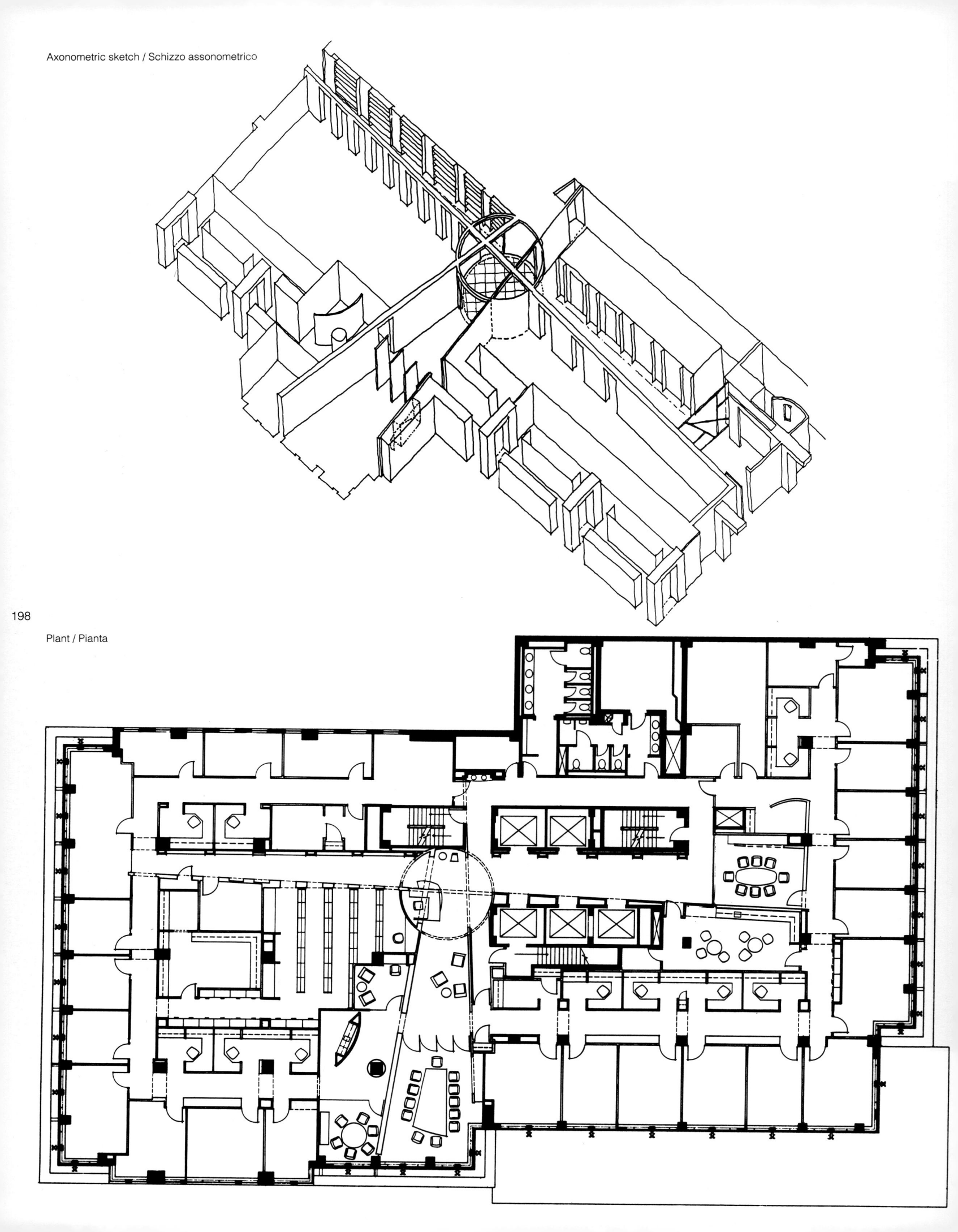

Plant / Pianta

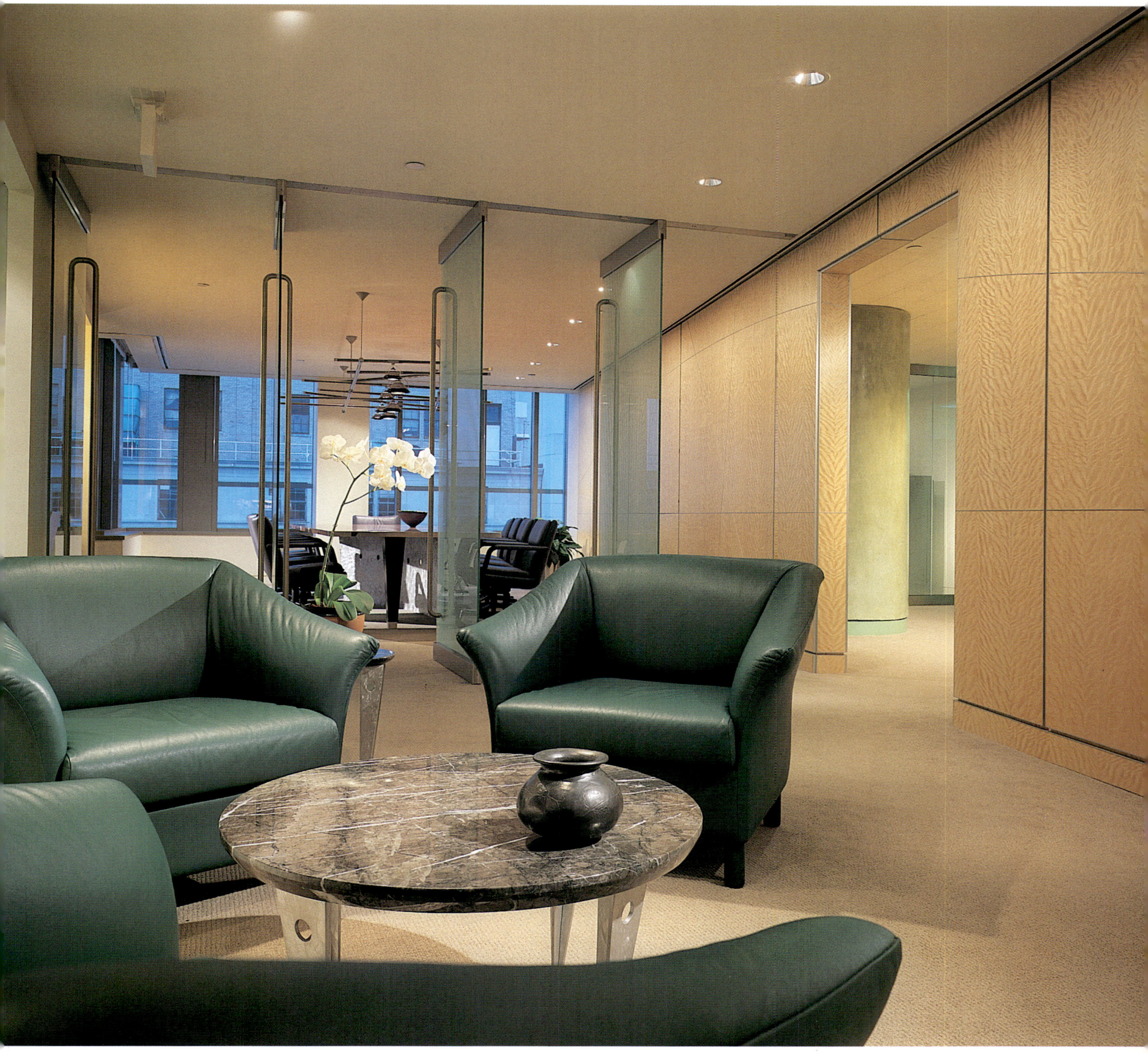

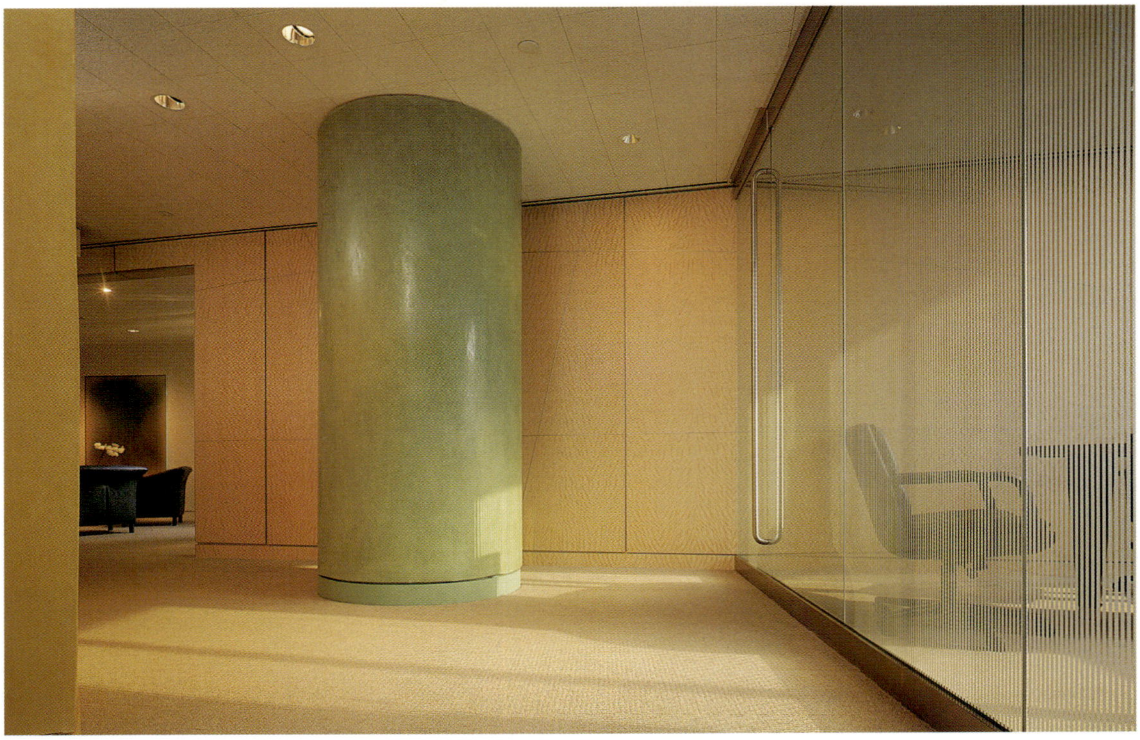

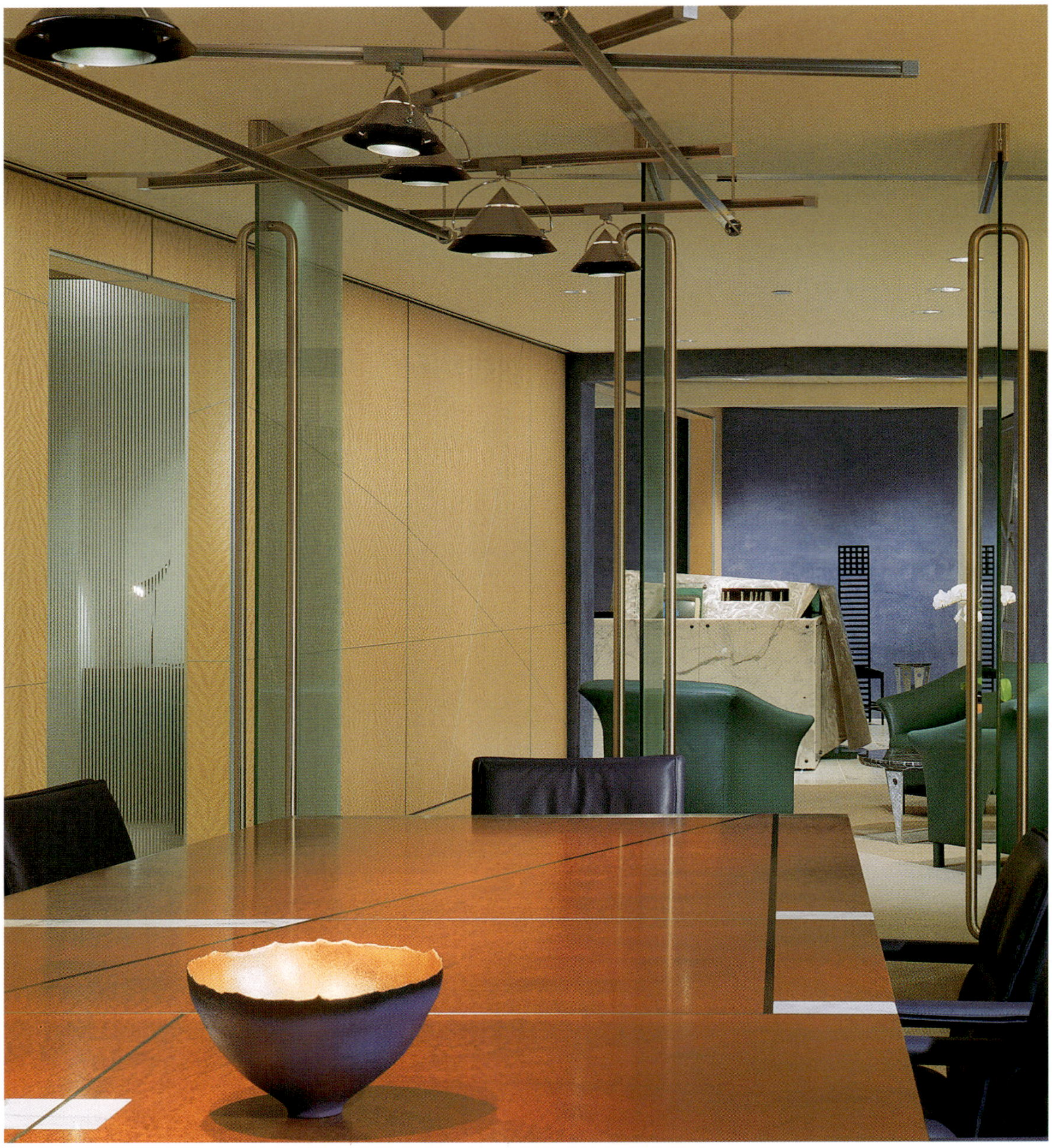

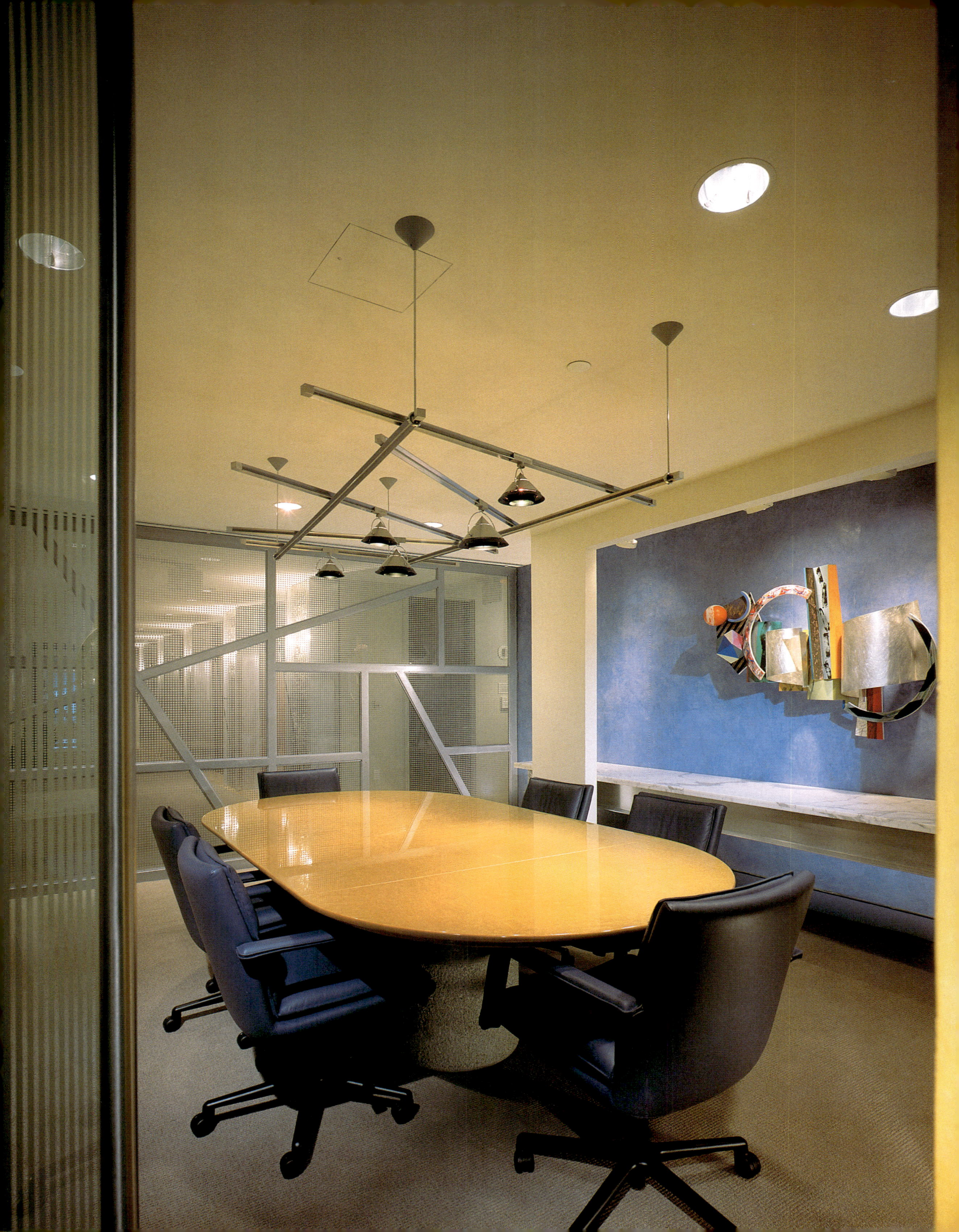

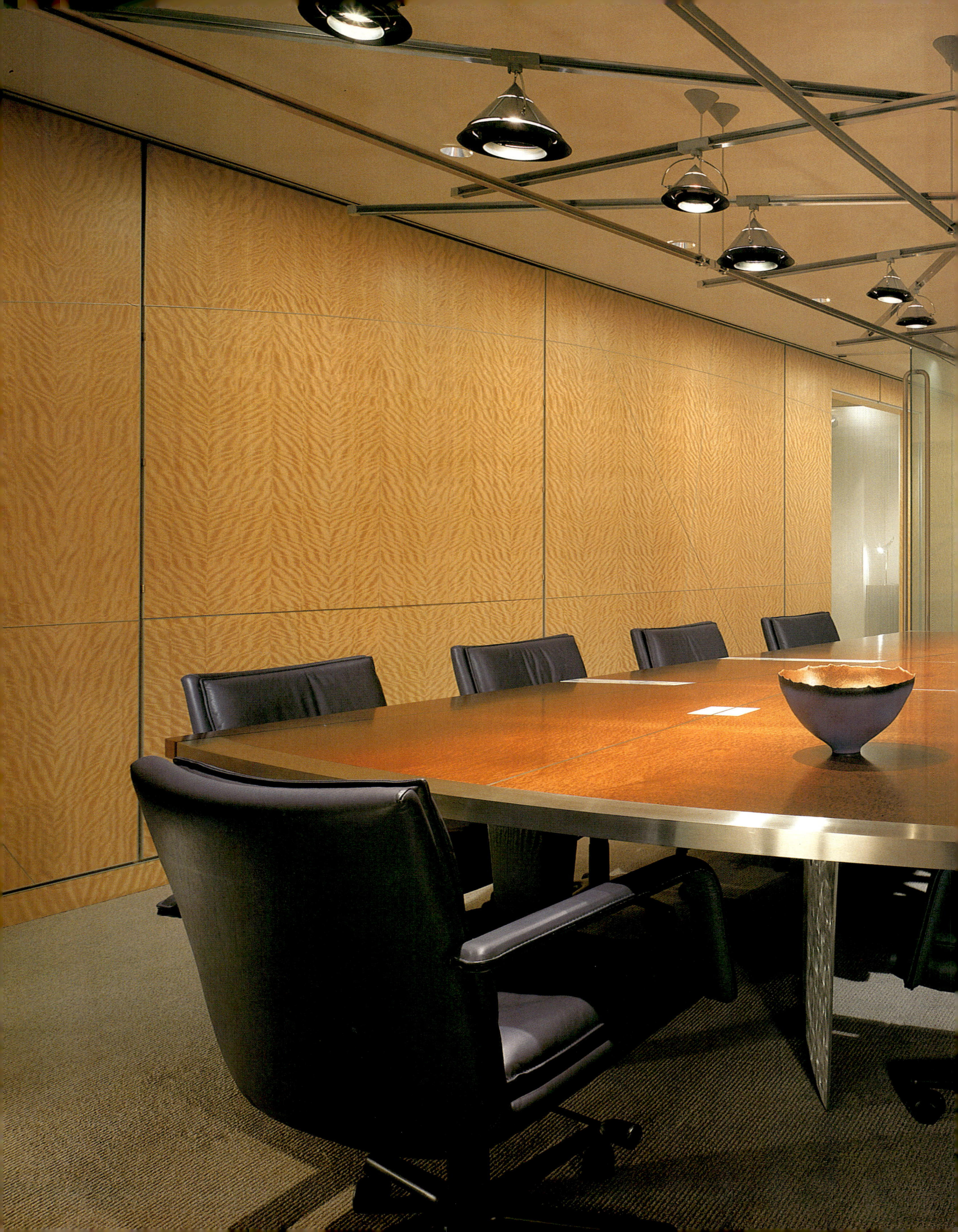

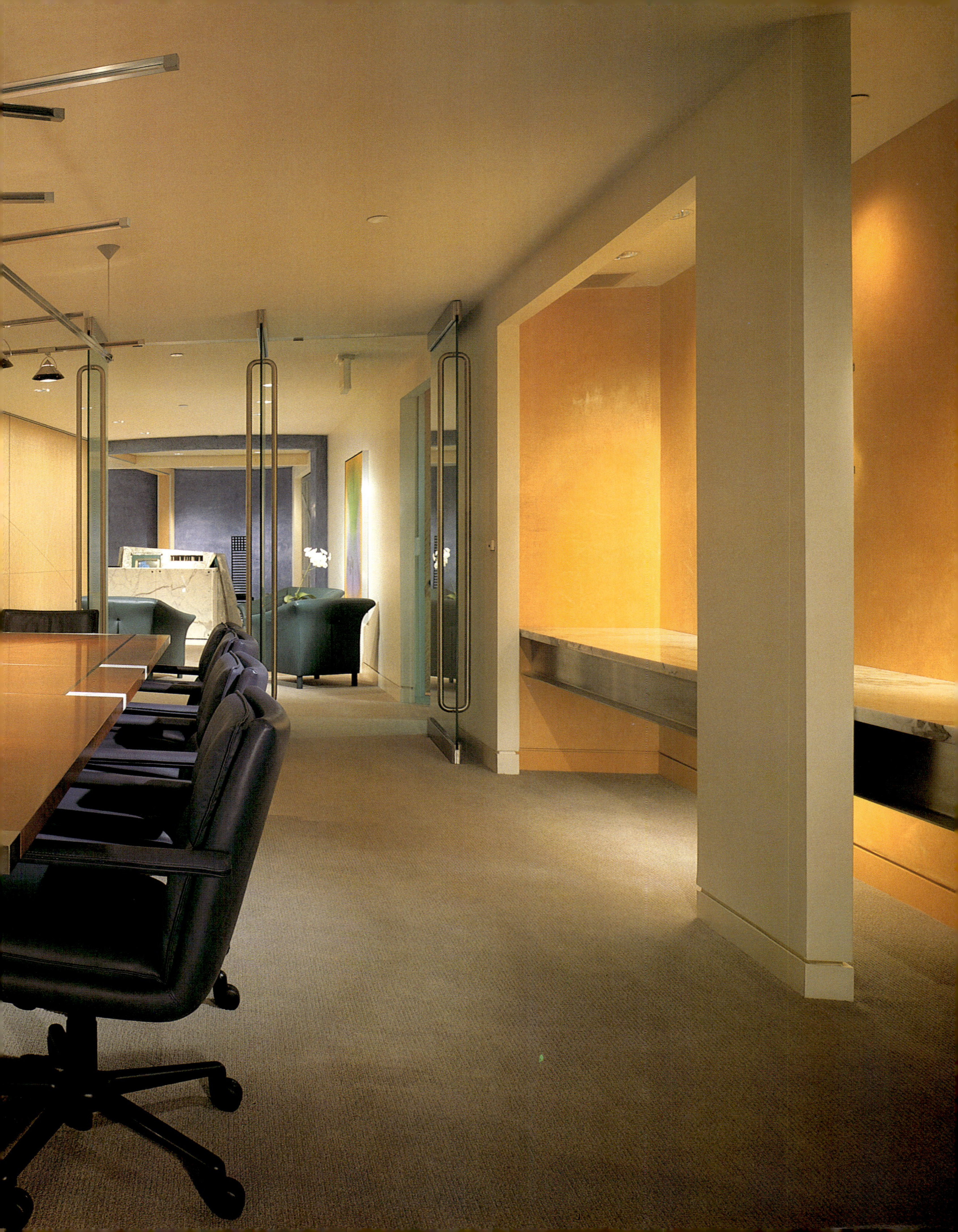

W.B. DONER

KressCox Associates, P.C. Baltimore, MD, 1994

Distributed on two stories of the host building, the corporate headquarters of W. B. Doner present an interesting gamut of different types of workstation whose adroitly optimized layout is devised to take complete advantage of the available floor space. The individual offices and meeting rooms are ranged around the building perimeter, and separated from the interior by an elaborate custom-designed wall-system composed of alternating wooden panels and sanded glass which stop shy of the ceiling, thereby allowing the natural light to penetrate the interior of the suites. The elevator lobby leads straight into double-height atrium, forming a distinctive gathering and distribution point from which a striking staircase leads off to the upper office level. This spacious foyer area takes good advantage of the full-height glazing in the south prospect, offering a superb panoramic view of the harbor. Close by the entrance area, with its handsome floor in gray slate echoing the color of the water in the bay outside, is an elegant and brightly lit visitors' lounge in front of a circular reception desk. Still in the reception area, a cylindrical column in unfaced concrete props up the corner of one of the upstairs presentation rooms, notable for its cladding of galvanized metal and sheets of oxidized copper, a device adopted for the other principal working rooms of the headquarters (i.e., conference and presentation rooms); like other features of the interiors, these materials all pay homage to the industrial streetscape of the port below. The main presentation room, set frontally to the preceding one, is distinguished by a large sloping window that describes a sweeping curve, an invention that is echoed in the curvature of the large conference table at the center. The industrial scenario in the harbor also prompted the decision to leave all the cables, tubes, and ducting visible, and allow an unabashed view of the concrete ceilings with their network of coffers painted white with black "shadows" following the pattern of the grille-like bulkheads suspended from metal stays. The ceiling patterns are also mirrored in the carpet design, with patches of light and dark, reiterating on two levels (ceiling and floor) the scheme of the suspended grille, which extends through the open spaces providing visual continuity.

Sviluppati su due livelli, gli uffici della W.B. Doner offrono diverse tipologie di posti lavoro all'interno di uno sfruttamento ottimale e razionale dello spazio disponibile. Lungo le facciate sono disposti gli uffici operativi e le sale riunione, separati dall'interno con un elegante sistema-parete su disegno composto da pannelli di legno e vetro sabbiato alternati che, senza arrivare al soffitto, permettono di illuminare con luce naturale anche la zona centrale. L'atrio a doppia altezza, direttamente aperto sul pianerottolo di arrivo degli ascensori, si propone come spazio di riferimento, cerniera architettonica distributiva da cui si sviluppa la scala che collega i due livelli degli uffici. Il grande atrio sfrutta al meglio la vetrata di facciata che offre, lungo il fronte sud, il panorama scenografico del porto. Nella zona d'ingresso, dal pavimento di ardesia, grigio come l'acqua del bacino portuale, è organizzata un'elegante e luminosa zona di attesa di fronte al banco reception circolare. Questo è posto sotto una delle sale di presentazione del piano superiore, sostenuta da un pilastro circolare in cemento a vista e riconoscibile, come gli altri importanti luoghi di lavoro della sede (sale conferenze e di presentazione dei lavori), per l'inconsueto rivestimento in metallo galvanizzato e foglie di rame ossidate, materiali che vogliono, come altri elementi del progetto e dell'arredo, citare il paesaggio industriale e marittimo del porto sottostante. La sala presentazioni principale, posta frontalmente alla precedente e pensata come architettura compiuta e autosufficiente, è segnata da una grande vetrata in curva inclinata, cui si riconduce anche il disegno del grande tavolo interno. All' atmosfera industriale del porto si rifanno anche le scelte di lasciare a vista tutti gli impianti e di denunciare con chiarezza il disegno del soffitto di cemento a cassettoni. Questo è tinteggiato in bianco e nero per simulare l'ombra del controsoffitto in rete metallica, sospeso con tiranti metallici e contenuto da una struttura di profilati in acciaio. Gli stessi motivi vengono ripetuti nel disegno della moquette in tinte chiare e scure alternate, ribaltando così su due livelli (soffitto e pavimento) la figura della rete sospesa, sviluppata nelle parti comuni e negli open space quale elemento di riferimento visivo.

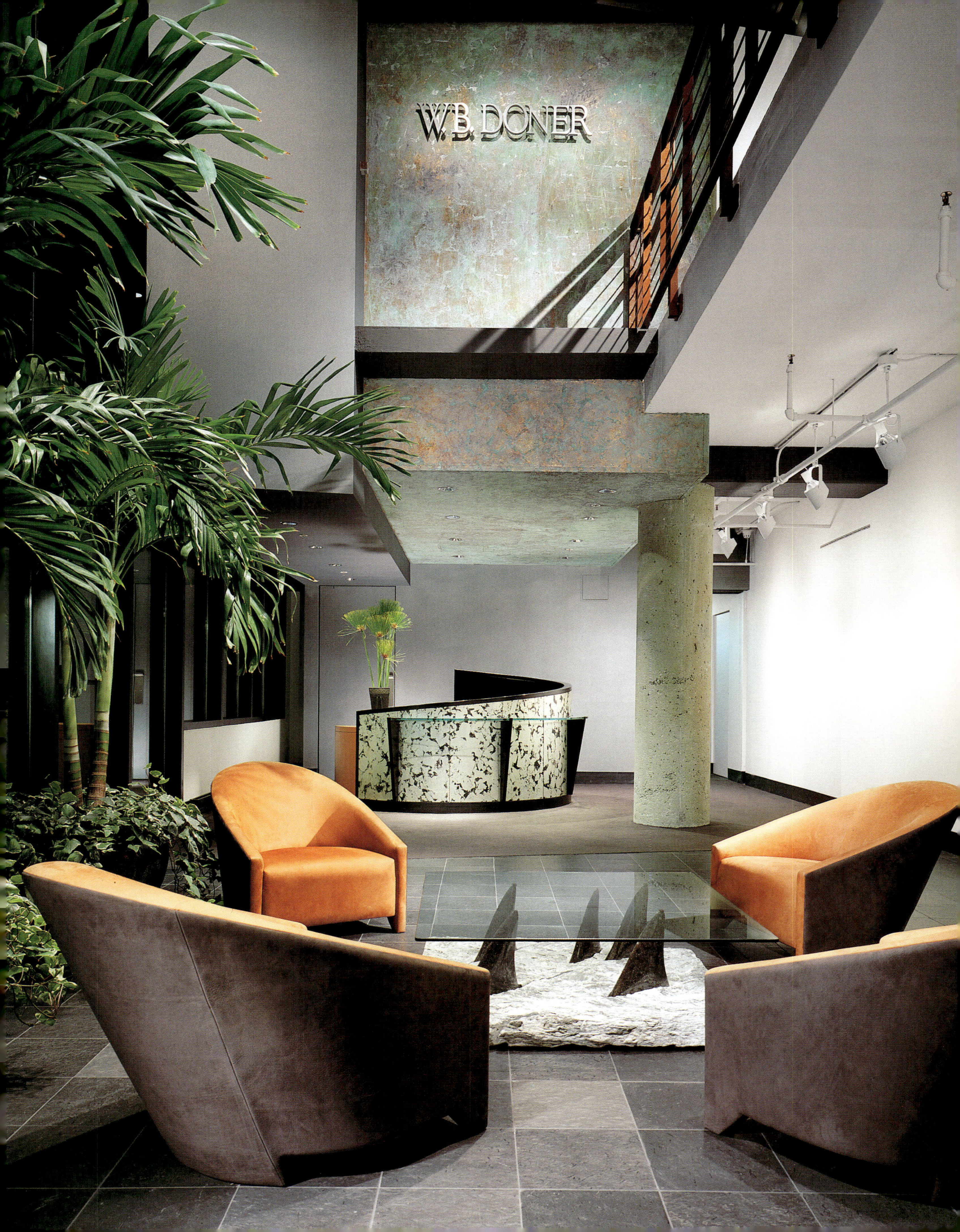
W.B. DONER

W.B. DONER

207

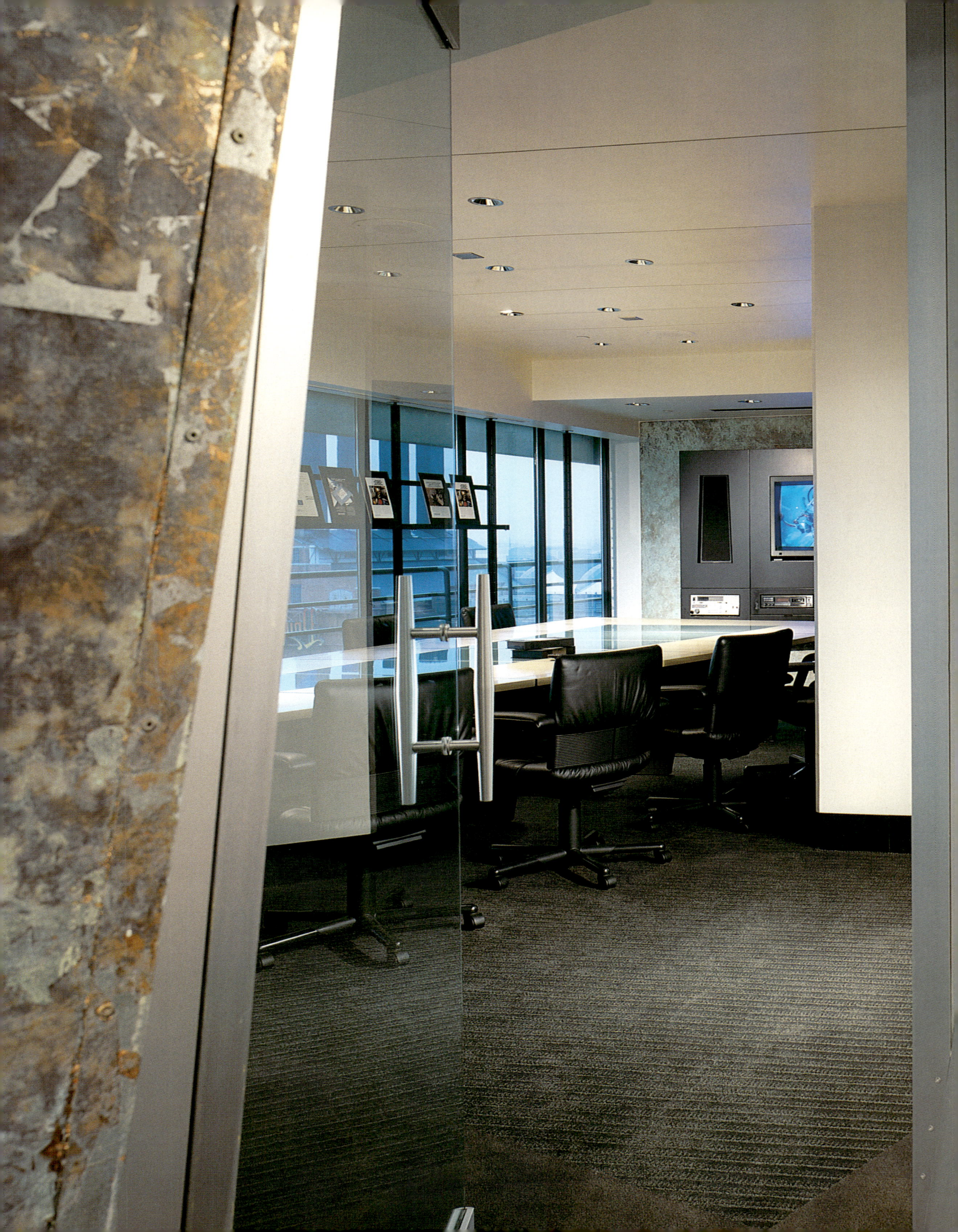

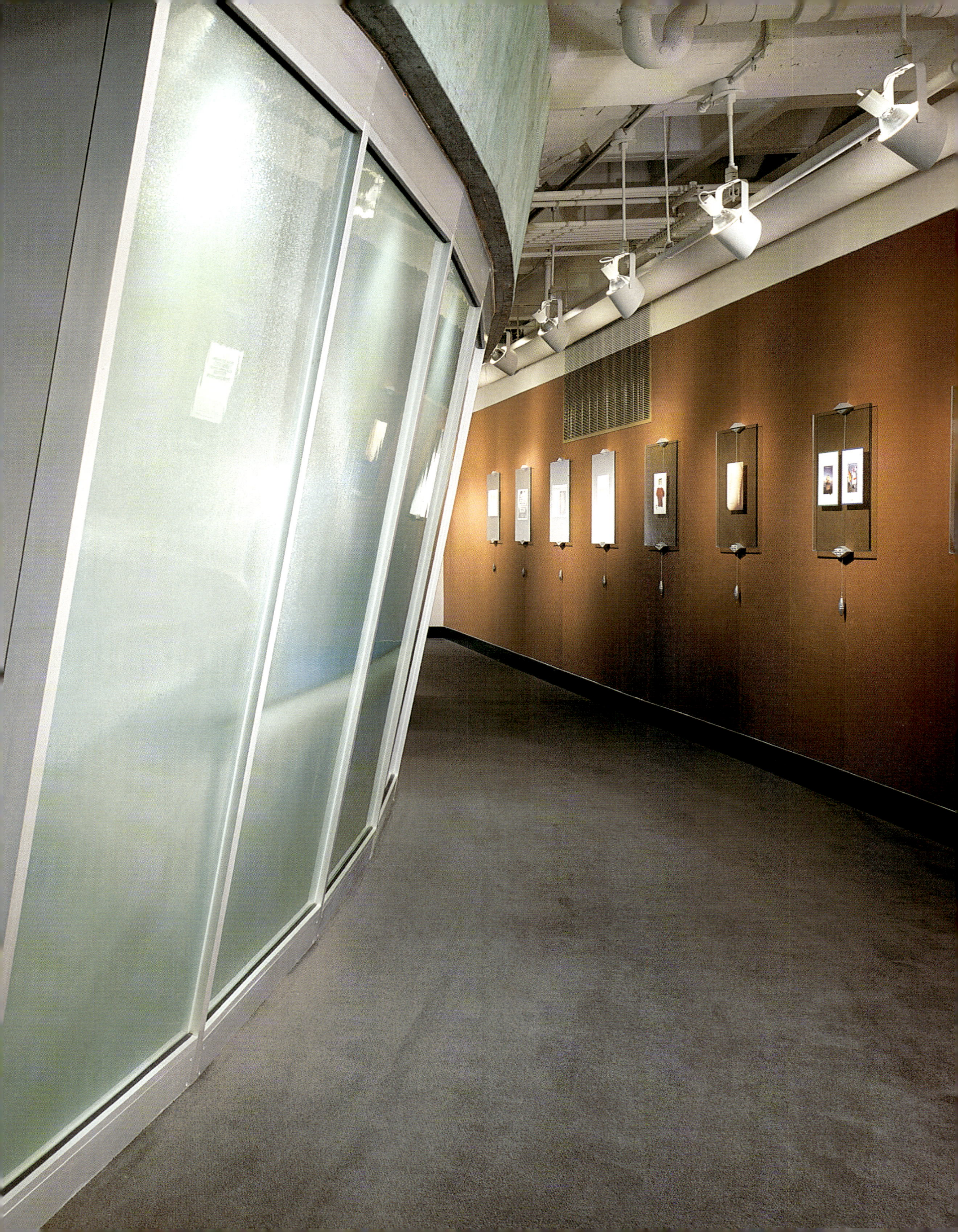

210

ome people spend hundreds of hours
mastering the fine art of cooking.
Lighten Up
The Creative Illustration Book
SONY

Tenth floor plan / Pianta 10° piano
1. Elevator lobby / Arrivo ascensori
2. Atrium / Atrio/Reception e Attesa
3. Presentation room
   Sale presentazione lavori
4. Commons / Salottino comune
5. Resource center / Archivio
6. Perimeter offices / Uffici Perimetrali
7. Core / Servizi igienici

Eleventh floor plan / Pianta 11° piano
1. Elevator lobby / Arrivo ascensori
2. Atrium / Atrio/Reception e Attesa
3. Presentation room / Sale presentazione
4. Commons / Salottino comune
5. Perimeter offices / Uffici Perimetrali
6. Core / Servizi igienici

SCHEDE TECNICHE
TECHNICAL DATA

ALTSCHILLER REITZFELD DAVIS TRACY-LOCKE
New York, NY, 1990

Private commission
Total usable (net) square feet 12,000
Total cost including furnishings and fees $1,400,000

Partner in charge: Henry Smith-Miller
Project Architect: Ruri Yampolsky
Design Team: John Conaty, Annette Fierro, Knut Hansen, Alexis Kraft, Charles Renfro, Jennifer Stearns, Kit Yan

Consultants:
Structural Engineers: Severud Associates, New York
HVAC Engineering: Carlo Marzot and Associates, New York
Lighting Design: Smith-Miller + Hawkinson Architects
Richard Eisenberg and Associates, New York
Electrical Engineering: Robert Gruder and Associates, New York
Sanitary Engineering: Andy Szewczuk and Associates, New York
General Contractors: Nico Construction, New York
Custom Woodwork: Materials Design Workshop and Philip Meskin and Partners, New York
Custom Metalwork: MetalForms, New York
Furnishings and Furniture: Furniture Consultants, New York (Knoll, Artemide, Storwall, and others)

The existing building's structure and utilities participate in the definition of the "office."
New work is juxtaposed with existing to render a sense of the building's frame and organization. New partitions, screens, and glass are understood as additions.
The program for the offices for an advertising agency, located on a high floor of a midtown office building configures office, presentation, and production spaces to take advantage of perimeter daylight and city views.
The elevator lobby entry sequence defines criteria for the entire floor: the large steel rolling panel with glass transom is reiterated in wood and aluminum-clad panels at each office; the exposed concrete slab in the waiting area occurs in all western offices; a rotated section of the dropped ceiling recalls the urban condition of Broadway and foreshadows the geometry of the executive suite; windows offer access to views available throughout the space.
The use of clerestory windows and sandblasted screens modulate and refract available daylight toward the more interior spaces. A minimal palette of natural materials – shotpeened\aluminum, brushed steel, clear and sandblasted float and textured glass, stained ash, industrial carpeting and resilient flooring – unifies the plan which wraps around two existing building cores. The use of standardized structural aluminum elements reinforces the idea of economy and provides consistency in detail.

APPLE COMPUTER, INC.
Glastonbury, CT, 1990

Client: Apple Computer, Inc.
Project: Regional Sales Office
Location: Glastonbury, CT
Principal: Scott Gentilucci
Manager: Peter Hapstak
Completed: 1990
Size: 17,000 SF
Service: Full Interior Architecture

This project consists of 17,000 square feet of space in Somerset Square, primarily composed of client sales areas, private offices, and workstations for the sales staff. Entry occurs under a lattice of beams which begin as an arbor and are transformed into a series of "electrified bolts" across the open office area, establishing visual continuity front to back.
Conference and demonstration areas are contained within stepped forms, composed of fractured geometric planes. Non-customer areas are contained within curvilinear forms creating, by means of contrast, the spatial layering key to the concept.
The shapes of a cylinder, a cross, and a square enliven the open areas of the plan. The cylinder contains the employee break room, private offices, storage, and conference rooms. The cross contains copy, mail, and storage space. The square contains training spaces. The forms are cut and carved as necessary to provide access and to create the transitional duality of forms.

BABCOCK & BROWN
Corporate Headquarters
San Francisco, CA, 1992

Client/ Project Background

Babcock and Brown Inc., an international investment bank headquartered in San Francisco, requested a design for office space that would reflect the corporate culture of a young and aggressive firm as well as reinforce the image that a firm headquartered in San Francisco could be competitive in the international investment world.
The space is located on the top floor of a reinforced concrete and masonry building built in 1926 on the San Francisco waterfront south of Market Street. The original structure was built for a single user who stored and roasted bulk coffee on the lower five floors. The top floor, with its 18-foot ceilings and commanding views of both the bay and downtown, was shared by the corporate headquarters and the special roasters for testing and blending new coffee.
Prior to starting the build-out of the Client's space and as part of a full-block redevelopment, the entire building underwent a major renovation which included seismic upgrading, a new central atrium running through the entire building, new common services including elevators and cores and other amenities required to transform the building from a mixed-use warehouse into a first-class office building.

Design Solution
The idea of a medieval town inspired the design concept:
- a hierarchy of spaces derived from the varying needs of public and private space.
- circulation linking these events evolved naturally, not by artificial grid.
- natural features of light and views determined the siting of key elements.

The medieval town typology was overlaid on the traditional concept of exterior perimeter offices and interior support space. As a result, six distinctive neighborhoods, each with its own public space were created. Four were formed by corner cluster, two by raised platform. The East Conference room and several key private offices were sited for the best views. Executive offices were located in a private "cul de sac" guarded by a symbolic "gatehouse" of the Office Manager. Open space in front of the conference rooms allows people to gather, similar to a parvis in front of a cathedral. Other internal functions were further delineated with freestanding elements and by residual open space.
To provide city and bay views throughout the space, two interior clusters were built on raised platforms. By glazing perimeter offices, views were brought into the interior. Access to one interior "hill top" work area is achieved via a meandering ramp; the other "hill top" area can be reached by either a more formal stair or ramp.
Throughout the project, new and old materials and vocabularies are juxtaposed, alluding to an evolution of man's habitat and modes of transportation. Airplane wings, ship's handrails, birds, clouds, and other elements of motion, flight and transportation resonate throughout the space, a reference to the client's specialization in transportation leasing finance. Huts, villas, and triumphal arches found in the space evoke man's habitat.
The original concrete structure of the building, stripped to its previous tenant's finish, was left unfinished, contrasting with the insertion of the building's use and new materials. New materials include: stone, concrete, plaster, steel and glass, cables, steel and aluminum, both curved and bent.

Size in sq. ft./meters: 33,000 s.f. / 3,085 m2
Lighting: Custom fixtures by STUDIOS & Neidhardt Lighting General – various manufacturers
Furniture and fittings: Custom workstations, reception desks & conference tables by STUDIOS
Modular workstations by Steelcase, "Context" product line
Flooring: Custom carpets by Pacific Crest Mill; Custom pattern sand-blasted granite tiles in entry.
Walls and partitions Integrally colored plaster, steel & glass conference rooms and entry walls, custom-designed by STUDIOS
Perimeter office; standard aluminum store front
General: gypsum wall board

BURGER KING CORPORATE WORLD HEADQUARTERS
Miami, FL, 1993

After Hurricane Andrew devastated downtown Miami in the Fall 1992 leaving only the roof and structural frame of Burger King headquarters the fast food giant reviewed its business culture and operations, and renew both with a renovated office. Burger King Corporation's new design contributes to a strong corporate community environment.
Imaginative integration of color and pattern reinforce the urban plan concept by delineating "Main Streets" and "Neighborhoods" with distinctive mixes of shapes and hues drawn from the elements of Burger King Corporation's condiment toppings.

Consultants (Specialty): PGAL (Core + Shell Architects); Spillis Candela & Partners (Mechanical/Electrical); Bliss Nyitray (Structural)

Product manufacturers/suppliers:
Seating: Larsen Furniture; The McGuire Furniture Company; Design America; Bright Chair Company; International Contract; Furnishings, Inc.
Upholstery Fabrics: Arc-Com Fabrics, Inc.; Deepa Textiles; Donghia Textiles; Design-Tex; Maharam Fabric Corp.; Spinneybeck; Bernhardt; Unika-Vaev, USA; Architex
Tables: Herman Miller; Intrex; Hickory Business Furniture; The McGuire Furniture Company; Falcon Products,Inc.; Davis Furniture Industries, Inc.
Desks: System Furniture: Herman Miller
System Furniture Dealer: Office Pavilion
Storage/Filing Equipment: Meridian
Lighting:
Fabrication: Metalux
Fixtures: (Lamps) Howard Lamp Company
Floorcovering:
Carpet: Harbinger
Walls: Not Available
Ceilings: Armstrong
CAD System Used: Auto CADD 11.0

CLEARY GOTTLIEB STEEN & HAMILTON LAW OFFICE
New York, NY, 1990

This law firm wanted a design that would reflect its democratic organizational structure and lack of departmentalization. The design response was to organize six 40,000 square foot floor plates into 45 "neighborhoods," each with a working cluster of partners, associates, para-legals, and support staff. Two atriums were developed to bring in as much natural light as possible and allow for efficient communication between floors. The atriums also offer the added benefit of allowing both visitors and employees to enjoy spectacular views of lower Manhattan, the harbor and the Brooklyn Bridge. Stone, metal and wood finishes are utilized in the atriums and adjoining reception and lobby areas to create consistent features that unify the space.

Client: Cleary, Gottlieb, Steen & Hamilton
Facility: Law firm with two multistory atriums, legal offices, secretarial space, cafeteria, kitchen, library, records room, conference center, and computer room on six floors.
Size: 255,000 square feet
Status: completed 1990

Structural system: concrete slab and steel beam; part of original structure demolished to install atriums.
Major Materials: Anigre architectural woodwork; glass walls; wood and glass doors; stone, oak wood, ceramic tile, and carpeted floors;gypsum board and acoustical tile ceilings
Mechanical systems; existing base building system with supplemental units for special areas.

Credits
Interior Art: Elizabeth Levine
Seating: Atelier International, Knoll
Tables: Brickel
Workstations: Peerless Woodworking Corp, Pilot Woodworking
Carpet: Prince St. Technologies, Edward Fields (custom)
Lighting: Linear Lighting, Edison Prise
Stone: Lanzilotta & Sons Steel Rails, Bronze Cables Burgess Steel Products
Sandblasted glass: Metralite
Oak Floor: Design Wood Floors
Paint: Shewin Williams
Millwork: John Langenbacher Woodworking Co

D.E. SHAW & COMPANY
New York, NY, 1991
Program: Office and Trading Area
Client: D.E. Shaw & Co.
Architect: Steven Holl Architects, P.C. with Thomas Jenkinson and Janet Cross
Net floor area: 10.561 sq.ft.

Concept:
The top two floors of a midtown Manhattan skyscraper are the site of an experimental project exploring the phenomena of spatial color reflection or "project color."
D. E. Shaw & Co., a financial trading firm founded in 1988 by a physicist, works with the minuscule drift of prices for financial instruments measured over short intervals of time. The firms' computers are connected to financial markets by satellite and by telephone lines, at rest only between the time the Tokyo exchange has closed and the London exchange has not yet opened. One room in the facility contains more than 200 small computers.
This curious and intangible business program has a parallel in the design concept of interior. The metal framing and sheet -rock with skim- coat plaster was carved and notched at precise points around the central 31 -foot cube of space at the entry. Color has been applied to the back or bottom surfaces of these notches, invisible to the viewer within the space. Natural and artificial lights project this color back into the space around walls and fissures. As the phenomena greatly reduces the intensity of the color being reflected, a range of fluorescent colors could be utilized on the unseen surfaces. One consequence of the exploration was the presence of the project seen from the street as a fluorescent green backside on the top floors of the tower. The interior has a mysterious calm glow with surprising views as one moves around observing one field of reflected color through another and vice versa.

ESQUIRE MAGAZINE-THE HEARST MAGAZINE COMPANY
New York, NY,1993

Completed: July 1993
Client: Esquire Magazine / The Hearst Magazine Company 250 West 55th Street New York, NY
Program: 24,000 sf office interior
Architect: Francois de Menil, Architect, P.C.
Francois de Menil, Principal-in-Charge
Jeffrey Bacon, Project Architect
Dwight Long, John Blackmon, Bryce Sanders, Elizabeth Adams, Agatha Klepacka
Engineers: Jack Stone Engineers, P.C. (Mechanical/Electrical/Plumbing)
Consultants: Carl Hillman Associates, Inc. (Lighting)
Construction Managers: Edward Robbins Construction Corporation, Robert Schoenbach, Project Manager

Project Description:
The Hearst Magazine Company's program called for a renovation of three floors (24,000 square feet) of a 1920's mid block industrial building in midtown Manhattan for the offices of Esquire Magazine. Each of the three floors would house one of the main departmental divisions of the magazine: editorial, art & production, and publishing. The architecture is informed by the need to bring natural light into the spaces as a major presence and by a desire to invoke the buildings industrial origins.
Each floor is organized around a large loft-like interior workspace with executive/editorial offices on three sides. The orientation of these perimeter offices is reversed so that they face into rather than away from the interior workspace. The glazed hollow metal storefront system at the offices uses both clear and translucent panels to provide privacy while allowing daylight from the exterior to filter through to the open workspace. Offices, primarily on the west, have angled walls and ceilings with light scoops at the windows to amplify the light to the inner core. A further light-enhancing device is the curved and luminous Lexan wall enclosing the conference room. This light wall supplements light to the interior spaces and establishes privacy for the conference room.
The industrial origins of the building are evoked several times throughout the project: in the establishment of a simple palette of construction materials, the exposed structure of the ceiling in the central core; the hollow metal storefront system; and the steel stair connecting two previously separate floors. This industrial character is also evident in the design of the workstations. The workstations are designed as a "kit of parts" to achieve maximum flexibility. They are conceived as continuous returns of custom lengths with modular desktops and files clipped on as required. The power and signal distribution occurs overhead in visible troughs suspended from the ceiling and drops via shielded cables to each row of workstations. It is then distributed along the length of the return. The "kit of parts" components comprise particle board, galvanized steel legs and angles and plastic laminate tops.

Materials and Finishes:
Floor: Black vinyl composition tile by Armstrong Broadloom carpet by J.P. Stevens / Gullstan Mill
Ceiling: Gypsum board painted white Acoustical tile by Armstrong
Walls: Gypsum board painted white
Conference Room Wall: "Lexan Thermoclear" polycarbonate sheets by General Electric Stair: Custom fabricated steel
Windows: Existing steel windows
Doors: Solid-core flush wood doors with plain sliced maple veneer

Storefront
System: Hollow metal steel frame by Curries, with factory finished powder coating Custom
Workstations: Particle board partitions Plastic laminate desktops Metal brackets, frame and fittings by B-Line Systems, Inc.

Furniture: Custom desks, conference tables, cabinetry. Equa Chair from Herman Miller, Classic modern sofas, chairs, and tables

HENRI BEAUFOUR INSTITUTE
Washington, DC., 1992

This project is the US headquarters of a French pharmaceutical company. The jury might feel that submission to the Interiors category would be more appropriate. However, this distinction --Architecture/Interior-- suggests a qualitative difference between the issues that confront an architect when faced with a "building" project versus those inherent to an office interior. This project is included in the Architecture group as a statement suggesting that this supposed distinction and categorization should be questioned. The issues are the same--site, materials, orientation etc.- We ask that the jury to judge this project on its architectural merits.

Comprising approximately 30,000 sq. ft., the requirements of the project were at once commonplace, client/site-specific and subtle. Doctors and nurses make up the staff but this belies a program of standard hierarchies and needs. A variety of office types – executive, mid-management and support; a range of conference rooms – small, medium, large; clerical areas, lunch room and storage areas.

Our primary intention was to focus on a basic architectural issue: the relationship of the building to the site, an issue which is often ignored in commercial interior work. This is accomplished by establishing an ongoing dialogue between the base building architecture (the site) and the offices (the insertion). While each is made up of the same kit of parts – columns, walls, floors, roofs, cladding – they differ in scale, materials and sense of permanence. By extension, we established an equation that says the insertion is like the base building which in turn, is like the buildings throughout the city. The various systems overlap heightening one's awareness of standing simultaneously within all three scales – the office, the building and the city.

The base building architecture is rendered in painted drywall or raw concrete. The insertion architecture is made up of a rich, natural palette -- sycamore walls, ground face concrete block, slate, stainless steel, sisal...

Seeing the insertion architecture as a series of fragmented assemblies – wood panels, floating wood ceilings – the cellular nature of the program breaks down and the space unfolds to allow a dialogue between the base building and the offices. The scrim-like quality of the insertion architecture enables one to understand that each room is part of a complex of rooms, all of which exist within the base building. Within this context the work stations, made of perforated aluminum and maple, are understood as pavilions; buildings within a building.

Other issues: A common palette to play down normal official hierarchies. A conference room and table which lent itself to viewing slides versus across-table discussions. This was solved by designing a trapezoidal table. And, a sloping structural column in the lobby area posed a problem, which was dealt with by surrounding the column with a painted plywood jacket designed by a Danish artist.

The project is approximately 30,000 sq. ft. (about 2700 sq. meters) on two floors of a Washington, DC office building (refer to the attached project description that I sent along.) The history of the project; This was a fast track job. I won the job the last week of September 1991 or 1992, I forget, and the 100% construction documents were due the first week of January. Basically, I went into a four-month charrette along with the project architect -- Robert Dudka. The company, as you know, is a French pharmaceutical company. The president for the company here, and her administrator, were Danish. From this European mind grew an interest in something very different than what is typically seen here in DC.

It was a wonderful learning process for them and us. We investigated materials we hadn't used --the "Colorlith" lab top along the stair, English sycamore panels, the ground face concrete blocks, etc. We were able to travel to Copenhagen to review and purchase furniture and I worked with Danish artist Per Arnoldi to develop a design to mask the sloping column that sits in the middle of the reception room.

List of materials: Floors-- slate tile, sisal rug and white oak; Ceilings--sycamore panels, painted gyp. brd. and acoustical tile; Furniture--main conference is custom made of quarter sawn maple, chairs by Knoll, reception chairs by Cassina, small conference "Brno" chair, coffee tables by Paul Kjerholm side tables by me. Walls--ground face concrete block, sycamore, painted gyp. brd. Stair-- cantilevered steel w/maple treads, stainless steel rail, back wall "colorlith." Artwork-- posters that I chose and posters by Per Arnoldi.

HUMMER WINBLAD VENTURE PARTNERS
San Francisco, CA, 1997

Project Name:
Hummer Winblad Venture Partners
2 South Park
San Francisco CA 94107

Scope of Services: Full Architectural Services
Square Footage: 6,000
Staff Number: 22
Completion date: June, 1997
Client Background & Project Brief

Hummer Winblad Venture Partners is the first venture capital fund exclusively focused on investing in software companies at every stage of development from start-up to "mezzanine."

Holey Associates – who was just completing design of its own new design studio in the same building-- worked closely with Hummer Winblad on the very fast-track design. The client requested "downtown" amenities combined with an envelope characteristic of the warehouse buildings in the South of Market, South Park area which is home to many emerging software companies. Ann Winblad played a central role and was involved in all aspects of the design project.

The new space includes 9 private offices, including 2 larger partner offices, 8 open workstations for administrative, accounting and office management functions and 2 conference rooms – one public, the other more private.

Design:
Throughout the offices elements of the existing original warehouse architecture are played off against a new, more modern design language inserted into the space.

A soft, arcing curve adjacent to the central circulation marks the division between the office's inside space and the more public zone of the reception area. The reception area announces arrival at a successful venture capital firm with its more finished treatment of the ceiling, custom-designed reception desk and furniture appointments.

While the overriding impression is one of refinement, heavy timber warehouse loft design elements announce that one is in a space different from the usual venture capital office – one that honors the roots of the start-up firms which the venture capital firm invests in.

From the reception area, the visitor can also see over the soft curve to the heavy timber columns from the existing warehouse loft. The workspace behind this area is screened by textured glass which provides visual privacy.

These two rows of five original heavy timber columns define the open administrative zone located in the center of the office space. Private offices along the perimeter facing the street allow light to enter the interior administrative zone through the glass window walls. The open administrative space is terminated by offices for the human resources director at one end and by offices for the accountant at the other. While the ceiling allows one to see exposed duct, the floor is covered with the new, softer element of carpet.

Attention to details extended to the careful placement of exposed conduit runs and mechanical ducts, lighting and even screws on the existing original warehouse heavy timbers.

The result is a new office for Hummer Winblad that evokes the successful union of both the emerging software start-ups and the more established world of venture capital.

Holey Associates Project Team:
Principal – John E. Holey
Project Manager – Julie Dwyer-Gower
Project Designer – Paul Loeffler
Team Member: Patrick Booth

Consultants:
Acoustics Paoletti Associates (Gasper Sciacca)
Lighting – Auerbach + Glasgow (Larry French)
Contractor – Cannon Constructors (Ken Herguth, Mike Nebozek)

Materials and Furniture
Millwork: custom fabricated by Fink & Schindler plain sliced American cherry
Pattern Glass: Bendheim
Laminate: Nevamar
Metal work & Counter inset by South Park Fabricator
Files: Meridian
Resilient Floor-:Forbo – Marmoleum
Signage: Vivid Image
Wall Plaster: Custom Cement by Tony Olea

Seating: Knoll International with Design Tex fabric
Chairs: Geiger Brickel with Design Tex fabric; Keilhauer Chair with Spinneybeck Leather; Ted Boerner Chairs with Spinneybeck Leather
Carpet: Jack Lenor Larsen
Rug: Jack Lenor Larsen
Tables: Cast Concrete Top by Buddy Rhodes; HBF
Table Base: Stoneline Designs cherry and terrazzo
Desk: Creative Wood
Reception Desk: Custom designed by Holey Associates Fabricated by Fink & Schindler
Light Fixtures: custom from Neo Ray; Tizio by Artemide; Luce Plan; Zumtobel
Spot Fixtures: Stonco
Spot Lights: Stonco
Door Hardware: Schlage

KIRSHENBAUM BOND & PARTNERS
New York, NY, 1996

Project:
Kirshenbaum Bond & Partners, advertising agency office expansion and renovation, 145 Sixth Avenue, New York, NY.
Completion: April, 1995 (Phase one; 5th & 6th Floors)
March, 1996 (Phase two; 3rd & 4h Floors)

Owner:
Kirshenbaum Bond & Partners; Richard Kirshenbaum, chief creative officer, Bill Oberlander, creative director, Robb High, chief operating officer, (212) 633-0080

Architects:
Asfour Guzy Architects – Project team: Peter Guzy, Edward Asfour, Matt Read, Fredrik Svenstedt & Jiwook Kim.

Consultants:
Alexander Isley Inc. (Graphic Design), Asfour Guzy Architects (Lighting design, Interior design & Custom furniture design)

Engineers
Marcy Ramos (mechanical), Severud Associates (structural), Robert Wolsch (electrical)
General Contractor
Wonder Works Construction Corporation
Manufacturers' Sources
-Brazilian Cherry floors: Haywood Berk Flooring Co. Inc.
-Bayone Gris Limestone at elevator lobby: Stone Source.
-Tinted plaster: Art-in-Construction.
-Lighting fixtures: Ellipticar, Modular, Louis Poulsen, Fontana Arte, Luce Plan, Flos, & Halo. Custom fixture in stairway design by Asfour Guzy Architects and built by Metalum through MSK Illumination, Inc.
-Steel and glass doors & steel and glass curtain walls: Kern/Rockenfield.
-Carpet at reception area: Odegard Roesner.
-Steel stair fabrication: Lee Consulting.
-Chair at reception: Knoll.
-Chairs in conference rooms: ICF.
-Receptionist's desk, main conference room table, side tables, TV stand in main conference room, & round table at reception area: designed by Asfour Guzy Architects and built by Kern/Rockenfield. These pieces all employ stainless steel with linoleum by DLW.
-Large gold sofa at reception area: Designed by Asfour Guzy Architects and built by Park-Serpico.
Furniture in principal's office: side table and coffee table; Dialogica, stool; Chris Lehrecke, carpet; Entree Libre.
-Work stations on 5th & 6th floors; Designed by Asfour Guzy Architects and built by Christiana Millwork, Inc.
Paint – Benjamin Moore.

Project Description
An advertising company, occupying 20,000 sq. ft. located in a classic Soho loft building, required a 15,000 sq. ft. expansion to accommodate an additional 100 staff members as well as a comprehensive renovation of their existing space. Initially meetings were conducted with all department heads including accounting, creative, graphic services, public relations, media, food services and operations. Goals for these departments were established while potential organizational schemes were examined and reviewed. At the same time, a clear idea for a new visual spirit of the office, a critical component for both clients and staff of an advertising agency, was created through working closely with the partners. As a result of the master plan, a final project and its scheduling were established.
The project was constructed in stages, which permitted the agency to continue its growth and operation during the construction. The new spaces, with the help of a large open stairway and a central space which was initially left empty, created a unified user-friendly office over 4 floors, and incorporated and facilitated a variety of departments and functions while at the same time anticipating flexibility for the future. Special elements of the original building -notably the original wood columns and beam structure- were uncovered and celebrated in the design. Using a few special materials sparingly, such as plaster, wood, glass and steel, the new spirit of the agency was achieved at a reasonable cost. Custom designed light fixtures and furniture helped to buttress this new spirit.
The final construction cost was $1,250,000.00 which was divided between 14,000 sq. ft. of renovated existing office space and 23,000 sq. ft. of new construction.
The following is a text which was prepared to describe the spaces on the 5th and 6th floors:
Kirshenbaum Bond & Partners is a young fast growing advertising agency whose clients include accounts like Citibank, Prudential, Target, Moët & Chandon and Olympus. Late in 1994 the firm found itself at a difficult juncture: with only three years remaining on their lease, they needed space for an additional 100 staff members. Moving to new space was too disruptive to the operation of the agency. Two partial floors of raw space above their existing space, which is located on two floors, was leased to get them through the next three years. The parameters of the project (phase one) were defined in terms of a highly economical solution and rethinking the way that the agency works. The client requested that the architects formulate a strategy which would facilitate a high density semi-open office plan while at the same time as providing the types of shared enclosed spaces which are essential to the way that internal business is conducted. The new spaces were to be used as laboratories for work, which reflected Richard Kirshenbaum's conviction that the agency is a high energy operation which develops and produces ideas. Client meetings remained in conference rooms located on the agencies two existing floors.
The architects established a concept which embraced the requests of the client while at the same time offering new solutions to standard office design problems. Both floors, which are connected by a new stair, employ the same two main components: open work stations located on the glazed perimeter and solid central cores which contain mini-conference rooms and support functions. These cores are composed of slightly angled walls to facilitate movement and to create, at the larger sections of the circulation areas, some common spaces where people can interact. The open work station system promotes an egalitarian arrangement which provides each person with a similar workspace. The agency had determined that, unlike other alternative office arrangements, each person still needed their own individual work space.
The architects designed a custom work station/panel system which permitted a high density layout, allowed for a comfortable amount of privacy, and yet helped retain an open feeling with the penetration of natural light to typically dark deep spaces. As well, the work station/panel system was produced and installed at about a quarter of the cost of conventional open office systems, and can easily be disassembled and reinstalled at the agencies next space. The work stations use a standard industrial shelving system for its structural components. Maple veneer plywood panels provide the dividing elements and laminated natural cork is used for tackable surfaces. Exposed electrical conduit and outlets are affixed to the vertical members of the shelving system which substantially reduced the electrical installation cost. An open metal trough incorporated in the structural system provides for communication and data wiring and permits daily changes as required. The panels, which allow privacy for the work stations, are made of translucent fiberglass and maple and are supported by standard plumbing pipe and sandblasted standard aluminum brackets. The fiberglass intensifies natural light in the circulation areas and provides a constantly changing screen of light and shadow throughout the day.
The mini-conference rooms are the key to the concept. These rooms hold up to four or five people and provide spaces for a variety of uses: private phone calls, meetings between individuals and creative team brain storming sessions. Some of the rooms are devoted to specific accounts. This allows for a home base with which a large team can identify. The mini-conference rooms have been furnished either with a table and chairs for work sessions, or with a small sofa and lounge seating for more informal discussions. The walls in these rooms are painted in four different colors, to contrast with the rest of the white, gray, black and maple interiors. One of the walls is cork with a steel ledge which provides flexible presentation possibilities. These rooms also feature a standard exterior grade sliding glass door, which is an excellent sound insulator, brings in a large amount of natural light and does not take up the precious space of a standard door.
Considering the entire space, the square footage per person is 95 square feet, which is over half of the required area which is considered standard.
The offices, which were recently occupied, appear to be succeeding beyond the client's expectations. Separating the actual individual work spaces from the meeting/discussion spaces proved to be the critical generator for the project. Giving all the people collectively the prime windowed spaces, which are usually reserved for just a limited number of offices, empowers and unifies the agencies main resource: its people. This inside-out scheme, with the enclosed spaces at the center and the work stations at the perimeter is an exciting model for office design. This model, as envisioned and developed, is operational and is providing a new type of environment which, through minimal investment costs, allows for an easy flow of the agencies work, flexibility for the future and helps give the sense to the people that they work in a special place.

LANCASTER GROUP WORLDWIDE, INC.
New York, NY, 1994

Design firm: Quantrell Mullins & Associates Inc
Project name: Lancaster Group Worldwide, Inc.
Client name (if different):
Client business: international cosmetics and fragrances firm
Job location: New York City
Location type: New location
Job size: 75,000 square feet
Cost per sq. ft (optional): Confidential
Number of floors and area per floor: 3 floors
Services performed: Building search and evaluation; design and space utilization studies; project budget and schedule development; programming and test layouts; space planning and interior architectural design; furnishings design and coordination; furnishings selection and management; accessories coordination;

cost and schedule tracking; bid and award; construction administration and project management; move coordination and management.
Number of employees housed in this installation: 140
Facilities provided: Private offices; open office workstations; conference rooms; videoconferencing rooms; product storage areas; computer rooms; offices for affiliated public relations agency.
Unusual program requirements: State-of-the-art a/v international conferencing requirements; flow and maximizing space without feeling crowded; flexibility since company restructuring was in progress; integration of new corporate logo; client wanted a Class A building in Midtown Manhattan; light penetration all the way to the core.
What were the chief design problems and your solutions?
- Penetration of exterior lighting throughout in allegiance to European standards: Generous use of glass panels and millwork storage components reflect light and also function as space dividers; interior glazing.
- Image: Wanted to be different from competition. Developed a contemporary, clean image with updated Art Deco styling; new corporate logo was integrated and interpreted with waves, stars and stripes that are etched on glass and recur throughout the space.
- Flexibility and function: Consistent size and type of offices and to allow for easy re-organization; compact layout and built-in vertical storage maximize space usage.
 - Extensive cabling to provide communication and data access: Used stainless steel floor-to-ceiling columns to contain cables and add aesthetic appeal; wanted futuristic capabilities.
- Manage project for overseas client: Used total process design management to coordinate all aspects of the project; client liaison to all consultants (brokers, owners, insurance, European); cost and schedule tracking for fast-track project.
Quotation or statistic indicating client satisfaction that can be used in article: "Quantrell Mullins & Associates was the integral force behind the organization, management, planning and design of our corporate headquarters relocation. Their creativity, professionalism and sensitivity to our needs set them apart."- Peter Harf, CEO
 Furnishings: Contemporary; adapted custom-designed and custom-designed.
Spatial organization: Vertical and horizontal planes
Color scheme: Sophisticated; light and airy; bright blue carpet with black/white and glass and stainless steel accents.
Lighting design: Mixed sources of light; low-voltage downlights and ambient torcherers to illuminate vaulted ceiling.
Principal materials used: Sycamore wood; stainless steel; glass; white marble with black inserts; black marble with white inserts.

NEW LINE CINEMA-EAST
New York Headquarters
New York, NY, 1992

Private Commission
18,000 square feet
Partners-in-charge: Henry Smith-Miller and Laurie Hawkinson
Project architect: Jorge Aizenman
Project Team: Eric Cobb, Eugene Harris, Charles Renfro, Jane Wason, Fritz Read, John Conaty, Kit Yan, Belen Moneo, Yolande Daniels

Consultants:
Structural Engineers: Severud-Szegezdy, New York
Mechanical Engineers: Carlo Marzot and Associates, New York
Lighting: Claude Engle and Associates, Washington, D.C
Audio/Visual: Harry Joseph and Associates, New York

Contractor:
NSC Construction, New York

Manufacturer Sources
Task Lights: Artemide (Tolomeo)
Locksets: Schlage, Allgood; Stanley
Perforated Ceiling: Simplex
Reception desk, cabinetry and custom woodwork:
Custom design by Smith-Miller + Hawkinson Architects,
Custom fabrication by Hird-Baker and William Somerville
Custom Metalwork: Treitel-Gratz
Parabolic downlights: National
Linear-indirect pendants: LiteControl (Mod Series)
Recessed downlighting: Edison Price
Low-voltage spots: Harry Gitlin

Situated on contiguous high floors, just south of Central Park, the offices enjoy commanding views of Central Park, Seventh Avenue, and the Hudson River.
The narrow floor plan and an L-shaped perimeter appear to lend themselves more to an open layout, rather than a spatially layered plan. However, an approach different from these two was taken. The disparity between the building perimeter as a trace of urban and political constraints, and the programmatic concerns of the corporate structure as evidenced in the office plan, provided the conceptual point of departure for the project's development.
Adjustments mandated by an unaccommodating building volume and by a less than ideal floor plan established the design parameters. A spatial language for the project was developed which allow for the discrepancies between the – over-determined – existing spatial conditions and the oblique inserted plan to be registered rather than repressed.
Diverse formal structures are utilized; folded ceiling plates, displaced volumes, and disjunctive operations articulate the "negotiated" plan. The glazed clerestory mediates between ceiling and plan. Aligned and non-aligned systems – volume and plane, material and color – contribute to a visual fabric that offers workers and visitors diverse impressions and "points of view."
The ceiling plates are sloped to maximize the window views at the building perimeter. In this way a connection is made to the surrounding urban fabric, and the insularity of the private office space is challenged. Thus, the anonymity and generality of the idealized modernist space is supplanted by a contemporary specificity which situates functional spaces in a historical register.

OFFICE HEADQUARTERS
New York, NY, 1992

Five thousand square feet of office space was renovated for a single floor tenant in Carnegie Hall Tower, New York. This suite of offices serves both as a busy corporate headquarters and as a gallery for a significant art collection.
The design focused on the issues of control and letting go, on materiality, and on how the space could best serve the people using it. Creating personal space, relieving or building tension, and achieving balance were important considerations. The office became a kind of stage set for human dynamics. How to use the space, how to achieve harmony in interaction, and how to facilitate productive work required research. In the end, resolving issues of concern to the people working in the office also served the company's desire for a new office demonstrating professionalism and elegance.

Area: 5,000 sq. ft.

Credits
Architects:
Tsao & McKown Architects
Principal-in-charge: Calvin Tsao
Project architect: Gary Morgenroth
Project team: Ted Krueger, Ross Wimer, Werner Franz
Engineer: Flack & Kurtz
Project engineer (mechanical, electrical, plumbing): Robert S. Roth
Consultants: Theo Kondos Associates
Project designer: William Armstrong (lighting)
Stephen A. Pine (specifications)
General Contractor: Alexander Wolf & Son
Project Manager: Antony Patryck

Manufacturer Sources:
Casework, paneling, and cabinetry: Kird Blaker.
Limestone and marble floor tiles: MarbleTechnics.
Paints and stains: Benjamin Moore & Co.; Pratt & Lambert.
Ceiling: USG Interiors, Inc.
Tinted plaster: Art-In-Construction. Laminate surfaces: Formica Corp.
Wall switches: Lutron.
Tracklighting: Edison Price.
Cold-cathode lighting: National cathode.
Pendants: custom by architects, fabricated by Bergen Art Metal.
Diffusers: Gray Glass.
Window shades: MechoShade.
Mirror light: Alko.
Office furniture: Knoll (Morrison).

PUTNAM, LOVELL, DEGUARDIOLA & THORNTON
San Francisco, CA, 1996

Context
Built in the 1920s, the historic "head-buildings" of the finger piers running along the Embarcadero formed one edge of the city. With their grand portal entry arches they connected maritime and commercial uses of the city as the symbolic entry gate to San Francisco from the Pacific. With the passing of 'break-bulk' cargo ships came the end of the traditional working waterfront and the vacant piers deteriorated or were removed and an elevated freeway of the 1960s became the symbolic edge. Behind it the long narrow head-buildings lay vacant or were adopted to a variety of small commercial uses on a month to month basis. As part of the waterfront renaissance following the Loma Prieta earthquake in 1989 and the demolition of the elevated freeway along the Embarcadero, the head buildings, now listed as historic structures, once again formed

the urban edge and have become a vibrant asset to the city.

As part of this renaissance, Putnam, Lovell & Thornton, an investment bank, with offices in New York London and Los Angeles, leased 5,000 square feet of the head building of Pier 5, which had lost its finger pier. The lease included, for the first time, the right to develop the space inside the forty foot high volume behind the central arch. With the build-out of the arch space and the addition of a mezzanine, the usable space grew to almost 8,000 square feet.

Design Concept

During demolition, the entire space was stripped, the existing trusses and arch structures, exposed, sandblasted and bleached, and the full height existing roll doors removed and replaced with new glazing system sympathetic to Pier 3 to the south. One enters the offices through the Pier 5 grand portal entry arch to a double height reception area. The original railroad tracks curving through this zone were retained. Access to the main office floor is up by a par of stairs located in the building to take advantage of the city views from the glazed central arch.

To further take advantage of the dramatic views of the city and the bay, the primary offices and analysts' workstations are located on the building's second floor, in the old wing previously used for customs offices and shipping company freight forwarders. The volume under the central peaked roof behind the grand portal entry arch was infilled with the principal's office flanked by two conference rooms. New sixteen foot high windows were added to these rooms, offering panoramic views of the Bay Bridge and the East Bay beyond. In plan, elevation and section, the walls and ceilings of these new spaces respond to the waterfront's maritime heritage with walls reminiscent of ship's hulls: either smooth skinned (the conference rooms' curved painted plaster), or the more archaic ribbed hull (the private offices' curved glass panels inset between sloped aluminum stanchions). The imagery and waterfront reference is further reinforced with a palette section of metal gratings, steel stairs and able stanchions, red primed structural steel, expressed fasteners and exposed ducts.

To celebrate the historical importance of both building and waterfront, the 15 foot long conference table is a steel and glass assemblage celebrating the materials of a steel ship and culmination in the sand blasted glass table top depicting a plan of the 1920's city waterfront.

Program
Ground Floor: Entry, Reception, Server Room, Storage and Parking
Mezzanine: Research/Library, Copy Room, Toilet Rooms
Second Floor: Private Offices, Analysts Workstations, Conference Room & Support, Visiting Office, Partners Office, Upper Reception & Fax/Copy Room

Credits

Client:
Putnam Lovell & Thornton Inc.
Don Putnam
Pier 5, The Embarcadero
San Francisco, CA 94111

Architects:
Architecture & Light
Darrell Hawthorne, Peter VanDINE, Partners in charge

Project Team: Yvonne Dunworth, Lee Loomis, Sean O'Connor, Lynn Soleski

Presentation: Isabella Shvetsky, Tania Rutherford

Lighting: Architecture & Light, Darrell Hawthorne, Partner in charge

Structural Engineer: Teyessier Engineer Inc.

Electrical Title 24: Randall Lamb Associates

Mechanical/Plumbing: Ted Jacobs Engineering Group Inc.

Furniture: Coordinated Resources, Inc.

Contractor: H.A.P. Construction

SILICON GRAPHICS COMPUTER SYSTEMS
Product Demonstration Center, Building 6
Mountain View, CA, 1992.

Client/ Project Background

Silicon Graphics is a Silicon Valley firm which manufactures high performance computer workstations and software with 3-dimensional graphic capabilities. Applications of Silicon Graphics' products are wide-ranging and include the medical, engineering and design fields.

While this two-story, 33,600-square-foot product and demonstration and briefing center for potential clients and members of the press projects a high tech spirit appropriate for a leading-edge firm, it also retains a warm, human, and egalitarian ambiance reflective of Silicon Graphics' company culture.

Although visitor traffic was envisioned as high, a modicum of privacy was needed for key executives located on the first floor.

Design Solution

A circle is used as a processional device to link upper and lower floors. The spiral stair, the first element which visitors see upon entering, provides a clear circulation path to the upper floor, easily conducting a series of first time users around a "technology tower." The demonstration area and briefing center located on the second floor take advantage of the panoramic views of the entire campus.

The circle reappears as a soffit demarcating a private executive area at the first floor perimeter. An executive boardroom is also located in this more private perimeter zone. Orthogonal walls at the base of the staircase shield executive work areas from public traffic.

Three white gypsum display forms capped by custom copper mesh and hanging light fixtures draw the eye upward. On the reverse side, the gypsum turret forms at the second floor contain product demonstration niches. A splayed circular segment in a stone pattern carries through to the second floor, continuing the stair's spiral. A clerestory window at the top of the rotunda area brings in natural light.

A number of private conference rooms used for press briefings and client meetings are located off the main product demonstration area. The demo area is organized as a trade show floor, encouraging flexibility in the display of several products. Demonstration niches encourage visitors to explore at their own pace. An interesting interplay exists between elements evocative of the technologically sophisticated environment and features suggestive of the more human, even elemental aspects of the space.

The procession of the exterior--entrance lobby--staircase--second floor recalls an almost ritualistic circling around a sacred object, underscoring the important space where the firm's product is exhibited on the technology tower. Graphic computer images on the technology tower evoke the hieroglyphics of a modern culture's Rosetta stone. Eventually, the tower will invite more visitor interaction as virtual reality software products are added.

Several elements underscore Silicon Graphics Inc.'s egalitarian company culture. The tabletop of the cappuccino coffee bar is an erasable marker board which allows executives to explore ideas over cappuccino----or leave behind graffiti thoughts. A sliding bulletin board displays messages which can be read from a distance throughout the work area. As a counterpoint to these "softer" elements, exposed ducts and double volume space recall the high tech nature of the manufacturing area located in another building.

The design of the product demonstration and briefing center communicates an image of the human transformed by technology and technology informed by the human.

Size in square feet: 33,600 s.f
Lighting: Cable-hung industrial light fixtures
General – various manufacturers
Furniture and fittings:
Perforated aluminum sheet metal, Copper screen, Maple wood veneer, Plastic laminate, Ceramic tile
Flooring: Quartzite stone floor tile
Carpet tiles/ rolled goods
Walls, ceilings, partitions:
Exposed HVAC system ducts
Exposed shell structure: girder, joist and columns, Typical steel studs with gypsum, Fiberglass and woven wire (aluminum) ceiling tiles
Stairs: Steel stair with cable rails

SONY MUSIC INTERNATIONAL
Miami Beach, FL, 1995

Project Description:
The offices for Sony Music International's Latin and South American headquarters are located in Miami Beach and occupy 20,000 sq.ft. on two floors. The building, an Art Deco structure built in 1933 is situated on the Lincoln Road Mall. Lincoln Road, a broad, six block concourse limited to pedestrian traffic, was planned by Morris Lapidus in 1958 as the prototypical outdoor shopping promenade. Lapidus' design implemented brilliantly colored paving patterns with an eccentric series of sculptural planting and water elements, and fanciful pavilions punctuating an absent median. These urbanized "follies" create ad hoc points of congregation, shading from the sun and a locus for outdoor activities which contribute to the promenade features of what is essentially a formulated piazza. Sony Music's decision to locate in Miami's South Beach district was in part based on the image of casual style, visual exposure and chance encounters which characterize the Beach and Lincoln Road in particular. Their program was somewhat conventional in its organization of perimeter offices along the window walls with administrative functions at the core. Yet Sony was also interested in

those same qualities which brought them to the Beach and which define the experience of Lapidus' promenade. On the street, the availability, however transitory and incidental between participants engaged in the act of seeing and being seen, provides a sense of immediate connection to a larger social context. Visual accessibility between colleagues, the openness from offices to public spaces, furnishings which de-emphasize the hierarchy between levels in favor of a cool and flexible vocabulary of interchangeable shapes and surfaces is intended to provide a similar linkage and immediacy between staff members. Using the boulevard as a conceptual model for the office interiors, the design incorporates strategies more typically associated with exterior spaces. The circulation is oversized with long vistas which suggest views beyond. Special elements of visual interest are partially withheld from full view and sequentially revealed as one progresses through the space. Circulation is connected to the facade of perimeter offices by the membrane of an aluminum and glass wall. These transparent skin walls allow light to filter from all four of the building's exposures into the core spaces throughout the course of the day while the exterior brise-soleil ledging partially deflects the sun's strong directional rays. Long horizontal soffits situated at 3.5 meters above the floor echo and extend those brise-soleil elements into the interior spaces and serve to hide ducts and indirect lighting sources. They also establish a datum which links the activities within each office or group much as the building canopies do at street level along the concourse. The circular disks which occur at points of significant transition are suspended at a height of 3.0 meters above the floor level provide a series of stop points defined as overhead pavilions. Cut away openings in the ceiling plane reveal the fabric of the original plank formed concrete slabs lending texture and suggesting continuity between different uses. The interplay of the horizontal soffits, the disks and the original slab surfaces creates a highly dynamic field of alternating levels of light and dark, new and old surfaces. These ceilings elements are intended to radically reverse the conventionality of the basic floor plan by providing a floating continuum throughout the space which visually activates the interstitial areas between the private offices and the core. The interplay which juxtaposes inside and outside has long defined architectural strategies in benign climates. Our objective was to add social history and temporality to that mix. The Sony offices present a vibrant pulse of overlapping fields of sound, video and motion which compete, collide and activate the space in a highly energetic and visually open manner. This locus for the production of music and entertainment suggests a street which is syncopated by contrasting beats and rhythms, incorporating the old and the new in a series of intersections at which connections can be made, sights seen, excitement generated and, conversely, a certain calm and tranquillity are also available.

Manufacturers/Sources
Seating:
Office Seating: Kita Chairs, ICF
Visitor Seating: Oscar Chairs, ICF
Cafe Seating: Handkerchief, Knoll International
Executive Visitors: PFM Chair, Dakota Jackson
Desks & Workstations. Unifor
Files: Office Specialty
Carpet: Crossley
Millwork: [Custom] Altura Studios
Aluminum & Glass Walls:[Custom]Kern-Rockenfield
Specialty Glass: Asahi Lamitone
Fabrics: Unika-Vaev YOMA
Lighting: Zumtobel Edison Price

SQUIRE, SANDERS & DEMPSEY
Cleveland; Ohio, 1992

Client
Squire, Sanders & Dempsey

Project
Law Firm Headquarters

Location
Cleveland, Ohio

Service
Master Planning,
Interior Architecture

Size
170,000 sq.ft.

Completed
1992

Relocating for the first time in its 100-year history, this firm sought to portray a progressive, forward outlook while communicating the quality and strength associated with its long tradition. In addition, the design challenge involved incorporating state-of-the-art technological capabilities to enhance productivity. Strong but simple planning and form geometries are utilized to organize and animate the facility while a rich palette of materials provides comfort and stability.
Vertical integration was an important planning determinant since the firm moved from three large low-rise floors to eight small high-rise floors. A series of two-story stacked atria, in concert with a connecting stair, significantly enhance interaction among the occupants. A vertical conveyor provides effective delivery of service to each floor where a manned service center ensures immediate support to the attorneys and staff.
Australian black bean wood, multicolored African slate tiles, Andes granite and bronze materials are utilized throughout the facility. The materials are enhanced by extensive use of translucent glass in walls and doors to bring in daylight to the occupied interior areas. Highly functional task and ambient lighting systems are combined with custom sconce, elevator lobby, and cove lighting to establish rhythm and continuity throughout the space.

STEVE GOLD PRODUCTIONS
New York, NY, 1995

Project Team:
Principal in Charge: Thomas Sansone
Project Architect: Skip Boling, Patrocinio Binuya, Carlos Sifuentes, Kim Sippel, Robert Thorpe, Ileana Fernandez
Associated Architect: Gustavo Ramos
Structural Consultants: Gilsanz, Murray, Steficek
Mechanical Consultants: Steven Feller and Associates
Lighting Consultant: Thomas Thompson

Manufacturers/Sources
Seating:
Office Seating: Kita Chairs, ICF
Visitor Seating: Oscar Chairs, ICF
Cafe Seating: Handkerchief, Knoll International
Executive Visitors: PFM Chair, Dakota Jackson

Desk & Workstations: Unifor
Files: Office Speciality
Carpet: Crossley
Millwork (Custom): Altura Studios
Aluminum & Glass Walls (Custom): Kern-Rockenfield
Specialty Glass: Asahi Lamitone
Fabrics: Unika-Vaev YOMA
Lighting: Zumtobel, Edison Price

TIME OUT
New York, NY, 1996
Site: 10.000 square foot loft space, 627 Broadway, New York City
Program: Provide work space for electronically published weekly magazine of arts and entertainment listings, allowing for flexible working groups with smaller private working and meeting areas.
Issues: The unusual time and budget constraints for this start-up enterprise required a combined design and construction schedule twelve weeks at a cost of USD 34/sf for construction and furnishings.
Concept: Planes of translucent corrugated fiberglass panels and oriented strand board (OSB) partitions stained with bronze and aluminum dust are the elements dividing and defining the functions of the space. Computer workstations for 70 persons made of composite panels of OSB and Tectum tack surface create flexible groupings. Private offices at several perimeter locations allow light transmission to the interior through fiberglass partitions and accommodate small meetings and computer workspace with triangular desks and trapezoidal OSB tables. Requirements for air, light, staff interaction and electronic networking were met by partial-height partitions crisscrossed overhead by triangular-section steel ducts, data/voice controls and fluorescent lighting. Workstations were assembled using a slotted gravity system.

TOMMY BOY OFFICE
New York, NY, 1992-1997

Project Description
The most recent addition to the offices of Tommy Boy Music more than doubles the area of the existing premises. Turett Collaborative Architects had designed the initial 1350 m2 space in 1992 housing the corporate offices. The expansion encompasses a partial floor above this and a full floor below, rounding out the entire area to 3000 m² of office.
The lower floor (see floor plan accompanying these documents) is occupied by several new smaller music labels which are offshoots of the Tommy Boy parent company. Turett Collaborative Architects dealt with this disparity by creating

three separate wings of office area with three distinct characters. These wings spiral about the central entrance form, the rotunda, pierced by the entry stair. As one enters the floor (accessible from the main lobby entrance above) by this stair, they must choose which of the three pathways to take, color coded in blue, yellow, and green.

Additional elements which make this a somewhat unusual office are the inclusion of progressive exercise facilities for Tommy Boy. The yoga/dance, weightlifting, and aerobic rooms are the secondary focuses of this floor, and add to the unusual character of the expansion. Color and form play important roles in the way these rooms are presented differently from the typical offices – bold blue and green stucco set these apart as special.

Another key to the success of these offices is the allowance of natural light to penetrate the inner spaces which make up the assistant areas. In each case, outside light filters through the perimeter offices' translucent walls so that artificial lighting in these spaces is kept to a minimum. With the overhead translucent "wing" elements, they have an outdoor feel to them.

Incorporating the client's philosophies
Tommy Boy, an established rap label, encourages the notion of individuality both in its music and in its staff. The design of this expansion, enlarging their offices by twice to a total of 30,000 square feet, is an attempt to foster this idea through the expressive use of color, form, materials, and light. Unusual combinations of these elements create an environment of comfort and boldness suited to this user.

A major concern of the client was that the design should adhere to the general principals of the ancient Chinese practice of *feng shui*. A *feng shui* expert visited the site with us to determine the appropriate layout of spaces, materials, colors, etc – elements which effect *feng shui*.* These principals were incorporated by dividing the project into its component wings and using color, in association with direction, to enhance the *ch'i*.** The three wings are individually unified by the three colors green, blue, and yellow. Within the private offices, an accent colored wall is opposite the user as they are seated at their desks.

As a notation, the chinese symbols for *ch'i* have been incorporated into the curved wall just beyond the rotunda, the center and entry to the floor at the bottom of the stair to the main level of Tommy Boy offices. Occupants pass by these everytime they enter the floor.

Another way that *ch'i* can be enhanced is through the demonstration of *Yin* and *Yang*.*** These two opposing forces have been expressed throughout the floor by the constant juxtaposition of opposing colors (i.e. the placement of the blue gymnasium adjacent to the green meeting/yoga room), opposing forms (the rotunda pierced by the linear stair), opposing materials (i.e. combinations of wood and metal, plaster and concrete), and opposing qualities of light (the normally dark inner courts of the assistant areas are daylit on one side by the translucent edge of the offices on which they face).

* *Feng shui* is the enhancement of ch'i to improve one's life and destiny.
** *Ch'i*, the force that links man and his surroundings, can be broken down into five elements,
each of these elements associated with a color, and each associated also with a direction:
metal – white – west
water – black – north
wood – green – east
fire – red – south
earth – yellow – center
*** *Yin* and *yang* are the two complementary forces which govern the universe and make up all things.S l

On Being Green
The shell of this project has been constructed using common building techniques standard for New York City and commercial loft construction. But the finishes used are somewhat less ordinary. It has become our standard to use environmentally-friendly materials and building methods. We have attempted to employ as many renewable resources, recycled materials, environmentally-safe products, and energy-saving devices as we could:
carpet recyclable
passes most stringent CRI Indoor Air Quality tests tackless (non-gluedown)
concrete floor/ceiling reuses existing surface
homasote recycled material (old newspapers)
mdf wood panels recycled material (sawdust by-product from milling process)
environmentally-safe (formaldehyde-free)
user-friendly stains (aniline dye)
end-grain fir floor sealed with oil and wax
wood common wood species (non-endangered) poplar, birch, ash, Douglas fir furniture Meridian approved by EPA for manufacturing standards Hermann Miller Aeron chairs 100% recyclable, approved by EPA and green
lighting dimmer switching to reduce wattage sensor switching for auto turnoff when no user
daylight translucent panels clad the offices in two wings assistant area artificial lighting usage reduced during daylight

Design: Wayne Turett and Stuart Basseches, Turett Collaborative Architects

Production: Lewis Chu and Maura Abernethy Turett Collaborative Architects
Assistance: Silke Rorig, Simeon Siegel, Kirk Lenard, Jessica Shaw, Turett Collaborative Architects
Construction:
Robert Werthamer, Robert Cook, S. Christopher Mountain, Alliance Builders
Bill and John MeleMele Construction
Fabrications: Karol Popek, Modelsmith
Cabinetry: Bruce Gardella and Paul Pickard, Modelsmith
Lighting: custom fixtures Turett Collaborative Architects
Electrical: Lalomia Electric
Desk fixtures: Artemide
industrial Stonco, Killark
Flooring: poured at rotunda Stonhard
Plaster: Stucco Lustro Veneziano

VARET MARCUS & FINK
Washington, D.C., 1992

Client: Varet Marcus & Fink
Project: Law Office
Location: Washington, DC
Service: Full Scope Interior Architecture
Size: 14,500 s.f.
Completed: 1992

In responding to Varet Marcus & Fink's desire to be "more than just another Washington law firm," the critical challenges were to make very efficient use of the available space while giving a small firm a larger presence and capitalizing on spectacular views.

The design is ordered by two pairs of converging walls that meet in a reception "rotunda." One pair of converging walls extends from the elevator lobby and connects a conference room to the south and the library to the north. From the reception area, a second pair of walls extends to the west window-wall and encloses the main conference room. Each architectural feature is designated by a different construction and finish.

The lobby/library walls pair a massive wall of pale ochre plaster with a wall assembled of mahogany panels, aluminum fins and rotary brushed stainless steel panels, the former giving the sense of a solid, pre-existing structure while the latter refers to the ground floor building lobby. The reception/conference room walls of painted drywall and of bleached reinforce the natural light from perimeter windows and indicate the transition to the more functional areas of the law firm. The four walls intersect the reception area, a cylinder of deeply tinted blue plaster.

Where the architecture of the lobby, conference, and reception areas explore forced perspectives; the use of natural and industrial materials; and the illusory qualities of richly grained wood, brushed steel and waxed plaster, the architecture of the attorney areas is ordered, rhythmic and less elaborate in the use of materials. The architecture is one of open, well-lit working areas, and reflects the importance of the team working relationships and direct flow of work amongst attorneys and secretaries.

W.B. DONER
Baltimore, Maryland, 1994.

Material Descriptions:
Floors: Flooring colors and patterns are used to define differing spaces in direct coordination with ceiling elements. Carpet in a variety of colors and patterns is the materials used throughout most of the project; the reception area has slate; some back-of-house areas have VCT.
Ceiling: Much of the ceiling is exposed, concrete waffle-slab of the base building, painted white with black "shadows" following lines of dropped ceiling elements. These feature elements are ordinary suspended ceiling grid and curving metal edging system with wire mesh inserts. Suspended drywall ceilings with recessed lighting are used in executive offices and presentation room.
Furniture: Most of the office furniture and seating is Vitra's "Metropol" line, selected for its high-tech appearance, versatility, and ergonomic design. The special group-use spaces -the commons, presentation rooms, lobby- have custom furniture.
Walls: Walls, in coordination with floors and ceilings, are in a constant state of flux, changing materials frequently and dematerializing altogether in some locations. Corridors are defined with solid, full-height, fabric-covered partitions on the core side and 8'-tall screens of alternating stained flush wood doors and art glass panels on the perimeter office side. Wall surfaces include art glass, distressed metal panels, special paint techniques, and fabric wallcoverings.
Stair: The feature stair in the 2-story reception area remained from the previous tenant. It was stripped down to its concrete structure, and new metal railings designed to express the movement and thrust of the stair were added.
Inside structure: The concrete structure of the base building -waffle slab and large round or square columns- was exposed in most instances and painted.

BIOGRAFIE
BIOGRAPHIES

Architecture + Light
Pier Five, The Embarcadero
San Francisco, CA 94111
tel. 415-6763999 - fax 415/3974375
e-mail: archlight@batnet.com

Architecture + Light is a San Francisco design studio led by Darrell Hawthorne, Mark Stevens and Peter VanDine. Founded in 1994, the firm has established a reputation for both architectural and lighting design on the west coast and the Far East. Recent projects include two brewery restaurants for Gordon Biersch Brewing Company in Las Vegas, restaurants in San Francisco and the Bay Area and the O'Brien Center for Scholarly Publications at the Hasting College of the Law. Lighting design work includes the flagship stores for the Banana Republic in Chicago and Miami, as well as numerous other stores for the Gap, Old Navy, and Banana Republic. Far East work includes the Venetian Restaurant at the Shangri-La Hotel in Bangkok and the Les Saveurs in Tokyo. Putnam, Lovell and Thorton which is currently undergoing a phase-two expansion, received a San Francisco Chapter AIA Interior Design Award in 1996

Asfour & Guzy Associates Architects
594 Broadway, suite 1204, New York, NY 10012
tel: 212-3349350, fax 212-3349009

Asfour Guzy Architects, founded in 1988 by Edward Asfour and Peter Guzy, is a multi-disciplinary firm involved in projects including institutional, commercial, retail, residential and industrial design, planning, interior design, furniture design and restaurant design.
Asfour Guzy Architects has completed over 100 projects in Europe, Canada, California, Florida and the new York City Area. Presently, some of the firm's projects include, offices for TVT Records, several residential projects, a photographer's studio and residence in the Hudson Valley, The Blue Ribbon Bakery and cafe in New York, and the renovation of a warehouse in Greenwich, CT. for the corporate offices of Chalk and Vermilion, an art publishing company. Edward Asfour began his career at the San Francisco office of Skidmore, Owings & Merrill. He subsequently taught architectural design and methods and materials of construction at the Swiss Federal Institute of Technology in Zürich, Switzerland and at Ohio State University in Columbus. Mr. Asfour, after studies at the Architectural Association in London and with O.M. Ungers in Berlin, received his B.ARCH. from Syracuse University in 1981.
Peter Guzy began his career at the office of Werner Seligmann in Cortland, NY. He subsequently taught architectural design at the Swiss Federal Institute of Technology in Zürich, Switzerland. Prior to joining with Mr. Asfour in New York, he established the office of Peter Guzy and Associates, Architects in Zürich, which completed a wide range of projects during a five-year period. Mr. Guzy received hi B. ARCH. from Cornell University in 1979. He was subsequently awarded The Eidlitz Fellowship which was completed in residence at the American Academy in Rome.

Carl D'Aquino Interiors, Inc.
180 Varick Street, 4th floor, New York, NY 10014
tel. 212-9299787, fax 212-9299225

Carl D'Aquino, ASID, principal of his own Manhattan-based interior design firm, earned a degree in architecture from the City University of New York.
Prior to establishing Carl D'Aquino Interiors, Inc., he worked with Alan Buchsbaum, Giovanni Pasanella, and Peter Blake, among others.
Architect, painter, and sculptor, Paul Laird has been affiliated with D'Aquino since 1982. He studied painting and architecture at the Cleveland Institute of Art and earned a degree in architecture at the Cleveland Institute of Art and earned a degree in architecture from Cornell University.
John Chow joined D'Aquino in 1986 after working with artist Arakawa as a project architect for the Tokyo Bay landfill master plan, and with Diane Lewis Architects. He received his B. Arch. from Cooper Union School of Architecture and M. Arch. from Harvard University.

Francois de Menil, Architect P.C.
21 E. 40th St., New York, NY 1007
tel. 212-7793400 - fax: 212-9474381
e-mail: fdemenil@fdarch.com

Francois de Menil, Architect, P.C. is a sole proprietorship professional corporation providing a range of commercial, retail, residential and institutional architectural services. The company was established in New York State in 1991. Francois de Menil is the president and senior design principal. The office seeks to have no more than three to four clients/projects at any one time in order to be able to concentrate on design and provide a high level of attention to the client's project throughout the process. The firm has completed work in the United States and Japan.
Mr. de Menil, a graduate of the Chanin School of Architecture of The Cooper Union, was an established documentary film-maker for many years before entering Architecture School. After graduation and prior to establishing his own firm, Mr. de Menil worked in the offices of Richard Meier and Partners, Kohn Pederson Fox Associates, P.C., and Nagel and Lesser Architects. His work has been exhibited at The Cooper Union's Houghton Gallery, Rice University's Farish Gallery, The Schafler Gallery at Pratt Institute and The Chang Gallery at Kansas State University. His work has been published in *A+U*, *Interior Design*, *Progressive Architecture*, *Abitare*, *Architectural Record*, and *Architecture*. He is a registered Architect in New York and Texas. He is a member of the National AIA, the NYC/AIA Chapter, and certified by NCARB (National Council of Architectural Registration Boards).
De Menil's work is rooted in a search for an architecture of essence and simplicity that enhances the human spirit.

Margaret Helfand Architects.
32 East 38th Street, New York, NY 10016
tel. 212-779 7260, fax 212-779 7758

Margaret Helfand, principal of her own firm since 1981, has gained recognition through awards and publications for her innovative design approach to a broad diversity of projects ranging from institutional buildings to experimental interiors and from campus planning to the design of functional objects. The last decade of this work is honored in a monograph by the Monacelli Press to be published in the summer of 1998.
Her work is characterized by logic, simplicity and sensuality, geometry, materials and details are the three axes along which all projects are conceived and developed, creating strong continuity through a diverse portfolio of work.
Helfands earned a Master of Architecture degree from the University of California, Berkeley after studies at the College of Environmental Design at Berkeley and the Architectural Association, London. Before founding her own firm, she was an Associate with Marcel Breuer Associates, and earlier worked with Archigram in London. She serves frequently as a guest critic in architecture studios at schools including Columbia University, Pratt Institute, SCI-ARC, Yale University and the University of Pennsylvania. She has lectured on her firm's work at Columbia, SCI-ARC, Northern Illinois University, the American Craft Museum in New York and the Cooper-Hewitt Museum.
Ms. Helfand is currently Vice President of the AIA New York Chapter and President of Art Awareness, an artists' community in Upstate New York offering residencies for visual and performing artist developing new work.

Holey Associates
2 South Park
San Francisco, CA 94107
tel. 415-5370999 - fax 415/5370953
e-mail: ashley@holeyassociates.com

Holey Associates identifies integrated and inspiring design solutions that build business – while preserving the heart and soul of company culture. This is smart design and smart business. This is thoughtful innovation.
In a global and digital economy it's more important than ever to work smarter and faster. While the rapid adoption of communication technologies offers many new choices for how we work and live, sifting through all the options for today's work environment becomes more complex. Holey Associates has developed a unique expertise that addresses the transformation of the work environment.
Since its founding in 1984, Holey Associates has created workplaces for many of the nation's more dynamic companies - from established industry leaders such as the Monsanto Company, CBS tel.evision (add another) CUC International *Robertson Stephens / Bank of America* and Andersen Consulting - to fast growing start-ups such as America Online, Hummer Winblad Venture Partners, Idea Factory, Wired Ventures, Revo Sunglasses, and Univision tel.evision Group. From its studios in San Francisco's lively South of Market area, Holey Associates works throughout the United States. Holey Associates' designs, commentary and forecasts concerning the changing workplace have appeared frequently in leading national and international design publications, as well as in the business press, including *National Public Radio, The San Jose Mercury* and the French National Press.
Design is a tool for increasing competitive edge. The design process opens the possibilities for working smarter, as well as faster.
It's a speeded-up world. With greater freedoms – and complexities – thanks in part to global competition and the need to be as fast and nimble as possible. Design provide the opportunity to bring
Technological advances are changing how we work.

We can work in a number of places. There is a tremendous freedom that can be seized for expanding the range of possibilities. It requires an analysis and redesign of how we work and live.

Holey Associates presents integrated design solutions.
Integrated Workplace Solutions
Design as Competitive Edge in Business

Team
Creativity thrives on diversity.
Our office hires a talented staff with varied backgrounds and experiences.
You will find us expert and interesting people.

Steven Holl Architects
435 Hudson Street New York, NY 10014
tel 212-9090918 fax 212-4639718
e-mail: sha@walrus.com

Steven Holl, principal
Steven Holl (b. Bremerton, Washington, 1947) established Steven Holl Architects in New York in 1976. Holl is an honors graduate of the University of Washington. He studied architecture in Rome, Italy in 1970, and did post-graduate work at the Architectural Association in London in 1976.
In 1989, the Museum of Modern Art presented Holl's work in a special two-man show, purchasing several drawings for their permanent collection. In 1991, Holl's work was featured in a solo exhibition at the Walker Art Center in Minneapolis, in the series entitled "Architecture Tomorrow" curated by Mildred Friedman. This exhibition was moved to the Henry Art Gallery in Seattle, Washington and in 1992-3 exhibited throughout Europe. In 1992 Holl received the National AIA Interiors Award for the offices of D.E. Shaw & Co. in New York City and in 1993 the National AIA Honor Award for Excellence in Design for "Texas Stretto House" in Dallas, Texas. That same year, Steven Holl Architects was awarded the winning design among 516 entries in the competition for the new Museum of Contemporary Art, Helsinki. The project is scheduled to complete construction in January 1998. Among his most recent honors are the 1995 New York Honor Awards for Excellence in Design for "Chapel of St. Ignatius" in Seattle, Washington, and the "Cranbrook Institute of Science" addition and renovation in Bloomfield Hills, Michigan. Holl's 190 unit Makuhari Housing in Chiba, Japan, which won an A.I.A. award for Design Excellence, recently completed construction in March 1996.

Professional affiliations
NCARB Registered - New York, New Jersey, California, Michigan, Washington, Ohio, Florida, Texas
American Institute of Architects
American Association of Museums
Honorary Whitney Circle, Whitney Museum of American Art

Teaching
Columbia University Graduate School of Architecture and Planning, New York:
Tenured Professor since 1989; Adjunct professor since 1981
University of Washington, Seattle
Pratt Institute, New York
University of Pennsylvania, Philadelphia

Honors
1990 Arnold W. Brunner Prize for Achievement in Architecture as an Art - American Academy and Institute of Arts and Letters

Tomoakil Tanaka, registered architect, Japan
4 years with Steven Holl Architects
Waseda University, Japan
Yale University School of Architecture, Honors Graduate
Project Architect: Makuhari Housing, Japan Project Team: Museum of Contemporary Art, Helsinki,
Finland; Villa den Haag, The Netherlands;

Justin Russli, registered architect, Switzerland
3 years with Steven Holl Architects
Eidgenossische Technische Hochschule Zürich, Switzerland dipl. arch. ETH
Columbia University Graduate School of Architecture, MSAAD
Recipient of Eternit Award for Postgraduate Studies; Award for Excellence in Design, Columbia University
Project Architect: Zollikerberg Housing, Zurich; Düsseldorf Harborfront, Düsseldorf. Project Team: Museum of Contemporary Art, Helsinki

Chris McVoy
2 years with Steven Holl Architects
University of Virginia, BS Architecture
Columbia University Graduate School of Architecture
Guggenheim Studentship, 1985; William Kinne Travel Fellowship; American Scandinavian Foundation Grant
Project Architect: Cranbrook Institute of Science

Pablo Castro - Estévez, registered architect, New York
1 year with Steven Holl Architects
3 years with Richard Meier & Partners
Universidad de San Juan, Argentina, Honors Graduate
Columbia University Graduate School of Architecture
1st Prize San José Veteran's Memorial Competition
Project Team: Museum of Contemporary Art, Helsinki, Cranbrook Institute of Science, Michigan

Janet Cross
6 years with Steven Holl Architects
University of California, Berkeley, BA Architecture, Summa Cum Laude
Project Designer: Walker Museum Exhibition, Minneapolis; Z-House, Millbrook; Competition Museum of Contemporary Art, Helsinki; Third and Fourth Floor Exhibition, Whitney Museum of American Art, New York

Timothy Bade
2 years with Steven Holl Architects
Arizona State University, BS Architecture
Columbia University Graduate School of Architecture
Arizona AIA Travel Fellowship, McKim Prize, William Kinne Travel Fellowship
Project Architect: St. Ignatius Chapel, Seattle University, WA

Bibliography of Published Work
GA International '95, May 1995; Museum Contemporary Art, Helsinki
Architecture, May 1995, pp. 43; Cranbrook Institute of Science.
de Architect, April 1995, pp. 28-49; Selected Projects.
Archis, April 1995, Selected Projects.
GA Houses #45, April 1995, pp. 76-82; Makuhari Housing, Zollikerberg Housing
"The Periphery" *Architectural Design Profile* No. 108, 1994, pp. 86-89; Edge of a City.
"Steven Holl" *Die Bauwelt* - The Week in Review, August 1994; Exhibition Review
"Inside Out" INSITE, May 1994, pp. 43-45; Storefront for Art and Architecture, New York.
"A Clean Sweep." *New York Times Magazine*, 10 April 1994, pp. 20-24; Texas Stretto House.
Architecture and Urbanism, April 1994, pp. 28-38; Kaistrasse 18, Dusseldorf.
Archithese, March/April 1994; Selected Projects.
L'Architecture d'Aujourd'hui, February 1994, pp. 86-115; Selected Projects.
International Interiors, 1993; D. E. Shaw & Co., New York.
Progressive Architecture, September 1993; M.O.C.A. Helsinki.
Light & Architecture, September 1993; D. E. Shaw & Co, New York.
Casabella, September 1993; Selected Projects.
Lotus #77, August 1993; Texas Stretto House.
Artemis. August 1993; Selected Projects.
GA Houses #38, August 1993, pp. 32 - 59; Texas Stretto House.
GA Architect #11, January 1993; Collected Works.
Quaderns #197, November - December 1992, pp. 48 - 87; Selected Projects.
Domus, December 1992, pp. 56-65; Texas Stretto House.
GA Houses #34, Project 1992, pp. 34-37; Port Ludlow
"Stream & Consciousness" *Progressive Architecture*, November 1992, pp. 54-63; Texas Stretto House
Abitare, October 1992, pp. 207-212; D. E. Shaw & Co., New York.
"A Design That Taps Into the 'Informational City" *The New York Times*, August 1992. p. 32; D. E. Shaw & Co., New York.
"Virtual Reality" *Architectural Record*, June 1992, pp. 114-119; D. E. Shaw & Co., New York.
Domus, October 1991, pp. 42-51; Fukuoka Housing Project, Japan.
"The Japan Architect" -- *JA Housing*, Autumn 1991, pp. 92-103; Fukuoka Housing.
"A Cross Cultural Concert in the Far East" *Progressive Architecture*, August 1991.
"Holl Explores City's Edge at Walker" *Architecture*, June 1991, pp. 33-34.
"Steven Holl in Walker's Last Look at Tomorrow" *Progessive Architecture*, June 1991, pp. 28-29.
"A Once Modest Architect Lets Out the Stops" *The New York Times*, 26 May 1991, p. 28; Walker Review.
"Quinta Monstra Internazionale di Architettura" La Biennale di Venezia, 1991, pp. 102-117.
"Work in Progress," *Architectural Record*, April 1991, pp. 134-137; Texas Stretto House.
"1991 AIA Honor Awards" *Architecture*, March 1991, pp. 65; Hybrid Building.
"38th PA Awards," *Progressive Architecture*, January 1991, pp. 114-116; Fukuoka Housing.
Technologia y Arquitecture, December 1990, pp. 132-165; Berkowitz-Odgis House

L'Architecture D'Aujourd'Hui, October 1990, pp. 122-6.
"House echoes, embraces water" *Texas Architect*, September-October 1990, p. 44.
"Master Alchemist" *Elle Decor*, May 1990, pp. 92-99.
New York Architektur, 1970-1990, August 1989, pp. 148-152; five projects.
Progressive Architecture, August 1989, pp. 59-67; Hybrid Building.
Architecture, May 1989, pp. 140-143; Berkowitz-Odgis House.
Architecture and Urbanism, July 1989, pp. 3-14; review of the M.O.M.A. Exhibition.
Architectural Record, June 1989, pp. 65; American Memorial Library, Berlin.
L'Architecture D'Aujourd'hui, June 1989; review of the M.O.M.A. Exhibition.
Abitare #274, May 1989; Metropolitan Tower Apartment.
Architectural Record, March 1989, p. 33; Ambasz and Holl at M.O.M.A
Quaderns D'Architectura i Urbanisme (Vol. 181-182), April-September 1989, pp. 164-169; AML, Berlin.
Progressive Architecture, March 1989, p.33; M.O.M.A. review.
"A Dreamer Who is Fussy About the Details." *Time Magazine*, March 20, 1989, pp. 75-7.
The New York Times, Sunday 12 February 1989; review of the M.O.M.A. Exhibition.
Wrede, Stuart, ed. Emilio Ambasz/Steven Holl: Architecture, The Museum of Modern Art Exhibition Catalog, New York, February, 1989.
The Architectural Review, February 1989, pp. 33-39; five projects.
Casa Vogue, January 1989, pp. 66-85; five projects.
Paris-Architecture et Utopie, 1989, pp.74-77.
"Meet the Architect." *G.A. Houses* #25, 1989, pp. 164-227; ten projects
"House for Mr. and Mrs. B." *Utopica Two Architecture/Nature*, 1988, pp. 64-69.
"The Conviction of This Project Is..." *Off Ramp* (Sci-Arc Journal), 1988.
New York Architecture Vol. 1 New York Chapter AIA. 1988 Design Awards Program. 1988, pp. 11, 16-7, 51-52, 58-61.
Fischer, Thomas. "A Literary House." *Progressive Architecture*, December 1988, pp. 62-67.
Russell, James S. "Skin and Bones." *Architectural Record*, Mid-September 1988, pp. 122-12; Metropolitan Tower Apartment.
Byron, Elizabeth S. "The Holl Truth." *House and Garden*, September 1988, pp. 184-91, 245.
"Architects Review Furniture: 7 Leading Architects Think About What Works, What Doesn't --And Why." *Architectural Digest*, August 1988, pp. 52,56.
"Awards." *Occulus*, vol. 50, March 1988, pp. 6, 11.
"Three Projects." *A+U*, January 1988, pp. 39-58.
"The Emerging Generation in theUSA: Steven Holl." *GA Houses Special* 2, 1987, pp. 92-97; Berkowitz-Ogdis House.
Guerrera, Giuseppe. "Steven Holl." *New York Architects*, 1987, pp. 109-113.
"Le Citta Imaginate." XVII Triennale Di Milano Catalogue (Milan: Electa), 1987, pp 292-295; Urban Proposal Porta Vittoria.
"Porta Vittoria Project Area." *Lotus International* #54, 1987, pp. 96-193.
Bethany, Marilyn. "What's Modern Now? Suprise Package." *New York Magazine*, 28 September 1987, pp.64-67; Giada Clothing Shop.
Stein, Karen D. "Portfolio: Steven Holl Architects." *Architectural Record*, September 1987, cover and pp. 90-101; Museum Tower Apt., Giada Clothing Shop
Di Giorgio, Manola. "Una Piccola Galeria a Manhattan." *Domus*, June 1987, pp. 5-6; Pace Collection Showroom.
"Showroom for the Pace Collection." *A+U*, May 1987, pp. 89-94.
"Steven Holl, Three Projects." *AA Files* #14, Spring 1987, pp. 18-24.
34th PA Awards: Citation - Hybrid Building. *Progressive Architecture*, January 1987, pp. 108-9.
Nicolin, Pierluigi, ed. "Commercial Buildings with Residences." *Lotus International* #50, 1986, pp. 27-29.
Nicolin, Pierluigi, ed. "Bridge of Houses in Manhattan, Individual Characterizations, Urban Houses in North America." *Lotus International* #44, 1986, pp. 41-50; projects and research.
McNair, Andrew. "40 Under 40." *Interiors*, September 1986, p. 175
"Works: Steven Holl." *A+U*, August 1986, pp. 59-74.
Smith, C. Ray. "Tale of Two Interiors." *Unique Homes* (City Living), June/July 1986.
"New York Showroom." *Nikkei Architecture*, May 1986, pp. 82-87.
Gandee, Charles K. "Pace Maker" Architectural Record, April 1986, pp. 93-103.
Adams, Janet. "The Avant Garde Grows Up." *Blueprint* #35, March 1986, pp. 34-5, 38.
33rd PA Awards: Citation -- Berkowitz House. *Progressive Architecture*, January 1986, pp. 104-6.
Expressions: 5 New Design Stores" The New York Times, 16 January 1986, Section C-1.
Bethany, Marilyn. "Setting the Pace." *New York Magazine*, January 1986, pp. 44-6.
"Record Interiors, 1984." *Nikkei Architecture*. 1985, cover and pp. 179-18.
Bartos, A. "A Humanistic Approach to Building Design." *Esquire*, December 1985, p.84.
"Modernism Takes a New Turn." *Home Decorating*, Fall 1985, pp. 30-35.
Davis, Douglas. *Newsweek*, 12 August 1985, p. 64.
"Cohen Apartment." *Occulus*, May 1985, p.3.
Greenstreet, Bob. "Law: Who Really Owns Your Designs." *Progressive Architecture*, April 1985, p. 63.
Gandee, Charles, K. "Homework." *Architectural Record* Interiors, Fall 1984, pp. 153-163.

Phillips, Patricia C. "Steven Holl at Facade Gallery." *Artforum*, October 1984, p.93; review of exhibit.
Giovannini, Joseph. "An Unbuilt House Sets Up a Quandary." *The New York Times*, 18 October 1984; Van Zandt Residence.
"Accent on Grandeur." *Newsweek*, 3 September 1984, pp. 70-71; Cohen Residence.
Regnier, Constance. "Ein Kuehnes Experiment Mit 3 Deimensionen." *Ambiente*, August 1984, cover and
pp. 3, 118-127.
Bethany, Marilyn. "The Look of the 80s." *New York Magazine*, 16 April 1984, cover and pp. 54-56.
"Steven Holl." 'Architecture in Transition' Neue Architecktur: Sieben Junge Architekten aus Amerika, Deutschland, Endland und Italien, exhibition catalogue, April 1984, pp. 44-53.
31st PA Awards - Van Zandt Residence. *Progressive Architecture*, January 1984, pp. 102-3.
"Deposito de Casas de Seguridad/Estudio de Escultura y Casa de Baños." *Arquitectura*, September/October 1983, pp. 66-68.
Viladas, Pilar. "Banca Rotunda." *Progressive Architecture*, September 1983, pp. 100-103; Guardian Safe Depository
Giovanni, Joseph. "Designers are Creating Etched Glass Renaissance." *The New York Times*, 11 August 1983, pp. C-1, C-10; Sandblasted Glass
Filler, Martin. "A Poetry of Place." *House & Garden*, May 1993, pp. 78-81.
"Pont de Maisons: Projet pour Manhattan." *Architecture DAujord'hui*, February 1993, pp. 9-10; Bridge of Houses.
Iaccuci. "Projects: Poolhouse by Steven Holl." *Archetype*, vol II, no. IV, Fall 1982, pp. 26-29.
Miller, Nory. "Braving the Elements." *Progressive Architecture*, July 1982, pp. 78-81; Poolhouse and Sculpture Studio.
"Neue Tendenzen in den USA: Steven Holl." *Werk, Bauen & Wohnen*, May 1982, pp. 40-43.
"Works: Sculpture Studio by Steven Holl." *A+U*. April 1982, pp. 46-50.
"New Waves in American Architecture: 3." *GA Houses* #10, March 1982, pp. 128-137.
Weinstein, Edward. "Steven Holl: Hybrid Architect." *Arcade*, February/March 1982.
29th PA Awards - Metz House. *Progressive Architecture*, January 1982, pp. 152-155.
"Three Projects." *A+U*, April 1981, pp. 73-84.
Miller, Nory. "Interventions: Good Fences." *Progressive Architecture*, February 1981, pp. 92-93.
Emery, Marc. "Consultation Internationale sur le Quartier des Halles, Paris." *Architecture D'Aujord'hui*, April 1980, p. 7.
Maroni, Angioli. "Tre Edifici." *New Americans*, 1979, p.55.
Domus, December 1979, p. 7; Sokolov project.
Archetype, vol. 1, no. 1, Spring 1979, pp. 29-30.
Battisti, Emilio. "Tre Giovani Architetti Americani." *Controspazio*, April 1979, pp. 49-53.
"Retreat for M. Sokolov." *A+U*, February 1979, p.22.
Selig, M. "Gymnasium-Bridge: Checkerboard Site Plan to Signal Hope and Despair." The Harlem River Yards: Bridging a South Bronx Community Need, 1978, pp. 6-8; study.
25th PA Awards: "Haunting Image by a Young Architect." *Progressive Architecture*, January, 1978, p. 81.
Architecture of Self-Help Communities. January 1978, pp. 66-71.
Baumeister, October 1976, cover.
"Prelude au Congres de Vancouver Habitat '76." *Architecture D'Aujord'hui*, no. 185, May/June 1976, pp. 90-91.
Wagner, Walter F. "International Design Competition for the Urban Environment of Developing Countries." *Architectural Record* 5, May 1976, pp. 136-139.
Hilgenhurst, Ch. A. "Back from Niagara." *Architecture Plus*, April 1973, pp. 74-75.

Kohn, Perdersen, Fox Associates, P.C.
251 W 57th St., 14th Floor, New York, NY 10012
tel. 212-3971100 - 2373408 - fax 212/9562526

Introduction
Founded in 1976, KPF offers full architecture, master planning, space planning, programming and building analysis services. The firm's work in the United States and abroad has earned KPF recognition as one of the most respected architectural design firms in the world.
In 1990, Kohn Pedersen Fox became the youngest firm ever to be honored with the highest honor granted by the American Institute of Architects, the AIA Architectural Firm Award, in recognition of years of achievement and contribution to the built environment.
The following year, *Architecture* magazine conducted a poll, asking its readers, "of today's practicing architects, whose work do you admire?" Kohn Pedersen Fox Associates tied for first place, cited for their "principled and intelligent" approach to design.

International Reputation
In the 1990s, as more commissions have originated from abroad, the firm has expanded its reach to over 28 foreign countries, solidifying their reputation, designing buildings and master plans for some of the world's most respected companies and organizations.

Diversity of Experience
KPF has developed proficiency in the design of a variety of project types for both the private and public sectors. KPF believes a strong and diverse background is the key to design excellence and approaches each new project as a unique challenge.

Design Reputation
Having substantial prestige as a top architectural firm, KPF is continually hired by many of the world's most established companies and institutions to design and construct millions of dollars worth of facilities. KPF is especially attentive to the Client/User's special needs and interests as well as the site and region of each project. Because of this relationship and KPF's track record as firm that has persistently delivered quality product, the majority of the firm's clients have commissioned Kohn Pedersen Fox for more than one project. The American Broadcasting Company, for example, has hired KPF to design 15 projects over the last 15 years.

Firm Philosophy
Kohn Pedersen Fox does not have any one specific architectural style. KPF's design is always the product of each individual situation. Enormous pressure is placed on architecture to be the willful expression of personal originality. However, architects often forget the human and physical context and create an architecture of mere self-indulgence. The philosophy of Kohn Pedersen Fox holds as its premise that this condition must be resisted.
Rather than being driven by an overriding design style, KPF is driven by an overriding design intent. If KPF is to be known for anything for its work as architects, it is to be known as architects of structures that are intimately connected to function and context; structures which hopefully achieve a degree of craft and concern for detail which elevates them to the highest level of both beauty and practicality.

Design Approach
The philosophy of KPF begins with an insistence on design excellence, partner commitment, and superior management. The partners, together with a team of architects, are involved in the supervision and design of each project from the initial stages of planning through construction and post-construction.
Every architectural problem brings substantial variation to each design solution, and KPF has been successful in translating both the mission and the vision of its clients through our designs. Meaningful architecture has been achieved through creating a balanced dialogue between three sets of conditions:
- functional and programmatic issues
- a building's physical context
- concerns arising from an owner's desires and aspirations

Abstract intellectual ideas, human considerations, and environmental concerns are all part of a carefully considered process that is rooted in basic budgetary and programmatic needs.
Through this method KPF is better able to open their minds to the potential of an architectural problem. It also enables the Clients to enter into a more meaningful dialogue with KPF. The firm's intent is to demystify the design process and to subject each of the possibilities to the harsh light of informed questioning.
All phases of the work, from the broadest to the most detailed, evolve from such a comparative method. The end results are humane spaces that are functional as well as beautiful.

Conclusion
KPF works with its clients to help design projects which architecturally express their identity while ensuring that their program is fulfilled with maximum efficiency and flexibility for years to come.

Interior Design Experience
Designing an efficient, flexible workplace
Kohn Pedersen Fox's design of the office work environment began with a corporate headquarters for AT&T in Oakton, VA in 1980, for their "Office of the Future." Today, KPF continues to be a leader in developing innovative work environments with the Worklife Center for Steelcase. Just completed last year, it is the office and showroom for the most cutting edge and flexible office work systems. During the past thirteen years, KPF has planned and designed more than 12.5 million square feet of interior space, and currently has work in the United States, South America, Europe, and Asia.
Key to the successful design of an efficient interior space is KPF's investigation of the way the Client is organized and uses the space. KPF carefully integrates the interior planning and program elements within a flexible and cohesive building form, functioning with the highest degree of efficiency. In KPF office projects, for example, one finds state-of-the-art facilities which integrate high technology with flexibility for the future, both in terms of the adaptability of the spaces and ability to handle future changes in technology and telecommunications cabling and wiring.
Expert cost effective coordination of mechanical systems, cabling, and structural changes, that is to say all those things behind the walls and above the ceiling that one never sees but are critical to good design is what the KPF interior design staff specializes in. As well, KPF has a state-of-the-art computer system and uses CADD to document all design projects.
KPF maintains an extensive resource library, and has a full-time research staff trained to investigate materials, fabrics and furniture. The design and research staff also analyzes other important factors like environmental forces and sociological considerations that are vital in shaping the direction of a project. KPF staff members are completely familiar with the technical requirements of the Americans with Disabilities Act, and have established guidelines for using products that conform to the highest standards of design excellence while fulfilling the functional requirements of this law. This dedication to research and analysis allows KPF to create truly three-dimensional solutions geared to the specific needs of a client.

A well-designed interior does not evolve arbitrarily, but out of a rigorous design process. Each KPF project uses a set of architectural ideas in which the laws of geometry, the principles of proportion, and the intrinsic qualities of the materials are explored to formulate a precise concept. The goal is to give each client a finished product that captures their own unique imagination and identity.

KressCox Associates, PC
2909 M Street NW, Washington DC, 20007
tel: 202-9657070, fax 202-3349009

KressCox Associates PC is a nationally recognized, architectural design, planning, programming, space planning and interior design firm with a professional staff of 25 based in Georgetown, Washington DC. Founded in 1981, the firm has distinguished itself as a leading design force in the Nation's Capital, winning 38 national and local awards to date, with the following 7 being award in 1996-97: 1 of the 13 National AIA Honor Awards for architecture, 2 of the 11 National AIA Awards of Excellence in Religious Architecture, and 3 of the 18 Washington Chapter /AIA Awards for architecture.

KressCox architects and designers have many diverse talents; therefore the firm's portfolio is broad, including commercial, retail, civic, institutional, governmental, educational, industrial, religious, transportation and residential design, as well as specialized studies and reports. In addition, the firm employs specialists in historic preservation, accessibility design, environmental design, energy conservation, life cycle costing, value engineering, building codes, variances and waivers.

In eighteen years, KressCox has put its signature on much of the Washington, D.C. cityscape in addition to areas across the country. *Progressive Architecture* included KressCox among a select group of architects on the forefront of innovative design in Washington, D.C. In April, 1991, Architecture magazine included the design of the new office building at 1331 F St., N.W. in a group pictorial of "a new generation of increasingly urbanistically sensitive buildings, especially in the commercial core." The magazine's editors placed KressCox among "a younger generation of local architects" who "turn away from the polite historicism of 1980's Washington" and who "design buildings that relate to their surroundings without looking like period architecture."

The prestigious awards and critical praise KressCox received from its inception, have established the firm as a major local and national force in architectural design. The firm has earned such recent awards as a 1997 AIA Honor Award from the National American Institute of Architects for Arlington National Cemetery Facility Maintenance Complex; 1996 AIA/Washington D.C. Chapter Award of Merit in Architecture for the Arlington National Cemetery Facility Maintenance Complex and Connelly Chapel of Holy Wisdom; a 1995 AIA/Washington D.C. Chapter Merit Award for Historic Preservation for Founders Hall at Georgetown Visitation Preparatory School; and a 1997 National AIA Award of Excellence in Religious Architecture for Western Presbyterian Church and Connelly Chapel of Holy Wisdom. The jurors praised the KressCox design of Western Presbyterian Church for its successful integration of the past and present "without destroying the delicate architecture of the old, and without mimicking what was there before." They also praised KressCox's design of Connelly Chapel of Holy Wisdom by stating [they] "took a banal set of apartment buildings and wonderful but somewhat menacing chimney and created a composition so strong that it actually grabs all of its surroundings as well."

Right around the corner from The White House stands the Colorado Building, whose design has also won several awards for KressCox, such as the 1990 Reconstruction Award from Building Design & Construction magazine as well as the 1990 Cornerstone Award. Washington Post architecture critic Benjamin

Forgey described KressCox's restoration and addition to the Beaux-Arts building "as poetic a piece of architecture as exists in the city." The 1903 office building has been recognized as a Category III Historic Landmark on the National Register.

Several other designs have also received high accolades from architecture critics. When the Columbus Georgia Museum won the 1989 AIA Design Excellence Award, Josiah Sumbry of The Columbus Ledger-Enquirer called the building "a visual sensation . . . a masterpiece." Architecture magazine also featured it in their June issue of that year.

The 1930 Manhattan Office Building, one of the few remaining examples of Art Moderne architecture in Washington, D.C. won the three top architectural awards of Washington in the same year: the AIA Design Excellence Award; The District of Columbia Mayor's First Place Design Award; and the Art Deco Society Preservation Award. It was featured in Historic Preservation magazine, and Benjamin Forgey of The Washington Post called the restoration "pure and simple," which "calls for and merits attention and applause." Forgey also gave the Art Deco-inspired new Shirlington Theater accolades for "artful design" and "good, conscientious architecture," as it too recalls the grand designs of the period.

The firm's award-winning sense is rooted in its strength to make each project strike a critical balance between sensitive design considerations and pragmatic technical requirements. Questions of aesthetic balance and visual delight are as important as sound engineering and energy conservation. Beauty and economy carry equal weight. Cost effectiveness, energy efficiency, environmental quality, building code and zoning adherence are all important factors in the generation of a total design.

A strong commitment to meeting the client's needs and a subtle understanding of the complexities of inserting new construction into existing neighborhoods yields consistent success for the firm in winning design approval from regulatory authorities. KressCox has cultivated the delicate knack of navigating the maze of influential review and approval bodies, such as: The Board of Zoning Adjustment; The Zoning Commission; The National Capital Planning Commission; The Fine Arts Commission; Pennsylvania Avenue Development Corp.; The Advisory Neighborhood Commissions; The Historic Preservation Review Board; the State Historic Preservation Officers; The Department of the Interior; and building permit review and approval authorities.

For example, residents of Columbus, Georgia were concerned about the potentially negative impact of the size of the new 200-room Hilton Hotel. A local newspaper typified citizen reaction and approval ". . .I think KressCox did an excellent job in making it blend in with the surroundings. . .We've been nothing but impressed. It's not an intrusion at all . . . It's a good thing for the city as a whole and especially for this district."

KressCox's award-winning designs, and its special ability to integrate divergent concerns -- client needs, neighborhood elements, municipal codes, engineering practicalities, budgetary factors, and aesthetic inspiration -- stand as the firm's hallmark, and forms the basis for growing public recognition and professional success.

Previously owner of Kress Associates, as well as Principal and Director of Architecture for a large architectural/engineering firm, Jerrily R. Kress, Managing Principal of KressCox Associates, has over twenty-eight years of architectural experience. She has administrated, managed and coordinated complete architectural and engineering services for numerous large projects -- among them, several stations of the Washington metro system, Spacelab support facilities for NASA, and the Hirshhorn Sculpture Garden for the Smithsonian Institution in Washington, D.C. She also has a strong background in computer-aided financial systems, expertise in historic research gained with the Historic American Buildings Survey, and she is a certified value engineering specialist.

Ms. Kress extends and enriches her professional effectiveness through her active involvement in municipal and public service organizations; she is currently serving a four year term on the D.C. Zoning Commission. She was appointed by the Mayor and City Council and was unanimously elected Chairperson by the four other members of the commission. As Chairperson, Ms. Kress also serves as a rotating member of the Board of Zoning Adjustment and was the 1991 President of the D.C. Chapter of the American Institute of Architects. Additionally, she serves on the Board of Directors of the Greater Washington Board of Trade, she is a member of the D.C. Occupational Safety and Health Board, and is chairperson of the D.C. Building Codes Advisory Committee, which recently rewrote the building codes for the District of Columbia and is now in the process of adopting the 1996 BOCA codes with amendments

David Cox's thirty years of architectural design encompass a broad range of award-winning commercial, civic, and residential projects. He has extensive experience with preservation and adaptive reuse projects, as well as neighborhood revitalization projects, community centers, and multi-use complexes. Prior to establishing his own firm -- David Cox, AIA, Architects -- he worked as Senior Associate with a large architectural firm for over seven years. His work includes large scale office and retail centers, housing developments, theaters, schools, and medical facilities. He has also performed urban design work for the downtown districts of Nashville, TN, Fort Wayne, IN, Norfolk, VA, Baltimore, MD and Columbus, GA.

Under this leadership, KressCox has seen fourteen years of projects that range from a new multi-million dollar urban waterfront development combining an extensive plaza with four city blocks of high-rise office/retail structures to a small block of shop fronts for a corner in Georgetown.- from a Department of Defense electronics R&D lab to a museum of fine arts. - from an inner-city low income housing project to an award-winning luxury condominium residence incorporating two historic mansions. - .from an urban planning/transportation study for the politically and economically sensitive Georgetown waterfront to a master planning study for the corporate headquarters of a major media organization.

At the present time, the firm is working on a wide range of commissions, including: the $280 million office headquarters for the World Bank in Washington, D.C., which combines new construction with renovation of existing structures; a new Performing Arts Center & Outdoor Amphitheater and Gymnasium at Georgetown Visitation Preparatory School, various projects at the George Washington University; the Washington Ballet in northwest Washington; NSDAR Constitution Hall; and the addition/renovation of the Lyndon House Arts Center in Athens, Georgia as well as numerous residential commissions.

NBBJ Architecture Design Planning
111 South Jackson Street Seattle, Washington 98104
tel. 206-2235555 - fax 206-6212300
e-mail: srooks@nbbj.com

Founded in Seattle in 1943 and driven by design excellence and high standards of service, NBBJ has grown to become a national and international practice, grounded in design-focused leadership. During the past 55 years, NBBJ has grown in size and in the quality of its work, while developing a national and international practice. Today, NBBJ is the second largest architectural firm in the United States – and the fifth largest in the world – and employs over 700 professionals in six U.S. cities: Seattle, Columbus, San Francisco, Los Angeles, New York, and Research Triangle Park (N.C.). NBBJ's wide range of services include: Architecture; Programming; Interior Design and Space Planning; Facilities Management; Economics and Financial Feasibility; Land Use Planning; and Graphic Design. The firm's markets include health care, corporate design/interiors, sports & entertainment, airports/transportation, commercial/mixed-use, higher education, hospitality & resorts, justice, senior housing, research and advanced technology, graphic/environmental design, and urban design. NBBJ is currently working on projects throughout North America, Asia, Europe, and Latin America.

Quantrell Mullins & Associates Inc.
999 Peachtree St. NE, Atlanta, GA 30309
tel. 404-8746048 - fax 404-8742026
e-mail: qmainc@mindspring.com

In 1974, Bianca Quantrell founded Quantrell Mullins & Associates in Atlanta, Georgia and serves as its president today. The firm's focus is commercial interior architectural programming, planning and design, with an emphasis on creative solutions, functional efficiency and budget adherence. Projects range in size up to 1 million square feet and include regional, national and international locations. The firm has worked with clients in Canada, Germany, France, Italy, Luxembourg, New York and throughout the southeastern United States. Projects include corporate headquarters and offices, financial institutions, medical facilities, hotels, clubs, retail shops and private residences.
Quantrell Mullins was founded in response to the need for an independent interior architectural specialist. The principals believe it is this independence, with no allegiance to architects, manufacturers or dealers which provides the freedom of design needed to create optimal space usage, efficient layouts, and aesthetically pleasing interior environments. Quantrell Mullins' services include master planning, building evaluation studies, programming, space planning, conceptual design, construction documentation, furnishings specifications, construction administration, product design, graphics and art programs, project management and facility management.

Smith-Miller + Hawkinson Architects
305 canal Street New York, NY 10013
tel. 212-9663875 - fax 212-9663877
e-mail: TAYLOR@smarch.com

Henry Smith-Miller began his private practice in 1977 following a seven-year association with Richard Meier and Associates where he was a project architect for several nationally recognized architectural projects: The Athenaeum at New Harmony, Indiana, the Albany Mall Art Museum, and the Bronx Developmental Center. He received an undergraduate degree from Princeton University, a Masters in Architecture from the Graduate School of Architecture at the University of Pennsylvania, and a Fulbright Grant to study architecture in Rome, Italy. Henry Smith-Miller has held visiting adjunct professor positions at Columbia University, the City University of New York, the University of Virginia, the University of Pennsylvania, Harvard University, the Thomas Jefferson Professor in Architecture at the University of Virginia, and the Saarinen Chair at Yale University. He has also served on the Board of Creative Time and is a member of the Associate Council of the Museum of Modern Art in New York. He is a registered Architect in New York, Pennsylvania, Maryland, Connecticut, California, North Carolina, Virginia, Maine, Colorado, and NCARB certified.

Laurie Hawkinson received her Masters in Fine Arts from the University of California at Berkeley, then attended the Whitney Independent Study Program in New York and received her Professional Degree in Architecture from The Cooper Union in 1983. Currently an Associate Professor of Architecture at Columbia University, Laurie Hawkinson has held visiting adjunct professor positions at SCI-Arc, Harvard University, Yale University, Parsons School of Design, and the University of Miami. She is a board member of the Architectural League of New York, a past member of the Board of Governors of the New York Foundation for the Arts, and has served as a panelist for the New York State Council on the Arts in Architecture, Planning and Design from 1986-1989. Collaborative projects include the North Carolina Museum of Art "Master" Site Plan and project, now built, for an outdoor cinema and amphitheater with artist Barbara Kruger and landscape architect Nicholas Quennell, LA Arts Park Competition and the Seattle Waterfront Project, also with Kruger and Quennell. Laurie Hawkinson is a registered Architect in New York and NCARB certified.

Smith-Miller + Hawkinson Architects, founded in 1983 is an architectural firm in New York. The firm consists of two principals, Henry Smith-Miller and Laurie Hawkinson, and fourteen employees. Smith-Miller + Hawkinson's projects span a very wide scope, from small to very large and complex interiors, from additions to free-standing single or multi-use buildings.

Recent projects include a new mixed-use building for Samsung in Seoul, Korea; the North Carolina Museum of Art project, which opened in April 1997, for an outdoor cinema and amphitheater with artist Barbara Kruger and landscape architect Nicholas Quennell; The Wall Street Ferry Terminal for Pier 11 in Lower Manhattan; Design Guidelines for the Battery Park City Authority and New York's Hudson River Ferry Terminal; and The Corning Glass Center 2000 Project, a 3-phase, $30 million millennium project, presently under construction. Smith-Miller + Hawkinson were one of six American Architects invited to exhibit in the Italian Pavilion at the 1996 Venice Biennale for Architecture, and one of four firms participating in the exhibition, "Fabrications," with an installation in the sculpture garden at the Museum of Modern Art in the Winter of 1998. Smith-Miller + Hawkinson, a monograph, was published in 1995 by Gustavo Gili Editoriale and the firm is also included in the film "The New Modernists", by Michael Blackwood.

Smith-Miller + Hawkinson bring to the firm strong interests in a general culture of architecture: its design and technological histories, as well as its complex and changing relationship to society. Of these changes, the firm is particularly interested in focusing on the ways in which the architectural program – the location and accommodation of functions, activities, and services – can be developed through innovative interpretations that are sensitive to and transformative of contemporary cultural needs and ideas.

Studios
588 Broadway, Suite 702, New York, NY 10012
Tel 212-4314512 - fax 212-4316042
e-mail: jacobs@studiosarch.com

Linda Jacobs
Linda Jacobs was educated at Cornell University, (B.S. 1977) and has practiced Interior Design in New York City and on the east coast of the United States for corporate, legal, and financial firms for twenty years. Ms. Jacobs joined ISD in 1979 and rose to the position of Vice President, undertaking projects for clients such as Price Waterhouse, A T & T, Baker & Botts, Hunton & Williams, MGM/UA, and Exxon. She continued at ISI (the successor firm to ISD), completing this assignment for Fischer, Francis, Trees & Watts after she left the firm. Currently at STUDIOS Architecture, Ms. Jacobs runs their New York office, focusing on high technology, advertising, and corporate projects. In addition to her management and design responsibilities, she has a specialty in pre-lease consulting and feasibility studies.

Ms. Jacobs is married and lives in Maplewood, New Jersey, USA. She can be contacted at (212) 431 4512. Ms. Jacobs has been published in *Interior Design Magazine, Interiors, Corporate Design*, and *The National Law Journal*.

Jon Nathanson
Jon Nathanson is an architect interior designer, product designer and painter. Educated at University of Maryland (B.Arch 1977) and Yale University (M.Arch. 1980), Mr. Nathanson studied with an array of artists and architects including Ann Truitt, Frank Gehry, Cesar Pelli, Richard Serra, Peter Eisenman, as well as many others.
Jon worked for large architecture and interior design firms for fifteen years, including Skidmore, Owings and Merrill; Swanke, Hayden Connell; Perkins & Will; ISD; ISI; and The Office of the Architect of the Capitol. He held the positions of Associate, Principal, Vice President, Design Director and Managing Director during his corporate tenure.
In 1994, Mr. Nathanson retired from the corporate milieu to focus on living with AIDS. During this period, he has made a renewed commitment to smaller scale design projects demonstrated in designs of his residences, painting and landscape design. His life has been enriched and nourished by his partner Richard Feldman and his dog RJ.

STUDIOS Architecture DC
113 Connecticut Ave. N.W., Washington DC 20036
tel. 202-7365951 - fax 202-7365959

STUDIOS Architecture SFO
99 Green Street, San Francisco, CA 94111
tel. 415-3987575 - fax 415-3983829
e-mail: gong@studiosarch.com

Established in 1985, STUDIOS Architecture (STUDIOS) is a recognized industry leader with a world-wide reputation for excellence in architectural design. Providing services in strategic design, architecture, and interior architectural design, STUDIOS combines creative problem-solving with a clear focus on the client's strategic objectives.
With offices in San Francisco, Washington DC, New York, Paris, and London, STUDIOS has established a strong international presence with many projects underway in Europe and Asia.
STUDIOS' clients include: Silicon Graphics Computer Systems, 3Com Corporation, American Express, Morgan Stanley, Credit Suisse First Boston, Andersen Consulting, AirTouch Communications, MCI, Excite, and Petronas Bhd.
The firm has garnered more than 70 design awards and has been featured in more than 100 publications for its work around the world.

Tas Design
145 Hudson Street, New York, NY 10013
tel. 212-3348318 - fax 212-3348025
e-mail: Bongabilia@aol.com

TAS Design Firm Profile Established in New York City in 1983 by Thomas Sansone, TAS Design employs Architects and Designers with collective experience on projects throughout the United States and in Europe. TAS Design's primary commitment is to create highly crafted interior spaces which carefully orchestrate clients, functional priorities with an enhancement of their visual and spatial environment. Within many different contexts and at varying project scales, the design intent is always to create spaces of serenity, expansion and reflection. The primacy of an intelligent plan is the generating principle whether the design is for a new structure out of the ground or for the conversion of existing spaces to new uses. Thomas Sansone Principal Thomas Sansone is the principal of TAS Design. He received his Bachelor of Arts degree from Williams College and his Masters of Science degree in Environmental Art and Architecture from the Massachusetts Institute of Technology. Mr. Sansone began his practice as a designer and builder of highly crafted residential and commercial interiors. In 1986, Mr. Sansone worked as part of the team organized to develop the Massachusetts Museum of Contemporary Art, an historic rehabilitation, converting 800,000 square feet of a former mill complex in North Adams, Massachusetts, to a new museum of contemporary art and related public facilities. In 1988 he began work with the Guggenheim Museum directing their extensive reorganization, design and construction projects. Thomas Sansone served as Director of Capital Planning for the Guggenheim Foundation in New York from 1988 - 1993. In this capacity he was responsible for directing and coordinating the museum's expansion program totaling $65 million of construction. Under his direction, TAS Design provided research for the restoration of the Frank Lloyd Wright building, formulated the application for its landmark status, oversaw construction administration, provided design services for all interior renovations and assisted in the development and strategy of their capital campaigns. From 1993 - 1997, TAS Design worked extensively in Miami on a number of projects; the renovation of a commercial art deco office complex; a private facility for the Rubell art collection; and new corporate headquarters for Sony Music International. In New York, design services for the National Urban League's new headquarters on Wall Street were completed as well as various commercial and residential projects.

Project Team
Thomas Sansone, Principal in Charge
Skip Boling, Project Architect
Patrocinio Binuya, Carlos Sifuentes, Kim Sippel, Robert Thorpe, Ileana Fernandez, FF & E Associated Architect, Gustavos Ramos Structural Consultants, Gilsanz, Murray, Steficek, Mechanical Consultants
Steven Feller and Associates Lighting Consultant
Thomas Thompson

TsAO McKown Architects
41 E. 42nd St., Suite 1610
New York, NY, 10017
tel. 212-33738100 - fax 212-3370013
e-mail: mullan@tsao-mckown.com

The partnership of Calvin TsAO and Zack McKown was established formally in 1984 and the first major commission came in the same year: a 28-story residential building in Shanghai, completed in 1989. In 1987, the partners started work on Suntec City, in Singapore. Their responsibilities included locating the site, working with the owners and representatives of the Singapore government, and leading the design from concept through construction. With a construction cost of US$1.2 billion, Suntec City is among the world's largest privately owned developments. Construction has been phased. Southeast Asia's largest convention and exhibition center opened in 1995 and three of the office towers and approximately half of the planned 1.2 million sq. ft. of retail space opened in 1995 and 1996. The remaining office tower and a retail/entertainment complex are scheduled to open in 1997.
In 1990, TsAO & McKown began the design of Menara IMC, located at the major crossroads of downtown Kuala Lumpur, and took this project through construction. The 30-story office building and corporate headquarters is recognized for establishing new standards of building design and technology in Southeast Asia. For the same developer, the firm is now designing a 1.5-million-sq.-ft. primarily residential project in central Kuala Lumpur; this project is scheduled for completion in the year 2000.
TsAO & McKown is unusual among young firms in having a major body of built work. The firm has earned an international reputation for its ability to transform complex building projects into architecture memorable for its humanity, attention to detail, and embrace of diversity. The work also includes many smaller projects considered significant, among them interior design and furnishings for Morgans Hotel, in New York; a museum interior in Montreal; high-fashion boutiques and other retail shops; apartment and townhouse interiors; and objects ranging from much-copied sinks and bathtubs to dinnerware and candlesticks sold in Barneys department store and to picture frames sold at the Museum of Modern Art. Set designs for dance, museum exhibitions, fashion presentations, and film design continue to be critical aspects of the firm's practice.
This diversity of practice is not a contradiction. The unity of the work derives not from style, geography, typology, or scale but from a process of distillation wherein all facets of work inform the other. Operating in the arena of life with all its complexity and uncertainty is how the principals find meaning, personally and professionally. This is the core of the firm's work.

Calvin Tsao
Calvin Tsao brings to TsAO & McKown a broad range of design experience in international and domestic projects ranging from designer boutiques and hotels to major commercial and residential developments, including Suntec City, which includes office towers, a civic center plaza, and retail complex. In addition Mr. Tsao is known for his design and art direction of film, dance, and theatrical productions. Mr. Tsao is a founding partner of TsAO & McKownand is based primarily in the firm's New York office.
Calvin Tsao graduated in 1974 from the University of California at Berkeley with a Bachelor of Arts degree in Architecture. During his last year at Berkeley, Mr. Tsao was the artistic director of the Berkeley Repertory Theater and received the Eisner Prize for directing and stage design and a fellowship to direct *Les Chants de Maldoror*, by Comte de Lautremont. Mr. Tsao continued his theater training as a graduate student at Carnegie Mellon, where as a Fulbright scholar, he studied directing. In 1975 he entered Harvard Graduate School of Design, where, in 1978, he earned his Master of Architecture degree and received the Henry Adams Medal from the American Institute of Architects for ranking first in his class. Currently Calvin Tsao is a visiting professor of Architecture at Harvard's Graduate School of Design.

Zack McKown
Zack McKown brings to TsAO & McKown extensive experience in the design of large-scale and technologically sophisticated corporate, residential, and retail projects. Mr. McKown has also received recognition for his product and furniture design. Mr. McKown is a founding partner of TsAO & McKown and has spent nearly seven years in the Singapore office to oversee the design of Suntec City, a 5-million-sq.-ft. mixed-use project.
Zack McKown graduated cum laude from the University of South Carolina's honors college in 1974 and obtained his Master of Architecture degree from the Harvard Graduate School of Design in 1978.

Turett Collaborative Architects
86 Franklin Street, 3D Floor
New York, NY 10013
tel. 212-9651244 - fax 212-9651246
e-mail: info@turettarch.com
www. turettarch.com

Turett Collaborative Architects was founded in 1984 by Wayne Turett. Established on the principle of creative design, it has grown into a multi-disciplinary practice with the ability to produce a range of design solutions from architecture and interiors to graphics and industrial products.
The current architectural project profile is comprised of commercial, retail, restaurant design, and corporate planning. Examples of recent projects include the design of Tommy Boy Music Offices (1997), Penalty Recordings Offices (1998), America Restaurant Las Vegas (1992 +1997), The Grille Room Restaurant (1997), Hale and Hearty Soups at 3 locations (1997), The Atrium at 237 Park Avenue (1997), Priority Records offices (1993 & 1997), Newsbar's 4 locations (1992-1997), Majestic Theater renovations (1996), and Kenneth Cole Shoes at 4 locations (1996).
TCA has received numerous accolades and the projects have appeared in many domestic and international journals. The Market at Newport received Best Restaurant Award for 1996 and was nominated for Best Restaurant Award by the James Beard Foundation. Tommy Boy Music received Best Office Design of 1994 by Interiors Magazine. Newsbar received Best Coffee Bar from New York Press and Best Menu Design Award. Mr. Turett has also won the New York City Art Commission Award for Design Excellence for a newsstand located at 81st Street and Columbus Avenue and was also a finalist in the 1988 Newsstand Competition.

Williams & Dynerman Architects
1751 N Street NW Washington DC 20036
Suite 202
tel. 202-6598080 - fax 202-6591030
e-mail: wdarch@erols.com

Williams & Dynerman Architects is a nationally recognized design firm that has earned a reputation for design excellence for a range of projects types: commercial interiors, schools and university institutions, historic preservation, and residential. Its expertise extends from site selection and master planning through full-service building design and coordination with master craftsmen to the detail design of furniture and light fixtures. The firm's work has won local and national design awards, and been published in Architectural Digest, *Interior Design, Metropolitan Home, Southern Accents, Architectural Record*, the *Washington Post* and the *Washington Times*. The fimr was included in the recent AD 100 listing of top architects and designers.

Alan B. Dynerman
Alan Dynerman's practice covers a range of work and project types: corporate offices here and in Asia, a Montessori school, weekend retreats in the mountains of Virginia. In each case, Mr. Dynerman's work has been characterized by a few overarching interests: a sensitivity to the site and the unification of the architecture and the landscape; an intense attention to detail and assembly, and a love of natural materials. The list of published work and many design awards--national and local-- attest to the level of recognition and achievement he has attained.
Along with his professional practice Mr. Dynerman has continued to teach. He has been a guest critic and lecturer at a number of universities. Currently, Mr. Dynerman is an adjunct at the University of Maryland. His interest in teaching stems from Mr. Dynerman's commitment to the profession, its future and his personal efforts to broaden his views and keep his work fresh.
Currently, Mr. Dynerman is directing the firm's work in the following areas: The Grand Hyatt service apartments in Malaysia, offices for the Academy for Educational Development and a number of high-end residential projects.
Mr. Dynerman is originally from New York City and for the early chapters of his life stayed close to home. He entered Columbia College in N.Y. in 1973 and graduated in 1976 with a BA in architecture. After a few itinerant years as a cabinet-

maker and carpenter Mr. Dynerman enrolled in the University of Virginia graduating with a Masters of Architecture in 1981.

Richard P. Williams
During the course of his practice Mr. Williams has developed a body of work that speaks to his interest in the integration of building and site. This, combined with his knowledge of traditional architecture has produced a number of unique projects. The many design awards and list of published work give evidence to this claim.

Mr. Williams is intensely involved with historic preservation and urban planning concerns. He has been a board member of the District of Columbia Preservation League - DC's most important citizens' preservation organization - for the past seven years and chairman of its issues committee for four. In this capacity he has both reviewed and presented a broad spectrum of architectural and planning projects.

Alan B. Dynerman, A.I.A.

Education
1981 University of Virginia School of Architecture: M. Arch. w/ Honors
1976 Columbia College, Columbia University: B.A.

Professional Practice
Oct. '86-Present Williams & Dynerman Architects, Washington, D.C.

June '83 - June. '86 Hartman-Cox, Architects, Washington, D.C.
Project Architect: Law Offices of Fried, Frank, Harris, Shriver & Jacobson; Washington, D.C.
Staff Architect: Law Offices of Caplan & Drysdale, Washington, D.C.
Staff Architect: Headquarters for the HEB Grocery Company, San Antonio, TX
Staff Architect: Cafritz Residence, Washington, D.C.

Aug. '81 - June '83 Rubin and Smith-Miller Architects, New York, N.Y.
Project Architect: New Line Cinema Offices, New York City
Project Architect: Hudson Residence, New York City
Project Architect: Schmertz Residence, New York City
Project Architect: Shipper Residence, New York City
Staff Architect: I.B.D. Factory; Hartford, CN
Staff Architect: Determined Productions Headquarters; New York
Staff Architect: Kalisman Residence

Awards
1998 Custom Home Magazine Design Awards; Grand Prize
The Grass Farm; Shepard/Jaffe Residence, Markham, Virginia
1997 National AIA; 1997 Honor Award in Interior Architecture
The Henri Beaufour Institute, USA; Washington, DC
1997 Washington Chapter AIA: Award for Excellence in Interior Architecture
 Lobby of 927 15th Street, Washington, DC
1997 Virginia Society of Architects *Inform Magazine* Award:
Offices of MYCOM Berhad, Kuala Lumpur, Malaysia
1996 Washington Chapter AIA; Merit Award in Interior Architecture
Offices of MYCOM Berhad, Kuala Lumpur, Malaysia
1995 Washington Chapter AIA: Award for Excellence in Architecture
Fellows Housing: Center for Hellenic Studies
Trustees for Harvard University, Washington, DC
1994 Institute of Business Designers: 1994 Best Project of the Year
Offices of the Henri Beaufour Institute, USA, Washington, DC
1994 Institute of Business Designers: 1994 Will Ching FIBD Design Award
Offices of the Henri Beaufour Institute, USA, Washington, DC
1993 Washington Chapter AIA Award: Award for Excellence in Architecture
Pool/ Tennis Complex, Rappahannock County, Virginia
1993 Washington Chapter AIA Award: Merit Award in Interior Architecture Offices of the Henri Beaufour Institute, USA, Washington, DC
1993 Virginia Masonry Council: Excellence in Masonry Award
Pool/Tennis Complex, Rappahannock County, Virginia
1993 Virginia Society of Architects *Inform Magazine* Award:
Offices of Henri Beaufour Institute, USA
1993 Selected as participant in the International Young Architects Forum
1990 Excellence in Design; Village of Falls Church, Preservation Society, Pender Residence
1988 Washington Chapter AIA Award: HEB Headquarters
1981 Henry Adams Prize for Excellence
1981 University of Virginia: AIA Scholarship Award
1980 Virginia Society of Architects Award

Publications
1988 - Present Interior Design, August 1997, Lead article, "New Design in Asia: Holding Pattern"
Architectural Record, May '97 "1997 Honors & Awards"
Architectural Record, Jan '97 "Record News: 28 Firms Win 1997 Honors"
Washington Times, Dec.22, '96 "3 Local Firms Find Honor" by Ellen Sands
Architectural Digest, September 1995, "The AD 100"
Architectural Digest, May 1995, cover + article, "A Neoclassical Pool Complex: Balancing Nature and Design in the Virginia Countryside", by Pilar Viladas.
Interior Design, January 1995, cover + article, "Williams & Dynerman- Will Ching Award Winner", The Henri Beaufour Institute, by Edie Cohen
Inform Magazine, 1994- number one, "Classicism on the Rise", by Edwin Slipek, Jr.
Architectural Digest, June 1994, "Old Virginia Redux: Improving on Venerable Traditions", by Pilar Viladas
Washington Post, Nov. 5, 1993, "Architects Nab Design Honors", by Benjamin Forgey
Inform Magazine, 1993- number three, "Sign of the Times- 1993 Inform Awards"
Washington Post Magazine, Oct. 3, 1993, Fall Home & Design Issue, "By Things Possessed" by Nancy McKeon and "The Last Detail" by Candy Sagon
Metropolitan Home, March 1992, "Suburban Renewal", by Julie Iovine
Produced by Tim & Karen Ward: The Cafritz Residence, cover and feature
Washington Business Journal, March 4, 1991: "FOCUS - Young Architects on the Rise", by Leslie Aun
Remodeling Magazine, March 1990, "Top Jobs" The Dynerman Residence
Washington Home and Garden, Winter 1990: "More of Less", by Constance Stapleton: The Hedden House
Museum & Arts Washington, March/April 1988, "Inside Stories" - Fried, Frank Library
Interiors, October 1986, "40 Under 40" - The Sward House in Seaside, FL.; with Deborah Berke
Global Architecture, Volume II, New Waves in American Residential Architecture"
Princeton Architectural Journal Volume II, "House in New Castle, Delaware"

Teaching Experience
Spring 1994 University of Virginia School of Architecture, Visiting Critic
Sept. '83-present University of Maryland School of Architecture, Adjunct Professor of Design
Summer 1988 University of Maryland Foreign Studies Program, Directed Studio Program in Italy
1989-91 Catholic University Annual Urban Design Charrette, Team Leader
Sept.'83-May '84 George Washington University, Landscape Design Program

Lectures/ Symposia
The Corcoran Gallery of Art: "Imaginary Spaces: Architecture of the television Family"
University of Virginia, "With-In-Site"
University of Maryland, "With-In-Site"
"The Work of Williams & Dynerman Architects"
"The Villa Savoy and the Typological Diagram of Retreat"
Andrews University, "With-In-Site"
Catholic University, "The Work of Williams & Dynerman Architects"

Juries
Columbia University
Yale University
University of Virginia
New Jersey Institute of Technology
Ohio State University
Catholic University

Exhibitions
1994 "Visions of Home": National Building Museum, Washington, DC
House in Markham, Fauquier County, Virginia
1991 "Give us Your Best": National Building Museum, Washington, DC
Williams & Dynerman Current Work
1991 Third International Contemporary Furniture Fair, New York City

Activities
1996-97 University of Virginia School of Architecture: Dean's Forum Development Co-Chairman
1995-96 Washington Chapter, AIA:
Board Member, Chairman of Awards Committee
MODO-Architectural Club of Washington founding member.
1994 Aidan Montessori School: Building Committee Member
1990-93 Calvary Women's Shelter; Board Member
1993 District of Columbia Warehouse Survey Advisory Committee
1990 District of Columbia Baseball Stadium Charrette; Director

Professional Registration
Commonwealth of Virginia
District of Columbia
State of Maryland
State of New Jersey

Fotolito: San Patrignano - Rimini
Stampa: Euroteam - Ciliverghe di Mazzano (BS)
Legatura: Pedrelli - Parma